Boston Against Busing

Boston

Race, Class, and Ethnicity

Against

in the 1960s and 1970s

Busing

by Ronald P. Formisano

The University of North Carolina Press

Chapel Hill and London

Library of Congress Cataloging-in-Publication Data

Formisano, Ronald P.
    Boston against busing : race, class, and ethnicity in
the 1960s and 1970s / by Ronald P. Formisano.
        p.   cm.
    Includes bibliographical references (p.) and index.
    ISBN 0-8078-1929-8 (alk. paper). —
    ISBN 0-8078-4292-3 (pbk. : alk. paper)
    1. Busing for school integration—Massachusetts—
Boston—History.   2. School integration—
Massachusetts—Boston—History.   3. Social classes—
Massachusetts—Boston—History.   4. Boston (Mass.)—
Race relations.   5. Boston (Mass.)—Ethnic relations.
I. Title.
LC214.523.B67F67   1991
370.19'342—dc20   90-12587
                                                            CIP

The paper in this book meets the guidelines for permanence
and durability of the Committee on Production Guidelines
for Book Longevity of the Council on Library Resources.

Manufactured in the United States of America
98   97   7   6   5   4

For Erica

Contents

Illustrations

Tables

Map

Preface

I just want to let you know how opposed *I am to your* forced *bus-sing order, but opposed though we are, my husband and I are trying so hard to be law abiding and set a good example for our 6 children, 3 of whom attend the South Boston-Roxbury District. We have si-lently protested and aloud to each other, but never marched or felt violent or even angry about your decision, so on Sept. 12 my children all went to school even though they were frightened, and among the very few in South Boston who did so.*

[But] I haven't sent my 3 older children since that first day, why— because I'm terrified 24 hrs a day. Living if that's what you can call it in a nightmare, helicopters over head, police everywhere (for which I'm thankful), but which are constant reminders, people so full of hate, I never dreamed possible. I guess I'm quite a fool, I never thought a lot of people I see in church so often were so unchristian like, it truly hurts, and makes the job of being a parent so much harder.—South Boston mother to Judge W. A. Garrity, Sept. 23, 1974

In September 1974 I was living in Cambridge, Massachusetts, and commuting to work at Clark University in Worcester. From the comfort-able remove of Harvard Square I watched with dismay the violence that erupted as Boston began to desegregate its public schools under court order. Unlike many throughout the country who associated Boston with an abolitionist past and a liberal present, as a historian I was better prepared to understand the conflict. I knew that there had been several Bostons whose diverse cultures had often generated religious bigotry, nativism, and ethnic and racial conflict. I knew that discord between Irish Catholics and African-Americans extended back to before the Civil

War, and that pluralist tolerance had its limits in the case of the black minority. The events of 1974–75 nevertheless astounded me.

Like many others of my generation, I was powerfully affected by the Southern civil rights movement in the early 1960s. The rights of black Americans to full citizenship had been deferred too long, and I cheered their efforts to tear down the caste system of the South, rejoiced at the embracing of their cause by Presidents Kennedy and Johnson, and applauded Congress's passing of the 1964 Civil Rights Act and 1965 Voting Rights Act.

But even while celebrating these changes, on reflection it was clear that in the early 1960s the South was once again playing its role as the nation's villain, once again attracting northern moral passion to right wrongs—and the southern caste system was evil and did need to be dismantled—and becoming the focus of a national morality play. What, I wondered, about racial prejudice and discrimination in the North? What about class lines in the North and the virtual caste lines that excluded blacks almost completely from white suburbs? It was especially troubling that desegregation schemes usually began and ended by mixing poor blacks and working- or middle-class whites, while the lives of upper-middle-class and rich whites remained untouched.

In 1974 my response to the Boston desegregation troubles was to offer a course on the topic in the spring semester. My students and I began the semester as liberals committed to the goal of an integrated society, and probably with some disdain for those opposing school desegregation in Boston's neighborhoods. We ended the semester desiring integration no less and feverently wishing for peaceful desegregation, but having lost an elitist bias against working-class or local people with values different from ours.

Our initial assumptions reflected the ease with which affluent and liberal whites, including scholars, assume that the Archie Bunkers are the only racists in our society. Most whites benefit from the institutional arrangements that keep a huge proportion of the black population in a subordinate position. From this perspective, those "expressing intolerant attitudes are not the only racists and their racism is not abnormal. . . . racism is quite characteristically American and . . . it can be found in different forms throughout the class structure."[1]

Considering the central role of slavery and racism throughout American history, the nation has from one perspective come a long way in overcoming racism since World War II. The "Second Reconstruction" of the 1960s removed Jim Crow public segregation from the South and gave Southern blacks political leverage that they have used to good advantage. Job programs and affirmative action helped to create a new black middle class, and white Americans have increased social interactions with educated, better-off blacks considerably during the last two decades.

But the "American Dilemma," as Gunnar Myrdal termed it in 1944, persists in a new form: the incongruity between the promise of American democracy and the grim reality of ghetto poverty for those whom Harold Cruse recently described as "the magnified black millions of the Eighties existing below the poverty line—the black unemployed, the fatherless families, the high school dropouts, the petty criminals, the urban homeless, the unskilled, the welfare survivors whom the nation and its uplift forces and agencies cannot rescue."[2]

Most whites of all classes avoid contact with the black underclass trapped in urban ghettoes.[3] Middle-class blacks similarly try to escape the unstable black poor. More affluent blacks who live in the ghetto take pains to insulate their families from the social undertow of the underclass.

What happened in Boston illustrates the persistence of race and class discrimination and the counterproductiveness of some solutions that are imposed on it. Imposed on people, rather; and we learn much by scrutinizing what gets imposed on whom.

This book focuses primarily on the white antibusers and on the complexity of antibusing. First of all, racism alone is too simple an explanation of the resistance to court-ordered school desegregation, especially if by racism one means simply overt expressions of prejudice or hostility. Of course, racism, however defined, was important. It has been a fact of life in Boston. And there were those in the antibusing movement whose failed lives, broken dreams, or warped spirits found release and redemption of a kind in a movement that allowed them to hate without restraint. But many impulses moved and shaped antibusing, and thousands of decent, moderate whites across the city cannot be said to have been racists.

Neither can antibusing be reduced to a neat dialectic of class conflict, though some writers have tried to do that. Antibusing action and opinion arose rather from the interplay of race and class, in admixture with ethnicity and place, or "turf." All these must be considered together in disassembling the complexity of antibusing. All must be considered, too, in historical perspective.

As a historian and social scientist, I have tried to bring a fair amount of analytic rigor to this inquiry. At the same time, I have tried to make it accessible to lay readers, and especially to give voice to ordinary persons buffeted by conflicting forces. Many of these average people were caught in a no man's land, struggling with the dictates of common decency, common sense, and uncommon demands on their concern for their own self-interest and the well-being of their children. In the later chapters, particularly, the reader will encounter these voices. They will not necessarily speak with clarity and may echo the ambivalence of the South Boston mother quoted at the outset, or of the thirteen-year-old schoolgirl who wrote to Judge W. Arthur Garrity, Jr. to admit that she was a racist, though she had never thought about race before. "I do not call black people niggers out loud and I never will. A nigger is a very ignorant person and if we are able to call others the word then we are niggers ourselves for being so ignorant to use the word. In other words, I am not a Negrophobe." But she called herself a racist because "now I distinguish the color of the skin instead of whats deep down inside I never did this before [*sic*]. . . . Another thing is that I have a black girlfriend whom I write to and we are very good friends because she was bused to my school last year." But the writer now wanted to leave her West Roxbury school because a black girl had picked a fight with her, and two days later three black girls slapped and roughly pushed her into a locker. Still, this youngster gave the judge suggestions for making school desegregation work better: start busing "when children are young because their to young [*sic*] to understand color. Then they will be bused together through the years and be friends, not enemies. Kids 12 and up should be left alone."[4]

Many of these voices will be filled with anger at being forced to send their children to areas they regarded as dangerous, or for having taken away from them the decent schools that they had worked hard to live near, or because they knew their cousins in the suburbs were wholly exempt from "the law." They will express anger, too, against the judge, and sometimes against blacks in general, but often against blacks for specific acts against their own. But many of these voices will convey also the anguish of mothers and fathers genuinely fearful for their childrens' safety. These were parents who saw children—sometimes teenagers—

crying and nauseous in the morning as they prepared themselves to go to school. There was the aide in South Boston High School who told of a fifteen-year-old girl she found sobbing in the lobby, who pleaded with the woman to ask her mother to allow her to quit school. The youngster had not eaten lunch since the start of the school year because she feared going into the cafeteria, scene of numerous fights. The aide's own daughter, a senior, sometimes cried and screamed in the morning for fear of going to school. This South Boston mother also empathized with the black children who rode the buses each day into a hostile, terrifying place.[5]

Some of the voices—antibusing voices—will be those of whites who struggled in their homes against the poison of racial prejudice. One of these was the Brighton mother who had served on court-created biracial parents' councils working to smooth implementation and to encourage racial cooperation. But she had taken two children out of Boston Technical High School because she feared for their safety and "because they saw numerous incidents that were making them racists." Another child who attended Boston Latin was beaten by black youngsters on his way home from school, receiving severe bruises to one side of his face. He now "has different racial feelings than myself, that I have not been able to change. It does not help me to understand his feelings, as I accept all people as HUMAN BEINGS." This mother was determined to let no further harm come to her children. She now called herself "a consciencious [sic] objector against forced busing."[6]

I have tried to portray organized antibusing with understanding, and from what is a perspective hitherto unexplored. But my greatest sympathy has resided with those like the Brighton father, a city employee, whose son was transferred to a school in the middle of the ghetto. His son already attended an integrated school, for which he paid high taxes, but now the boy must go to "one of the worst schools, in one of the most dangerous parts of the city. . . . When that black family moved in down the street, who told everyone to live and let live? Me! When the antibusing crazies had their march, who said ignore them, they're only trouble makers? Me!" But in frustration this man falsified his son's home address and sent him to school in Quincy, ironically a long bus ride away.[7]

Aside from wanting to give voice to some of the many involved in Boston's desegregation who have felt voiceless, I wrote this book to try to present in as clear and unvarnished a fashion as possible what happened in the antibusing protest and why. There are unpleasant truths here for the whites of Boston, but I hope that they and many other white Americans will find in the pages that follow something useful. Blacks also will find hard truths here, and some may resent a book so heavily focused on whites. Indeed, it has often occurred to me that *Boston Against Busing* will be damned for its empathy for the diffuse mass of nonracist moderate whites who opposed court-ordered busing, while the antibusers themselves will find it far too critical of themselves and some of their leaders. These risks are worth taking.

The attempt to understand antibusing is fraught with further difficulties. Many are quick to moralize and pass judgment on antibusers without recognizing that there existed many different kinds of opponents to the court orders in Boston. But the epithet "racist" springs easily to the lips of middle-class persons who live in suburbs or college towns, or who if they live in urban retreats possess the resources enabling them to avoid sending their children to schools that are populated with the poor, working class, or black. Calling attention to the class and cultural dimensions of antibusing can prompt from those anxious to display their moral credentials the often eager criticism that one is somehow exonerating racists, or, a lesser sin, simply ignoring racism. In discussing race and antibusing in Boston, however, one must consider also class, religion, ethnicity, and turf. One must emphasize, too, that there were several different antibusing movements in Boston.

I want Bostonians to read this book. It is about their city and their travail. But I also want other Americans to read it. Of course Boston is unique, and its distinctive history and geography had much to do with the course of events during its modern school wars. But Boston is an accentuated case of what exists elsewhere in the nation. As can Bostonians gain self-understanding from this history, so can others.

Acknowledgments

Many persons have helped with the making of this book, including above all many Clark University undergraduates who, over a decade or so, participated in one version or another of a course focused on school desegregation and opposition to it ("the busing course," everyone called it). Students who wrote papers that were directly useful will find their names in the notes. Clark University also gave me great practical assistance in the form of several Faculty Research Grants and an entire sabbatical year in 1987–88.

Alan Lupo, a very good journalist (who is also a superb teacher when he sometimes ventures onto campuses), not only provided me with notes and research materials that he had used in writing a book on this subject, but also took the time to read an earlier draft of this manuscript and to deliver detailed and constructive criticism, saving me, through his abundant knowledge of Boston, from many errors. J. Anthony Lukas, another journalist-historian whose writing in this area is well known, also generously allowed me to use photocopies of his research materials dealing with ROAR. Judge W. Arthur Garrity, Jr., a key actor in the events described, allowed me to look at a large collection of letters in his possession and graciously granted two interviews. Similarly, K. Marie Clarke, another participant, trusted me with many boxes of papers and tirelessly answered questions.

Several Clark University colleagues helped in various ways. William Koelsch read an earlier draft and in addition called to my attention countless books, articles, and newspaper stories, clipping many of the latter for me and sending them not only through the campus mail but even to Italy during the 1989 spring semester, where I continued to work on the manuscript while on a Fulbright. His criticism throughout, based on his knowledge of the urban landscape and Boston's in particular, has been most valuable. Richard Ford, with his usual cheerfulness, ensured that my personal computer and printer were always working, printed several copies of the manuscript at crucial times, and corrected spelling and other errors. Doug Little read parts of the manuscript at various stages and otherwise helped simply by being a splendid colleague and friend. Simone Caron from time to time provided excellent research assistance.

Robert Levey of the *Boston Globe* was once that paper's education reporter in the early 1960s. He also happens to be a good friend who facilitated many of my trips to Boston and to the *Globe*. The latter's library staff were always helpful, particularly David Jennings and Jean Mulvaney. John Mulkern of Babson College made available to me the typescripts of a large number of interviews that he conducted with Boston officials regarding desegregation. Sandra Eisdorfer supervised the publication process of this book and Martha Rappaport provided meticulous copyediting. Robert Berkhofer made a timely suggestion regarding the title.

Special thanks also go to Robert Blumenthal, William Crowley, Coleen Gladden, and Charles Glenn of the Massachusetts Department of Education, Robert McDonald of the Office of the Boston City Council, Helen Mamiadas of South Boston Library, and also Julie Aubuchon, Bill Baller, Sandra Batchford, John Blydenburgh, Margaret Campbell, Forest Cason, Jason Chin, Mary Colvario, Neil Corwin, Frank Couvares, John Curran, Laura DeCesare, William Densmore, Amy Jo Freeman, Anne Gibson, Ellen Goodman, James Hannon, David Harmon, Howard Husock, Alison Jennings, Melanie Killen, Jeff Lambert, Ann McKinnon, Robert McMahon, Peter McMillan, Ione Malloy, David Miles, Sandra Mitchell, Tyke Patriquin, Trudy Powers, Robert Pressman, Ann Roisman, Robert Schwartz, Joseph Wallace, Stephen Young, The *Boston Phoenix*, and the staffs of the Boston Public Library, Clark University's Goddard Library, and the Worcester Public Library.

Boston Against Busing

1

Not Little Rock But New Orleans

During the fall of 1974 shocking images of racial bigotry and violence emerged from Boston, that graceful, cosmopolitan city known for the excellence of its educational, cultural, and scientific institutions, a city once called "the Athens of America." As court-ordered desegregation of the public schools began, entailing entensive crosstown busing of both black and white pupils, racial conflict that had been escalating for over a decade overflowed into streets and schools.

In 1974 the tough, mostly Irish, working-class neighborhood of South Boston became as much a symbol of white racism as Selma, Alabama had been in 1964. Wild, raging mobs of white men and women confronted armies of police, while youths in their teens and younger hurled rocks, bottles, and racial epithets at buses carrying terrified black youngsters to school. Clashes with police erupted frequently and schools in other white neighborhoods became armed camps. The violence continued, arising alternately from whites and blacks, engulfing the innocent as well as the engaged a black man stalked and beaten with hockey sticks; a white student carried out of Hyde Park High with a knife wound, then another stabbed by a black at South Boston High; a white man dragged from his car and beaten to death; a black lawyer beaten on the steps of City Hall by young white protesters and struck with the staff of an American flag used as a spear. Some observers, recalling a dramatic outburst of Southern opposition to desegregation in 1957, now called Boston "the Little Rock of the North."

Organized resistance to desegregation, or what its opponents called "forced busing," ground on for three grim years. Opposition to the court orders became, in the words of the United States Civil Rights Commission, "the accepted community norm. Behavior in defiance of the constitutional process seemed to many—albeit erroneously—to be a legitimate exercise of individual rights."[1] The intensity and duration of the antibusing resistance in Boston dwarfed that encountered in any other American city. The federal district court judge who decided the case in June 1974, W. Arthur Garrity, Jr., shepherded implementation for eleven years, issuing 415 orders and becoming more involved in the everyday school operations than any judge in the history of desegregation. For some of those who tried to keep the peace in Boston, comparisons to Belfast in Northern Ireland seemed more appropriate in conveying the sense of "hopelessness" and "protracted struggle leading to no solution."[2]

Though a relative peace eventually prevailed in the schools (urban schools in the 1970s were hardly oases of tranquility), incidents of racial violence persisted at a high level and did not taper off until the 1980s. Although Boston's racial climate has improved steadily since former antibuser Raymond Flynn's election as mayor in 1983, many wounds fester. Remnants of the antibusing movement persisted into the 1980s, and Boston still wears the reputation, at least partly deserved, of being a racist city, a reputation which clings to it like a bad odor that all the winds of the Atlantic cannot blow away.

To label an entire city racist, however, clearly violates common sense, and to explain the antibusing movement as primarily racist also is far too simple. By antibusing movement I mean in part the organized groups, principally ROAR (Restore Our Alienated Rights), that were dominated mostly by antibusing's Mother Superior, Louise Day Hicks of South Boston. I refer also to the vast number of white Bostonians who were not ROAR members but who participated in protests of some kind.[3] Eighty percent of white parents thought the court orders to be bad policy, and their responses varied greatly. Many moderates throughout the city agonized over the conflicting demands of conscience, duty, and the law and what they saw as potential danger to their children's welfare. The travail of many decent whites caught in a whipsaw of decent intention and negative experience is a story that has not been told.

Explanations of antibusing also err, I believe, in attaching too much importance to the role of individual leaders.[4] Louise Hicks, for example, became synonymous with antibusing, beginning in 1963 when as chair of the school committee she contested the demands of the local National Association for the Advancement of Colored People (NAACP) for better schools for blacks. But consistent majorities on the school committee, with or without Hicks, pursued essentially the same policies for a dozen years.

Antibusing in Boston, especially its organized active expressions, can be seen as a case of reactionary populism, a type of grassroots social movement that has flared frequently in American history. From "regulators" in the eighteenth century, to nativists and agrarians in the nineteenth, to urban Progressives in the twentieth, these movements have been bundles of contradictory tendencies seeking greater democracy or opportunity, perhaps, while simultaneously expressing intolerance or denying the legitimacy of certain group interests. Our modern populisms especially seem to be inhibited, to be cramped by limited horizons, and they easily go sour from a lack of faith rooted in a sense of powerlessness. Yet many antibusers shared with other protesters of the 1970s at least the attempt to regain control over their lives.

Social scientists too often homogenize such internally diverse movements by stamping them as either liberal or conservative, radical or reactionary. Sometimes the labels are justified, but grassroots insurgencies often defy ready classification. Hence this description of Boston antibusing as reactionary populism, while an oxymoron, should not be seen as unusual. Indeed, in Canarsie, New York, in the early 1970s, white reaction to desegregation, according to Jonathan Rieder, "was a disorderly affair. Backlash contained democratic, populist, conspiratorial, racist, humanistic, pragmatic, and meritocratic impulses."[5]

Reactionary populism is used here as a term of neither blame nor praise, but descriptively. Boston's antibusing movement was populist in that it sprang from the bottom half of the population, from working-, lower-middle- and middle-class city dwellers who felt their children, neighborhoods, and status to be threatened. Like many other citizens' movements of the 1970s, antibusing expressed rampant citizen alienation from impersonal government, drawing on an ingrained, deeply felt sense of injustice, unfairness, and deprivation of rights.

Several neighborhoods that became strongholds of antibusing tended to see the fight against the court orders of a suburban, "out-of-town, out-of-touch" judge as a continuation of wars waged in recent years against the depredations of highway construction, urban renewal, and airport expansion promoted by social engineers, bureaucrats, and above all, outsiders. Antibusing exuded the same anti-elitism and fierce class resentments that had erupted in these earlier struggles of neighborhood defense.

Yet while populist in many ways, Boston's antibusing movement was not reformist. It sought little more than a return to the status quo in the school system that existed before the court orders. It did not challenge established political and economic power, and militant activists too often expressed hostility, or at a minimum, insensitivity, to the just demands of black citizens for a full share of their rights. Fear of blacks, specifically of poor ghetto blacks, fed antibusers' feelings of being trodden on, while their outrage at injustice and feelings of powerlessness often fed their hostility to blacks.

This book is not essentially about blacks but about whites, though many blacks in fact opposed the court orders and mandatory desegregation, and some resisted the implication of racial balancing of schools that black youngsters could not learn unless they were in a classroom with white youngsters. The black struggle for decent schools is recounted here in two chapters that argue that school segregation in Boston sprang largely from the democratic interaction of a school committee elected at-large and various of its constituents.

That democracy and segregation were linked was only one of the many ironies involved in Boston's trauma. Several other "jokes of history" derived from the impact of the 1960s. The white antibusers, for example, consciously and unconsciously imitated black civil rights activists. More generally, the antibusers were in many ways children of the 1960s. The enormous cultural and social upheavals of that decade, above all the loosening of public standards of conduct and the decline of authority, powerfully shaped organized antibusing. Numerous protesters during the 1960s—blacks, students, youths, hippies, opponents of the Vietnam War, women, Native Americans—as well as the rise of a new permissiveness in popular culture, all contributed to a climate of civil disobedience and disrespect for authority. Sitting before their televisions and watching—usually with disdain—the protesters of the 1960s and 1970s, the antibusers had learned powerful lessons that they would seek to apply against school desegregation.

Of course the greatest irony of all was the activist antibusers' imitation of the black civil rights movement, which had served as midwife to most 1960s movements. Antibusers frequently staged demonstrations aimed at gaining media coverage and affecting public opinion in the way that they believed civil rights protesters had done a few years earlier. The antibusers usually failed to realize that the civil rights movement had gained widest public support during its nonviolent phase, whereas antibusing in 1974 quickly became associated with violence. Still, they wanted to see themselves portrayed with the sympathy the media had bestowed on the followers of Martin Luther King, Jr.; that is, as victims. By replaying the strategy of civil rights activists, they hoped that the media would legitimize their cause.

When antibusers compared themselves to black activists, they usually ended up seething with bitterness. "They were heroes and martyrs," they lamented, "but we are racists." Who regarded the antibusers as racists? The liberals, suburbanites, elite politicians, outsiders, and especially the media. For antibusers these groups not only overlapped, but "the liberal establishment" and the media were virtually the same thing: a hated enemy who presumed to judge them from the safety of their "lily-white" suburbs. The media doubly frustrated the antibusers by portraying them as racists and by refusing to anoint them with victim status, much less to bestow on them a mantle of morality. But the liberal media earlier had readily legitimized black demonstrators and hairy, unruly youth. For the antibusers, the contrast was infuriating.[6]

Aside from the antibusers' conscious imitation of civil rights and antiwar movements, the 1960s affected them in other ways just as profoundly, though perhaps not as consciously. The decline of authority, or rather, of respect for authority, spread from the young and rebellious throughout much of the population. Traditional mores and values came under scathing questioning and attack from all quarters, not just from radicals, intellectuals, or those on the margins. Irreverence burst into the mainstream, and that most powerful domestic agent of change, television, reflected and promoted the decline of confidence in public and private institutions. Television was, both in its news and entertainment programs, perhaps only the most ubiquitous of debunking agents.[7]

The antibusers of the 1970s sprang mainly from groups who in the 1950s had tended to be orderly, conformist, and self-conscious about their public demeanor. In the 1960s they were at first repelled by the outrageous behavior of black and antiwar protesters and shocked by deviant lifestyles. Richard M. Nixon had labelled them "the silent majority": decent, hard-working, reflexively patriotic, and trusting in authority. But they too lost respect, lost faith, and when pressed themselves, many turned to modes of action that a short time before had marked those whom they scorned and resented. It is hard to imagine ethnic neighborhoods mobilized in street protest during the 1950s—but then that comfortable, seemingly secure postwar world had suddenly changed.

The civil rights movement had done most to define the new era, acting as a generative force of this axial decade leading out of postwar triumphalism and self-congratulation. The black crusade had revealed a lie and a sickness at the core of American society, and once self-doubt began it spread, especially among the young who now inhabited college campuses in record numbers. The civil rights movement went through several phases, however, changing from nonviolence and heroic suffering in the South to aggressive demands for "Black Power" in South and North. Legal victories in Congress in 1964–65 did not relieve the poverty and lack of opportunity that defined living conditions for many blacks, and a mounting sense of relative deprivation gave rise to massive urban riots in black ghettos in the mid- and late-1960s. Militant black separatists such as the Black Panthers used revolutionary rhetoric and went armed, further frightening many whites and provoking lethal responses from local police and the FBI.

Both separatist and integrationist black leaders exhorted blacks to nurture self-love, pride in their history, and a self-conscious African-American identity, and this helped to inspire similar upwellings from other inhabitants of America's cultural salad bowl. Those European groups who had been part of the great immigration of 1890–1924 and who had been intimidated by the ideology of the "Melting Pot" now began to emerge from the shadow cast by British-American dominance of the nation's identity. The cry of "Black is Beautiful" taught those of Irish, Polish, Italian, or Slavic background, among others, to look at their roots with new reverence. Many urban ethnics thus were caught up in a cultural chauvinism that often fed the backlash.

Several recent writers have argued that the ethnic revival of the 1960s came at a time when ethnicity was in fact fading—and was in part a product of that recession. Being "ethnic," like being African-American, was often an act of will. Ethnicity had changed from being "a taken-for-granted part of everyday life" to being "private and voluntary," from "the status of an irrevocable fact of birth to an ingredient of lifestyle." Yet even the forces that submerged ethnicity also contributed to raising barriers against blacks: the black influx into central cities, by arousing consciousness of race, helped make various white groups less conscious of their ethnic differences and diverted white antagonisms to blacks.[8]

On balance, "ideological ethnicity" reinforced the backlash by providing it with a rhetoric for resistance to desegregation. The ethnics of the "urban villages" of the North often felt most vulnerable to blacks in the latter's efforts to break out of the ghetto, and for the urban ethnics theirs was foremost a vulnerability of place. It was their schools and their blocks into which blacks would be coming.

Furthermore, not only did New England and Boston tend to be more ethnicity-aware than other parts of the country, but Boston's neighborhoods commonly swelled with a localist pride that made their residents highly conscious of turf.[9] Within neighborhoods, pockets of ethnicity, class, and place flourished, often identified by parish, squares, corners, hills, and the like. These small worlds often reacted with instinctive hostility to any outsiders.

Besides the militant, organized antibusers, opposition to Judge Garrity's court orders and the plans of 1974–75 also involved many thousands of moderate whites who did not join ROAR, who disapproved of violence, and who rejected illegal activities, including school boycotts. Many moderates believed fully in integrated schools; some had been sending their children to schools that were integrated. Hundreds and thousands of individual families grappled conscientiously with the fear, anxiety, and vicissitudes of sending their children to schools and streets they saw as dangerous, and which often were. The moderates' story has not been told.

The Boston Home and School Association (HSA) constituted one moderate group whose role has not been appreciated by earlier histories. The Boston HSA, similar to parent-teacher associations, has been viewed as militantly antibusing and as a creature of the Boston School Committee.[10] But while local chapters were diverse, most citywide leaders were pragmatists.

As individual and group responses varied across the city, so did neighborhood expressions of antibusing. The sound and fury of South Boston and Charlestown captured media attention, but at the opposite end of the neighborhood spectrum from Southie was semisuburban, middle-class West Roxbury, where antibusing opinion was nearly as intense as in South Boston but where antibusing *action* found expression in a very different *style*. South Boston's militants tolerated no dissent from their hard line. They engaged in every form of protest but were best known for their collective actions: marches, motorcades, rallies, disruptions of traffic and meetings, and violent street clashes with police. By contrast, West

Roxbury's style tended to be individualist, pragmatic, and legalist, tolerant and permissive of different views, and cool to boycotts and street demonstrations.

A small minority of antibusers deliberately practiced terrorism against blacks and especially whites for at least three years. Their targeting of white moderates—most of whom strongly disagreed with the court orders but tried to comply—probably affected the course of desegregation more than the harassment of blacks. Antibusing vigilantes, based especially in South Boston, exercised a disproportionate influence because they were tough, because the moderates lacked leadership and also perceived the court orders as unfair, and because it takes only a few incidents of violence to intimidate one's neighbors. Of course racism added an ugly, frenetic charge of ferocity and violence to many antibusing protests. But as powerful as racism was, it formed only a part of the story.[11]

Both the sweeping nature of the court remedy as well as the powerful resistance to it owed much to the Boston School Committee's long resistance to even the most limited attempts to implement desegregation. From 1963 to 1974 majorities of the five-member, elected school committee engaged routinely in blatant discriminatory practices, heedlessly letting evidence accumulate on the public record that would create ironclad proof of their guilt. A series of politicians, playing upon and being tossed about by their constituents' fears, stepped forward as pied pipers of the white backlash.

These backlash entrepreneurs, joined by neighborhood populists cast up from the grassroots, *virtually created an antibusing movement before busing ever existed.* They also caused racial fear and hostility to be much worse than it would have been. The entrepreneurs' actions sometimes sprang in part from genuine concern for preserving neighborhoods. They arose, too, from the desire both to gain office for access to patronage and sometimes to try to ride antibusing to higher office. Whatever the motivation, the Boston School Committee ran a dual school system, and its leaders kept telling their constituents that busing would never come to Boston.

To an astonishing degree, many citizens of Boston simply could not believe that busing would actually happen. This mind-set, along with its offspring notion that busing could be stopped somehow by protest, arose in part from Boston's unique political culture in which many citizens believed that "everything is politics," that all issues were negotiable, and that interest groups competed for tangible rewards while talk of principles and laws were mere camouflage. Thus the belief persisted, especially among working-class whites, as William A. Henry, III, said, "that busing was not a constitutional remedy for previous lawbreaking and political abuse, but was simply some sort of political maneuver that could be 'fixed' like a traffic ticket."[12]

If the antibusing politicos had done the most to create an antibusing movement up to 1974, the judge and his advisers helped to sustain antibusing after 1974. Anyone who reads Garrity's decision in *Morgan v. Hennigan* will understand why he found the school committee guilty of segregative practices. But the judge then imposed on the city a desegregation plan with which he was barely familiar. Designed by officials working for the State Board of Education, which had been battling the school committee for years, the plan appeared to be punitive, particularly in its pairing of the antibusing hotbed of South Boston with the ghetto of Roxbury. When the school committee refused to review or revise the plan, it defaulted on the chance to eliminate some of its worst features. Implemented by a reluctant and sometimes subversive school administration, the plan's reality often became horrific for thousands of parents.

Of course the intensity of antibusing after 1974 depended on many other causes as well, including the hostility or neutrality to the court orders of most of the city's political and institutional leaders; the permissive attitude of the police and local courts to antibusers arrested for disorderly conduct; and the physical absence from the city of the economic and status elites, who from the safe distance of their suburban retreats were unable or unwilling to ameliorate the situation.

The civil rights movement, which came into being after World War II, generated powerful and contradictory responses among white Americans. The South reacted with massive resistance to the Supreme Court's 1954 decision in *Brown v. Topeka Board of Education*, which struck down the region's "separate but equal" system of segregated schools that had been established by state and local law. Many northern whites, meanwhile, became allies of the black civil rights struggle. Ironically, an Irish Catholic from Massachusetts, John F. Kennedy, placed the awesome moral weight of the presidency behind the black quest. The civil rights movement would peak after Kennedy's assassination with Congress's passage of the Civil Rights Act of 1964 and the Voting Rights Act of 1965. This legislation, sometimes called "The Second Reconstruction," sought to undo the caste system of the South. But civil rights agitation, a mostly southern phenomenon until the early 1960s, already had moved

North. And some northern whites were reacting fearfully to black demands for equal opportunity. When spectacular urban riots exploded in black ghettos after 1964, whites would feel additionally threatened by demands for affirmative action to move blacks ahead at a faster pace to compensate for generations of discrimination.

White reactions in Massachusetts and Boston presented a microcosm of differing reactions in the nation. On the one hand, sympathetic whites mobilized a constituency of conscience to promote black aspirations, which in Boston had become fixated on improving the educational facilities available to black children. A coalition of liberal and cosmopolitan whites succeeded in gaining passage of a state Racial Imbalance Act in 1965 whose intent was to desegregate the state's schools, and particularly those of Boston. On the other hand, the Boston School Committee, dominated by Irish politicians and highly sensitive to aroused local groups, adamantly resisted demands for school reform. Indeed, Boston and Mrs. Hicks became symbols as early as 1963 of the "white backlash" that was perhaps the most significant northern white response to the civil rights movement.

The Boston ruled by Brahmin merchants and Yankee Protestants and famous for its abolitionists, feminists, Mugwumps, and exotic native radicals had long ago faded into history and folklore, its politics taken over by the Irish, who had grown from an often despised, exploited, and discriminated-against minority to a political majority. Political patronage was hardly invented by the Irish Americans, but they brought to politics a particularly intense ethos of interest-group politics and "spirit of patronage." Enjoying several advantages over other immigrant groups, they seldom practiced politics as a way of maximizing the public good, but rather, in nonideological fashion, as a means to upward mobility by gaining status and patronage, and distributing jobs, favors, and contracts to kin and friends. Their ethic was personalist, particularist, and competitive.[13]

Boston's political culture, in short, was predisposed to receive inhospitably a moralistic movement (civil rights) promoting a particular group (black) interest. In addition, a long history of Irish-black hostility dated back to before the Civil War, generated in part by Yankee reformers tending to be sympathetic to black slaves and freedpersons but hostile to Irish Catholic immigrants. Native Protestants often treated the poor Irish "Papists" as "niggers," and the Irish then vented their resentment against a class that they regarded as pariahs. The insecure among the Irish could reassure themselves by making sure that the blacks were kept below them. Blacks and Irish Catholics often have continued to regard one another with hostility across cultural barricades that are composed in part of perceptions and stereotypes, but also real differences, both cultural and material.

The Irish, with select allies from other ethnic groups, used the public schools less as an educational than as an employment system. Having earlier wrested control of the city and its patronage from the Yankees, the Irish assumed that politics was a street fight in which interest groups competed for the rewards of power by mobilizing voters, winning elections, and making deals. They were not inclined to give away anything to the black civil rights leaders who seemed to be seeking leverage by assuming for their group a special moral status based on white guilt. Yankees or Jews might have been susceptible to such an appeal—most Irish were not.

Thus when the Boston NAACP went to the school committee in the early 1960s, complaining of inferior schools and degrading teaching and demanding that school officials admit that de facto segregation (arising from residential patterns) existed in the schools, the committee balked at most black demands. So began a struggle that would last until 1974, during which time the school committee would rebuff all attempts to end its many practices that maintained or promoted segregation.

The close, powerful tie between democracy and segregation that existed in Boston's schools was nourished in large part by the committee, which had served for years as a stepping-stone for aspiring politicians. This point has been well recognized, but it has tended to obscure the fact that, for some politicians, election to the committee, because of its patronage power (it was nonpaid), was an end in itself.

If political culture, race, ethnicity, and place contributed to antibusing in Boston, so too did class. Judge Garrity always regarded *Morgan v. Hennigan* purely "as a race case." But various studies of the controversy have emphasized class and status resentments—as well as race—as powerful forces in antibusing.[14] The role of class was connected to broad changes that took place in the distribution of blacks within the United States during the twentieth century. As blacks continued to migrate from South to North and into central cities after World War II, white movement to the suburbs from cities accelerated enormously. It was, in fact, the greatest exodus in United States history. It drained the white population out of the city limits and engorged the near and far suburbs.[15]

In the 1950s Boston's suburbs grew from two to three million, spurred by the growth of electronic industries on Route 128 girdling Boston. By 1960 Boston's ratio of population in the central city to population in its adjoining metropolitan area was one of the lowest in the country (.27, compared, for example, to .46 for Philadelphia and .73 for New York). Of course, the suburbs were almost entirely white, while blacks, Hispanics, and later Asians were ringed into the central city by the suburban noose.

Thus metropolitan patterns of segregation created a situation throughout much of the nation and in Boston that called for *metropolitan* solutions to desegregation.[16] In 1972 a federal district court judge tried to bring the city of Detroit, whose school population was overwhelmingly black, together with outer county districts to create viable school desegregation. But in 1974, as the outcry against busing among whites and in Congress reached a fever pitch, the Supreme Court, by a five to four split decision in *Milliken v. Bradley*, declared that no proof had been given that state or local governments had been responsible for the racial composition of the Detroit schools or for residential patterns in Detroit. For the majority, Justice Potter Stewart said that the concentration of blacks in Detroit was "caused by unknown and perhaps unknowable factors such as immigration, birthrates, economic changes, or cumulative acts of private racial fears." In contrast, as Professor Thomas Pettigrew pointed out, there are many things in social science that are "unknown and perhaps unknowable," but the "tight, unremitting containment of urban blacks over the past half-century within the bowels of American cities is not one of them."[17]

Indeed, the federal government did most to abet suburban residential apartheid. The government provided massive aid to the housing industry, to localities, to banks, and to individuals in the form of mortgage insurance and loans, and subsidized the suburbs further through highway programs. And rural towns insured their transformation into white enclaves with large-lot zoning, restrictions on multifamily dwellings, the waste of buildable land, and resistance to various social services. Of course bankers and realtors engaged in discriminatory lending and channeling practices as they had for decades. The government also subsidized the Route 128 high-tech boom, which created jobs where blacks (and the poor) did not live and were not likely to find housing. From 1958 to 1967 over 66,000 new jobs came into being in the Route 128 complex, while several thousand jobs were lost in Boston, just as the city was experiencing its largest black in-migration. Blacks did not live near the new jobs and lacked the means to get to them. The state Commission Against Discrimination belatedly labelled Route 128 "Boston's Road to Segregation."[18]

Throughout the country the segregation of minorities was paralleled by a less complete but nevertheless pronounced clustering of less affluent whites in central cities. Some working-class whites chose to live in cities. Others were trapped by lack of resources. In either case, when the Supreme Court decided to prohibit metropolitan remedies for school segregation, it was insuring that desegregation remedies would involve mostly the black and white lower classes, while middle-, upper-middle-, and upper- class whites would be largely excluded. Further, once desegregation began those whites in the city with the most resources could more easily escape "the law of the land" by sending their children to private schools or moving out.[19]

The results of the postwar migrations were exaggerated in Boston because it was so small in relation to its metropolitan area, in territory as well as population. The roots of this ran back to the late nineteenth century when Boston began to annex contiguous suburban towns even as many native Protestant whites began to move to those towns in search of rustic purity and to escape the burgeoning political power of the Irish. Ironically, the native middle class saw annexation in part as a way to keep the city government in their hands and away from the Irish while also tapping new sources of tax revenue. But in 1873 Brookline declined annexation and halted Boston's growth. Prosperous towns like Brookline had already provided themselves with waterworks, good schools, and other municipal services, and suburban and rural Yankees wished to keep separate from the city, from its high taxes, and the Irish. So Boston entered the twentieth century as one of the most geographically truncated cities in the country.

In 1970 some half a million persons lived in Boston, but another million and a half, perhaps 99 percent white, lived in the metropolitan area. They enjoyed the superior facilities of a cosmopolitan downtown, often held jobs in the city, but had no part in any of its attempts to deal with the burning national issue of racial discrimination.[20]

Further, had more of the middle classes remained in Boston, they might have exerted a moderating influence on the city's school politics. But a large part of what remained of the Jewish middle class had been driven out after 1968 by a well-intentioned program to aid minorities

and create integrated housing. In the wake of Martin Luther King's assassination, Mayor Kevin White had persuaded a consortium of Boston
banks (BBURG, Boston Banks' Urban Renewal Group) to provide $27
million in mortgages to low-income black families. Unfortunately, realtors and bankers quickly exploited the program to make money and to
turn a thriving Jewish neighborhood into a black ghetto. BBURG selected Mattapan, which ran through two Irish neighborhoods and was a
thriving self-contained Jewish community, and "redlined" it—granting
mortgages to blacks only within that corridor. BBURG expected less
trouble from Jews than from the Irish or Italians, in part because of their
reputation for liberalism. Real estate agents suddenly showed up on
white doorsteps warning that blacks would be moving in by the hundreds and saying "Your neighbor across the street is selling to a black. I
thought maybe you'd be interested in selling." Some residents fought
back with a biracial group that tried to put realtors out of business, but
in three years Mattapan became 90 percent black, the ghetto had been
merely enlarged, and more white middle-class moderates were driven out
of the city.[21]

In a different way the extensive system of Catholic parochial schools
also removed a potentially calming element, since these families tended
to be somewhat better off or aspired to be. Some one-third of all school-
age youngsters went to Catholic schools, with their parents paying taxes
for public schools as well as the extra fees that went to the church. The
Catholic schools also figured prominently as havens for fleeing white
families once busing began.[22]

For a long time Boston's economy had been relatively stagnant, lacking growth industries and an expansive infrastructure. New workplaces
almost always were built outside Boston, whether factories in the 1840s
or laboratories in the 1950s. By 1970 the old city had been transformed
primarily into a "postindustrial administrative and service center." The
Irish had succeeded in politics but as a group depended heavily on jobs
with government or with utilities such as the phone company, which
enjoyed an unusually high degree of job security. This contributed to the
Irish sense of anxiety when facing black demands for integration. Boston's economy, politics, and heritage of ethnic rivalry all made for a lack
of generosity and openness among ethnic groups.[23]

In 1970 Boston had become one of the costliest cities in which to live
in the continental United States. At the same time the median family
income ranked only twenty-fourth out of the largest thirty cities. Then in

the early 1970s a national economic recession hit Boston with particular severity. The hard times brought by stagflation, a rare combination of both higher inflation and unemployment, made black-white relations, already tense along a number of fronts, even worse.

Meanwhile, school desegregation was just one way in which the white and predominantly Irish hold on public employment was being challenged. In a series of affirmative action suits and decisions beginning in 1970, blacks, Hispanics, and public agencies challenged the patronage and kinship networks of recruitment in the Police, Fire, and Public Works Departments. In November 1971, Federal District Judge Charles E. Wyzanski, Jr. found that police department exams from 1968–70 had discriminated unintentionally against minorities and had favored whites. Wyzanski's attempts to get the police to hire minorities turned into a protracted struggle over the next three years, even as women began to be added to the department during 1972–73.

It was not just that the Irish of Southie, Charlestown, or Dorchester heavily staffed these agencies but also that sons and nephews followed routinely in the steps of fathers and uncles. The Fire Department especially was "one big family," literally, up to 1974 when a U.S. district judge ruled its entrance exams discriminatory and ordered the firemen to bring minority representation up to levels comparable to the Boston population as a whole. In 1975 the United States Supreme Court declined to hear a challenge to the order by the firefighters' union, and after that the department hired one member of a racial minority for every white.[24]

White workers in the construction industry, where the jobless rate climbed as high as 50 percent, similarly felt themselves under siege. Firstly, employers began hiring young, out-of-town, nonunion labor, stirring demonstrations in downtown Boston by angry hardhats. But by 1976 the competition for jobs between black and white workers took center stage and formed another part of the racial conflict that already centered in the schools.[25] In 1974 the city, construction companies, and unions had agreed to aid minority workers by requiring 30 percent minority employees on construction jobs in inner-city areas of dominant minority residence. But soon the Third World Jobs Clearing House, a lobbying and hiring agency supported in large part by city funds, was demanding that the minority quota be raised to 50 percent. That spring, groups of mostly black workers began picketing jobs in ghetto areas, with violence breaking out at several places. A construction site in Dorchester suffered $4,000 worth of vandalism, and workers were forced to flee. Radical members of the Third World Workers Association declared their intention of closing down more sites. The South Boston Marshalls, a vigilante group which provided security for antibusing parades, began to appear at construction yards in a show of solidarity with white workers.

In April union representatives complained of harassment to the city and then on May 7, 2,000 boisterous white construction workers marched on City Hall to protest job stoppages and to demand that the city stop funding the Third World Jobs Clearing House. Union men insisted to reporters that their protest was not over race: "It's my job. I need a job. You been workin' 10–12 years, some guy comes along from this Third World and grabs your job. What the hell?" sputtered one union man. An unemployed white worker from South Boston complained, "Every time I try to join a carpenters, electrical or iron workers union they tell me they are only taking minorities. But if you don't have a union card you can't work and if you aren't black you can't get a union card." Third World spokesmen countered by asserting that companies should not be allowed to operate in the city if they were not hiring Boston residents (and many white hardhats lived outside the city): "Boston jobs for Boston people. We feel it is outrageous for suburbanites to come into Boston to work on construction sites when 12 percent of Boston residents are unemployed." The minority workers' agitation threatened white workers generally because they feared that their sons and nephews would not be able to use preferential apprenticing systems to get access to good jobs. This coincided with what they saw happening to their kids in the public schools, so they saw themselves doubly at risk.[26]

Several writers have drawn a direct connection between unemployment and antibusing activity. Two neighborhoods with the most antibusing, South Boston and Charlestown, were indeed among areas with the highest levels of unemployment.[27] Yet antibusing sentiment and action cut widely across the ranks of the unemployed and employed and raged in both prosperous and depressed neighborhoods. Still, the economic slump, added to Boston's long-term stagnation, certainly made matters worse. As the Mayor's Committee on Violence said in June 1976, too many Bostonians lacked money, work, decent housing, and hope. "They see neighbors with good-paying jobs sending their children to private schools. They see those with better jobs living in the suburbs, where, they believe, you don't have to fear opening your door or walking down the street. They also see that society and the establishment orders their children bused. Then, the whole focus of their grievances is directed toward that issue."[28]

"Their children" indeed were bused, if by that is meant Bostonians at the lower end of the economic scale. In 1972–73, for example, 76 percent of the city's public school students came from families with incomes low enough for them to get free or reduced-price lunches. During 1974–75 the pool of poor left behind grew larger as the more affluent families tended to be the first to leave the schools. In 1976, 61 percent of an estimated seventy-eight thousand pupils came from families at or below the federal poverty level.[29]

As woeful as many Boston schools may have been by middle-class standards, the fact is that their localist, working-class clienteles cherished them, especially the neighborhood high schools. These old, often dilapidated but beloved buildings served less as educational institutions providing upward mobility and more as community socializing agents. For the working-class kids of Southie, Charlestown, or East Boston, high school days were often the best times of their lives, after which many moved on to unexciting, dreary jobs or became mothers and fathers soon after bringing their youth to a close well before middle-class youths who attended college. One Southie young woman told me that while growing up she was "just dying to go to Southie High," and "thought it would be the greatest thing in the world to go to the senior prom." The sports teams of these schools commanded deep affection and passionate loyalty. Young men grew into middle age wearing their high school letter sweaters or team jackets.[30]

The desegregation planners, however, looked upon the Southie Highs of the world as at best anachronisms, and at worst as narrow, parochial places perpetuating distrust of outsiders, prejudice, ethnic and racial stereotypes, and outmoded and ineffective modes of education, trapping their students in a cycle of immobility. The planners (e.g., Board of Education employees, Judge Garrity's advisers) believed that it was right on both moral and utilitarian grounds to "take away" the Southie Highs from their communities. The planners assumed the superiority of their middle-class and cosmopolitan values to those of persons and groups they judged to be localist, uneducated, and, unlike themselves, bigoted.

Thus, Boston's desegregation controversy was very much a contest over whose values would prevail. Those trying to defend localist, ethnic, and communitarian values were at a distinct disadvantage because their efforts too often resulted in violence, too often soured into racial hatred, or sometimes had been prompted by it in the first place. This did not mean, however, that the self-righteous cosmopolitans seeking to change localist life-styles were necessarily morally superior.

Social scientists have conducted an extensive debate, often highly technical and arcane to the layman, to assess the role of racism in motivating protest against school desegregation. Some scholars maintain that racism in some form plays the major role in stimulating opposition to desegregation, while others argue that nonracial factors count more heavily.[31] Researchers reemphasizing racism maintain that most whites oppose busing, especially two-way busing, because they calculate that the benefits are not justified by the costs.[32] Although such studies of Boston have demoted racism as an explanatory factor, the relative importance of the causes of opposition to desegregation promise to remain "very much at issue."[33]

The different findings arise in part as they normally do from different assumptions, methods, and cases chosen for study. They also spring from some fairly massive incongruities that have existed in national public opinion over the past two decades. Since World War II the American public has moved increasingly toward acceptance in principle of an integrated society. By 1970 support levels in the North for integrated schools were reaching 90 percent. But then something happened. As the busing controversy heated up, support for specific policies to implement school desegregation dropped sharply, and the decline seemed directly related to federal efforts to implement school desegregation. Meanwhile, racial isolation in the nation's schools, particularly in the Northeast, actually increased. By 1986, as Harold Cruse put it, "despite the *Brown* decision . . . legal segregation has been almost universally replaced by *de facto* segregation in public schools; and in both South and North, most black and white schoolchildren are as 'separate' as in 1954, *if not more so.*"[34]

It seems puzzling that "white Americans increasingly reject racial injustice in principle but are reluctant to accept the measures necessary to eliminate the injustice."[35] They endorse school integration in the abstract, expect it to happen, and seem to be accepting contact with middle-class blacks in many social relationships. But when faced with potentially extensive contact with poor blacks, which arouses fears of schools and neighborhoods being "invaded" or "overrun" by the black underclass, then resistance skyrockets. Most Boston antibusers bitterly resented being tagged as racists, in part because they saw themselves as having attitudes very much resembling most white Americans. They were right insofar as most whites shared their ambivalence and unwillingness to implement school integration through involuntary busing.

White Bostonians also found themselves wondering about a state of affairs in school desegregation that had evolved from a 1954 Supreme Court decision which said it was wrong to bus a black child in Topeka, Kansas, past a white school in her neighborhood to an all-black school across town, to a federal court decision requiring their children to be bused past their neighborhood school—which in a few cases was integrated at least partially—to schools in black neighborhoods across town. They wondered, in effect, how the "color blindness" sought in the 1950s had become the "race consciousness" of the 1970s, in which children were assigned to schools solely on the basis of race.

In fact, the 1954 *Brown* decision had been freighted with ambiguities, including a tension between simply providing blacks with equal access to white schools and requiring that schools be balanced racially. Moreover, the 1964 Civil Rights Act explicitly mandated color blindness in its implementation, particularly in those sections that gave federal officials leverage by requiring nondiscrimination in schools receiving federal money. But a race-neutral approach disappeared as "the push for racial equity [came] to rely on racial information as a way of gauging, first, the pace of desegregation and, later, the effects of various measures on black advancement."[36]

Boston's Catholics possessed additional reasons to be confused. The Roman Catholic church historically opposed state intervention into the private affairs of families and nowhere had its objections been greater than in the area of childrens' education. Catholic doctrine defined the family as anterior "in idea and in fact to the gathering of men into a commonwealth." Though in recent years church teaching has swung behind state intervention to aid the poor and propertyless victimized by unjust or oppressive social structures, family rights in childrens' education had been vigorously defended by the hierarchy for over a hundred years in its efforts to get Catholics to provide parochial schooling. Catholic parents had been led to believe for generations that they held a "right in usage, if not a right in law, to control educational choices for their children."[37]

Working-class and Catholic Boston was not in the end "the Little Rock" but rather the "New Orleans of the North." In 1957 Governor Orval Faubus of Arkansas was seeking reelection to an unprecedented third term, and he manufactured the crisis at Central High School in Little Rock. Several schools in the state already had desegregated peacefully, but Faubus declared a state of emergency, sent in the national guard to keep out black children, and roused segregationists throughout the region to descend on Little Rock and demonstrate.[38] The Little Rock crisis resulted mostly from one man's ambition.

In 1960 a desegregation controversy in New Orleans, however, anticipated Boston's in several ways, just as the graceful, old tourist city itself more resembled Boston. The nation's second busiest port, it was a city of high culture as well as heterogeneous ethnic groups, home of liberal French Catholicism as well as rabid segregationism, a city with an aristocratic elite as well as a polyglot underclass.

Violence erupted in November 1960 when four black first-graders entered two previously all-white elementary schools. Whites by the thousands rioted through downtown, hurling rocks and bottles. For months a crowd of women (whom reporters called "the cheerleaders") gathered in front of the schools every day, forcing small black children to run a gauntlet of obscenity, spittle, and shoves, while harassing the few whites who ignored a school boycott.

New Orleans and Louisiana differed greatly, of course, from Boston and Massachusetts. Segregationism was avowed openly in Louisiana by major politicians. The mayor was allied with segregationists, while the state government and legislature uniformly expressed hostility to desegregation. But given the differences, consider the similarities: a federal court ordered desegregation after protracted resistance by a school board that continually acted as if the schools would never be integrated; the Catholic church at first advocated desegregation, then fell silent; a mayor with a "reform" reputation disappointed integrationists; no viable political parties existed, no political machinery by which desegregation could be promoted; an influential civic-business elite, based on old money and high status, toyed with politics only sporadically and shunned desegregation; and finally and most importantly, the schools chosen to be desegregated were in one of the city's poorest neighborhoods.

The choice of schools ironically illustrated the naïveté of those who think that controversial policy decisions can be done "scientifically" and "without politics." Moderate members of the school board used a computer program to select a tiny number of black children who would desegregate. Elaborate screening produced a handful of well-scrubbed black youngsters. Little care, however, was taken in the choice of the white schools. Since they needed to be schools with median grades low enough to admit the black children, two elementary schools in rundown, poor, white Ward 9 were selected. The ward housed an ethnic potpourri of working-class and welfare families, many of whom lived in housing projects. The neighborhood was the most neglected in the city and, to make matters worse, abutted St. Bernard Parish, controlled by boss Leander Perez, a rich segregationist who hired pickets to protest and who made his own schools available as refuges for the boycotters.

The school board claimed "the machine did it," but in choosing schools the board ignored advice to use other sections of the city where black children already lived. They also refused offers of help from affluent white parents who volunteered to have their schools desegregated first. One sign carried by a protester in the Ninth Ward signaled the message thus delivered: "If you are poor, mix; if you are rich, forget about it; some law."[39]

A year later, in 1961, desegregation went very differently in New Orleans. The elite of old families and rich businessmen called for peace; the mayor gave the police firm orders to disperse crowds; and the school board did not hide behind a computer but chose schools in the silk-stocking wards. Now violence subsided, and on its second try New Orleans peacefully began the desegregation of its schools. Thirteen years later Boston finally would begin its desegregation, unfortunately with many of the dynamics in action that made New Orleans' first attempt disastrous. Coincidentally, 1961 marked the beginnings of a new phase of the black struggle for decent schools in Boston, a struggle which, along with the reaction to it, is the subject of the next chapter.

2
Democracy and Segregation, 1961–1965

On January 19, 1964, a pantheon of political and religious celebrities attended a memorial service in Boston for the late President Kennedy. Catholic, Protestant, and Jewish clergy joined together in honoring the native son, and a venerable Boston historian thought he saw in the proceedings "the spirit of Bishop Cheverus and his neighbors of the first quarter of the nineteenth century. . . . The memory of John F. Kennedy had reunited Boston." Later that year, however, a black Roxbury mother observed sadly about Boston: "I used to feel that things like boycotts and demonstrations belonged in Birmingham and Mississippi. Now I know that . . . this is the Boston problem as well, here in the deep North."[1]

Earlier, on August 26, 1963, over 250,000 black and white marchers gathered on the mall at the Washington Monument in the nation's capital and heard the Reverend Martin Luther King, Jr. speak with transcendent eloquence of the dream of racial integration and brotherhood. Ten days before this historic event, in Boston, local NAACP leaders had met with the city's all-white school committee to present demands regarding public schools in black neighborhoods. When black activists tried to discuss first de facto segregation in the schools, Louise Hicks, committee chair, abruptly gaveled adjournment and the meeting ended in less than fifteen minutes. The angry black men and women stalked out. That fall, as Hicks was reelected to the school committee by an enormous majority, the national media launched her and Boston's committee into prominence as a symbol of the white backlash.

Both educational reformers and civil rights activists found much to lament about the structure and functioning of the Boston School Committee, but a key point that tends to be overlooked is that the five-member committee was democratically elected, chosen at-large in non-partisan elections for two-year terms. To a great extent the committee

22

responded to the will of its constituents. That the city's black minority possessed no representation, that at-large elections, together with low black voting, tended to make a black's election to the committee highly unlikely, and that the committee turned a deaf ear to most demands of blacks, no one can dispute. The system provided poorly, if at all, for the protection of minority interests. Yet large majorities of white voters elected and reelected members who stood-up to what many whites perceived as unwarranted black militancy.

Since the 1960s comparative studies of desegregation have revealed the discouraging truth that elected school officials, in contrast to those appointed, have been far less willing to promote desegregation. This springs from many causes, especially the fact that elected officials who vote to desegregate tend not to get reelected. "The more perfect the means of popular control, the worse for racial equity."[2] In Boston, the resistance to desegregation was from the start a problem intimately associated with what Tocqueville called the tyranny of the majority.

The long local saga of black efforts to gain better schools began before the Civil War and contains many scenes of déjà vu filled with much irony. During the early nineteenth century separate primary schooling for blacks had been created by white charity, black contributions, and a pittance from the thrifty school committee. By the 1840s, however, reformers found the "African" grammar schools "unhealthy and inadequate" and Boston's small black population tried, with the help of white abolitionists, to eliminate segregated schools. Both the white and black populations divided angrily within themselves on the matter, with some blacks anticipating the "community control" position. But in 1849 the reformers brought a suit to the Massachusetts Supreme Court involving a black child, Sarah Roberts, who walked a mile across the city every day, past white schools, to attend the segregated black school. In 1850 the court decided against integrating the Boston schools, but five years later the state legislature, now under complete control of the upstart Know-Nothing party, required that the Boston schools desegregate. Significantly, Boston's first desegregation, like its last, was imposed from the outside by nonlocal authorities.

Just as importantly, and ironically, the 1855 desegregation sprang very much from an anti-Irish Catholic animus that propelled the brief, spectacular, and controversial career of the Know-Nothings. The nativists sought to cleanse the city and state of what they regarded as corrupting influences emanating from foreigners and Catholics, but especially the

Irish Papists. The nativist movement also contained antislavery and evan-
gelical elements in conflict with the Irish, because the latter tended to
defend slavery, to vote stubbornly for all Democrats, including southern
Democrats, and to oppose favorite Yankee Protestant reforms such as
temperance. In addition, many Irish were Negrophobic, so it was not
surprising that the *Boston Pilot*, a Catholic weekly, opposed the desegregation law and said it probably was meant "as an insult" to Catholics.
Indeed, one nativist Boston legislator had urged passage of the law on
the grounds that "well-scrubbed" Negro children on the outskirts of
Boston were forced to go long distances to the black school, while white
children, including "the dirtiest Irish," could step from their homes to
school next door.[3]

Less than twenty years after the Civil War, blacks again were clustered
in separate schools. For the next century, too, Boston's black population
remained relatively small, residentially segregated, and economically and
politically weak. At-large elections or outright gerrymanders often excluded them from representation in the state or city governments. Like
blacks throughout the nation, they remained clients of the Republican
party until the 1930s, receiving token patronage through local community leaders not particularly interested or able to fight for civil rights.

World War II laid the foundations for the modern civil rights movement, as it did for the forward thrust of many minority groups. War-
engendered prosperity and mobility lifted blacks' social condition as well
as their aspirations. Nazism and the death camps discredited racism, at
least among educated classes and elites, and by the early 1950s the Cold
War competition between the USSR and the United States made discrimination in America embarrassing to a nation that boasted of the superior
morality and fairness of its way of life.

The Supreme Court's 1954 *Brown v. Topeka Board of Education* decision called for an end to the South's legally established (de jure) systems
of racially segregated schools. The Court thereby overturned the doctrine
of "separate but equal," which had provided the rationale for school
segregation since 1896. The next year the Court told lower federal courts
to implement the *Brown* decision "with all deliberate speed," but the
Deep South had embarked already on a program of "massive resistance"
that would maintain southern caste lines for another decade.[4]

Meanwhile, a social movement akin to a religious revival had galva-
nized southern blacks, and they began to challenge segregation in such
well-publicized episodes as the Montgomery, Alabama, bus boycott of

1955–56 and the 1960 college student sit-ins at lunch counters in Greensboro, North Carolina. By the early 1960s these and other events captured the nation's attention as television joined newspapers, magazines, and radio in creating a media coverage that became itself part of the powerful array of forces at work.

During the late 1950s and early 1960s a kind of national morality play, set in the South, unfolded before an ever larger audience whose sensitivity to discrimination against southern blacks rose with each new act in the drama. In the Montgomery bus boycott a young, black preacher, King, had arisen as a charismatic and eloquent spokesman of an oppressed people, and he impressed on this phase of civil rights his philosophy of nonviolence and civil disobedience. Southern blacks, for generations submissive, downtrodden, and exploited, now confronted the power of white southern society as had Gandhi's legions in British India: quietly, soberly, and firmly; not backing down; absorbing the blows and curses, beatings and killings that rained down upon them.[5]

To many whites outside the South, the civil rights assault on explicit forms of discrimination and the often brutally violent southern defense of the caste system seemed a stark struggle between good and evil. Given the tendency to see the mote in the other fellow's eye, and the South's retention of the lion's share of movement and media attention until 1965, the ambivalent northern response stayed in the background during this period.

In Boston, postwar changes within the black population would have far-reaching consequences. From 1940 to 1970 the black population increased by 342 percent to a total of 104,000. At the same time many middle-class whites left Boston for the suburbs (31 percent of whites left between 1950 and 1970), and so blacks rose from about 3 to over 16 percent of the city's population. Boston's blacks became more concentrated even as the borders of the ghetto expanded from Roxbury and the South End to Roxbury Highlands, North Dorchester, and Mattapan (map 2.1).

The black influx came just as native blacks enjoyed their most significant advance in economic mobility in at least a century. The more established, middle-class blacks viewed with trepidation the mostly poor, rough-edged newcomers. Rivalries and cultural differences existed among old natives, new southerners (called "Homies"), West Indians, and others. Before 1945 the small black community possessed a secure, though subordinate, working relationship of the patron-client type with the

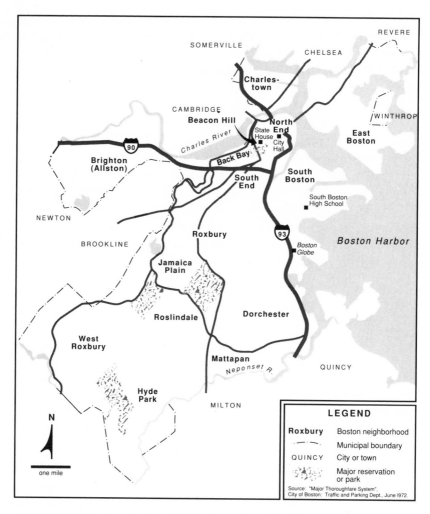

Boston's Neighborhoods, about 1970. Courtesy of Clark University
Cartographic Service.

white power structure. By the 1950s its middle class was expanding just
as the arrival of poor newcomers caused the black population as a whole
to lose status and the quality of schools in black neighborhoods to
plummet.

As the ghetto grew and became more visible to whites it did so mostly
in terms of problems and crime. On the FBI index in 1960 black males

reportedly represented 5 percent of Boston's population but 24 percent of people arrested for crimes. Ironically, before whites acquired a perception of a black crime threat, respectable blacks were far more acutely aware of the connection between young black males and crime and all the more anxious to protect themselves.[6]

Thus, the emergence of a school desegregation movement in the early 1960s resulted from the confluence of national events, internal strains in the black population, improved economic conditions for native blacks, rising aspirations, and of course the desperate condition of schools in black neighborhoods. Young professional blacks moving into Boston during the 1950s waged an uphill battle to politicize the apathetic rank and file and to ignite a mood of defiance in a black population long known for its quiescence. Ruth Batson, who became a psychologist at Boston University, fought a lonely struggle with the school department about the treatment of her three daughters in the early 1950s. Soon she was joined by new young leaders such as Paul Parks, Melvin King, the Reverend James Breeden, Thomas Simmons, Thomas Atkins, and Ellen Jackson. Parks, for example, an engineer, came to Boston in 1951. He had been educated at Purdue University where he had already participated in protests against discrimination. Thomas Atkins was a graduate of Indiana University who in 1961 began to study East Asian affairs at Harvard, then became active in the NAACP and entered law school in 1966. The Boston-born King was the son of West Indian immigrants who came to Boston after World War I and typified the activist posture of that cultural group. This new generation barely concealed its impatience with the older community leaders whose power, said King later, was "more illusory than real," and who seemed oblivious to the "fantastic and fanatical racism" all around them.[7]

The middle-class professionals leading the schools fight had been affected by the broad national currents at work unleashed by World War II, prosperity, the Cold War, and the *Brown* decision.[8] These upwardly mobile blacks also accepted the myth of education as uplift, which exerted its charm more powerfully on blacks than on other Americans. The NAACP had decided to focus on schools in the 1930s because discrimination in public schools was relatively easy to demonstrate, because government played such a central role in education, and because blacks bought into the ideology that "education will set you free." That schools were enhancers of mobility was an article of faith, despite the fact that economic opportunity depended on many other factors, and that groups

that had profited from schooling had the advantage of particular historical conditions while not facing the same degree of prejudice as blacks.[9]

Boston's blacks also found inspiration from blacks in New York City,
where from 1954 to 1960 a controversy over school integration had
produced black demonstrations in Harlem and white boycotts of schools
in Queens. By 1963, when Boston's relatively moderate blacks finally
held a modest school boycott, in New York civil rights demonstrations
had become "a daily occurance."[10]

In 1961 the NAACP asked the Massachusetts Commission Against
Discrimination (MCAD) to investigate the Boston schools, but the
MCAD concluded that race was not a determining factor in the assignment of pupils or in the quality of schools. Next the NAACP engaged in
talks with school superintendent Frederick J. Gillis, who insisted that the
department did not classify students by race, so he could not assess the
NAACP claims regarding black students. At this point, Boston's fledgling
civil rights movement was just beginning, with a small group of activists
trying to pressure companies that did business in black Roxbury to hire
blacks, while the racially integrated Citizens for Boston Public Schools
(CBPS) in 1961 ran a slate for school committee that got more votes in
white West Roxbury than it did in Roxbury.[11]

By spring 1963 the NAACP brought its case directly to the school
committee, and in doing so set off a reaction that energized both a more
broadly based civil rights movement and an even more powerful white
backlash. On May 23 the new chair of the school committee, Louise
Hicks, visited a meeting at Freedom House in Roxbury arranged by Paul
Parks of the NAACP and CBPS. Hicks actually listened sympathetically
to black grievances, came away "deeply disturbed," and invited black
spokesmen to come before the school committee. At this stage the CBPS
even considered endorsing Hicks in the fall elections.[12]

But in the next three weeks the NAACP and a Hicks-led committee
majority parted ways, particularly on the apparently symbolic question
of whether de facto segregation existed in the schools. The NAACP
insisted that the committee admit to it, pointing out that this did not
mean that the committee was guilty of creating segregation itself. But
Gillis, Hicks, and a majority of the school committee refused to acknowledge any condition of segregation.[13]

The school committee and NAACP representatives came together
again on June 11, with NAACP sympathizers packing the 125-person-

capacity committee room, while 200 allies who could not get in rallied outside. During an eight-hour session, NAACP representatives asked that de facto segregation be recognized, that white teachers be trained to remove their prejudices against black children, that discrimination in hiring teachers be ended, and, in general, that the committee act to ameliorate the inferior facilities, materials, and teaching to which black children were subjected. In retrospect, the black demands seem moderate, but the committee and school administrators found it impossible to admit that segregation existed or that any of their actions constituted discrimination. The committee agreed to discuss certain points but adamantly refused to admit to de facto segregation.[14]

That same night, in reaction to events in Alabama where Governor George Wallace had sought to prevent desegregation of the state university, President Kennedy had gone on television with a dramatic call for civil rights legislation to end discrimination in public places and to promote school desegregation. In Boston, negotiations between the school committee and black activists continued for several days, then broke down for good.

On June 18 the NAACP sponsored a "Stay Out For Freedom Day," and an estimated four to eight thousand high school students, many of whom apparently were whites simply finding an excuse for a holiday, boycotted school. From this point on, the NAACP and the committee routinely talked at rather than with one another, usually via the media. Hostilities simmered through the summer, until on August 18 the NAACP representatives again came before the committee. Mrs. Hicks had agreed to the meeting on condition that there be no discussion of de facto segregation. But that was what the NAACP was determined to discuss. As soon as Mrs. Batson mentioned the term, the meeting ended.[15]

In Washington, D.C., less than two weeks later, the great civil rights demonstration took place, and the Kennedy administration continued to be pushed along by events in the South. Boston, however, was creating something of an embarrassment for the president from Massachusetts. Telephone calls from presidential advisers and then from JFK himself did nothing to deter Mrs. Hicks, who was now marching at the head of the white backlash parade.[16] Most analysts of the Boston school controversy have given much emphasis to Hicks's role, as if she single-handedly created the white backlash. But social movements do not usually arise because of one leader. Leaders and constituencies normally shape one another. Hicks was just as much a creature of the backlash as she was one of its creators.

Hicks joined the school committee in 1961 after a bland, standardly reformist ("take politics out of the schools") campaign in which her best assets were her South Boston base and a well-known political name, always a factor to be reckoned with in Boston. Her father had been a popular political figure and municipal judge for whom Day Boulevard in South Boston is named. After his death in 1950, Louise Day Hicks (she had married a New York electrical engineer in 1942 and had sons in 1945 and 1946) went back to school for a B.S. in education and then a law degree. Earlier, she had taught first grade in affluent Brookline and clerked in her father's office. It was nevertheless, as J. Anthony Lukas commented, "extraordinary" for a South Boston mother of two to attend law school in the 1950s. With a law degree and various volunteer good works on her resume, in 1961 the forty-three-year-old Hicks, an unknown quantity, ran a respectable fourth in the September primary, then third in the general election.[17]

A perfect image of maternal, lace-curtain propriety, Hicks's political appeal certainly derived from attributes other than her appearance, especially in a city that has so often elected macho males with flamboyant styles. "Her round, outsized baby-doll face, her high-pitched, singsong voice and elocution-school manner, and her orchid-corsage style of dress could hardly be called political assets."[18] She looked as if she were perpetually en route to a confirmation or christening and spoke in that excessively formal, hypercorrect English characteristic of Boston school teachers turned politician.

During the summer of 1963, Hicks not only continued to deny that segregation in any form existed in the Boston schools but also began to lash out at the NAACP for its militancy. She quickly acquired a reputation for gutsiness and a willingness to stand up to "them," at a time when many other white leaders seemed to be cowed by fear of offending blacks and white liberals. "*De facto* segregation is an inflammatory term," she pronounced. "It implies prejudice." She denied that blacks received an inferior education and pointed instead to blacks' advantages in having extra expenditures for remedial programs. She argued that the problem was not with the schools but with black pupils who were poorly equipped by their families and culture to learn.[19]

In the preliminary election of September 1963 Hicks topped the field of school committee candidates with 78,665 votes—21,000 more than the incumbent mayor, John Collins, received. In the weeks before the election, the NAACP and its allies staged sit-ins at school committee headquarters, and two days before election day, a "March on Roxbury." The several thousand black and white marchers stopped at one point at the Sherwin School, which Melvin King called an "atrocious example" of a black school. The next day it mysteriously burned to the ground. Before the election political forecasters believed that Hicks had committed political suicide in so recklessly embracing the white backlash. But after the votes rolled in, Hicks saw now that "every time the Negroes demonstrated, they campaigned for me."[20] In her victory speech Hicks blasted the NAACP leaders as "not the true leaders of the community. They are not speaking for the community in the sit-ins they staged . . . the demonstrations they fostered . . . and the boycott of classes they called last June. The real harm done by the NAACP was to the very children they said they were aiding. They drew a color line where none had existed before."[21]

For the November election a coalition of civil rights activists, educational reformers, and liberals entered the lists against Hicks. They endorsed Melvin King, a black social worker at the South End Neighborhood House, as well as incumbent committee member Arthur Gartland. But the anti-Hicks candidates failed badly, while Gartland barely won reelection. All five incumbents were reelected and Hicks, receiving over 128,000 votes (Gartland had just over 58,000), nearly 69 percent of those voting, not only led the ticket and received more votes than Mayor Collins but also set a record for the greatest number of votes ever received in a city election. There now could be little doubt that white majority sentiment in Boston had set itself firmly against the local civil rights movement. In 1961 only a third of all registered voters had turned out in the city election, while in 1963 almost 61 percent cast ballots. Since Hicks led Mayor Collins by some 20,000 votes, clearly the school committee election had created this remarkable electoral surge.

Hicks appealed to groups and neighborhoods across the city, receiving over 80 percent of the vote in working-class enclaves such as Charlestown as well as in middle-class West Roxbury. She failed to get over 50 percent only in black Roxbury and liberal Back Bay and Beacon Hill precincts where young, affluent, or educated voters predominated.[22] Hicks was now ensconced as the darling of the white neighborhoods. She rode antibusing furthest, to the city council, to two unsuccessful runs at mayor, and to a term in Congress. When many antibusers became disillusioned with their political leaders, they still opened their hearts and clapped their hands for "Louise." But if Hicks had not come to the fore as the champion of fearful, reactive white Bostonians, then other local politicians would have done so. Over the next dozen years and more, several did.

During 1964–65 the national civil rights movement enjoyed its most spectacular successes as "The Second Reconstruction" climaxed. Capitalizing on the emotional momentum created by Kennedy's assassination, President Lyndon Johnson guided the 1964 Civil Rights Act through Congress. By the time the president from Texas signed the bill on July 2, a coalition of civil rights and church groups had launched Freedom Summer in deepest Mississippi, where segregationists responded with the beatings of many and the murders of fifteen persons, though these did not attract national attention until the bodies of three young civil rights workers, one black and two white, were discovered on August 4.

Southern violence and brutality backfired, however, boosting national support for civil rights and bringing the next great and final legislative triumph the following spring. In Selma, Alabama, black demonstrators for voting registration attracted enormous media coverage and the scenes of peaceful demonstrators attacked by troopers with clubs, tear gas, water hoses, and cattle prods again saturated the media. By the time the demonstrations ended, white and black sympathizers from all over the North and West had gathered in the Selma marches. With a big, liberal Democratic majority in Congress, the Voting Rights bill of 1965 passed.

After Selma, though, the movement began to come apart. Tensions rose between blacks and whites, and between blacks and blacks. Labor unions became preoccupied with other matters. The Vietnam War, which Martin Luther King and other black leaders opposed, divided the Democratic party and helped rupture the black-labor alliance, as did the federal government's promotion of affirmative action. In 1966 the "Black Power" slogan emerged, as did radical black self-defense groups such as the Black Panthers. And each summer, from 1965 through 1968, television screens were dominated by scenes of rioting, arson, looting, and virtual military occupation of urban ghettos. All this fed a white backlash that in Boston was well established.[23]

In the presidential primaries of 1964, George Wallace, the Alabama governor who the year before had "stood in the schoolhouse door" (unsuccessfully) to prevent desegregation of the University of Alabama, traveled north to challenge civil rights legislation and to tap white fears of black militancy. In April and May he racked up surprising votes in Wisconsin and Indiana, with 34 and 30 percent of the Democratic vote, respectively, and almost won the Maryland primary with 43 percent. Wallace's surge gave impetus to the candidacy of conservative Barry Goldwater within the Republican party. In November, however, incumbent President Johnson buried Goldwater in a landslide, and the threat posed by Wallace seemed a momentary aberration. But as the civil rights movement left its nonviolent phase, and as riots and flames engulfed one northern ghetto after another, white fears and resistance steadily increased.[24]

In Massachusetts and Boston, as in the nation, two different currents flowed through the middle 1960s. One was liberal, optimistic, cosmopolitan, universalist, and pro-integration, while the other was reactive, fearful, localist, in part anti-integration and antiblack, and in part opposed to change, any change, of which there seemed to be a great deal in the mid-1960s.

The Massachusetts parallel to national events during 1964–65 included a state legislative victory for school desegregation. Boston's civil rights protests also continued to follow closely in the steps of activities in New York City, where on February 3, 1964, for example, blacks staged a huge school boycott, with 45 percent of all students staying out. In Boston, on February 26, about one-fifth of black students boycotted, with some attending "freedom schools" and others joining about fifteen hundred protesters at city hall. Though apparently pushed forward by younger leaders over the objections of NAACP veterans, Boston's boycott was relatively tame. More significantly, it was held in late February to coincide with the vacations of suburban schools.[25]

Once again state and local officials tried to discourage the boycott, while Mrs. Hicks requested the attorney general, who was Edward Brooke, the black Republican who later became U.S. Senator, "to inform the Negro leaders of state laws concerning compulsory education." Hicks and her allies stated often during 1963–64 that adults who encouraged student boycotts ought to be held legally accountable and punished.[26]

The boycott made little impact on the school committee and its implacability led integrationists to turn for help to sympathetic state authorities. The state commissioner of education, Owen Kiernan, appointed an advisory Commission on Racial Imbalance, loaded with college presidents, prominent business executives, educators, and religious leaders. Journalist Alan Lupo called it "one of the greatest collections of googoos ever assembled in Massachusetts."[27] More importantly, the blueribbon, cosmopolitan group was far removed from Boston's neighborhoods. The Kiernan Commission's preliminary findings revealed that fifty-five racially imbalanced schools existed in the state, forty-five of them in Boston. The commission delivered its final report in April 1965, in a climate pervaded by "The Spirit of Selma," as events in Alabama dominated Boston's headlines, pushing aside even the newly escalating war in Vietnam.

Boston and Selma suddenly became intertwined, symbolically and in blood. In early March Rev. James Reeb, a white Unitarian from Boston, was clubbed to death in Selma's streets, prompting Massachusetts to send to Selma an official state delegation headed by Lieutenant Governor Elliott Richardson. On March 12, fifty to two hundred college students began to sit in outside the office of the U.S. district attorney at the Federal Building in downtown Boston and said they would stay there until Federal troops or marshals went to Selma. Two days later, twenty-five to thirty thousand persons gathered on Boston Common in memory of Reeb. Several of the speakers compared events in Alabama with "the less bloody but, in the long run, no less destructive processes of injustice that were being carried out in the Boston public schools."[28]

In April, after the Kiernan Commission report appeared, a black minister, Vernon Carter, began what became a five-month vigil, joined by various clergy, students, and others, outside school committee offices. Then Martin Luther King came to Boston. Mrs. Hicks refused to see him and forbade him to enter a black school. But King did visit the governor and addressed the state legislature. He also led a march to the steps of the Boardman School where he denounced de facto segregation and then spoke to some twenty thousand people at a Boston Common rally. At the latter, Ruth Batson charged the school committee with committing "educational genocide on the Negro child in the Boston public schools."[29]

In more temperate rhetoric, the Kiernan report, Because It Is Right— Educationally, condemned racial imbalance as unequal, undemocratic, and educationally harmful to black and white children. Pervaded by optimism, the report was not written with a local audience from Boston's neighborhoods in mind. Rather, it was addressed to a national readership, perhaps even to the national conscience.[30]

The report included six research papers by social scientists, one of which contended that the neighborhood school, whose banner Hicks and her backers had raised aloft, was a myth. To the extent that it still existed in a highly mobile population, the paper held, the neighborhood school reflected not generational stability but simply concentrations of particular ethnic groups in various parts of the city. Educationally, in any case, the neighborhood school was of no value. Another paper purported to show the deleterious effects of ethnic group concentration.[31]

The attacks on neighborhood schools and ethnicity fit logically with the universalist, cosmopolitan, and egalitarian impulses feeding the civil rights and other reform movements of the 1960s. Yet they came also just as an ethnic revival was gathering momentum and launching the most powerful attack ever on what had been the nation's assimilationist traditions and dominant melting pot ideology.[32] The wave of cultural pluralism owed much to the civil rights movement and African-American self-consciousness. It received a boost in the fall of 1965 with the passage of an Immigration Act by Congress abolishing the national origins system, which since 1924 had discriminated against ethnic groups from Eastern, Central, and Southern Europe. Gradually, the tacit ignoring of ethnicity and the shame attached to it for many fell away, and by the early 1970s a new awareness of cultural origins blossomed across the country. In 1972 Congress gave its blessing in the Ethnic Heritage Studies Act.[33] Ironically, like those who wrote the Kiernan report, spokesmen from Boston's white neighborhoods could now call on history, social science, and official sanction to legitimize their values against those of liberals and blacks.

But the Kiernan report added another push to the already extensive lobbying to get the legislature to pass a law to abolish racial imbalance. Various dignitaries, including Governor John Volpe, Cardinal Richard J. Cushing, and the head of the Greater Boston Chamber of Commerce, endorsed the report and urged passage of such legislation. A statewide coalition formed behind it very similar to the array of political, social, and religious groups that had won passage of national civil rights legislation. In the legislature, Democratic party leaders teamed up with liberal suburbanites to guide the bill through continuing attempts to derail or gut it by Boston legislators. In Washington the civil rights movement crested in the Voting Rights Act of 1965; in Boston, in the Racial Imbalance Act of 1965. No other state passed such a law.[34]

The law defined a racially imbalanced school as one with over 50

percent nonwhite pupils and required that local school committees provide the Board of Education with an annual census of students by race;
any imbalanced school system could lose state funds.[35] In focusing on
racial imbalance rather than on how schools got that way, the law actually went further than the *Brown* decision. But at the same time it
granted parents the option of not allowing students to be bused, and any
school committee denied funds because of persisting racial imbalance
could get judicial review and thus delay implementation. Perhaps it is
sufficient comment on the law's effectiveness to note that the Boston
School Committee managed to delay its implementation for nine years.
But many non-Bostonians whose local school districts in no way faced
desegregation now possessed satisfied consciences. According to political
scientist Frank Levy's "Simple Theory of a Civil Rights Law," "the
probability of securing majority approval for a civil rights bill increases
as the proportion of unaffected districts rises."[36] Only one Boston legislator voted for the law.

The episode recalled for some the era of the "Boston Bills" when,
during the Irish Catholics' rise to political power in Boston in the late
nineteenth century, Yankee and rural legislators passed laws governing
Boston's internal affairs (e.g., appointing a police chief) as a way of
blunting the impact of Irish takeover. Once again outsiders, no longer
mainly Yankee or rural, were dictating to Boston's untrustworthy Irish
about how to run their city.

The school committee's reaction to the law could have been predicted
by its aggressive opposition to relieving racial imbalance during 1964–
65 and its success in making the term "busing" a shibboleth as early as
1965. Long before busing ever came to Boston and before anyone ever
proposed extensive busing as a solution, the school committee catered to
and fed the fears of its white constituency by raising the specter of busing. They, not the NAACP or its allies, made busing a household word in
the city.

Mrs. Hicks denounced the authors of the Kiernan report as hypocrites
whose own children attended private, all-white schools. Dismissing their
conclusions as the "pompous pronouncements of the uninformed," she
characterized the blue-ribbon commission as "a small band of racial
agitators, non-native to Boston, and a few college radicals" who were
key agents in a "conspiracy to tell the people of Boston how to run their
schools, their city, and their lives."[37]

Hicks pounced on one of the report's "suggestions," tucked away in an appendix, regarding "mutual exchanges of students" as a short-term remedy for imbalance in five elementary schools. Hicks found this "incomprehensible" and denounced it as "undemocratic, un-American, absurdly expensive, and diametrically opposed to the wishes of the parents of this city." It was not, she said, the way to address the "environmental disadvantages" of ghetto children. Rather, compensatory programs should be given to them in their own schools—busing them to white schools only harmed them and the children in the receiving schools.[38] By June of that year the *Globe's* education reporter observed that "busing" had surpassed "*de facto* segregation as the hobgoblin . . . that sets off flames of anger." It meant essentially racial integration and "when you talk about integrating the schools you have a fight on your hands."[39]

During the previous year the school department had proposed that several hundred black students from three severely overcrowded schools in Roxbury and North Dorchester (the Endicott, Greenwood, and Gibson schools) be bused to nearby schools in Dorchester and Brighton. The school committee at first had approved but then in August 1965, responding to phone calls and visits from aroused white parents, voted against the plan and instead proposed that an abandoned Hebrew school in Dorchester be purchased and that the black students be sent there. The thirty-two-year-old Beth El School would cost $175,000 to buy and renovate and an additional $100,000 to staff and supply. Transporting black students to underutilized white schools would cost far less, but the committee earlier had tried to avoid that remedy by proposing double sessions or reopening a sixty-four-year-old public school to relieve black overcrowding. Superintendent Ohrenberger, Governor Volpe, and Mayor Collins all opposed these options, and warned the school committee that it might now be engaging in acts that a court would eventually find to be deliberate acts of segregation.[40]

At this point a group of black parents decided to bypass the committee. Parents from the overcrowded schools, led by Mrs. Ellen Jackson and Mrs. Betty Johnson, organized the privately funded busing of black children to underused white schools. Under the city's open enrollment policy—which Hicks and school officials continually pointed to as evidence of the lack of discrimination—any student could transfer into a school provided there was space available. The catch was that the committee did nothing to aid black transfers and, indeed, much to obstruct them. But in early September the *Boston Globe* pitched in by publishing detailed tables showing where vacancies existed in every school in the city, and the new grassroots program, called Operation Exodus, began. It initially moved eighty-five students with donated buses and car pools. By September 12, two hundred students were involved. By 1966 money was coming in from the unions, suburban liberals, and bake sales and spaghetti suppers held by the black parents. At its peak, Operation Exodus would involve over six hundred students.[41]

Hicks and other white politicians misrepresented Operation Exodus and consequently, in many areas of white Boston, it was not perceived as a black bootstraps effort. It seemed rather part and parcel of what blacks and "outsiders" were trying to foist on the city. Hicks promoted obfuscation by lashing out against the "Negro leaders" she claimed were "misinforming parents and telling them half truths" about overcrowding; she distorted the fact that the leaders in this case were parents. The committee also threw obstacles in Operation Exodus's path at the last minute by, for example, requiring that children could not be transferred without "official" transfer slips. On September 9 Hicks made a dramatic appearance, with police escort, at the Blue Hill Avenue headquarters of Operation Exodus to tell the black parents that "without these yellow authorization slips, your children will be turned away by the busload." Despite protests by white parents and Hicks's obstructionism, Operation Exodus continued.[42]

On the heels of Operation Exodus came the Metropolitan Council for Educational Opportunity (METCO). METCO began in 1966 when seven suburban school committees voted to join together to bus black students from Boston into their usually superior schools. Leon Trilling, an MIT professor and Brookline School Committee member, obtained a $259,000 federal grant and an additional $126,000 from the Carnegie Corporation. Busing 220 black students in 1966, METCO by 1971–72 bused 1,580 blacks into thirty suburbs and had a waiting list of 1,300. By 1969 the state legislature had taken over funding of METCO and by 1972 the state was spending just under $2 million to operate it. In 1974–75 METCO was busing nearly 2,500 and still had a long waiting list, and Boston's direct cost was still zero.[43]

As the 1965 school committee elections approached, no one now expected antibusing to hurt Hicks or her allies. One of the reformist CBPS candidates said of the voters: "All they ask me is are you for busing? are you for Mrs. Hicks?" Even the CBPS issued a flyer saying that they opposed busing as a permanent solution to racial imbalance, but it did little good. In an off-year election, with only the committee and city council being elected, a record 48 percent of the electorate turned out, and 65 percent (93,056) voted for Hicks, who led the field. Hicks's strength was all the more impressive given her reliance on low-cost, nonmedia, campaigning with a solid neighborhood base. Arthur Gartland, the liberal incumbent who had opposed Hicks, failed reelection.[44]

By now Louise Hicks and Boston had acquired national reputations as being in the forefront of the white backlash. What that meant was fairly complex, as a study of Boston voters' attitudes before and after the 1965 election showed. Like most other white Americans, Bostonians during this time showed a greater willingness (if polls are to be believed) to favor black rights and condemn injustice in the abstract. Almost none expressed any objections to sending their children to school with a few blacks, and only 22 percent objected to sending them to a school that was half black. However, 64 percent would not want to send them where more than half the pupils were black.[45]

On the other hand, striking differences turned up between pro-Hicks and anti-Hicks voters. Hicks drew support especially from persons more firmly rooted in the city who perceived a threat to *"familiar, secure, and comfortable ways."* Their position on the schools constituted a first line of defense—they were most worried about integration of the neighborhood, "the inner citadel." Beyond that was the "fear that the old, good ways of life will change if Negroes move in." Hicksites agreed more often that it was best to keep Negroes "in their own districts and schools" and that "white people have a right to keep Negroes out of their neighborhoods if they want to."[46]

Hicks voters also scored higher on questions that tapped tendencies to conformity, general conservatism, and fear of "unsettling change." Regarding the latter, Hicks already was in tune with her constituency. After her thumping victory in 1965, she began to broaden the scope of her message, as she clearly set her sights on a run for the mayor's office. Hicks not only began an unrelenting campaign to repeal the Racial Imbalance Act but also added to her speeches denunciations of Vietnam War opponents, of the countercultural emblems of long hair and drugs, of "pseudo-liberals," of "the filthy-speech movement . . . at Berkeley, California," and of "radical agitators" and all who took a challenging or deviant posture toward traditional values and authority. "The current wave of 'street democracy,'" she said, "is the greatest threat to our cherished free society." Further anticipating the backlash mounted by Richard Nixon and Spiro Agnew after 1968, she also condemned the news media as part of society's problem.[47] Thus the backlash included not just a reaction to black civil rights militancy but also to the social and cultural upheavals that accelerated through the late 1960s.

The civil rights leaders of Boston have been faulted for focusing excessively on a symbolic, even a semantic issue (de facto segregation), rather than presenting concrete plans for alleviating racial imbalance or for creating better schools.[48] But the initial complaints of the civil rights leaders—and concerned parents behind them—focused initially on the dilapidated and overcrowded conditions in black schools. The sheer decrepitude of ghetto schools, as well as the attitudes of their mostly white staffs, provided the motivation for those blacks who believed that a good education was essential to their childrens' prospects for any kind of success in life.

It was not at first apparent that the average white school in Boston was no prizewinner for educational excellence, and some were in quite shabby condition. But black schools monopolized the bottom of the barrel. In 1962 a team of Harvard University consultants found that of thirty-five schools enrolling 60 percent or more Negroes, twenty-seven were built before 1914. Several, ranging from 65 to 95 percent black, were simply hazardous to the health of their occupants, such as the Bates School, a seventy-eight-year-old structure in the South End beside the Cathedral Housing project. It had wooden stairways, small outside grounds in need of resurfacing, an exterior charitably described as "deteriorating," while inside, said the consultants, "the window sashes and frames are rotting; the classrooms are drab and in need of paint and the toilet facilities require a great deal of renovation."[49]

In February 1964 a Harvard Divinity School report showed that school department expenditures were 10 percent lower for textbooks in ghetto schools, 19 percent lower for library and reference books, and 27 percent lower on health care per pupil. In elementary schools that were mostly black, expenditures ran lower than in comparable white schools on nine major items in the educational budget. For Boston overall, in-class expenditures averaged $275 per pupil; in the Negro schools, $213.

Given the unarguably sorry state of ghetto schools, why did it prove so difficult to address the problem of just fixing them up and making them better? To begin with, Boston schools in general suffered from being the stepchild of school committee politics. In December 1965 the *Globe* ran a series on the schools that highlighted deteriorating conditions in black schools and also provided details on the sad state of affairs in all schools, for example: the absence of school libraries in the 175 elementary and junior high schools, the relatively low scores of Boston students on national tests, the lack of guidance counseling, and so on.[50] Yet many whites thought that the blacks, not the schools, were the problem. As William O'Connor, a successor of Hicks as chair of the school committee, said, "We have no inferior education in our schools. What we have been getting is an inferior type of student." In this context those who ran the schools actually believed that they were doing well by Boston's blacks. The Boston Irish did not feel responsible for slavery or the long history of black oppression. They believed that the blacks should raise themselves up as other immigrant groups had done before them. The Irish had gotten ahead largely through mobilizing votes, of course, but not (they now thought) by staging sit-ins or protest marches.[51]

The school committee also resisted black demands because it was an elected body used as a stepping-stone by ambitious politicians. They were unlikely to risk offending the white majority and, indeed, had no incentive to do so.[52] But the political calculations of committee members were only the most visible parts of a political culture whose past forecast a pugnacious response to black protest. The school committee had been overwhelmingly Irish for most of the century; only four non-Irish men had served since 1942. Up until the late 1960s teachers were overwhelmingly white and Irish Catholic female, though the top administrators, of course, were male Irish Catholics. The school committee spent most of its time dealing not with educational but with patronage matters, and that was the heart of the matter. The Irish were not about to hand over to the blacks a share of their security blanket, which they had won according to the accepted rules of big city politics.[53]

Further, the blacks' criticism of the schools struck most Irish politicians and schoolmen as attacks on them personally. The NAACP seemed to be putting the Boston Irish in the same moral category as racist southern sheriffs. The whites who ran the schools probably were unconscious of their own patronizing attitudes toward blacks, whom they seemed to regard as dependent and unfortunate clients. Now these backdoor citizens were knocking, loudly and rudely, on the front door, demanding to be let in, and doing so at a time when their voting strength was still negligible.

The Irish schoolmen reacted most negatively to the blacks' confrontational style, which was rapidly becoming the protest mode of the 1960s but which in Boston simply reinforced a white reaction that would have been defensive anyway. Irish Catholics historically felt little sympathy for blacks. The Yankee Protestants who had run the city eighty years before might have responded more favorably to appeals to conscience, but the Irish (as well as the Italians) were not susceptible to civil rights leaders playing on guilt and shame.

Politics in Boston had long since become, in William Shannon's words, "an Irish family affair" marked by "inbreeding and a complacent parochialism." Though the Irish had wrested power from the Yankees, they had made few inroads on social and economic power. The glorious past of the Yankees and their rigid caste reaction to the Irish had produced in the latter "a massive inferiority complex." The long economic decline of New England and Boston in the twentieth century had done nothing to dispel the Irish's inordinate focus on security and status. As observers saw at the time, the Boston Irish in 1960, despite the election of John Kennedy to the presidency, and despite their constituting some 60 percent of the population, still saw themselves as a minority. One wit described them as "the only oppressed majority in the world."[54]

In their rivalry with the Yankees the Irish had viewed city politics "not as a conflict over how to obtain the best government for the lowest cost but as a struggle for power among competing groups." They looked at blacks similarly, as a competing group with no claim to a better moral position. Senator William Bulger of South Boston expressed this view of the NAACP well; he described it as simply another "political organization like any other—it can be right, it can be wrong; its demands have to be assessed on that basis."[55]

For several decades the schools had been in the hands of one close-knit branch of the Irish family. Many administrators and teachers actually had attended not the public but Catholic parochial schools and had absorbed their values. While Boston State College provided the system with many teachers, in 1967 all but one member of the board of superintendents were graduates of Catholic Boston College. These were men imbued with a sense of "discipline, hierarchy and authority." Such men did not welcome criticism under any circumstances. Indeed, their governance was notable for its resistance to questioning and innovation. Deviancy and nonconformity amounted to heresy.[56]

During the 1960s the Boston public schools and their Irish keepers came under attack as never before. Most of the criticism came, of course, from blacks and their allies, but some of it was simply directed at the overall mediocrity of the schools. And the Boston Finance Commission, a watchdog agency established by Yankee mistrust in the early years of the century, had since 1944 issued reports calling for elimination of political corruption in the school system. But Boston had long since developed, in Shannon's words, "a straight-forward acceptance of graft as necessary and inevitable." The schools were performing many functions with which their white users were relatively satisfied. Many whites who knew that political connections, kinships, and plain bribery resulted in jobs, better jobs, or transfer of children into preferred schools, simply accepted the system as it was. The following excerpt from the novel *Firewatch* was written during and about the busing crisis:

> "I was trying to get a promotion," Peter explained. "I didn't get it."
>
> "You'd be surprised how often these things work out for the best."
>
> "I was willing to pay for it. I was ready to pay for it. A thousand dollars in the right hands. Was all arranged. But the job, it went to someone else. A foul up."
>
> "Oh well," the priest never blinked, "you don't want a job on those terms."
>
> "Those terms? Father, there are no other terms. You pay the money and move along or you don't move along. Everybody does it. Sometimes it's a ticket to a dinner or a contribution or just working in somebody's campaign. But it all comes to the same thing. Jobs are hard to get and good jobs in good schools are harder to keep. You don't wanna get transferred one day to some zoo middle school, you gotta have friends. You don't much care how you get them. I know for a fact, there's a girl in the Grant School who slept with Monelli to get her job. She tells people. Laughs about it, like it's funny. Some joke, huh? You want a job, a promotion or a little security? These are the things that hafta be done."[57]

3

Democracy and Segregation
Part Two: The School Committee
Holds the Line

*[In dealing with English courts the Irish developed] the art of
soft deception ("blarney") and the disingenuous oath which is not
an oath at all. These were the acts of an imagination designed to
oblige the bearer with the fiction of compliance while preserving
fidelity to one's own conception of justice.*
—*William V. Shannon,* The American Irish:
   A Political and Social Portrait

*The affinity of the Irish for verbal innuendo, ambiguity, and meta-
phor have led the English to coin the phrase 'talking Irish' to describe
the Irishman's style of both communicating and not communicating
at the same time. . . . It is likely that their tradition of verbal obscurity was at least partially owing to their history of oppression by the
British. (Black Americans are another oppressed people who developed verbal mechanisms to disguise meaning.)*
—*Monica McGoldrick,* Ethnicity & Family Therapy

For nine years after the passage of the Racial Imbalance Act, the Boston School Committee, with or without Louise Hicks, refused to take
steps to bring about any significant school integration. Through delay,
counterattacks, and the most transparent obfuscation and tokenism the
committee held the line against a growing black population. Meanwhile,
the number of racially imbalanced schools climbed upward.[1]

As residential segregation increased the committee in no way tried to
ameliorate the situation; instead, in most cases where it could choose it
acted to perpetuate or even actually to increase imbalance in the city's
schools, as would be demonstrated conclusively in the 1974 federal court

44

decision. But that cataclysmic event seemed unlikely during the second half of the 1960s when the school committee's strategy of delay looked as if it might buy enough time to win legislative repeal of the Racial Imbalance Act.

The committee consistently refused to do simple acts that might have reduced racial imbalance, such as redistricting or locating new schools on the borders of neighborhoods, thereby creating mixed schools without needing to transport students. In 1965 neither the NAACP, black parents, the state board, nor anyone else was suggesting extensive two-way busing. But the school committee acted as if this was the threat, or, if they gave an inch, soon would be. The plan that the federal district court imposed nine years later fulfilled the worst fears of thousands of Bostonians—fears which the Boston School Committee had first propagated and made into a self-fulfilling prophecy.

The first round of the struggle between the state board and the committee began in the fall of 1965 and came to a close in the spring of 1967, rehearsing in its tortuous maneuverings the basic pattern of board-committee interaction into 1974. The first racial census of Massachusetts schools detected fifty-five imbalanced schools, forty-six in Boston (table 3.1). As required by the Racial Imbalance Act, the board in October asked the committee to submit a desegregation plan. In December the committee submitted a plan whose impact on racial imbalance it would have taken a theologian to discern. After finding the committee plan inadequate in April 1966, the board suspended Boston schools' state funding. In late May the committee and board began exchanging plans in ping-pong fashion. By August, both combatants went to court. The committee undertook not only to free the money held by the state but also filed suit to test the constitutionality of the Racial Imbalance Act.[2]

The Suffolk Superior Court ruled that the board had acted improperly in impounding funds, but on appeal the State Superior Court in January 1967 overturned the decision and at the same time ordered the school committee to submit an acceptable plan within ninety days or lose permanently the funds in question. Shortly thereafter the committee sent a new plan that the board, with reservations, approved as a "first step" by a six to two vote. Board Chair William G. Saltonstall said lamely that the plan "was more than a token, though perhaps not very much more" and added: "We are dealing with a situation where not only the law is involved, but politics."[3] Obviously the board had decided to accept *any*

Table 3.1. Racial Imbalance in the Boston Public Schools, 1965–1973

	Number of imbalanced schools	Nonwhite percentage in imbalanced schools
1965–66	46	68.2
1966–67	49	69.7
1967–68	52	69.7
1968–69	57	71.7
1969–70	63	73.5
1970–71	63	76.4
1971–72	65–67	78.6
1972–73	75	78.9

Source: Adapted from Emmett H. Buell, Jr., with Richard A. Brisbin, Jr., *School Desegregation and Defended Neighborhoods: The Boston Controversy* (Lexington, Mass.: D. C. Heath and Co., 1982), p. 77.

gesture from the committee, hoping to coax it toward compliance. Some board members thought the committee was faking, while others emphasized the double-edgedness of recent court decisions. The board also did not acquire, until 1969–70, full-time staff whose duties would focus entirely on desegregation.[4]

The board's attempt to soft-pedal differences with the committee coincided with the growth in the number of Boston's imbalanced schools from forty-six to sixty-two in 1969–70. It also paralleled efforts of the school committee, Mrs. Hicks, and their allies to try to dismantle the Racial Imbalance Act. When the Supreme Court of Massachusetts in June 1967 ruled unanimously against the committee's suit on the unconstitutionality of the Racial Imbalance Act, the committee appealed to the U.S. Supreme Court, which in January 1968 refused to hear the case. Yet Hicks and her South Boston colleagues (Senator William Bulger and Representative Raymond Flynn) continued every year to file bills in the legislature to amend or repeal the Racial Imbalance Act. Thus the board's policy of moderation simply played into the committee's strategy of buying time.

Another element of the pattern of the nine years of school committee stonewalling also appeared in round one during the spring of 1966 when the committee received from the board a plan involving redistricting that would immediately affect racial imbalance. News of the board's suggestions created an uproar in the white Dorchester neighborhoods affected, and committee chair Thomas Eisenstadt received over one hundred phone calls from angry whites. Mrs. Hicks and two other committee members quickly appeared at a Home and School Association meeting in Dorchester and assured this pocket of constituents that there would be no redistricting.[5] This would not be the last of such scenes.

The committee's actions in other areas also indicated the futility of the board policy to "go slow." Claiming that overcrowding had been exaggerated to provide "a camouflage for racially balancing schools," the committee voted in October 1966 to classify 670 Chinese students as "white," as a way of keeping the number of imbalanced schools lower. One wit suggested that perhaps the committee intended to extend "Operation Whitewash" to 700 million Chinese.[6]

In 1967 Mrs. Hicks ran for mayor, playing heavily upon her opposition to desegregation ("You know where I stand") and upon her populist defense of Boston's neighborhoods from outside forces ("Boston for Bostonians"). Bashing suburban liberals such as Beryl Cohen, a state senator from Brookline and coauthor of the Racial Imbalance Act, made for perfect campaign fodder. "The racial imbalance law does not affect Brookline, so he smugly tells the elected officials of Boston what they should do. I, for one, am tired of nonresidents telling the people of Boston what they should do." Hicks challenged suburbanites to "help the poor city correct the situation. Take the Negro families into your suburbs and build housing for them and let them go to school with your children."[7]

Hicks could not have chosen a better year than 1967 to try to ride the backlash into the mayor's office. Black urban riots peaked during the summer of 1967 as enormous conflagrations erupted in Newark and Detroit. Boston too seemed on the brink of explosion. In early June a group of black mothers sat in at a welfare office and when police roughly tried to clear them out, several hundred demonstrators began throwing rocks, then went on a spree of looting and arson along Blue Hill Avenue. The next day young blacks began three days and nights of rioting in Dorchester, resulting in forty-seven persons injured and several buildings burned.

Though the lid stayed on in Boston, political and business leaders began to fear, rightly or wrongly, that a Hicks victory could light up the city Detroit-style. The media, and particularly the national media and the *Boston Globe*, treated this "uncommonly loquacious woman" as an object worthy of ridicule and fear.[8]

Hicks's principal opponent, Kevin White, also in his first run for mayor, benefited from the fear Hicks generated among liberals and the business community. Accordingly, White "was consecrated, canonized, raised from the status of a semi-obscure secretary of state to the pedestal of great White Hope." White handled the desegregation issue gingerly, and Hicks's presence allowed him to present himself as a moderate, even a liberal. Hicks won the September primary with 28 percent in a crowded field, while White placed second with 20 percent. In November, however, White garnered some solid black support and many white voters who supported Hicks for school committee chose not to vote for her as mayor. As one observer predicted six months earlier, Boston's voters knew Hicks's value to them as well as her limitations. "They don't want her as mayor, they want her standing guard at the school committee."[9]

The committee continued to hold the state board at bay through 1970, but internal changes in the Department of Education were under way that would soon lead to a dramatic showdown between the board and committee. In 1969 Neil Sullivan, an integrationist who had presided over the 1966 desegregation of schools in Berkeley, California, and whom Hicksites quickly dubbed "The Berkeley Buser," arrived to be the new commissioner of education. In 1971 he appointed Charles Leslie Glenn, Jr. to oversee racial balance efforts and soon made him head of the newly created Bureau of Equal Educational Opportunity. Boston officials viewed Glenn as a "hard-liner" and detected a new aggressiveness in the state board's attitude.[10]

Charles Glenn would play a key role as a desegregation planner over the next few years. To some, he was a hero; to many more, a villain. The grandson of a carpenter from Northern Ireland, Glenn was the son of an Episcopalian priest whose churches included St. John's Lafayette in Washington, D.C., "The Church of Presidents," and prestigious Christ Church in Cambridge, Massachusetts. Born in Cambridge in 1938, Glenn's well-developed social conscience and pietism may be gauged by his having waded into community activism as early as 1955, during his freshman year at Harvard. Well before other white middle-class youths discovered the black poor and civil rights in the 1960s, Glenn was doing the Lord's work in urban ghettos. Becoming an Episcopal priest himself, Glenn was assigned to Roxbury and from 1962 on lived in Boston, becoming one of the organizers of the black student boycotts. In 1967 he moved to Jamaica Plain and lived in an integrated neighborhood through the 1970s, one of the few principles in the entire process who sent his children to the Boston schools. His interests steadily became more secular, however, as his neighbors elected him to local urban and antipoverty boards. From 1968 to 1970 he took courses at the Harvard Graduate School of Education, writing a dissertation on low-income parental involvement in schools. Glenn brought a dedication and zeal to his work that led some of his enemies to think of him as a modern abolitionist. A self-described "Calvinist," Glenn told his parish in Jamaica Plain in a 1977 sermon that "I have tried to act in faithfulness to the Gospel during this difficult time."[11]

By 1971 Glenn, Sullivan, and the state board were ready for a showdown with the school committee on open enrollment and said that in the future students could request transfers under open enrollment only if it would relieve racial imbalance. The committee had paid lip service for years to open enrollment but in practice made it difficult for black students to use it, while routinely granting transfers for white students whose parents knew the system. In addition, the committee had never given Operation Exodus anything but harassment. Fifty black parents, aware that the committee brazenly claimed Operation Exodus as part of *its* efforts to reduce imbalance, had brought suit against the committee to try to recover 3½ years of Operation Exodus costs.[12]

On May 25 the board voted unanimously to withhold state aid from Boston because of the committee's refusal to cooperate on open enrollment. "Now is the hour," said Commissioner Sullivan, "after these long years, to truly test the act." Intensive negotiations followed over the next two to three months and by August the committee agreed to conduct open enrollment to reduce imbalance.[13]

But the committee's key concessions involved the redistricting of four elementary schools in Dorchester. Two of them, the Joseph Lee and John Marshall schools, were spanking new schools built with 25 percent state aid on the promise that they would open balanced, and thus had been built in mixed neighborhoods. But the racial composition of the area had changed to virtually all black during construction, and the gleaming new Lee School would open imbalanced unless district lines were redrawn.

At first the school committee gave white parents at the nearby Fifield and O'Hearn schools the option of having their children attend the Lee, but under intense pressure from the state board, a shaky three to two majority of the committee agreed to redraw district lines. In May, at a committee meeting to discuss traffic and safety, parents packed the meeting and expressed fears that busing would be required and spoke out against it. In July Deputy Superintendent Herbert Hambleton warned that any redrawing of district lines would fail because white and black parents "have told the school committee in unmistakable language on numerous occasions that they want to send their children to the local school."[14]

On August 31 the board approved the committee's new plan, whose concessions prompted the board to release Boston's state money. That same day, newspapers in Boston and across the country featured photographs of ten yellow school buses firebombed in Pontiac, Michigan by arsonists protesting impending desegregation. In Dorchester, the fires were raging in the emotions of many parents affected by the redistricting.

On September 7 Rev. Leonard Burke, a Catholic pastor of St. Matthew's parish, led a group of forty Dorchester white parents to a school committee meeting, where unruly parents forced a recess. Committee chair Paul Tierney was drowned out by parents' shouting. Yelled one: "Our kids are going to the Fifield. I'll stand on that. We'll go to jail or anywhere else if we have to." As Tierney adjourned the meeting, the shouting continued, "You're chicken, you're yellow. Run away, run away!" That same night nearly two hundred white parents met in Dorchester and vowed not to send their kids out of the Fifield and O'Hearn schools into the Lee School. Their state legislator, Paul Murphy, Democratic whip in the House, offered to be their legal adviser, while Mrs. Hicks lashed the crowd into a frenzy by exclaiming that "our children are the innocent victims" and that parents should not send them to the "far-distant Lee school where we know the hazards that are presented to them. . . . Should we be forced to send our children into an area where we know what harm can come to them?—I say no, a thousand times no." And the audience agreed with stomping, thunderous, visceral applause.[15]

On the first two days of school, 250 white children showed up at the Fifield and O'Hearn instead of going to the Lee where they had been reassigned. At the latter, 692 black and 149 white children were in attendance. The committee's plan had called for a racial balance at the Lee of 585 white and 520 black students. But many black parents had also defied the reassignments because they were bitterly opposed to sending their children to the Fifield and O'Hearn, where they were not welcome. Besides, the Lee contained a modern gym, a pool, a theater, carpeted classrooms, and a curriculum described as "one of the finest in any elementary school."

The black protesters lived across from the school in the run-down Franklin Field housing project, so close to the Lee that, as one black mother said, "Your mouth waters when you look at it." Thus many black parents showed up at the Lee and gave false addresses. One black group demonstrated and threatened to "hold a class" in the lobby of the Lee until their demands were met, and some black parents joined Father Burke and white parents meeting at St. Matthews the night of September 9 to plan strategy. The next day 136 white parents presented a petition in Suffolk Superior Court for an injunction to prevent the school committee from transferring their children to the Lee. Thus over four hundred white and black students refused to abide by the redistricting that constituted so important a part of the bargain struck by the committee and state board.[16] The thorny complexities of the Lee School controversy caused some integrationist leaders to draw back. Even Thomas Atkins, now a City Councillor, visited the Lee and pronounced the Racial Imbalance Act "unworkable." "The city and state have fiddled around so long with the law, it makes no sense to implement it now."[17]

On September 17 the white parents seeking an injunction were refused, but four nights later, at a hearing held by the school committee at the O'Hearn auditorium, they gained everything they wanted. Four hundred or more persons crammed into the small assembly hall while several hundred outside listened to loudspeakers as their spokesmen berated the committee, in particular John Craven, who had earlier switched his vote to provide the three to two majority for compliance with the state board. Mrs. Hicks was there, of course, campaigning for mayor a second time, calling for the committee to reverse itself again. Craven, running for city council, soon cracked under the pressure, telling the audience that the board and the school department had given him erroneous data. After having been cursed on his way in, Craven was cheered on his way out. Father Burke, however, was the crowd's favorite. Dozens of mothers "threw their arms around him," kissed him, and most said at least a "thank you, Father" or "God love him."[18]

The board hardly joined in the rejoicing but angrily concluded that the school committee had reneged on its promises. They charged that the committee had taken official action to increase racial isolation and to violate the Fourteenth Amendment to the U.S. Constitution. It voted unanimously to withhold $14 million in state aid and to suspend approval of all new school construction in Boston.[19]

A *Boston Globe* editorial lashed the school committee majority for "crummy politicking . . . which plays on the fears of a hopeless community with utter disregard for the law and common sense." Other critics quickly attributed the Lee School uproar to racial prejudice, but racial fears were only part of the story. The Fifield, for example, where most of the Lee boycotters preferred to stay, was already 20 percent nonwhite (the O'Hearn, however, was less than 3 percent nonwhite). Still, the white protesters' complaints about dangerous streets or a bus ride were less than honest or consistent. The maximum walking distance for any child assigned to the Lee was .8 miles, hardly excessive. State law did not require the schools to provide transportation to elementary students unless the distance was a mile or more. The streets involved differed little from many others in the city. And when the schools offered shuttle buses to the parents, they then protested they would not have their children bused .8 miles. What they wanted to avoid, clearly, was having their children attend a school, new and attractive as it might be, in what was now an all-black neighborhood, and a school that they guessed would soon become an overwhelmingly black school.[20]

Representative Murphy charged that the Lee redistricting was merely symbolic politics by the state board, by which "for token purposes of public relations, a small enclave was selected to bear the rigors of the law in a pretense of implementation."[21] The charge was hardly accurate. It was necessary, after all, to begin somewhere. Yet the Lee controversy did show the complexities that could be involved in applying the law even to just one neighborhood.

The state board lacked not so much the will but the clout to get the committee to comply and to lead its constituents to integration. If any party was guilty of tokenism, it was the flimflamming school committee. Yet the sense of being "a small enclave . . . selected to bear the rigors of the law," of being picked on to bear the conscience of the state, the nation, and the hour, emerged in microcosm in the Lee controversy as it emerged at large throughout the city in its relations with the cosmopolitan representatives of nationalizing values.

The School Committee Helps to Build an Antibusing Movement

Its reneging on the Lee School made the committee more vulnerable than ever to legal action holding that racially segregated schools existed through its official action. In the next year and a half, while the state board employed the cumbersome legal means at its disposal, other government agencies also served notice on the committee that its time was running out, yet the committee ignored these warnings and also paid surprisingly little attention to the federal court suit activated in 1972.

At the time other events pointed to a possible victory for the long resistance to desegregation. After 1971, in the train of what Charles Glenn called "a worsening national mood," only liberal Republican governor Francis Sargent's vetoes prevented repeal or passage of crippling amendments.[22] School Committee members meanwhile stayed on the offensive and worked diligently to build an organized, grassroots antibusing movement. Indeed, the rise of an antibusing movement from 1971 to 1974 created a political climate so hostile to implementation of racial balancing that in many ways it looked as if the committee would make good on its promise to the white neighborhoods that "forced busing" would "never" come to Boston.

This almost romantic political strategy unfortunately led Boston's rank and file away from recognizing the realities of the situation. A legal case against the committee was building to a point that would be incontestable. In October 1970, for example, the Massachusetts Commission Against Discrimination had filed suit on behalf of the father of Christine Underwood, a black student denied entry to Roslindale High School. In June 1971 the MCAD found the committee guilty of discriminating in its operation of open enrollment and ordered the committee to eliminate racial imbalance. The committee ignored this and in October 1971 the MCAD filed suit seeking enforcement of the order, a case delayed for the next two years. Next, in December 1971, the federal Department of Health, Education and Welfare's (HEW) investigators in the Office of Civil Rights (OCR) charged that the city was violating Title VI of the Civil Rights Act by tracking minority students through middle schools and white students through junior highs. Months of negotiations and then legal review followed and resulted in April 1974 in an HEW review board and administrative judge upholding the OCR allegations.[23]

Of course the decisive sword stroke through the Gordian knot of delay woven by the committee began in March 1972, when civil rights lawyers filed a class action suit on behalf of black parents in U.S. District Court against the committee and board. The Boston NAACP earlier had considered such a suit too costly, but after the Lee reversal civil rights lawyers saw their opportunity. J. Harold Flannery, a former Justice Department lawyer now directing the Harvard Center for Law and Education, concluded that the Lee episode made the committee a "sitting duck" for a suit based on violation of the Fourteenth Amendment's guarantee of equal protection under the law. Federal district courts had held that when school boards adopt a desegregation plan, then revoke it, an act of de jure segregation is committed. Flannery, who happened to live in Cambridge in the same apartment building as Commissioner Sullivan, was already offering the state his expert advice as a civil rights lawyer. He and his colleague Robert Pressman soon joined forces with two young lawyers (Roger Abrams and John Leubsdorf) who had come together with frustrated black Dorchester parents through the Lawyer's Committee for Civil Rights. On March 15, 1972 they filed a class action suit on behalf of fifteen black parents and forty-three children, selecting as lead plaintiff a twenty-four-year-old mother of three, Tallulah Morgan. Since James Hennigan was chair of the Boston School Committee, the case became known as *Morgan v. Hennigan*.[24]

In 1970 and 1971 the school committee also began to hear suggestions that it be abolished or at least restructured. Some critics wanted to expand the committee and elect its members both by district and at large, arguing that at-large elections led to overrepresentation of a few wards and that blacks and members of other groups never won elections. Mayor White's Home Rule Commission suggested instead a committee wholly appointed by the mayor.[25] Yet none of these pressures exerted any effect in changing the committee's basic course. Its leadership became if anything even more aggressive in articulating antibusing rhetoric.

The Lee School rescission took place in the midst of a city election campaign in which Louise Hicks was making her second run for mayor. Hicks and the four incumbents seeking reelection to the school committee all presented themselves as unalterably opposed to "forced busing." Indeed, most candidates in the primary and all ten finalists opposed the Racial Imbalance Act. The one black candidate, Patricia Bonner-Lyons, preferred community control of black neighborhood schools, but as a last resort supported busing as "the best of bad solutions." Two incumbent school committeemen, James Hennigan, Jr. and Paul Tierney, were regarded as moderates because they occasionally pointed out the committee's growing legal vulnerability and opposed the Lee reversal. Yet their reelection and the defeat of Hicks for mayor hardly meant that the electorate had mandated a new era of accommodation in school committee politics.[26]

More revealing of the posture of the committee was the emergence of John Kerrigan as its dominant figure in the late 1960s. If Louise Hicks was the Mother Superior of antibusing, Kerrigan was its Papa Doc or Idi Amin. First elected in 1967, Kerrigan just narrowly squeezed into fifth place after a bland campaign in which he was helped—as so often in Boston—by having the name of a popular Boston politician. Kerrigan had lifted himself out of working-class Dorchester by going to law school at night and—as so often in Boston—by getting a big break from an influential friend. While working as an orderly at New England Medical Center he befriended convalescing Mayor John Collins and later became assistant corporation counsel in the Collins administration. In 1962 he ran unsuccessfully for state representative and then arrived on the school committee just as Hicks departed for Congress, leaving an opening for Kerrigan to assert himself.

Kerrigan was elected chair of the committee in early 1968 and by September 1969 had established himself as the committee member most adamantly against busing. "A conservative," opined Kerrigan, "is a liberal whose child just got on a school bus." He soon began to fill the role of the Boston politician cut in the Curleyesque mold—flamboyant, outrageous, and uncensored—but more vulgar than Curley and without any real compassion for the unfortunate.

A large, beefy man with a streetwise manner and ready wit, Kerrigan also followed Hicks in playing deftly upon the general backlash and class resentment. When Boston's schools were rocked by student protests and youth rebellion in the late 1960s, Kerrigan stepped forward as a blunt upholder of "law 'n' order." In his 1969 campaign he discovered the political benefits to be reaped from baiting the *Boston Globe*, one of the few voices consistently raised in favor of the Racial Imbalance Act. After Kerrigan led the field in the preliminary election, the *Globe* ran a story about a crony of Kerrigan's receiving a $50,000 no-bid contract from the schools and also revealed that Kerrigan himself held a moonlighting job at the Registry of Motor Vehicles. These stories, as well as others in the *Boston Herald* about Kerrigan's dealings, did not prevent him from topping the ticket in November. Like many Boston pols before him, Kerrigan asked, "What's wrong with a little patronage?"

Louise Hicks did not, as some writers have suggested, keep her distance from John Kerrigan, but campaigned with him and celebrated election victories together as a close ally. In 1971 Hicks sat beaming at a reception at which Kerrigan went into his *Globe*-bashing routine: "We have a newspaper in this city—the *Boston Globe*—that has endorsed a communist for School Committee and an ex-convict for City Council. The people of Boston," he said to rousing cheers, "ought to do something about this." Like Hicks, Kerrigan continually attacked outsiders who tried to dictate to Bostonians and also played upon cultural antagonisms. He said it was ironic that "in these days of liberalization of civil rights, government has made continued concessions to convicted felons, homosexuals, abortionists, and others, yet persists in ignoring the pleas of parents who ask that they be accorded their rightful privilege of sending their children to their own neighborhood schools."

Next to the *Globe*, the suburbs were perhaps Kerrigan's favorite object of scorn, giving him a chance to posture, as Hicks did, as a populist expressing working-class resentment against the arrogant gentry who would dictate to Bostonians. In 1972 he introduced a bill in the legislature calling for the busing of children from the suburban retreat of Dover into an inner-city school. He selected Dover because it was the residence of Governor Sargent, who had been vetoing repeals of the Racial Imbalance Act. The suburbs, he never tired of pointing out, refused low-cost housing for the poor and erected barriers against blacks becoming their neighbors while insisting that Bostonians bus their children into black neighborhoods. When the liberal watchdog group Common Cause queried Kerrigan about his campaign finances, he wrote back—in a letter which appeared in several neighborhood weeklies— lashing out against what he called the "Pride's Crossing" approach to city government, "which mandates that suburban patricians rule urban plebeians from 9 A.M. to 5 P.M. It seems to be an elitist concept which would rule the destinies of the great 'unwashed' (us) through inquisitions, innuendo and high-powered Madison Avenue scare techniques." On the night of his election victory in 1973, Kerrigan boasted proudly of having grown up on "the wrong side of the tracks."

In September 1974, as the court-ordered buses finally rolled, he waged an unsuccessful campaign for district attorney and eventually moved off the school committee after winning a city council seat in 1975. In 1977 Kerrigan's nonchalance toward petty graft and brazen patronage would finally catch up with him, but before then his importance in the early and mid-1970s was a sign of how much uglier the resistance to the Racial Imbalance Act had become.

With Kerrigan, the macho style was as important as any substantive position on issues. He often went out of his way to be vulgar and obscene and especially delighted in shocking liberals with uninhibited racial derogation of blacks. His vituperation of journalists as "snakes" and "maggots" was almost comically opéra bouffe by comparison, as were his continual references to his own and others' sexuality (he often wore a bowling jacket with the nickname "Bigga," a reference to part of his anatomy). In December 1974, during a break at a hearing in Garrity's courtroom, Kerrigan allegedly mocked a black TV reporter, Lem Tucker, by imitating a chimpanzee and saying: "You know Tucker? He's one generation away from swinging in the trees. I bet he loves bananas." While testifying before the U.S. Civil Rights Commission in June 1975, Kerrigan became angered by charges made by a liberal rabbi the day before that the school committee had conspired to keep poor people and blacks confined in city ghettos. Kerrigan replied that fifteen thousand Jewish families had fled the Mattapan section, but not because of the Boston School Committee. They left "to get away from the schwarzes." When asked what "schwarzes" meant, he said it was a "Jewish word" for blacks. When Commissioner Stephen Horn bluntly told school committeeman McDonough that it was the committee's responsibility to insure attendance and safety, and that it should prevent "the parents from throwing bricks at buses when blacks are on them," Kerrigan waded in saying, "Can I have Mr. Horn, Mr. Chairman, I want him bad. I want him bad because he is what is destroying our society." He then called Horn, the mild-looking vice-chairman of the commission, a "capon," a term which, coming from Kerrigan, suggested some kind of sexual inadequacy.[27]

Hicks and Kerrigan fed off one another, but Kerrigan did differ from Hicks in the sheer opportunism of his antibusing career. He once said that the worst thing that could happen to him politically was to have Garrity reverse himself: "That would put me out of business." During his run for district attorney a group of radical Progressive Labor party demonstrators came to Kerrigan's house on primary day. The candidate himself came out smiling: "Oh boy, a demonstration. . . . You're gonna win me this election. Why didn't you come yesterday when we could've gotten more coverage?" A reporter for the *Boston Phoenix* observed the scene and wrote: "The Progressive Laborites were genuinely nonplused. Not in their wildest fantasies about capitalist politicians could they have imagined someone as profoundly cynical as John Kerrigan. Here was a man who took nothing seriously except his vote totals, and he freely admitted as much. He wasn't a racist—black, white didn't even enter his mind outside of politics—just a demagogue who said and did what he had to in order to win."[28] Hicks and Kerrigan, like Richard Nixon during these years, thrived on cultural, class, and racial resentments, and by the early 1970s Boston had become a cauldron of such animosities.

Kerrigan and his allies on the committee also worked systematically to mobilize grassroots opposition to the Racial Imbalance Act. By late 1971 the committee was using, in particular, many local home and school associations as a political vehicle to lobby for repeal of the Racial Imbalance Act. Later, however, the Boston HSA would act as a constructive critic of the court.

In the 1960s Boston's home and school associations, essentially a loose confederation of autonomous units, were tied closely to the committee. A city official described them as "a kind of company union, with bylaws that pretty much say it cannot be cruel to the Boston School Committee." In fact, the HSA constitution forbade criticism of the schools. Its offices were at 15 Beacon Street and were headed by an administrator paid by the school department. All teachers belonged, and chapter presidencies alternated between teachers and parents. Of course, antibusing activities in the HSAs did not result primarily from school committee pressure but sprang up independently in most neighborhoods. In any case, the HSAs, especially those in Southie, East Boston, and Hyde Park, became "the backbone of the resistance."[29]

During the early 1970s, antibusing activities included an October 1971 meeting at Faneuil Hall with the entire school committee and superintendent present and an April 1972 motorcade from Southie to Governor Sargent's home in Dover. But the most massive effort each year focused on the State House, where annual hearings were held on the Racial Imbalance Act. On March 21, 1972, several hundred women packed a hearing before the Committee on Education on a bill filed by Flynn to repeal the act. Dozens more women, some calling themselves members of the Concerned Parents League of Boston, picketed outside. Charles Glenn sat in the front row of the auditorium, "with hostile mothers breathing down our necks," and noted that some officials testifying for the act "were shaken by the virulent racism which was expressed."[30]

In September 1972 the Suffolk Superior Court ruled that the state board had acted arbitrarily in withholding $52 million from the Boston schools because of the Lee School episode. At the same time, the court ordered that the committee prepare a racial balance plan at once and outlined a timetable to be followed. After more legal maneuvers, on February 15, 1973, the court directed the board to produce, on March 19, a new plan complying with the Racial Imbalance Act, and to hold hearings on it. The board then appointed Professor Louis Jaffe of Harvard University Law School, who held eighteen days of hearings.[31]

Thus in the spring of 1973 the antibusers' lobbying became frenzied. When legislative hearings on the Racial Imbalance Act resumed, several hundred opponents descended on the State House in buses from all across the city. Telephone networks in the various neighborhoods and local newspapers aided the school committee and HSAs in mobilizing the rank and file. Joining the antibusers in the State House was a contingent of a couple hundred black parents, smaller in size than the antibusers, but nevertheless one that provided an audible counterpoint of boos to the antibusers' cheers when Louise Hicks appeared to testify. Hicks later compared the situation to 1965: "The color line is deeper. I mean you can feel it in this room."[32]

Hicks, Kerrigan, and other antibusing politicians next focused the attention of fearful parents on the court-ordered hearings on the state board's desegregation plan, which began on March 20. While the school committee's lawyer and Hicks tried to derail the hearings, parents' groups and HSA locals continued to meet nightly throughout the city and antibusers picketed the State House and the state education building at 178 Tremont Street. On March 29 the school committee voted to endorse a march and rally on April 3 and ordered that pupils citywide be given notices to take home to their parents. A black parents' group tried to get a court order restraining the committee from engaging in such actions, but failed.[33]

On April 3 five to ten thousand parents demonstrated in downtown Boston at the State House and City Hall. Riled up by the failure of the governor or mayor to meet with them, mothers with children in strollers continuously chanted such slogans as "our kids aren't going anywhere." One hundred militants sat down in Beacon Street and tied up traffic for hours. After singing "God Bless America," the crowd began to disperse about 1 P.M. As they departed, Mrs. Hicks called them "great Americans." On May 2 two thousand again went to the capitol as the legislators debated the Racial Imbalance Act. Some antibusers formed a human chain encircling the building with the gold dome while thirteen leaders met with the governor for forty minutes.[34]

The lobbyists undoubtedly took encouragement from recent national events. For three years the Nixon administration had been pursuing its "Southern strategy," aimed not only at undercutting George Wallace and building Republican support in the South but also at attracting traditionally Democratic northern voters caught up in the backlash. Part of that strategy was to make clear that the national administration opposed busing. In August 1971, after reports of a weakening of his southern support, Mr. Nixon lashed out at busing, flatly announcing his opposition to it for purposes of "racial balance." The Supreme Court, in its recent decision *Swann v. Charlotte-Mecklenburg*, had said expressly that it was not approving busing for the purpose of achieving racial balance. But that did not prevent Nixon and his lieutenants from continuing to exploit the issue during 1972. Three days after Wallace's victory in the Florida Democratic primary, the president gave a televised address criticizing busing.[35]

The spring 1973 debates in the Massachusetts legislature over the Racial Imbalance Act proved inconclusive, and on June 25 the state board directed the school committee to put into operation in September 1974 the plan that recently had undergone review hearings.[36] In the fall of 1973, however, both houses of the legislature approved measures undermining the act, which again were stopped by Governor Sargent's veto. The Senate barely sustained his veto of a one-year suspension of the law.[37]

In the elections for school committee and city council that fall, incumbent leaders of the resistance ran very hard against the imbalance law and the governor, a Yankee Republican and suburban liberal who had protected the law. Though apathy was high and voter turnout would be low, it was still necessary for most candidates to hoist the antibusing flag. Kerrigan led committee candidates with just 38,354 votes, while Hicks topped the council field with 44,208, followed in second place by "Dapper" O'Neil. "Dapper" was a six-gun-toting ex-war hero who had showed up at racially troubled Hyde Park High the year before and told reporters: "I'm not going to stand by and let those niggers take over this school." Although three other committee incumbents also won reelection, the surprise of the election was the second place finish of a moderate newcomer, Kathleen Sullivan, daughter of Billy Sullivan, a wealthy Irish-American entrepreneur and owner of professional football's New England Patriots. Sullivan possessed a strong lace-curtain appeal as a former teacher and attractive, pragmatic do-gooder. The media referred to her as a "moderate," yet while Sullivan distanced herself from Kerrigan and Hicks, she too had said repeatedly that "I am opposed to forced busing."[38]

Meanwhile, the state supreme court rejected committee appeals and on November 14 ordered the committee to submit its modifications to the state's plan by December 11. The committee sent no response until hours before the court's deadline and, against the advice of its own attorney, voted to appeal to the U.S. Supreme Court. The court ordered the school department to provide the state board with information regarding assignments and academic resources, and the committee amended this action by delaying teacher-student assignments until September. In the following months the committee usually acted only after the board obtained a court order. Nevertheless, on May 17, 1974, the board could report to the state supreme court that a racial balance plan, including provisions for teacher assignment, was "sound and complete."

In November 1973 Governor Sargent's vetoes continued to save the imbalance act. While the state Senate overrode one of Sargent's vetoes, the House, despite intense lobbying, upheld it. Antibusing leaders of course singled out Sargent for condemnation. Fumed Hicks: "I blame the governor. . . . the governor, damn."[39] Actually, Sargent already had indicated that he was willing to reconsider the definition of an "imbalanced" school as well as other aspects of the law. Naturally he continued to be the subject of intense pleading from antibusing activists.

In the first three months of 1974 the antibusing movement grew bolder, if not stronger, by the week. Nineteen representatives and six senators from Boston, led by Ray Flynn, sent a letter to the mayor and council urging them to fight the edicts of the state board, which was treating Boston's parents as second-class citizens. Hundreds of families were preparing to leave the city, and they said, "forced busing has become a nightmare of divisiveness and bitterness between the races." The school committee again chose Kerrigan as chair, and he promised to spend most of his time organizing opposition to implementation of the state plan. Committee members John McDonough and Paul Ellison boasted that they would even be willing to go to jail. On February 5 Massachusetts Citizens Against Forced Busing (MCAFB) announced its existence, with Hicks and Flynn its principal leaders.

The mood of the movement was already intense and desperate. Representative Flynn said of the MCAFB: "I think this group is prepared to go as far as is absolutely necessary in protecting those rights of parents in having a say in those matters affecting the education of their children." At a meeting of the MCAFB in Dorchester, one of its officers told parents that they "had better remind the School Committee members that . . . you'll visit them in jail." John Kerrigan, however, replied that while he was sure "the majority . . . will go that far," it was "premature to talk about jail for School Committee members. Look, I can do more good on the streets than I can in jail."[40]

Through February and March MCAFB and other antibusing groups held meetings across the city and laid plans for a big demonstration in early April designed to influence the legislature and Governor Sargent to undo the Racial Imbalance Act. South Bostonians continued to lead in this activity, of course; with two hundred block captains already manning telephone networks, they easily amassed fourteen hundred persons for a February 27 meeting to discuss possible boycotting and alternative schools.

During early March the movement became focused on a special referendum proposed by Hicks and Flynn that would allow the voters to express themselves on the question: "Should Boston public school children be assigned to a particular school on the basis of race, sex or creed without the consent of his parent or legal guardian?" Five thousand phone calls inundated City Hall to persuade Mayor White to approve it after it sailed through the city council. On March 11 White reluctantly sent the bill to the legislature, which approved it. But then Governor Sargent asked the Supreme Court for an opinion on its constitutionality, and the Court did not reply until April 16.[41]

Meanwhile, the antibusers continued to get moral support from the Nixon administration and from Congress, which had become increasingly conservative on school desegregation. In late March Mr. Nixon once again denounced "excessive forced busing" and spoke in terms quite familiar to Boston's antibusers: "Bureaucrats in Washington cannot educate your children. Your children can only be educated by you in your home and by the teachers in their . . . neighborhood schools." Congress, meanwhile, was filled with antibusing proposals and on March 26 the House voted 293-117 to prohibit busing past a student's nearest school and required other remedies to be considered before busing. The next day it attached an amendment banning the use of federal funds for the purpose of achieving racial balance to an aid-to-education bill.[42]

Heartened by these events, an estimated fifteen to twenty-five thousand antibusing demonstrators assembled on Boston Common on April 3, 1974. Hundreds filled the auditorium in the State House where the Joint Subcommittee on Education heard eight hours of testimony calling for repeal or modification of the Racial Imbalance Act. The now familiar warnings and threats of disaster and civil disobedience rang throughout the day. More importantly, a group of leaders emerged from a meeting with Governor Sargent with the news that the governor was rethinking his position on the act.[43]

Sargent would not approve the antibusers' referendum, however, unless it were rewritten to be nonbinding and to record just an expression of opinion. When the referendum finally occurred on May 21, it was largely a sideshow with antibusers claiming it a great success because 95 percent of those voting opted against busing (30,789 to 2,282). Critics of the referendum, not all of whom backed the imbalance act, pointed out that only 10 percent of the eligible voters took part, the lowest turnout in the city's history. What it most likely measured was the intensity of feeling on the issue.[44]

The 31,000 "no" votes probably represented the minimum pool of adults in the city that antibusing cadres could draw upon for demonstrations, marches, and rallies. Beyond that, a huge majority of whites in Boston opposed busing. A 1971 survey of ten neighborhoods showed no neighborhood favoring busing, most overwhelmingly opposed, and only two, Central Boston and Roxbury, with pluralities in favor (42 and 38 percent, respectively). A *Globe* poll in May 1974 revealed that whites opposed busing by three to one, while blacks favored it by two to one. Spanish-speaking residents also registered opposition by 49 to 37 percent, and Boston residents with school-age children registered 79 percent opposed.[45]

During April, meanwhile, the political tide continued to run against the imbalance act. On April 22 Senate President Harrington announced his opposition, and soon after the legislature passed a repeal and sent it to the governor. On the night of April 30, Hicks led an all-night vigil of antibusing demonstrators outside the state capitol. On May 10, finally, the Governor announced his decision to replace the imbalance act with a new plan that would depend heavily on the voluntary busing of minority children into white neighborhoods, expansion of voluntary busing to the suburbs, and magnet schools. Soon Kerrigan, Hicks, Flynn, and Bulger were appearing with Sargent at a legislative hearing as friendly witnesses for his proposals.[46]

Thus, the antibusers apparently had achieved at long last their goal of undoing the Racial Imbalance Act. All the political dominoes had tumbled. Yet in late May and early June the situation was still laden with ambiguity. On one hand, the state board, the school department, and the mayor's office were proceeding as if the state plan would be implemented in September as ordered by the court. On the other hand, the school committee was busy declaring victory. Kathleen Sullivan later said that the committee believed that the general political situation and the Governor's action meant that "the state plan would not go forward." The feeling was still strong throughout the city that busing would not, could not come to Boston. This is not surprising, given nine years of delays, and with highly visible politicians still assuring the worried masses that their watchword was "never."[47]

Nevertheless, the decision in the federal court suit was still out. Then the worst came to pass. On June 21 Judge Garrity gave his decision, finding the school committee guilty of maintaining a segregated school system. Soon after he ordered that the state plan go into effect in September. For some antibusers, this was the final defeat, coming with brutal speed after what had seemed to be the final victory, and they gave up. But for many other antibusers, this was the greatest challenge, one which they would take up for months and years before burning out and realizing that the politics of protest—and even terror—could not change it.

In retrospect, an aura of unreality hangs over the frenetic campaign to repeal the imbalance act. That many, perhaps most, average citizens did not fully understand the situation seems likely. During the summer of 1974 Mayor White held a series of coffee klatches throughout the city in the homes of local activists, meeting with neighborhood groups to plead for peace in the fall. Some of them insisted that he could "stop the busing," and at one gathering one woman suddenly burst out, "Why doesn't Governor Sargent just fire Judge Garrity?"[48] The antibusing leadership, particularly the lawyers, knew differently. Yet they continued to ignore the federal court suit. Over and over again they urged meetings of agitated parents to lobby, to march, to rally, to protest, to fight.

An occasional *Globe* or *Herald* editorial might warn that a sweeping and unalterable desegregation ruling might come forth from the federal court no matter what the legislature, governor, or even state courts did. As *Globe* education writer Muriel Cohen wrote in April 1973, "No rhetoric from politicians and assurances from School Committee members greedy for next year's votes can change those . . . facts." Indeed, she added, if the federal court simply followed precedents set in other cities, extensive busing for desegregation inexorably would come to Boston.[49]

One must surely wonder about the failure of lawyers such as Hicks, Kerrigan, and their allies on the committee and council to warn their followers that the pending decision in the federal court would likely render irrelevant all of the zealous lobbying and demonstrating against the imbalance law. Some of them acted perhaps with more than just a dash of cynicism. This situation was an appropriate sequel to the overall behavior of the school committee in creating a clear-cut case of de jure segregation in the years from 1965 to 1973.

Yet leaders are shaped also by their followers, and it is clear that many second-level cadres and thousands of the rank-and-file activists really believed that the politics of protest had a chance to prevail. The neighborhood leaders and the parents they rang into action on the telephone networks truly believed that democracy was on their side. They could not accept the idea that "the system" could resist the kind of grassroots pressure they felt and knew themselves capable of mounting.

4

"A Harvard Plan for the Working Class Man"
Reactions to the Garrity Decision and Desegregation

The federal district court judge who decided the Boston case, Wendell Arthur Garrity, Jr., had been assigned the case from among a number of judges by a process of random selection. It is doubtful, however, that the luck of the draw would have made the basic finding any different. Any other judge, given the twenty-year history of Supreme and lower-court decisions preceding *Morgan v. Hennigan* also would probably have found the Boston School Committee guilty of maintaining a dual, segregated school system.[1] But the distinctive personality of Garrity had much to do with the timing of the decision and with the remedies applied.

That Garrity's father had been named by his grandmother after the well-known nineteenth-century Boston Brahmin abolitionist and reformer, Wendell Phillips, signified much. That his father, a prominent lawyer and member of a middle-class Irish Catholic family in Worcester, Massachusetts, was a member of the NAACP in the 1940s and 1950s also presaged his son's reaction to *Morgan v. Hennigan* as "pure and simple a race case."[2]

As did most male members of his family, Garrity attended Holy Cross College in Worcester, from which he was graduated in 1941. He left Harvard Law School during his second year and, despite nearsightedness, joined the army and became a sergeant in the Signal Corps. He participated in the Normandy invasion and won five battle stars during his service in France and Germany. Returning from war, he finished law school in 1946 and followed a typical career of interweaving minor public office, private law practice, and political work. The latter brought him into John F. Kennedy's orbit in the 1950s, and after meeting Kennedy at a

66

fund-raiser, he hitched his fortunes to the Kennedys. In 1958 he organized scheduling for JFK's U.S. Senate race and in 1960 managed the
state headquarters in Wisconsin for Kennedy's presidential primary run,
which resulted in a big victory. The next year the new president named
Garrity U.S. attorney for Boston. In 1966 President Johnson, on the
recommendation of Senator Ted Kennedy, made him a federal district
judge.

Trim, balding, and spectacled, with an aura of calm rationality and
kindliness about him, Garrity established a reputation as a liberal judge
concerned to a fault with fairness and orderly procedure. Active in the
Boston Bar Association, an upper-status group with a social conscience,
Garrity reflected the dominance in the courts of judicial activism and
liberal social philosophy. Yet in other ways Garrity fit several observers'
descriptions of him as "puritanical." In his personal habits, Garrity
tended to be highly disciplined—exercising regularly, eating sparely, and
sticking to tight schedules. As a judge in criminal cases he became known
for handing down stiff sentences in anything having to do with drugs,
pornography, and related moral issues. Above all, he was known for his
exacting, meticulous, and legalistic approach. As a prosecutor he had
earned admiration for letting "the facts and the law determine his course
of action, without emotion." And several young lawyers had learned to
their chagrin that coming late to Garrity's courtroom could earn them a
fine or a stern reprimand.

Before June 21, 1974, Garrity's name was not a household word in
Boston, but from that date on it became one of the best known in the
city's history, revered among many blacks and a small minority of white
liberals, hated throughout the length and breadth of the city's white
neighborhoods. Garrity's critics faulted him first of all for taking so long
to deliver his decision in a suit filed in March 1972. June 21 was the last
day of school: there would be only a short summer in which to prepare
for desegregation. Yet in Garrity's defense, the case was complex, involving over one thousand exhibits and several earlier court cases, and he
tackled it along with a large regular workload. In particular, Garrity
took exceptional care to make his opinion dovetail with earlier decisions of the Massachusetts Supreme Court. Garrity wanted above all to
present an order that represented "united judicial authority."

When Garrity finished his decision, moreover, he was determined that
there would be no delay. The Supreme Court, he explained several years
later, had mandated that the schools needed to be desegregated "*now*."

Aware of all the delays preceding his opinion, Garrity feared feeding the opposition's hope for further roadblocks.[3]

In Garrity's courtroom the Boston School Committee had not contested that segregation existed in the schools, but it defended itself by arguing that circumstances beyond its control had caused segregation. Against this defense Garrity marshaled overwhelming evidence of how the committee had in fact maintained and extended segregation by adding portable classrooms to crowded white schools, for example, rather than assigning white students to underutilized black schools a short distance away. In one instance, the school committee bought an old Catholic school in white Roslindale and bused black children into it past white schools with vacant seats. The school opened 93 percent nonwhite in the middle of a white neighborhood, while the 7 percent who were white in the school were mostly visually impaired students. Garrity also described how in constructing and locating new school buildings the defendants had ignored opportunities to decrease segregation and had acted in several instances to increase it. Moreover, said Garrity, the committee "made districting changes for the purpose of perpetuating racial segregation. . . . Year after year the defendants rejected proposals for redistricting carefully drawn with a view to lessening racial imbalance while at all times displaying awareness of the potential racial impact of their actions."

Garrity somehow managed to pick his way through the labyrinth that constituted the complex system of "feeder patterns" by which students were assigned to the city's high schools. Some high schools functioned more or less as district schools, while at least half drew students on a citywide basis. By manipulation of seat assignments and parent preferences and options in a discriminatory manner, Garrity revealed, the committee channeled students from predominantly black elementary and middle schools into mostly black high schools, while whites were tracked through mostly white elementary, junior, and high schools. In this "dual system of secondary education . . . one for each race," whites generally were given options "enabling them to escape from predominantly black schools; black students were generally without such options."[4]

In 1961 the school committee instituted an "open enrollment" policy that it frequently claimed allowed black students to enroll in schools of their choice. The state board, of course, had challenged this policy, which, it charged operated in practice to maintain segregation. In August 1971, therefore, the committee had substituted a "controlled transfer" policy purported to allow transfers only when they decreased racial imbalance. The judge concluded that both policies had been managed "with a singular intention to discriminate on the basis of race."

Teachers as well as students were also segregated by race in the Boston schools, Garrity found, though few black teachers and fewer administrators had even been hired. Garrity also decided that the special examination and vocational schools were operated in discriminatory fashion, though he had no specific evidence to that effect, but rather said that he was allowed to presume committee guilt on the basis of Supreme Court decisions and the rest of the evidence in the case.[5]

Garrity's decision should not have come as a surprise to anyone familiar with the course of Supreme Court decisions in the twenty years since *Brown*. Those decisions. particularly *Swann v. Charlotte-Mecklenburg* (1971) and *Keyes v. School District Number 1, Denver* (1973), also made clear that Garrity would enjoy wide latitude in ordering a remedy, including extensive transport of students, and that once deliberate segregation was demonstrated to exist anywhere in the system, then the remedy applied could be imposed everywhere in the system.[6]

Anyone who reads Garrity's opinion cannot avoid reaching the same conclusion as the judge. Thousands of moderate antibusers, and even some hard-liners, either agreed that the committee had been caught red-handed or tacitly conceded the point by offering no defense of the Committee's actions. But militant antibusers, as well as moderates, both reacted strongly against the desegregation plan that the judge imposed as a remedy.

Garrity, of course, took the only plan available in the spring of 1974—that which the Board of Education had developed as ordered by the state's highest court and of which Charles Glenn had been a principal architect. Ten years later Glenn himself described the plan as not as bad as its critics have charged, "but not a good plan either."[7] Glenn emphasized later that the chief mistake of the board was to be "*drawn into* devising a plan for Boston." (Italics mine.) Exactly. The committee persistently refused to devise a realistic plan acceptable to the state or courts at any time. When a plan finally emerged, the committee assumed its Pontius Pilate posture of blaming it all on the state or the judge. Glenn and his colleagues would clearly have wished for a reasonable plan from the committee, but the committee always acted in such a way as to make bad situations worse.

That said, the state plan that Judge Garrity decided to put into operation in September 1974, requiring the busing of some seventeen to eighteen thousand students, while not as sweeping a reorganization of the schools as some critics have claimed, was nonetheless a political and social disaster. Its most provocative feature was its pairing of Roxbury High School, in the heart of the black ghetto, with South Boston High, the pride of the Irish-dominated white enclave most associated with hard-core antibusing passion. South Bostonians were being asked to have their sophomores mix with blacks bused in and to send the entire junior class to Roxbury, while the senior class at both schools could choose either high school. "It was like the hostage system of the Middle Ages," explained Dr. William Reid, South Boston High's headmaster, "whereby the princes of opposing crowns were kept in rival kings' courts as a preventive against war."[8]

Even at the time it was difficult to see what was to be gained by transfers between two schools that, though they performed various functions valued by their communities, rated among the worst in the city educationally. Six different housing projects, all poor and highly segregated, would be included in the Roxbury–South Boston district. In 1973 Professor Jaffee, after conducting hearings on the state plan, recommended to the state board that South Boston, because it was "intensely hostile to blacks," be left out of the first year of desegregation. But Charles Glenn, his planners, and the board ignored Jaffee's advice.

Shock waves went through Roxbury as well as Southie when the plan was announced. Blacks knew better than Professor Jaffee, perhaps, the unwelcome that awaited their children, and when NAACP leader Ellen Jackson, who had worked with Glenn, told a May meeting of parents at Freedom House of their teenagers' assignments, the gathering was stunned. She explained to a shocked audience that her boss had "proposed [to the school committee] a compromise on that district many times. . . . I saw him agonize over that many a day, many a day."

Glenn has denied that this feature of the plan had a punitive intent. Yet state officials had battled the Boston committee for nine frustrating years. Glenn also described South Boston High before 1974 as "an ugly institution" where he said a young black who attempted to attend it was terrorized by being hung by his heels out a window: it "deserved to be changed."[9]

Many white liberals who would have championed a different plan could give only their reluctant cooperation to one they saw as punitive. A pragmatic liberal such as Robert Kiley, deputy mayor in charge of safety in 1974–75, regarded the plan as a "disaster"; and a compassionate, neighborhood-based liberal such as Fred Salvucci, a Little City Hall manager (later secretary of transportation), called it "absurd and crazy." Normally, reasonable citizens in neighborhoods, as Salvucci put it, control "the crazies." But the reasonable types were offended by the plan and left the stage to the militants. And all sorts of persons, all across the city, viewed desegregation as "a Harvard plan for the working class man."[10]

Well before Judge Garrity's decision the leaders of the opposition to the Racial Imbalance Act had been planning for the worst. In February Mrs. Hicks and friends had quietly called together neighborhood leaders. In mid-March this coalition declared its existence as the Save Boston Committee, but soon Hicks invented a new name for this umbrella group of antibusing networks, inspired, she said, by a toy lion in a friend's car: ROAR, Restore Our Alienated Rights.

Although ROAR became the most significant antibusing organization, it never encompassed all antibusing activists or sympathizers throughout the city. Many moderates kept it at arm's length, and it was strongest in more working-class and lower-middle-class areas such as South Boston and Hyde Park, considerably weaker in more middle-class West Roxbury or in areas accustomed to racial diversity, such as Jamaica Plain. Yet ROAR would play a very important role over the next months and years. On the night of Garrity's decision, Hicks brought the ROAR council together in the city council chambers to lay plans to resist the court's decision and to try to get it overturned. They agreed to begin by sponsoring a two-week boycott of schools which, ironically, Hicks had decried as illegal in 1963–64. Over the next three years, many similar ironies would follow.[11]

It was now evident that implementation would be a rocky road. Garrity's decision rallied neither community leaders nor those who would bear responsibility for implementing the plan. John Kerrigan, again chair of the school committee, appeared on the 11 P.M. television news on June 21, bristling with pugnacity, to promise an appeal and a trip to Washington. Five days later the committee voted, against the advice of its own attorneys, to appeal the decision.[12]

Similarly, the state legislature did not approve a June 29 request of Governor Sargent's for desegregation funds until a month later, and when Mayor White asked the city council for an extra $4.2 million for desegregation on July 12, it took two court orders to secure the funds in early August. School personnel, from Superintendent William Leary to maintenance workers, who wished to perform their jobs, not only struggled with their boss, the committee, but also in many cases with their own distaste or ambivalence toward the court order.[13]

As early as April 1973, Mayor White had shifted away from support of the Racial Imbalance Act, and proposed replacing it with an expanded version of METCO, a new magnet complex for Roxbury, and a restructuring of the school committee. While opposing "massive busing," White called attention to the class inequities between urban and suburban education. He did begin early in 1974, to his credit, to prepare for the safety and transportation requirements of the fall. Yet White defined his role as that of neutral broker and paid much deference to those who opposed the court order.[14]

Like the mayor, Governor Sargent vowed compliance with the court order but issued no ringing endorsement. The president of Boston's Chamber of Commerce urged support for desegregation, while top corporate executives—the elite group known as "The Vault"—did respond to school committeewoman Kathleen Sullivan's request that they pitch in and start using company resources to improve education. But they too kept a low profile.[15]

Black politicians eventually rallied to the court order, but on the eve of the court's decision the black state legislative caucus apprehensively proposed a compromise by which blacks would be given much greater control of schools in black neighborhoods, meanwhile protecting white jobs by having the state fund an absolute increase in the number of teachers. But community control had not been popular, and the Boston Teachers' Union refused to give up jurisdiction over any positions. Once Garrity spoke, however, Representative William Owens, a caucus leader, typically claimed blacks were "elated." Meanwhile, the NAACP, whose leadership during the previous year had been in "a shambles," reorganized in mid-July and chose an aggressive new leader, thirty-five-year-old Thomas Atkins, former city councillor and now an urban affairs official in the Sargent administration. In the months ahead, Atkins became perhaps the most persistent voice in support of the court order, which unfortunately served mostly to irritate the white majority.[16]

The clergy of the Catholic church completed the picture of a leadership divided or cowed. Many rabbis and Protestant ministers favored the court order, but too many of these no longer lived in Boston, and most of the flock being asked to comply with desegregation were Catholics.

Many priests did respond to the moral imperative of desegregation. But many openly aligned themselves with their parishes against forced busing. The church simply could not cope with the divisions and passions cutting through its ranks. At the top, Humberto Cardinal Medeiros had the misfortune to be the first non-Irish Cardinal of Boston in almost a century and a half and was indecisive. During April 1974 he appeared at the legislative committee hearing on the Racial Imbalance Act to testify in favor, an act of considerable courage given that most of the law's former supporters had melted away in the heat of antibusing lobbying. But soon Medeiros soft-pedalled his support of the court order, as his parishes and clergy remained deeply split.[17]

As the summer rushed on the neighborhoods seethed with a mixture of anger, apprehension, and confusion. No one doubted that trouble would greet the buses, the only question was how much. City authorities organized meetings at which persons responsible for safety spoke to parents to inform and reassure, but always within a context devoid of endorsement of the court order. At one such meeting in Dorchester, some two hundred young mothers brought together by the Little City Hall and the Pope's Hill Neighborhood Association listened appreciatively to city safety teams. Then John Kerrigan spoke and urged the women to participate in a September 9 march on the Federal Building. At another meeting in the Columbia-Savin Hill area, city officials were silenced by Kerrigan partisans who focused the meeting on angry promises to keep children out of school.[18]

Kerrigan, Hicks, and other antibusing politicians continued to play the Pied Piper, even as some of their most loyal constituents concluded that the school committee had misled them. James G. Colbert, publisher of the *West Roxbury Transcript* which was read mostly in West Roxbury, Roslindale, and Jamaica Plain, wrote that many parents "feel . . . let down by the School Committee." The parents said that the hard-line members "over-sold to the voters the idea that they would prevent compulsory busing. . . . It has always been clear to those who understand the situation that if the court ordered forced busing . . . that ended the argument. That is exactly what happened." Meanwhile, in their show of opposition, Colbert continued, the committee "probably missed opportunities to make revisions in the plan advanced by the State Board of Education."[19]

The committee's reputation slid further when charges surfaced that member Paul Ellison had been using his post to steal city money by setting up a phony assistant's job and routing the pay for it to himself. (A grand jury indicted Ellison in 1975 and he was tried and convicted in early 1976.) Polls for 1974–75 showed a decided slip in confidence in the school committee. Although hard-line antibusers remained willing to forgive the committee just about anything, moderates were much less willing to say that the committee had served well the citizens of Boston.[20]

Both judge and committee proved to be targets of grassroots rage on the night of August 24 at the Shaw School in West Roxbury. Two hundred and fifty parents listened to state legislators, local HSA officials, councillors, committee members, and others denounce the court order. Wild cheers welcomed suggestions to keep children out for two weeks. The only plea for caution came from a teacher who rose from the floor to say that it was irresponsible to advise parents to boycott the schools' appeals for monitors needed for safety. But that brave soul was shouted down.

A roar of applause burst out after a student speaker remarked that "perhaps the real culprits are the politicians, the so-called servants of the people." Later John Kerrigan joked lamely, "I didn't like the way everyone applauded when the young fellow said what he did about politicians." That met with a few laughs but more grumbles. "Its true," yelled someone; and another: "We don't care what you like," with some applause. Kerrigan then tried to save face by attacking his usual scapegoats, but members of the audience started arguing with him and yelling insults. Kerrigan finished by calling for support for the September 9 rally and walked off to restrained applause. Yet the standing ovation that greeted Louise Hicks suggested that disillusionment with antibusing politicians had its limits.[21]

As day one of desegregation loomed closer pleas for peace were heard more frequently. Politicians, public figures, and well-known athletes such as Carl Yastremski and Bobby Orr taped TV spots whose common theme was that Boston was a fine city and that the safety of children counted most. These ads always ended with the tag, "It won't be easy, but that never stopped Boston." Mayor White used that line as he brought the media campaign to a close on September 9 with a televised speech warning against violence. However distasteful the law might be, he said, we need to obey it. "We cannot avoid the situation that will be on us in three days. But we can, and we must control it."

Thousands of those adamantly opposed to the court order, however, remained angry, and many of them would welcome trouble as proof of the wrongness of busing. Countless other thousands were caught in the middle. These anxious citizens may not have been assured by John Kerrigan's taped TV spot that he opposed violence but would continue to fight desegregation in the courts. Meanwhile, he invited Bostonians "to join me and the school committee in non-violent activity. . . . I hope we will be so non-violent that we will win the Nobel Peace Prize."[22]

The Battle of Boston, 1974–1977

Although everyone expected trouble, most officials trying to keep peace believed that after an initial period of protest the schools—and streets—would settle down. These expectations underestimated the ensuing turmoil—its scope, intensity, and duration. Fights, riots, and protests, in and out of schools, broke out all year long. Racial tensions increased—certainly most Bostonians thought them worse than ever—and violence of white on black and vice versa flared up frequently as a spillover from reactions to desegregation. Throughout the year and beyond a small minority of antibusers conducted what amounted to terrorism against blacks and often against whites trying to cooperate, including their own neighbors.

The first days, weeks, and months constituted a wrenching experience for thousands of parents and children, resulting in many missed or disrupted school days for thousands of pupils. ROAR called for a boycott of the schools for the first two weeks, and in response to various incidents of "judicial tyranny" staged other boycotts later on. Much has been made of the success of the boycotts, particularly in South Boston, Hyde Park, East Boston, and elsewhere. In a system with a potential enrollment of 80,000, attendance fluctuated between 40,000 and 60,000 during the first year. But other factors besides antibusing solidarity caused parents to keep their children home, especially fear of violence. Attendance dipped sharply after each major incident, as well as during snow storms when fear of the weather joined fear of hostile encounters in schools and streets.[23]

Conditions in the schools then and later have continued to be disputed, with defenders of desegregation arguing that overall education went on as usual except for a few schools, while antibusers have maintained that school officials, police, and particularly the media played down and underreported difficulties, especially when black aggression against whites was involved.

Unquestionably, school conditions during 1974–75 did worsen more than reported in newspapers or on television. State troopers remained on duty at South Boston High for three years. During most of the first year, Hyde Park also required a strong police presence. Charlestown, excluded from the 1974–75 plan (known hereafter as Phase 1), nevertheless as early as the spring of 1975 began to be disturbed by protests, marches, and student boycotts. Roslindale, though less publicized, experienced frequent trouble at its high and middle schools, with police being called to the former five times. Often, disturbances in these trouble spots rippled into other schools, while small incidents pockmarked the entire city.

Before the first day of classes on Thursday, September 12, the antibusers rallied with Southie, as always, taking the lead. On Saturday, the seventh, a 250-car motorcade streamed out of Southie to generate support for the demonstration on the ninth. On that Monday before school began, some eight to ten thousand militants congregated at Boston Common and enjoyed Indian summer weather as they walked to City Hall Plaza to register their protest with the judge and the state's two U.S. senators, Edward Brooke and Ted Kennedy. Events at the plaza would show just how deeply alienated the antibusers were.

Brooke already had declined to meet with the protesters. Kennedy had agreed to meet with a small delegation at his office but on impulse unexpectedly went to the rally. He arrived just after Hicks's lieutenant Rita Graul had introduced two men in chicken masks, one white and one brown, who were stand-ins for Kennedy and Brooke. Boos and ugly jeers greeted Kennedy, and when he stepped to the microphone the shouting became a din. Then, in concert, the crowd began to turn its back on him (ironically facing the Federal Building named after his brother John). As Kennedy left, quick-stepping to the Federal Building, eggs, tomatoes, and curses splattered about. A woman punched him on the shoulder, a man aimed a kick. The words were uglier than the gestures. "You're a disgrace to the Irish. . . . Why don't you put your one-legged son on a bus for Roxbury. . . . Let your daughter get bused there so she can get raped. . . . Why don't you let them shoot you like they shot your two brothers." With Kennedy finally inside the building, the crowd pressed and pounded against the large glass doors until suddenly a large section of one of the doors shattered, surprising but pleasing the mob, which finally pulled back. "It was great," said another South Boston Hicks aide, Pat Ranese. "It's about time the politicians felt the anger of the people. We've been good for too long. They'd pat us on the backs, and we'd go home. No more."[24]

At night the tense neighborhoods seemed to be ticking bombs, but opening day went fairly well throughout the city except, of course, for South Boston, which dominated national news, while the local media underplayed it. Graffiti ("Kill Niggers," "Niggers Suck," "KKK") covered the high school, and an angry crowd jostled with police outside the building almost from dawn until school's closing. Several school buses carrying black children out of South Boston were bombarded with rocks, bottles, and other missiles—three buses somehow twice ran the same gauntlet of terror along Day Boulevard and nine youngsters and a bus monitor were injured by flying glass, none seriously. Citywide, eighteen buses sustained damages that day.

In many schools desegregation to all appearances went calmly. The headmaster of the Mary E. Curley School in Jamaica Plain, enrolling eleven hundred students from forty-five different elementary schools, called his the best opening in four years. The Frank P. Thompson Middle School in Mattapan-Dorchester experienced calm and quiet, though half the pupils assigned there stayed away. But in Southie, said a Swedish correspondent, "It's like Belfast. The women look the same, talk the same, and seem to be just as tough. Anytime there's any trouble, you see them egging the kids on."[25]

Mayor White and Deputy Mayor Robert Kiley during the summer had decided on a "low visibility" policy for police presence in South Boston. That policy ended with day one. On Friday, September 13, the city came into South Boston with a show of force; Hyde Park, too, would soon look like an armed camp. Antibusing leader Ray Flynn, outraged over the new policy, compared it to the Soviet takeover of Budapest in 1956: "They take our schools, now they take our streets. . . . This is the most degrading thing to South Boston." Over the weekend the mayor decided against letting Southie hold a protest march. On Monday, police broke up crowds of several hundred youths and adults. A mob of 300 took revenge by invading the Andrew Square MBTA station, assaulting blacks, ripping out phones, and trashing benches. Police arrested 24 by day's end. In five days the city police, perhaps half of them somehow related to South Boston by kin or origin, had become identified with "the enemy."[26]

After ten days buses were still being stoned in Southie, police were inside Hyde Park High, a shot had been fired through the door of Jamaica Plain High, and several rifle shots had been fired at the *Globe* building on Morrissey Boulevard bordering South Boston. The judge himself, surveying the first two weeks of violence, called it "intolerable. . . . Scores of young children, frightened out of their wits, afraid to go to school . . . what a situation." Garrity thought that too many opponents harbored unrealistic hopes that desegregation somehow would go away. But at the same time he believed fervently in the First Amendment guarantee of free speech and assembly: "That's the way the system works." So he took no action to prohibit demonstrations that often led to violence.[27]

Blacks too began to exercise their First Amendment rights. The night of day one Mayor White faced a vocal, furious throng of black parents at Freedom House in Roxbury, and the heavily protected buses that left Columbia Point the next morning were mostly empty. During the week, blacks at Columbia Point complained that carloads of marauding whites were driving through the project, and so blacks began to set up blockades while youth gangs skirmished with police. By late September police cars were being stoned and sniper fire came from the project.[28]

In South Boston marches became a way of life. When several hundred antibusers marched on September 29, that was just a warm-up for an October 4 march of five to ten thousand marking "National Boycott Day." Louise Hicks, state legislators, school committee members, and city councillors took part, while three hundred or so also rallied in Hyde Park. That night 300 antibusers drove to Wellesley, where they sang and chanted for an hour while helmeted police silently stood between them and Garrity's home.[29]

Although a flyer circulated through South Boston that day, addressed to "ADULTS ONLY," called for a "Human Barricade" to stop the buses, these demonstrations went peacefully.[30] Trouble, however, was brewing elsewhere. During the day members of the city police's Tactical Patrol Force (TPF), the elite 125-man riot-control unit that had already seen exhaustive service, clashed with stone throwers in Southie. That night, three officers were prevented from apprehending a stone thrower by twenty-five to thirty patrons of a bar, the Rabbit Inn. The next night a posse of TPF smashed into the bar, breaking everything and beating everyone in sight, sending ten men to the hospital and causing $20,000 worth of damage. Now the cries of "police brutality," already rife, became a standard part of Southie's litany of protest.

More was to come. The following Monday afternoon a black Haitian maintenance man, on his way to pick up his wife at a South Boston laundry, stopped his car at a red light. A nearby mob, frustrated by police from gathering to assault buses, chased the black out of his car and down the street, severely beating him with kicks, punches, and hockey sticks. The man was rescued by a police officer who fired his revolver into the air. Other incidents that day included the stoning of three buses of black students headed for Roslindale High and fighting between blacks and whites at the high school. When disturbances spread to the Washington Irving Middle School, the TPF rushed to the scene.[31] As pictures of the terrified Haitian struggling to get away from the mob filled the newspapers, Mayor White sent an urgent request to Judge Garrity asking for 125 federal marshals. White argued that 900 regular police officers and 125 TPF were overworked and that Southie especially was severely straining the city's capacity to keep order. More importantly, those arrested in South Boston strolled harmlessly through the local court with hardly a reprimand. In a federal court, it would be different. The law, White was saying, needed teeth.[32]

On October 8 young blacks in Roxbury added substantially to the rocks flying about in Boston. After some fifteen hundred students poured out of English High School following a false alarm, a mob moved into the Mission Hill area, "stoning everything in sight." By evening the MBTA canceled bus runs into Roxbury-Dorchester and the Mission Hill project "resembled a battleground . . . with pitched battles and skirmishes between young people, mostly black, and riot-equipped police." The toll for the day was 38 injured, 24 white and 14 black.[33] The next day the judge refused the mayor's request for federal marshals. Garrity conceded the need for more security, but said that it should come from local resources, because that was the way it was supposed to work.[34]

Ironically, on the very day that Garrity refused a federal presence, the president of the United States inserted himself into Boston's travail. Gerald Ford, having assumed office only two months earlier, following Richard Nixon's resignation in August, was questioned at a press conference regarding federal help for Boston. Ford took the occasion to deliver the gratuitous observation that the federal court's decision was "not the best solution to quality education in Boston. I have consistently opposed forced busing to achieve racial balance. . . . And therefore, I respectfully disagree with the judge's order."

The nation's top leader had just conferred on Boston's resisters an additional measure of legitimacy. Of course, the president deplored violence and said that citizens must obey the law, etc. He also, as became known several days later, had put the 82d Airborne Division on standby alert for possible Boston duty. Nevertheless, Ford's remarks had the effect of an elixir across the antibusing spectrum. "I was so happy when I heard his statement," said ROAR leader Fran Johnnene, "I felt like screaming."[35]

The first twenty-six days of school had produced, at a minimum, 140 arrests, 69 treatable injuries, countless incidents of harassment, and an enormous commitment of police to try to keep peace. South Boston had contributed a disproportionate share of the turmoil and some 40 percent of the arrests. The first serious incident within Southie High came in early October, when the cafeteria became filled with flying fists, trays, and spaghetti, and the TPF was called in. On the day after Garrity's refusal to bring in federal marshals, 150 state troopers marched down Telegraph Street in Southie. Tall, lean, tough, and tautly professional, the troopers awed onlookers as local police had not and brought a measure of calm to the high school and its environs.[36]

But the task of controlling violence in the city that fall was never done. As soon as the lid was secured in one place, violence boiled over in another. The fifth week of school opened with a stabbing (of a white by a black) at Hyde Park High School on October 15 and the TPF being rushed in. Governor Sargent reacted to the storm of white protest by calling up five hundred National Guardsmen—military police companies—and placing them in readiness in the City Armory. Shortly after, police arrested four white youths in Hyde Park who were driving near the high school with Molotov cocktails.[37]

Meanwhile, the antibusing movement remained in high gear, with rallies, motorcades, and a proliferation of neighborhood "information centers" opening in storefronts throughout the city. In mid-October ROAR leaders announced that they were beginning to target businesses for boycotting to bring pressure to end the court order. Stepping forward to boost this effort was John Kerrigan, who said so long as only poor people were affected by busing, "nobody cares, but if we start hitting the downtown financial community in their pocketbooks they'll start caring and they'll go down to see Judge Garrity. Money talks."

Near the end of October, South Boston mustered one of its biggest rallies to date, with ten thousand gathering at Marine Park; then a two thousand-car cavalcade, including many from the suburbs, snarled traffic all the way from Quincy to South Boston. On election day, November 5, a school boycott was widely effective. Five days later, over three thousand assembled for a Sunday rally at Billings Field in middle-class West Roxbury to celebrate the opening of an antibusing information center there and to hear Louise Hicks proclaim: "We're united . . . and together we're going to win." Around Thanksgiving a crowd of four thousand, mostly youngsters, entered East Boston Stadium in a police-escorted motorcade and heard speeches, led by neighborhood leader Pixie Palladino elaborating on the theme: "Eastie Will Never Be Bused."[38]

Fights and disruptions inside schools did not occur solely according to their own rhythms. Some were, of course, spontaneous. Some resulted from black retaliation or aggression. But some clearly were orchestrated by adults and youths from within the militant antibusing movement, particularly at Southie High and later at Charlestown High. Major fights seemed to coincide with increased attendance. On the day of the "spaghetti war" at Southie, for example, attendance had gone over five hundred for the first time since school began. The most militant boycotters wanted to show that the schools were unsafe—the more fights, the more parents would keep children out. Attendance did in fact decline sharply after major incidents.[39]

Tension remained high at Southie—scuffles and walkouts were normal. But elsewhere during November a state of affairs approaching prosaic prevailed. Citywide attendance cleared 70 percent, there were 230 fewer students suspended compared to October, and only seven as against sixteen assaults on teachers. At Southie, despite the angry mobs still yelling insults at black students every day, attendance went well over five hundred again. But Southie began to feel especially bitter around Thanksgiving—the highlight of sports-crazy Southie's year had been the annual football game with Eastie. There was no game—there was no football team. In early December incidents within the school became uglier. One student told Headmaster Reid that if a policeman were put with every student there would still be fights.[40]

Both white attendance and the crowds yelling outside had increased, but on December 2 the state police reduced their force by two-thirds. On December 6 adults from the South Boston Information Center (SBIC) entered the school in the headmaster's absence and incited a frenzied rally of white students in the auditorium and then throughout the school. Police finally ejected about three hundred whites. With turmoil continuing, a riot at Walpole State Prison caused the sudden and entire withdrawal of the state troopers the following Tuesday night. The next day, fighting had erupted before 10 A.M., resulting in the stabbing of a seventeen-year-old white, Michael D. Faith, who was rushed to City Hospital where doctors repaired his punctured lung and liver. An enormous crowd filled with hate and seeking revenge quickly besieged the school. State Senator William Bulger declined to try to calm them. Mrs. Hicks did plead with the mob to let 125 black students inside be bused "back to Roxbury," but even she was ignored. Finally, only a clever ruse by a bus company official, William Reilly, got the terrified blacks out in a narrow escape. A twelve-year-old Boston Latin School student who passed by the high school just after noon that day described it later: "What a mess! What a mob of people! I saw all the T.P.F. and the mounted police, and the smashed police car and some injured people."[41]

South Boston High remained center stage for the resistance in Southie. The militants sometimes acted as if they wanted the school closed, but had it been moved to a neutral site, the antibusing movement would have suffered a severe blow. Southie, after all, was the symbol of resistance. When word of the Faith stabbing reached Hyde Park High, two hundred white students walked out, along with fifty to seventy-five from a nearby annex. One teenager who left said "everyone seemed to be leaving and I didn't want to stay behind and get beat up by the blacks." Hyde Park and Charlestown marched to their own drumbeat of disruption, but as one Hyde Park student revealed after the Faith stabbing walkout: "Everyone passed the word around there'd be a walkout because of what happened in Southie. We help Southie and they help us."[42]

When Southie's long school year finally ended, with eighty to one hundred policemen still on hand, teachers left the building to the sounds of the "Hallelujah" chorus over the public address system. The year did in fact end quietly at the trouble spots as seniors focused on graduation, and most students simply melted away into warm spring weather. But there were no reasons to feel good about the future. Headmaster Reid of Southie said that in September he had estimated it might take three years before a viable climate of learning would be established. Now, in June, he regretted to say he thought it would take longer than three years. There simply existed no good will "on the part of the adult community."[43]

Although there were, on the other hand, all kinds of success stories during year one of desegregation, by May 1975 a majority of the city's white adults, 60 percent according to a *Globe* poll, said they believed the school year had resulted in an "almost complete breakdown" of public school education. To no one's surprise the poll also uncovered persisting high levels of opposition to busing among whites, and though a *Globe* poll a year earlier actually had found higher overall opposition to busing, the climate of opinion in the city was still unconducive to successful desegregation.[44]

During year one not all voices in Boston opposed the court order. *Globe* editorials and various religious leaders provided consistent support of the judge. Probusers marched in October and again in May 1975 when Roy Wilkins was the featured speaker. Some of the leaders of the largest Protestant denominations in the state issued a proclamation that not only backed busing but criticized ROAR for "your rhetoric, your strategy, your values," and for generating violence and refusing to condemn it.[45] But most elected officials continued to be vocal in opposition to the court order. The state legislature adopted a resolution calling for a national convention to draft an amendment to the United States Constitution to prohibit forced busing. The mayor tried to be neutral but also made clear his distaste for "the law."[46]

Some city and school officials, in the time-honored way of Boston, also managed to turn the bus-contracting business into private profit, while the logistics of transportation were horribly mismanaged. Before the end of 1974 the city's watchdog Finance Commission had begun investigating the bus companies, one of which owned no buses when its contract was secured, another of which seemed to have been running buses into South Boston on days when the schools were closed. Indictments and convictions would follow in the years ahead.[47]

The police, upon whom fell the most direct and dangerous part of the burden of peacekeeping, were themselves overwhelmingly opposed to the court order. Their Patrolmen's Association made no secret of its opposition, and its official publication was stridently antibusing. Some motorcycle police even flew colored ribbons from the handlebars of their cycles, with certain colors symbolizing solidarity with individual neighborhoods.

Other labor unions that spoke out on the issue tended to be antibusing. Firefighters Local 718 attacked Garrity and promoters of desegregation as vehemently as the South Boston Information Center. A convention of Teamsters Local 25, representing 12,500 members in eastern Massachusetts, in October 1974 adopted a resolution opposing busing while outside their meeting hall in Charlestown several hundred anti-busing demonstrators paraded on foot and in cars. That same month the Massachusetts Building and Trades Council, representing 70,000 construction workers, also lobbied by a South Boston motorcade, unanimously criticized the court order.[48]

The judge's softness toward the school committee also helped to create a climate that encouraged other outrageous and illegal acts of protest and additional disruption in the schools. Garrity gave the committee majority a long rope, long enough to hang all three, but when the moment of truth came, he refused to tighten the noose. During the summer of 1974 Garrity had directed the committee to have a desegregation plan for year two by December 16. Earlier, Garrity had given the committee a last-minute chance to submit a plan for year one, but the committee took the two weeks that the judge had given them, then met in a closed session during which John Kerrigan said "I can't vote for any plan where there is forced busing, and I never will." The committee also filed an appeal with the U.S. Circuit Court of Appeals to remand Garrity's June decision against the advice of its attorneys that it would be frivolous. On October 31 Garrity repeated his order for the school committee to have a plan by December 16. Meanwhile, the school department's Educational Planning Center (EPC), led by John Coakley, a responsible professional, prepared a desegregation plan involving extensive busing. On December 16 the committee rejected the EPC plan by a three to two vote, with Kerrigan, Ellison, and McDonough in the majority.

Earlier that month it seemed the committee would vote to approve the EPC plan rather than face the prospect of going to jail. Even Kerrigan had snapped at an antibusing delegation that he would not risk criminal contempt, disbarment, and a prison term. But the stabbing of Michael Faith at Southie High on December 11 had pushed Kerrigan, Ellison, and McDonough back to defiance. Indeed, the December 16 vote came at 12:20 P.M., twenty minutes after the deadline originally set by the judge. The committee's lawyer then decided to transmit the plan to the court anyway, neither "approved" nor "submitted," but simply as an action of an officer of the court. He and his firm then signed off on the case. In response to these events, the NAACP asked for harsh measures by the court against the three nay-sayers on the committee, including criminal contempt charges and fines of $300 per day.

The judge then summoned into court all five committee members on December 18, lectured them for nearly two hours, but told the defiant three that they were not in criminal contempt. He did warn that their failure to approve a plan could result in civil contempt and gave them until Friday, December 27 at 10 A.M. to show why they should not be so judged. He also asked the three committeemen to give him written answers to five questions regarding implementation of desegregation. The next day Garrity's position became even stronger as three federal appeals court judges endorsed his June decision in a thirty-six-page opinion, saying "we do not see how the court could arrive at any other conclusion" than that the Boston School Committee had acted to sustain and foster segregation.[49]

Nevertheless, when the three committeemen came back to Garrity on December 27 to answer his questions as to why they should not be held in civil contempt, the three conceded nothing to Garrity or desegregation. Justifying their actions as based on conscience, they gave the judge brief memoranda that consisted of antibusing platitudes and repeated that they would do only what the judge specifically ordered them to do. Garrity put each on the stand but got nowhere. John Kerrigan left the stand with a satisfied smirk on his face.

Garrity should not have been surprised by their behavior, since the committee had voted on December 23, five days after his lecture and warnings, to appeal Garrity's decision to the U.S. Supreme Court. The judge found the three in contempt of court but rejected the plaintiffs' lawyers suggestions that they be fined $500 a day until they approved a plan. Instead he delayed imposing sanctions and sent the three away over the weekend to work out a compromise, but by now Kerrigan and his cohorts knew they need not budge an inch. On Monday, December 30, Garrity told them that if they voted to authorize submission of a Phase 2 plan by January 7, they would be purged of contempt. Otherwise, coercive fines, geared to their ability to pay, would begin on January 9, and temporary disbarment proceedings would begin against lawyers Kerrigan and McDonough. The three committeemen probably no longer believed the judge's warnings. In any case, they called his bluff.

After leaving the courtroom on December 30, Kerrigan and the others returned to their offices to the cheers of antibusers, and they talked, as they had right along, of the court's "bullying" and oppression of the elected officials of the people of Boston. It was during a break in the courtroom proceedings on December 30, incidentally, that Kerrigan mocked ABC-TV correspondent Lem Tucker by imitating a chimpanzee. Shortly after this, Louise Hicks, deploring the possibility of Garrity's finding Kerrigan in contempt, defended the committeeman and compared him to Martin Luther King.[50]

On January 7, just one hour before Garrity's new deadline, the committee directed school department planners to give the court a wholly voluntary plan, one with no forced busing, and to file it promptly in compliance with the order for an authorized plan. To the surprise of his supporters, Garrity the next day accepted this sham and told the smiling men that they had purged themselves of contempt by filing "a" plan, though it was surely not "the" plan he had ordered them to authorize. "Despite all his tough talk," said a team of *Globe* reporters, "the judge decided to give the three men the benefit of the doubt. To their surprise and relief they were home free."[51]

The judge's defenders—and the judge himself—have justified his backing down by arguing that it would have been a mistake to make the three committee members into martyrs, and that their removal would only have created further obstacles. This thesis ignores the fact that by not risking making them martyrs, the judge made the defiant three into heroes. Bob Schwartz, Mayor White's education adviser, recalled that the feeling in City Hall "was that the School Committee was very vulnerable, politically, on issues having to do with management and . . . there was very little credibility. . . . at some level people must have understood that they had been played with. They'd been lied to . . . even though they'd been told what they wanted to hear." A *Globe* poll of April 1975 found that John Kerrigan had a favorability rating of 38 percent in the city, which was almost equalled by his unfavorability rating of 35 percent. Thus the judge missed the chance to exploit the erosion in the committee's credibility, as well as to deliver a lesson about the cost of law breaking.[52]

A few dedicated school officials trying to make the best of a bad situation had been hoping privately that the judge would free them from the obstructionism of the committee majority, not necessarily because they welcomed desegregation but simply from a desire to perform well whatever job they were called upon to do. "One of the leading professionals cried when he heard the news [from Garrity's courtroom on January 8]."[53]

Judge Garrity has also been criticized for refusing repeated pleas from the mayor to bring in federal marshals and to raise the costs of disruption for the violent minority among the antibusers. State and city officials who commented on this point before the United States Civil Rights Commission in June 1975 said almost unanimously that the absence of federal sanctions made things worse. As Kevin White argued often, and correctly, local arrests were not feared, but the likelihood of federal arrest and the consequences (said White: "You disappear") might have dampened some extreme protest, particularly the fomenting of trouble inside and outside the schools. The Civil Rights Commission, though careful to avoid any criticism of Garrity, nevertheless found that as persons arrested in South Boston were "broomed through" the local court, the assumption persisted that illegal disruption could be pursued at no cost.[54]

5

The Antibusing Spectrum
Moderation and Compliance

I myself am filled with prejudices, and I think we all are. I don't know if I'm a racist or not. Probably, like a lot of people, I have gone through periods when maybe I have been and didn't know it. I don't love all black people. I haven't known too many. Any time I've come across anybody [black] in a similar situation to my own, they've been terrific. I do know that hate is not good for the hater, much less for the one being hated. —Lorraine Faith, mother of Michael Faith, stabbed at South Boston High School[1]

I would say we were all opposed. You know, I feel so middle-of-the-roadish. . . . we were opposed to it [busing], but at the same time we didn't want any trouble. We didn't want any kids to get hurt, and were willing to go in and have students, both black and white, receive their education, without any violence. —Margaret Coughlin, South Boston mother, testimony before U.S. Commission on Civil Rights

To attribute the antibusing resistance to racism pure and simple is to ignore the complexity of experiences, actions, and attitudes displayed by Mrs. Faith, Mrs. Coughlin, and thousands of others caught up in Boston's desegregation. To focus only on the organized resistance, protests, marches, disruptions, and violence tends to obscure the great variety of individual responses.

Most white residents of Boston, and particularly most white parents of schoolchildren, were overwhelmingly antibusing in some way. Some fought the court orders in the ranks of ROAR or by acts of individual resistance. Some fled, putting their children in parochial schools or anywhere but in the Boston public schools. A few left the city. Many more during the first two years tried to give desegregation a chance by sending all or some of their children to the public schools.

Hundreds of parents did more than just send their children to desegregated schools. Judge Garrity had provided that a Racial-Ethnic Parent Council (REPC) be established in each school throughout the city, as well as a Citywide Parents' Advisory Council, formed entirely by parents. His Phase 2 plan added Community District Advisory Councils composed of ten parents elected by the districts' REPCs for each of eight new community districts. For Phase 2 Garrity also created a Citywide Coordinating Council (CCC), consisting of some forty members appointed by him, to monitor overall compliance with desegregation. The CCC initially included only three antibusers tied closely to parents, moderates K. Marie Clarke of West Roxbury, Jane Margulis of Dorchester, and Moe Gillen of Charlestown.

The REPCs and advisory councils involved many parents who thought the court orders and desegregation plans to be bad policy, yet they joined in to try to make desegregation work peacefully. Hundreds more served as aides in schools or as bus monitors or joined neighborhood groups. In October 1975, after letters went out to 80,000 parents asking them to elect court-mandated biracial councils, only some 3,000 turned out to do so, and just 1,326 of 2,000 seats were filled. But by that fall the court-ordered plans had alienated parents not once but twice, and the council elections coincided with the Boston Red Sox being in the midst of a thrilling World Series. Not until 1976–77, when ROAR finally began to fade, did the parents' councils begin to operate as effective vehicles of parental participation.

Those who did cooperate in the first two years risked threats, abuse, and harassment from antibusing militants. One South Boston woman came home from a council election night to find her home besieged by a raucous crowd of seventy-five, and then a motorcade circling her block. Six phone calls to the police finally got a response an hour later. Given the lack of protection moderates usually received from police and courts, their courage was even more remarkable. The militants called them traitors, or worse, yet most of the participants in implementation regarded themselves as antibusing and firmly disavowed the probusing label, whether affixed by militant oppositionists or liberal desegregators.[2]

The hard-liners sought to deter their neighbors from cooperating with busing in any way. They saw any compliance, even simple efforts to insure safety, as acceptance or tacit approval of busing. They brooked no middle ground. Thousands of parents, on the other hand, disdained the hard-liners' tactics. For many, ROAR implied something dangerous or disreputable. "Parents with kids in the schools will fight forced busing in any peaceful way," said Representative Angelo Scaccia of Hyde Park. "They get no fanfare. They run dances to get money for court appeals. They contribute to newspaper columns. They attend anti-busing rallies in their neighborhoods. They write to Congressmen. They are completely divorced from ROAR." But these moderates also subtly distanced themselves from those they regarded as liberal probusers, or suburbanite moralists, and they refused to advertise their distaste for ROAR.

Evidence of the majority's moderation appeared in a *Globe* poll of April 1975 that found that 57 percent of whites disapproved of school boycotts, 63 percent disapproved of demonstrations outside schools, and 87 percent said they disapproved of force to try to thwart forced busing. Of course these figures may be read another way. When, for example, over 10 percent of the adult population approves of violence to resist a policy there is going to be trouble. But the vast majority did hold essentially moderate attitudes.[3]

Many mothers who had been active in Massachusetts Citizens Against Forced Busing, home and school associations, and even ROAR, after September 1974 moved over into the moderate Citywide Educational Coalition, not because they were probusing but "to make the best of a bad situation" and to gain leverage to improve the court's plan or to improve education. Jane Margulis, with a daughter attending the McCormack School in black Columbia Point, helped organize a mutual aid society, then served on a biracial council and worked for the Citywide Education Coalition. She heard much criticism from former ROAR allies but regarded herself as still strongly against forced busing. Regarding harassment, Margulis said, "I can tread there too." She saw no alternative, however, once she decided to stay in the city and to keep her children in public schools. Similarly, Jacqueline Hill joined a Hyde Park REPC saying, "I'm anti-busing, but when you can't afford private school, you've got to send your kids to public school." Bernadette Malone, another Hyde Park antibusing mother (of five) said: "I disapprove of the law, but I felt that I'd be teaching the child to break the law if I boycotted. Also, I would not want [them] to form prejudices. Keeping them home would do more harm than good." Alice France, an MCAFB activist who lobbied in Washington in the spring of 1975, accepted election to a biracial council at the Jeremiah Burke School in the fall of 1975. She adamantly insisted she was not endorsing busing, rather: "Busing is here. You can't ignore it." And so it was with most of the three thousand parents who turned out for the elections to the councils.[4]

Most of them probably agreed with Rita Tomasini, an executive board member of MCAFB: "If you're on a racial council, you're called probusing, a pinkie, a communist, a nigger lover. . . . I have to participate because my son is going to school. I can't be keeping a kid out of school, and it's not going to do any good to keep him home. . . . If you're realistic, you have to realize it's going to take five years to change the federal busing law. If anybody thinks they can ride around the city and change it, they're losing their marbles."[5]

South Boston militants during 1974–75 did not permit the election of biracial councils there. After Headmaster Reid got some South Boston parents to attend a dinner at Freedom House, they returned to face fierce pressure in their neighborhood and never came back. Yet thirty-eight persons did serve as aides at the high school, persons who witnessed at first hand the difficult situation that some students faced as unwilling recruits in the busing wars.[6]

During the summer of 1975, when a nucleus of parents came forward to serve on the biracial councils, they were still subjected to harassment. One of those who joined the council said: "I was anti-busing and went to the first meeting last year. But the meeting was disrupted by loud people who weren't speaking for me. That's when I volunteered to do what I could." These hardy souls were buoyed for a time by an organization that had formed quietly the previous year, the Positive Action Task Force, an informal group of some twenty parents and clergy who met at the Laboure Center, a Catholic social service agency in South Boston's dilapidated lower end. When the group's existence became publicized, rocks came crashing through windows at the center. After the *Herald* ran a story lauding the efforts of one member, Tracy Amalfitano, a Southie mother who was also antibusing, about fifteen youths showered her house with rocks and bottles, breaking windows and furnishings within. For months that extended to "hell for three years," her car tires and windows were repeatedly destroyed. The newspapers, she concluded, after setting her up as a target were not much interested in the relentless terrorism conducted against her thereafter. Nor was the court.[7]

Not all the voices of moderation in South Boston were silenced during year one. Margaret Coughlin steered her own course independently of

ROAR and the SBIC, to whom she conceded nothing so far as being antibusing. Peggy Coughlin, fifty years old, who lived in a neat three-decker on Marine Road, had sent children to public schools for eighteen consecutive years, with six more to go. She went along with the boycott for two weeks and would not send one daughter to Roxbury because she feared the violence she saw as endemic there. Instead, she and her husband Francis, a disabled longshoreman, paid $820 to send her to a Catholic school.

Though Coughlin would accept black students in South Boston, she felt strongly enough about out-busing to write Judge Garrity a letter of protest. When Garrity did not answer, she sent a copy to the *South Boston Tribune*, which resulted in the *Globe* sending a reporter to interview her. Quickly, Peggy received the first of threatening calls and mail condemning her for not espousing a sufficiently hard-line position. But in December, at a private meeting of South Bostonians with the school committee following the Faith stabbing, Peggy spoke up again. Lorraine Faith had just finished a poignant plea to the committee to close the high school. But Peggy, whose son Kevin was a senior and star center on the hockey team, piped up that while she felt badly for Mrs. Faith, she believed that the children should not be deprived of an education in their own neighborhoods. Nancy Yotts, a ROAR spitfire, testily rebuked Peggy with a "Who are you?" to which Peggy replied, "I'm one of the mothers in this crowd who has a child at South Boston High."

Peggy was now well launched into the fray. In early January, as the school committee pondered closing South Boston High, committeewoman Sullivan asked Peggy if she would assemble support from parents to guarantee safety in the school. Peggy got on the phone, and at the committee's next meeting she appeared nervously, but smartly in a green pants suit, to report that over one hundred parents had agreed to patrol the corridors. Reassured by this and the efforts of Southie teachers to gain parental support, the committee decided to keep the school open. Significantly, all the parents rallying to Peggy were, she believed, like herself strongly opposed to busing.

Meanwhile, Peggy paid a price beyond the usual threats for, as she said, "opening my mouth." When a daughter, Michelle, had been assigned to the McCormack School at Columbia Point, Peggy, like many other Boston parents, gave a false address for her daughter to keep her at the nearby Gavin School. But after Peggy's prominence, hard-liners tipped off school officials and Michelle was taken out of the Gavin. Unwilling to keep the girl at home, a desperate Peggy went to see the McCormack principal, where she was charmed by the staff's welcoming tour of the school. Peggy was impressed and confessed to feeling "very sheepish because . . . I had done wrong and I had to admit this to all the people." Her daughter decided to try the McCormack and flourished. The school, Peggy told the U.S. Commission on Civil Rights in June, "is excellently staffed, and it's immaculately clean, and everybody is just really cooperative. *They don't take any bull from anybody.*"(Italics mine.) But Peggy, to "prove my point that I was against busing but still for education and against boycotting," drove her daughter to school and back every day.[8]

Was Peggy Coughlin a racist? She definitely feared crime in Roxbury, "a bad neighborhood." At the same time she could imagine "those mothers in Roxbury are scared to death, same as me." Peggy had worked as a banquet waitress with "colored men," with whom she had gotten along "just beautiful." Before year two Peggy reluctantly agreed to serve on a biracial council, which she knew local sentiment to be against.

The man who called Peggy and asked her to serve on the council was Jim O'Sullivan, a local community worker who directed refuges for the homeless, a halfway house for alcoholics, and a soup kitchen on D Street near Southie's poorest housing project. O'Sullivan thought that the judge's pairing of South Boston and Roxbury was insane, but while he opposed busing he was distressed even more when he walked into the high school in October 1974, which he remembered leaving in 1940 as a beautiful facility: "You could eat off the floor." Now its "appalling condition" dismayed him. "Down in the D Street project," he noted, "we have two temporary schools that you wouldn't put the pigs in." O'Sullivan decided to cooperate with "a terrible plan" because he wanted "to protect my children and my neighbors' children."

> I don't want any more obscenities. I don't want any more congregating in front [of the school] for purposes of terrorizing. . . . *I want the children to go to school like they do in Toledo or Weymouth or in Newton Center.* [Italics mine.] In the 1930s Boston had . . . one of the best school systems in the country. Today it has the worst. . . . I want all this turned around. I want a dollar for a dollar. I want my tax dollars to go to the schools. I want the people that work the schools to

keep them clean. I want teachers who . . . really want to teach to be allowed to teach. And I want to break down the terrible racism that's all around me.[9]

Coughlin and O'Sullivan were hardly racists. Neither were they the dominant voice in South Boston. In the end the moderates could not exert much influence there because the militants made the cost of dissent too high. Meanwhile, outside of Southie many hundreds and thousands of moderates who shared the decent impulses of Coughlin or O'Sullivan also shared the fate of lacking protection, leadership, or understanding.

Emily DeCesare of Roslindale was one such parent whose actions, experiences, and attitudes were probably closer to the norm than ROAR militants or embattled moderates such as Coughlin and O'Sullivan. DeCesare was living with her husband and two children in a clean, modest, middle-class section of Roslindale, where the houses tend to be small but well kept, on neat, tree-lined streets. A legal secretary before she married, her involvement with schools began in a limited way in the late 1960s when her children started school. In 1970–71 the fear that her children would be bused out of the neighborhood prompted her to get active in the local HSA. From the outset, DeCesare maintained that she and other parents would have accepted additional black children in nearby schools (there already were a handful); she conceded, however, that some parents would have resisted that as well. But she believed that she was not a bigot or a racist, and she resented that her position received little attention.

From 1970 to 1974 she attended meetings and knocked on doors with daughter in hand to lobby against the Racial Imbalance Act. The climax of this activity came in a demonstration at the state capitol, where DeCesare joined hundreds of other women trying to see Governor Sargent. She recalled this episode with mixed feelings: "We found an awful lot of women who were shocked that they were doing that type of thing. I mean here we were marching up at City Hall (chuckle). . . . I was involved that day at the governor's [office], and my God, the TV cameras [were] there and I said . . . if I'm ever on TV people are going to think I'm crazy to see me in this mess that I really didn't want to be in." Indeed, when some of the demonstrators (she supposed from South Boston) "became very vocal" and got into a pushing melee with capitol police, DeCesare was mortified. She returned home angry at the governor for not seeing them and irritated with the militants who made "things get out of hand."

When the Garrity decision came down, she gave up. "Our group of parents, we did what we could to fight it. But once it became reality . . . that was it." She blamed much of the outcome on the school committee for foolishly setting itself up for a law suit: "They got caught red-handed." Despite this and her generally moderate views, DeCesare voted for John Kerrigan most of the time, even while regarding him as "very crass." But parent groups like hers found Kerrigan accessible. "If we wanted to get something done . . . we got action from his office." Later on, the odor of corruption around Kerrigan did stop her from voting for him.

But she resented even more the *Globe* and other outsiders "telling us what to do." Here was the *Globe* "pushing something that they didn't know anything about. All of the people who work for the *Globe*, none of them live in Boston. . . . if they felt so strongly about it why didn't they move to Boston and put all their children in the Boston public schools?" Even more exasperating was the exclusion of the suburbs and the thought that "because I lived in Boston . . . my children had to be bused; whereas two miles down this way or . . . that way, in another town . . . Dedham is like two miles away . . . their children weren't in-volved. . . . Because [of] . . . the accident of living in Boston . . . I was being unfairly treated."[10]

It turned out that under Phase 1 neither of her children were to be bused out, so DeCesare kept them in the public schools. The results within this one small family were dramatically mixed. Her daughter, never before a discipline problem, began coming home from elementary school with black and blue marks all over her arms and legs. Gangs of small black boys and girls were hitting, punching, pinching, and kicking her; the girls especially were pulling Laura DeCesare's long brown hair. So the following year Emily put Laura in a parochial school. In contrast, her sixth-grade son encountered no unusual problems, even though she knew that other grades in his school were sorely troubled. To her relief, though, the boy moved on to Boston Latin the next year, making deseg-regation now something tried and abandoned by the DeCesare family.

All across the city parents similarly gave desegregation a chance. Some did not regret it; many did, and then retreated, some temporarily, some for good. The variety of their experiences defies summary. Even ardent antibusers who were local leaders gave the public schools a try during 1974–75. Richard Laws, active in his HSA as well as ROAR citywide, kept three children in the neighborhood elementary school because they were assigned there. But soon he believed that education was being disrupted as concern for safety became paramount. When his youngest son first came home with bruised knees, having been pushed down by a black, Laws did not interpret it as a racial incident. But when two weeks later in the school lavatory a fourteen-year-old black put a stranglehold on his first grader, Laws went to the school three times, demanding to see the black boy's parents. He finally learned that the boy was being raised by his grandmother, but that she was in the hospital and his sixteen-year-old sister was taking care of him. Although not all of his kids had met with trouble, "I came home . . . and said to my wife 'that's it, we're taking the kids out of that school.' "[11]

In Dorchester, as in Roslindale, the experiences within one family could be very mixed. One mother told of her two boys, eleven and eight, being bused to Roxbury and of "no trouble so far" (January 1975). But her daughter, age twelve, chubby, and with glasses, had been assigned to the Martin Luther King School and her shy vulnerability invited attack. On December 6, in the washroom, "four black girls grabbed her, broke her glasses, pulled her hair, and relieved her of 30 cents. She was so upset she ran from the school coatless. I have not sent her back nor do I intend to."[12]

Jim Costello, a thirty-four-year-old Savin Hill carpenter, and his wife, Arlene, decided to give integrated education a try before Garrity's order. In 1971 they put their daughter Kristine into a voluntary busing program at the Lee School. But they believed that tension in the school caused "the most important thing [to be] overlooked." Arlene visited the school and wondered "how anybody could teach in that atmosphere. All the teacher did all day long was to tell the kids to sit down." Kristine became one of a handful of whites in a class of fifty but appeared to be doing well. Then she moved to the Motley School where she wrote an essay about her time at the Lee, which included the thought "it seemed as if you were white, you should be afraid." As the number of whites at the Motley dropped, Jim and Arlene "felt defeated" and painfully transferred Kristine and her sister into a parochial school.[13]

One mother in the Codman Square section of Dorchester, a worker in the cafeteria at the Taylor School, which one of her sons attended, spoke for many when she said simply: "Just because parents are opposed to busing doesn't mean they are bigots." In March 1974 the Taylor was 50 percent black and according to Mary Antonino "the kids get a good education and there is lots of racial harmony. . . . It's a basic part of his education in life to learn and live with people who are not all Catholic and who are not all white." But her son would be reassigned to the Lee School in the fall, which she expected to be 80 percent black. Mary Antonino's tone changed and became tinged with anger: "He's already in an integrated school. I don't see why he should be bused."[14]

"I am not a racist," protested one Hyde Park mother to Judge Garrity. "I live in the Hyde Park/Mattapan area. I live and work with blacks. I have no objection to my child going to school with black children. I feel in this world, where we have to live with all kinds of people, that an integrated education is an advantage. I do not and shall not support forced busing to achieve racial balance in the schools. You cannot force people to get along."[15]

In the spring of 1974 one Dorchester mother described in a *Globe* column the unusual perspective from which she viewed the coming of "compulsory busing" in the fall. Evelyn Touchette found herself sympathizing "with both sides, pro-busing and anti-busing." She was the parent of four biracial, adopted children, and one white child of her own. Thus she favored busing if it held the slightest chance of her biracial children getting a better education. She told of how her most studious son had been transferred from a fifty percent mixed school to a 98 percent black middle school. After three months, the boy was losing interest and some of his teachers advised her to get him out as quickly as possible. But then she discovered (as Judge Garrity would explain a short time later in his opinion) how difficult it was for black children to get transfers. Touchette concluded that black children could never get "an equal education in a 'separate but equal' school system." At the same time, as a parent of a white child, she doubted that "fair balancing of the minority population of a city's schools" would result in equal education for all. Better education would not be automatic, and she lacked faith in the school committee's capacity to improve the quality of education. Because of "racism . . . in the black community," she did not want to bus her white child. Moreover, the white child goes into a mostly black school "with the implication that he will have to settle for a lesser quality education than he had previously." Touchette echoed thousands of Bostonians in saying that she strongly resented "having to allow the Federal or state government to experiment with my white child's future through his education, without any choice, or educational guarantees." And she echoed the plight of so many black parents by adding: "I also resent having to settle for an unequal (lesser) education for my bi-racial children because of white racism that keeps them socially and academically three steps behind."[16]

This selection of experiences of some white Boston parents hardly represents the experience of all those who cooperated initially with desegregation. It might be objected that these stories end for the most part with a flight from the public schools. Even though that emphasis is legitimate in a book about antibusing, that is not their primary purpose. These individual cases most of all reveal the good will that existed among many moderate parents throughout the city and their willingness to abide by the law. Some display a desire to do more than simply obey the law, indeed, they indicate hopes to further the cause of a peaceful, equitable, interracial society.

Judge Garrity, the Masters' Plan, and Phase 2

During the spring of 1975 there existed a chance that moderates might be rallied to some extent behind the desegregation plan for 1975–76, or Phase 2. Any gathering of support for Phase 2 would be an improvement over the negligible backing given by moderates to Phase 1. But a moderate coalition failed to materialize, and the causes of that failure have been the subject of considerable controversy.

By early February Judge Garrity had assembled a team of four masters, court-appointed experts who would devise a plan for Phase 2 that somehow would harmonize the conflicting requirements of educational concerns, neighborhood sensibilities, and racial balance. The group's chief was Jacob J. Spiegel, a retired justice of the Massachusetts Supreme Judicial Court, accompanied by Francis Keppel, former U.S. commissioner of education, Charles Willie, a black professor of education at the Harvard Graduate School of Education, and Edward J. McCormack, a veteran politician who served as Boston city councillor and state attorney general, nephew of longtime Congressional speaker John W. McCormack and a rival of the Kennedys. All commentators agree that for building community acceptance, South Boston-bred Eddie McCormack would be the key player. According to J. Anthony Lukas and other writers, McCormack succeeded in mobilizing moderate support for a plan that reduced the number of students to be bused and tried to balance racial integration with the craving of many parents for neighborhood autonomy.

But after the judge received it, and under pressure from the NAACP, plaintiffs' lawyers, and the Board of Education, Garrity decided to reject important parts of the masters' plan, to increase rather than reduce the numbers bused, and to ignore the political subtleties of the situation in favor of a by-the-numbers approach to racial balancing citywide. Thus the final Phase 2 plan was shaped by two academic experts upon whom Garrity relied heavily. This plan, announced May 10 (the masters' plan had been available March 21), scuttled any hope of mustering significant support for desegregation—or of damping down the fires of resistance.

Robert A. Dentler, then dean of the Boston University School of Education, and Marvin B. Scott, a colleague of Dentler's, shaped the final Phase 2 plan and remained as court experts for the duration of Garrity's involvement with the case. Dentler, who lived in the wooded, affluent suburb of Lexington, was originally from the mid-West, and before coming to Boston in 1972 had spent ten years at Columbia Teachers' College in New York City. An ardent integrationist and a polished technocrat, he became one of Garrity's few confidants and was extremely influential with the court throughout the balance of the decade.[17] Dentler has disputed sharply the contention that moderate support could have been rallied to the masters' plan or any plan, has challenged the figures used by Lukas and others in comparing the masters' plan to the court plan, and has held that Garrity had no choice but to change the masters' plan.

Lukas took the number to be bused under the masters' plan as 14,900 and said the court increased that to 25,000. Dentler maintained that the 14,900 figure should be increased by 4,000, because the masters did not count the estimated 4,000 who would be riding to magnet schools. Further, the number actually bused by the court was not Lukas's figure of 25,000 but 24,000.[18] If Dentler's figures are accepted at face value, the fact remains that the masters would not have increased busing over year one, while the Dentler-Scott plan raised the number by a minimum of four to five thousand. Aside from that, given the furor over forced busing, one may wonder about Dentler's quarreling with the masters' classification of the four thousand students who would have chosen to go to magnet schools.

The argument about numbers may go on forever because the whole situation was freighted with a high degree of unpredictability. It may be that the masters' projections were based on faulty data, as Judge Garrity and others have maintained.[19] The problem was that no one really knew how many students were going to show up in September, and any estimate was highly sensitive to parent reaction to the new plan. If parents perceived that plan as involving more busing and reassignments, then the number of white students would probably drop further, and projected enrollments would need to be revised downward. If they did not, then the enrollment estimates might be too low rather than too high.

More important than the dispute over the numbers to be bused, however, is the issue of whether the masters' plan could have rallied some moderate support. The unrevised plan not only won some moderate votes, but militant antibusing leaders greeted it with a very mixed response. Some flatly opposed it, as did both moderates and militants in Charlestown, which would be impacted heavily. Speaking in Charlestown, Ray Flynn of South Boston criticized the masters for not responding to the will of the people and eliminating busing totally. Yet even Flynn credited the plan for "its repeatedly stated intention of reducing forced busing to a minimum," and said it was too early to render a final judgment. The moderate Citywide Educational Coalition would have welcomed the chance to "have input into the . . . plan," while in West Roxbury moderate leaders focused on the plan's mechanics (as Charlestown would, winning some concessions). In Roslindale, HSA representative and antibuser Constance Maffei conceded that the plan improved on Phase 1: "It's certainly not as drastic as most people expected." Many antibusing leaders were simply muted or noncommittal, which in itself was a triumph of sorts.[20]

Contrary to the impression given by Dentler, Mayor White favored the masters' plan, though not publicly. White had asked for a delay of Phase 2 "until the inequities in Phase I are resolved," but members of his inner circle urged him to throw his weight behind the masters' plan. After warnings from Hicks that such action would bring retribution in the fall elections and fearing that Phase 2 could become identified as "the Mayor's plan," White backed off. But his education adviser, Robert Schwartz, sent a letter from the Mayor to Judge Garrity pleading with him not to accept "drastic" modifications of the masters' plan. Schwartz, Kiley, and other mayoral aides also tried informally to lobby the judge to support the original masters' plan—and got nowhere.[21]

The NAACP, led by Thomas Atkins, denounced the masters' plan as leaving too much segregation and insisted on strict racial balancing. The Boston Teachers Union opposed the masters' plan because it might eliminate jobs and promote interference from universities and businesses. One of the state Board's consultants, John A. Finger, Jr., who had designed Phase 1 with Glenn, labelled the masters' plan "a cleverly disguised one-way busing plan" that placed too much of a burden on the black population by closing more of their schools and requiring more black students to travel. On the other side, meanwhile, the recalcitrant members of the school committee were opposing it for going too far. Yet besides Mayor White, Governor Michael Dukakis (who otherwise kept a low profile on Boston desegregation) and his education secretary, Paul Parks, were pushing for the masters' plan. The state board, though publicly critical of the plan, quietly indicated a willingness to work with it, and disassociated its position from that of the NAACP.[22]

On April 17 Judge Garrity signaled that he was leaning to the NAACP position. He then put Dentler and Scott to work revising the masters' plan to install greater racial balance. On May 10 the final plan, with increased busing and new assignments, emerged from the court. The reaction now was almost universally negative. A few voices stuck by the revised Phase 2—WBZ-TV and radio bravely called it "a darn good plan"—but across the city moderates were crestfallen or bitter while militants found their voices again. Mayor White said he was "bitterly disappointed" and added that the cost of extra buses alone would be $3.6 million. Ray Flynn called the modifications "disastrous" and predicted a "mass exodus" from the city.[23]

Judge Garrity, in a recent interview, maintained that in fact he did not depart dramatically from the masters' plan, and that Dentler and Scott made use of information not available to the masters. The judge did concede, however, that the original masters' plan received a friendlier reception than the one offered in May, and that out in the city "perceptions changed" between March and May.[24]

Lukas wrote that when Garrity announced the new plan, Ed McCormack, who had labored to enlist backing for the original plan, felt betrayed. "Ed McCormack was so angry he couldn't bring himself to read the newspapers the next morning. . . . After encouraging them to build a consensus for the plan, the judge had kicked the props from underneath it." Dentler has commented that "these may well have been McCormack's views," but in any case the masters' plan "was incapable, as any plan would have been at the time, of establishing a common ground." Judge Garrity, when asked about McCormack's reaction as reported by Lukas, said that McCormack had never told him he felt that way.[25]

In a public interview just over a year after the events in question, however, McCormack said that it was "unfortunate" that Judge Garrity had made extensive changes in the masters' plan because it had "received such acceptance." ROAR would not support the plan, he noted, but it had not risen up in opposition either. To him that was "tantamount to a vote of confidence." Important elements in the Boston HSA, the mayor, the governor, and black leaders other than the NAACP and Atkins endorsed the plan, said McCormack. He believed, further, that the numbers the masters used were closer to the actual numbers enrolled, "but there was no way Judge Garrity could know that." If Garrity had accepted the masters' plan, McCormack concluded, there would have been much less continuing civil disobedience.[26]

Indeed, Garrity's May 10 ruling actually succeeded in reviving the militant antibusing movement, according to some observers. Factionalism had been growing in ROAR, but the masters' plan "would have crippled them more, in terms of retaining their numbers." Hyde Park activist Fran Johnenne's comment, though hyperbole, captured the elation of the militants: "Every time Judge Garrity opens his mouth, more people come to our side."[27]

In June 1975 Kathleen Sullivan explained to the U.S. Commission on Civil Rights why there was a problem with numbers and underscored the difference the masters' plan might have made: "A lot of parents said to me that . . . if Garrity had accepted the masters' plan which he should have in April . . . and put it into effect so that people would have had some sense about what they are going to do, that we would have been better off. But since he didn't, people in South Boston and Charlestown are saying they will not send their children to school next year either." The masters' numbers were more realistic, claimed Sullivan. They used a figure of sixty thousand enrollment because average daily attendance since January had been fifty-eight to sixty thousand. On the other hand, she conceded that some planners believed that if the masters' plan had been used, then many children would come back, which might have caused enrollment figures to surge up to seventy thousand or more.[28]

Several parents who wrote to Judge Garrity that spring and summer reflected exactly the reaction that Sullivan described. One "Boston Mother" of six children told the judge that her family's neighborhood school had been integrated through voluntary busing for the last decade or so. In Phase 1 two of her younger children were assigned to another school despite the fact that their school was 49 percent minority and 51 percent white. At first keeping them home, she then sent them to the new school only to discover that its actual ratio was 25 percent white and 75 percent nonwhite, "not a balanced school, hardly worth taking a bus for." Worse, her third grader was not accepted and called names. Meanwhile, their neighborhood school became predominantly black and she hoped her children could at least return there, a five minute walk from their home. But "the *experts* revised the Masters' plan and they are to be assigned to an entirely different school with a longer bus ride than last year. . . . We will *never* send them. We have been brought up to respect the law and those who represent it, this is something we can no longer do. . . . We will never allow our children to be used again in this social experiment."[29]

Charles Glenn, architect of the state plan used by Garrity for 1974–75, who called his own plan a "flop," has criticized Garrity and his experts for not building on that plan but rather for going through "the same fatal process again" and implementing "an entirely new plan which moved many students a second time from schools which were already desegregated by any standard, to produce an even greater 'flop' in September 1975." He continued, "and throughout these difficult years, school staff from top to bottom were able to answer parent complaints about virtually anything which went wrong by placing the blame on the state . . . or on Judge Garrity."[30]

Thus, an opportunity was lost in the spring of 1975 to rally moderates behind Phase 2. And as moderates fell into confusion or dismay during that season of uncertainty, the militant antibusers once again took courage and renewed their crusade. Vocal as they usually were, several antibusers called before the U.S. Commission on Civil Rights hearing in June refused to testify. Others turned the hearing into a forum for denouncing Phase 1 and for predicting continued resistance, white flight, and decline for Boston if forced busing were not stopped. While many moderates and a few supporters of the court order testified (and made a strong impression on the liberal commissioners), the defiant postures of Kerrigan, Hicks, and several local militants spread delight in the antibusing precincts.[31]

In August, before the commission released its initial report, Hicks held her own "civil rights" hearings at City Hall to offset the anticipated "biased" report of the commission. White parents and teachers trooped in to tell of assaults on persons and rights, and several complained of the FBI pressing investigations of criminal charges against whites but not blacks.

Racial violence as a spin-off of desegregation continued through the summer. The most publicized incident involved an assault on several visiting black Bible salesmen who stopped off for a swim one hot day at Carson beach, in South Boston. This spurred blacks to hold a demonstration at the beach, which only a strong police presence prevented from turning into a bloodbath. One reporter concluded that while there was not "an all-out [racial] war going on in Boston, even a quick survey of scattered incidents indicates pretty clearly that race relations have reached a low point, in Boston's poorer neighborhoods especially."[32]

As the time for the schools to open drew near, preparation once again was little and late. The school committee remained obstinate, hampering the efforts of those officials who were trying at least to do their jobs.[33] Perhaps epitomizing the lack of enthusiasm felt throughout the city was a front page *Boston Herald* editorial of late August that apologetically urged that compliance was the only course to follow. The *Herald* blamed no one for the regrettable fact of forced busing, saying Garrity was bound to act as he had, creating this "heartbreaking problem." The editors doubted that busing would either improve education or redress the historic grievances of blacks, but until the court order was set aside legally, it must be obeyed and given every chance to work without boycotting or violence. The editors commiserated with "the worried parents of Boston [who] are trapped. They are being asked to obey a law which, while not immoral, is repugnant and unjust in the eyes of a majority."[34]

Few in the city expected uniformly peaceful compliance. In Washington the assistant attorney general for civil rights, J. Stanley Pottinger, announced the federal government's contingency plans for Boston. The Justice Department stood ready to deploy, if needed, one hundred U.S. marshals and a squad of department lawyers. If needed, the 82d Airborne Division would be called upon as a last resort. To add to the rising tension, a group of young radicals calling itself the Committee Against Racism (CAR), some of them college students and most of them not from Boston, announced plans to conduct demonstrations that fall in support of Phase 2. The word came out almost gleefully from the South Boston Information Center that antibusers would greet CAR activists with "welcoming units."[35]

The first day of school in September brought scattered violence that continued throughout the week. In South Boston police arrested seventy-three members of CAR before school began, and a black reporter from out of town drove into Southie and was assaulted. Throughout the city buses were stoned, cars overturned, and in the worst incident, seventy-five white youths stormed into Bunker Hill Community College in Charlestown, trashed the lobby, and sent a black student to the hospital.

Mothers' prayer marches protested busing in Charlestown, Southie, Hyde Park, West Roxbury, and the North End throughout the week. In Southie an estimated 500 walked four abreast along Broadway on a mile and a half route to a local church, with Councillor Hicks at the front counting her rosary beads. Nearby, a mother pushed a carriage containing her twenty-month-old wearing a large badge—"South Boston—1775–1975—Resist." During the first week police arrested 112 for disturbances related to desegregation, and 16 policemen were injured. Meanwhile, of 76,000 expected students, only 52,000 showed up.[36]

Charlestown now drew heaviest media attention and an enormous armada of police cars, motorcycles, wagons, snipers, helicopters, and various police personnel called in from time to time, including the TPF. Charlestown High School also now rivaled Southie as a scene of continual disruption inside, and on National Boycott Day in October it was the Townies who with South Boston effectively emptied their school, while attendance elsewhere in the city was not much below normal. But Southie was still the heartland of resistance as seven to ten thousand marched two and a half miles with a host of city politicians leading the way.[37]

The 1975 city election did little to relieve the frustrations of the electorate. All candidates, of course, knew that an antibusing posture was the sine qua non of gaining or keeping office. But some did campaign hard to identify themselves with other issues. Mayor White survived a strong challenge from state Senator Joseph Timilty by saying as little as possible about busing and by focusing on a new threat, namely 100 percent property tax revaluation, which he said would destroy the city. Although Timilty's backing came largely from the same precincts as Louise Hicks's in 1971, the antibusing organization would not unite on a candidate. While most antibusers who voted probably chose Timilty, many stayed home, thereby helping White. Though Hicks was publicly neutral, behind the scenes she had cut a deal to help White.[38]

School committee and council candidates tried early to soft-pedal busing, but between the September 23 preliminary and the final elections all candidates gravitated massively to antibusing appeals. On November 4 warm weather and busing produced a large turnout, and the usual faces appeared at the top of the heap. Louise Hicks placed first in the council race with 80,777 votes, over 9,000 ahead of any other candidate, while prominent antibusers Dapper O'Neil and Kerrigan placed fourth and seventh, respectively.[39]

The school committee presented a mixed array of victors, with established hard-liners McDonough and Tierney easily winning reelection. Paul Ellison, the third veteran and Kerrigan crony, under indictment for larceny and perjury, lost. Sullivan was joined by a second moderate, newcomer David Finnegan. Yet both Sullivan and Finnegan had brandished their opposition to Phase 2 in the closing days of the campaign. Sullivan echoed McDonough by flatly saying that "busing is destroying the city." Finnegan, meanwhile, did his best to live down a *Globe* endorsement labeling him a "moderate," telling a television reporter shortly afterward "I am no moderate on busing." Although Sullivan and Finnegan won no votes at the South Boston Information Center, many voters seem to have been attracted by their posture of responsible opposition.[40]

At the same time, however, the voters put another newcomer on the committee—the passionate and flamboyant Elvira "Pixie" Palladino of East Boston, an ally of John Kerrigan. Palladino had risen from the ranks of antibusing mothers who had been the shock troops of the movement's lobbying the past several years and represented the thrust of grassroots fury into city leadership. She placed fifth, with 57,774 votes (Sullivan at the top had 81,393), but in the antibusing warrens of East Boston, Charlestown, and South Boston, Palladino led the school committee returns. Those precincts also voted heavily against a referendum proposal to replace the elected school committee with one chosen by the mayor. The overwhelming vote against "Question 7" reflected not only the majority's preference for an elected school committee but also its response to ROAR's appeal that the voters foil a mayoral power play and rebuke "judicial tyranny."[41]

Sullivan and Finnegan were polished candidates whose lace-curtain styles and media-oriented campaigning enhanced their appeal. Still, Sullivan's total could be interpreted as an indication of mixed currents at work in the electorate. In the same vein, so could the seventh-place finish of a black candidate, John O'Bryant, whose 45,556 total probably included 25–30,000 white votes. O'Bryant, a former guidance counselor and now an administrator at a community health center, had managed several of Mel King's early campaigns. Backed by black activists and King, who was now a state representative, as well as white liberals, O'Bryant would win in two years.[42] Of course, the name O'Bryant could very well have misled many white voters as to the candidate's ethnicity. And despite the victories of Sullivan and Finnegan, the overall impact of the election was to register the fact that the electorate still rewarded the antibusing politicians whose "never" had turned into "now," and that "moderation" still demanded a fervent and oft-stated opposition to Phase 2 or whatever label borne by court-ordered desegregation.

6

Defended (and Other) Neighborhoods

In some areas of the city . . . the opposition to desegregation is a more obvious one, a more visceral one. In other areas . . . maybe areas where college education is viewed as a goal, the opposition is less verbal and visceral, but takes the form of departure from the school system.
—*John Coakley, school administrator,*
  testimony before U.S. Commission on Civil Rights

There was no one antibusing movement. And one would be really hard pressed to come up with just two or three ways of describing it.
  It varied according to the community . . . according to the information that [people] got from the so-called leaders of the community.
—*K. Marie Clarke, president, Boston HSA*

During the 1970s the name of South Boston became synonymous with resistance to school desegregation. Not only did Southie militants make the drab, old high school on Dorchester Heights a symbol of racial strife, but Southie's activists carried the war to other neighborhoods, to hated enemy territory in the suburbs, to corridors of power in the state legislature and city hall, and beyond, more persistently and passionately than any other group. To this day the South Boston Information Center continues the crusade against "forced busing" and for "neighborhood schools."

In his Pulitzer-prizewinning book *Common Ground*, J. Anthony Lukas shifted the spotlight to Charlestown, another tough, working-class, mostly Irish white citadel, to illustrate the social dynamics at work in a fiercely antibusing neighborhood. Charlestown was cousin to Southie, often literally, as many families in the two precincts were related. Southie, Charlestown, mostly Italian East Boston on the other side of Boston harbor, and perhaps Hyde Park all constituted "defended neighborhoods."[1] Bounded to varying degrees by physical barriers, de-

108

fended neighborhoods shared a sense of separateness from the city. Each in itself contained many tribal domains of ethnicity, class, and turf, identified often with squares, corners, or parishes, but all shared an impulse to stop time, to resist change, and to hold fast to an ideal of society as it had been before the upheavals of the 1960s.

But the story of antibusing is more than that of South Boston or Charlestown, about which so much has been written. Antibusing activity flowed freely in all the white neighborhoods, including the middle-class bastion of West Roxbury, about which little has been written. Far from downtown, the partly suburban West Roxbury was slightly less opposed to busing than South Boston. But West Roxbury expressed its opposition in a style entirely different from South Boston and Charlestown. West Roxbury's protests did not generate news photos of rock-hurling mobs but rather images of middle-class individuals reading legal briefs, lobbying politicians and the media, and appealing in the courts. West Roxbury contained militants, surely, but it tolerated diversity of opinion. Moderates functioned there without serious harassment, and diverse antibusing elements coexisted. But in Southie "opening your mouth" could bring swift retribution, and antibusing expressed itself frequently in collective action in a distinctly working-class style.

No neighborhood was monolithic: each contained various factions, each used different methods. Yet busing forced each neighborhood into confrontation with the outside world, and, as Suttles has pointed out, "it is in their 'foreign relations' that communities come into existence and have to settle on an identity and a set of boundaries which oversimplify their reality."[2] Antibusing led to such definition and oversimplification. South Boston was surely the most antibusing of the neighborhoods, but it came to seem even more so because of the repression of many who were not whole-hog resisters.

Differences in neighborhood styles are important because most white Bostonians were so overwhelmingly opposed in principle to the court orders. Five surveys taken between October 1973 and July 1975 in six "neighborhoods" registered levels of opposition to two-way busing from 86 percent to 91 percent.[3] These figures were slightly higher than those appearing in various polls and surveys nationally during the mid-1970s.[4]

A poll of nine neighborhoods completed in August 1975 found that in no area did a majority strongly approve of busing, while strong disapproval (over 70 percent) centered in five of the nine: South Boston, Charlestown, East Boston, Hyde Park, and West Roxbury/Roslindale.

(The poll's neighborhood groupings are arbitrary and obviously too large in the case of West Roxbury/Roslindale, but they do allow for a contrast with the relatively self-contained localities.) Dorchester/Mattapan and Jamaica Plain strongly disapproved by 55 and 54 percent, respectively, while only just over a third did so in Central Boston and Roxbury. Yet in the latter two, both heavily minority, levels of strong approval registered only 23 and 27 percent, respectively.[5]

Even in the defended neighborhoods, however, conflict existed over the question of resistance versus compliance. "Some people say that there is nothing you can do about the situation, so go along with it," said Hyde Park's state representative, Angelo Scaccia. "Others say, 'like hell, it's wrong and we are going to fight it' . . . there is no middle ground."[6] Yet despite the pressure of polarization, diversity of opinion and action existed even within the most ostensibly unified enclaves.

Defended Neighborhoods: South Boston

South Boston lacked a strong parochial school system. On the contrary, it had a very strong public school tradition. Geographically, they have no alternatives. They have nowhere to go except into the sea. They don't border any suburbs. Dorchester is very much like South Boston yet it has been quiet. . . . the existence of a strong parochial school system in Dorchester explains the difference.
—Rep. William Galvin (D., Brighton), interview with John Mulkern

"Southie meant strong community pride, a fierce loyalty to one another, a distrust of any change, and—among some—a suspicion of those who might be different." South Bostonians shared "a chauvinistic pride. It is like the Marine Corps compared to the U.S. Army. . . . People like to say they are from South Boston."[7] Neighborhood defense that cut across class and ethnic lines certainly helps to explain Southie's tenacious resistance. Yet something peculiarly Irish impressed itself on the antibusing protest that in South Boston raged for some three years or more. Like the unreconcilables of the Confederacy's Lost Cause, a romantic aura of resistance for the sake of resistance emanated from the boasts of Southie pride.

Remarkably, antibusers engaged in protest despite recognizing that fighting would not change the situation. The 1973–75 surveys found that few protesters believed their actions would end busing. The majority in fact saw that goal as unattainable.[8] The 1975 poll showed that in

South Boston only 39 percent thought the court order could be reversed, but 59 percent believed the fight should go on, a 20-point difference, greater than in any other neighborhood (table A-2). Similarly, while 56 percent in Southie found busing inevitable, only 32 percent said people should cooperate with Phase 2, a difference of 24 points, again the highest among the districts.

An Irish Catholic tradition, termed "collective calculated violence" by one historian, to redress social and economic grievances or to subvert unjust laws, reaches back at least to peasant movements in prefamine Ireland. Irish history is littered with the bones of rebels and fighters who took on overwhelming foes and insurmountable odds. Thus as Jimmy Breslin observed in September 1975, busing was "the perfect fight for the Irish. They were doomed before they started. Therefore they can be expected to fight on."[9]

"It's something that had to be," said South Boston activist James Kelly in a 1983 interview. Kelly was now running for city council and had polished some of his rough edges, but the intense, short, stocky man still exuded a spirit of stubborn resistance. When asked in 1983 about his awareness in 1974–75 of the obstacles to reversing a court order, his eyes narrowed: "A man has to do what he has to do. . . . It [busing] was intolerable oppression . . . not to fight back would have been intolerable."[10]

But if Irish traditions stamped themselves on Southie's protest, South Boston was not homogeneously Irish. Poles and Lithuanians had settled there as early as the late nineteenth century, along with some Italians and scattered Jews. In the 1970s Southie contained a Greek church, an Albanian cathedral, and at least three small Protestant churches. But local politics and culture carried a distinctly Irish aura. Southie had served as one major base from which the Catholic Irish had spread out to wrest control of city politics from Yankee Protestants.[11]

South Boston was no more homogeneously working class than it was Irish. At the Point or upper end a middle- and upper-middle class occupied substantial town houses, some ringing the high school and commanding a lovely ocean view. The lower end, however, fended off spreading industrial development and held four housing projects, one dating from the 1930s. In 1970, not surprisingly, Southie's population of 38,500 (98 percent white) had a higher percentage of families on public assistance than the city average, a higher school dropout rate, more young unemployed males, and a median family income well below the city's. A psychiatrist who worked in the high school observed a different Southie from the one of which its politicians boasted, in which alcoholism was common as were families in the projects headed by single mothers. That Southie "has very little, it really does."[12]

Though the middle class on "the Heights" sent their offspring to parochial or private schools and projected a "keep-the-shamrock-flying respectability," Southie's style, when confronting the outside world, was distinctly working class and tough.[13] Southie kids learned early to be skillful with their fists. A state trooper posted at the high school in 1976 told of growing up there: "I literally had to fight my way from corner to corner. My last name was Lithuanian, though I had an Irish mother. The kids would mispronounce my last name and I would fight." Some graduated to more lethal weapons and to gangs. One neighborhood gang, the Mullens, seems to have existed at several levels, from recreational to criminal, with some toughs tied in with organized crime. During 1974 rumors frequently reached City Hall that the Mullens—meaning those who were armed and dangerous—planned to add their own mayhem to the protests.[14]

Southie's politicians incessantly preached unity, holding out to their tormented constituents the hope of winning provided they stayed together. At a rally at the Gavin School in mid-August, top antibusing leaders all incanted the same mantra: Kerrigan: "Stick together, fight together, and we will save Boston"; O'Neil: "Please for Christ's sake stay together and we will win"; Flynn: "We must stick together. No one will beat us"; Flaherty: "They have never run up against a Southie. United we stand, divided we fall."[15]

Southie had been drawing the wagons in a circle for at least a decade before 1974. Children had grown up hearing as much about the black threat as of the need to defeat "Eastie" in the annual Thanksgiving football game. Southie activists had preached antibusing at rallies, street corners, coffee shops, and the many bars and taverns. In April 1974, when an estimated twenty-five thousand marched on the capitol to urge repeal of the Racial Imbalance Act, five thousand South Bostonians led the way. Most of the buttons, bumper stickers, signs, and T-shirts protesters wore originated in South Boston.[16]

Southie activists pioneered in organizing a smoothly functioning telephone network with which to mobilize the neighborhood, and South Boston also took the lead in establishing the first antibusing "information center" in the city, which several other neighborhoods soon imitated. The idea for such a clearinghouse and rumor-control headquarters arose from Southie's distrust of city hall. During the first days of Phase 1, South Bostonians would call rumor control at city hall "and always get a reply that everything was fine." According to Nancy Yotts of the SBIC, "we started calling it the 'hunky dory' center and decided to set up our own."[17]

Southie's emphasis on unity and collective action meant that antibusing militants demanded absolute conformity from their neighbors. Sensitivity to issues of loyalty and betrayal ran deep in the Irish cultural heritage, and that too impressed itself on Southie's protest. As the legendary ward boss of New York's Tammany Hall, G. W. Plunkitt, once said, "The Irish, above all people in the world, hates [sic] a traitor." Southie's solidarity also fed off shared feelings of being put upon. "We're always fighting to keep from going under." said Hicks's lieutenant Virginia Sheehy. "But we do have solidarity. . . . if we don't look out for Southie, nobody else will."[18]

Although the district was actually sharply divided on boycotting and many parents would have preferred to send their children to school, the school boycott worked more effectively in Southie than elsewhere. Some parents kept children at home simply out of fear. One mother in the Old Colony Housing project kept five children out of school for the entire first year, with the kids living "just like a continuation of summer." When she sent them for Phase 2 she bought an expensive police radio to monitor the schools from her kitchen. At the first hint of trouble, she could be at the schools in fifteen to twenty minutes. Other parents sent out children only to have them return and report that there was "trouble at the school." Sometimes this amounted to their being harassed for trying to attend. One white boy (of two) who rode the bus to Roxbury on the first day of school had the misfortune of being interviewed by reporters and having his name broadcast. "I don't have to tell you," wrote his mother to Judge Garrity, "about the threats to his life if the 'nigger lover' boards the bus again. It seems he'll 'have his head blown apart' and 'be brought home to us in a box.' "[19]

The militants' ferocity toward those who tried to cooperate with desegregation exploded at a July 1974 HSA meeting. When the crowd learned that two persons had signed up as bus monitors, screams erupted: "Who are they? Get those bastards!" "You hear," said one community worker, "the word Judas a lot."[20]

One mother, a tower of strength in 1974–75 who "stuck her neck out" to be on a biracial council, threw in the towel just before Phase 2 began, lamenting, "I tried, God knows I tried but like so many others I cannot take another year like the passed [*sic*] one," a year "of notoriety" and "harassment." James O'Sullivan persevered and became a CCC member during 1976, despite continued hate letters and calls, public abuse, and damage to his property. As one thoughtful college youth, who himself remained silent, said, "People can't speak out in South Boston. Not if you want to live."[21]

Of course the voices of moderation in Southie were overpowered for reasons other than militant pressure. What many saw as the obtuseness of the court, the unjustness of the law, and the heavy-handedness of the police also silenced or converted some moderates. As one woman said at a parent-teacher meeting at Southie High in December 1974, "I was all for making desegregation work until last Wednesday, when I was chased down the street by a horse."[22]

Yet the ordeal of the moderates perpetrated by their own neighbors should not be underestimated. The force of community pressure was enormous. In June 1976 the Mayor's Committee on Violence concluded that "in some areas, the 'them-against-us' attitude prevents any meaningful participation by responsible moderates. If one tries to make the desegregation plan work in those areas where Judge Garrity's plan is opposed, he or she loses the status as 'one of us' and becomes identified as 'one of them.' "[23]

Although most Southie residents rejected violence, a 1976 survey found that over 52 percent of a random sample reported participating in collective protests such as marches, rallies, or lobbying; 47 percent partook of instrumental protest such as letter writing; while 13 percent admitted to engaging in expressive protest such as rock throwing. The percentage of rock throwers among eighteen- to twenty-four-year-old males, and even thirteen- to seventeen-year-olds, was probably higher. James Kelly claimed that "no adult ever stoned a bus," but said also that "hundreds" of men 18 to 45 were ready to march or to volunteer for more hazardous duty.[24] The stoning of buses leaving the L Street annex on the first day of Phase 1 made international headlines, but many other rocks were thrown in Southie over the next two to three years, at school buses, policemen, police vehicles, and blacks who unknowingly wandered into the neighborhood. Police and mobs ranging from fifty to several hundred engaged in repeated skirmishes and pitched battles.

Antibusing leaders alternately scoffed and raged in December 1974 at police revelations that the FBI was investigating a plot to blow up bridges into South Boston. Police officials also disclosed that the same persons suspected in the "bridges plot" were under investigation in connection with extortion of money from small businesses in South Boston to support ROAR. Antibusers responded by accusing the police of trying to intimidate them and to discredit their cause.[25]

Political leaders such as Hicks, according to James Kelly, were deliberately kept apart from militants' planning of street action. Yet the language of the politicians, filled as it was with talk of fighting, certainly did not discourage violence. In May 1976 the U.S. attorney general announced that he would not be intervening on the side of the antibusers in the Boston case. "In response," noted one acute observer, "Louise Day Hicks sent out signals: she prayed 'there will be no violence—people are so frustrated.'" That night vandals threw torches through windows of downtown department stores as well as the gift shop for the U.S.S. Constitution in Charlestown, which suffered $75,000 fire damage.[26]

But the focus of violence in Southie was the high school, an ancient structure that sat on Dorchester Heights where George Washington had placed the cannons that drove the British from Boston. For at least three years an atmosphere of hatred and violence prevailed in the school. Ione Malloy taught English there, and kept a diary that provides a chilling chronicle of the hell endured by students, teachers, and administrators.[27] The fear, anguish, and torment of the students, including the troublemakers, is painfully evident. The teenagers enjoyed little chance to develop good will on their own because adults—in Southie and then in Roxbury in retaliation—coached and bent them into belligerence. By the start of Phase 2 some blacks were campaigning to get the school closed and moved to a neutral site, while Southie militants complained that this was the cause of trouble at the school.[28]

The war over Southie High raged on and on, although it is difficult to see why anyone thought that blacks would be gaining much from a school (no matter what the dedication of individual staff) that was rundown, poorly equipped, and populated mostly by lower-class white children, few of whom went on to higher education.[29] But generations of working-class families loved it. For the daughters who married soon after graduation and the sons who went to work in blue-collar jobs, Southie High later evoked the fondest memories. For these immobile people the high school functioned as a socializing experience, reinforcing neighborhood values and identity and providing a shared cache of memories and traditions. Some dedicated teachers did work hard at Southie High, but "quality education" was not what Southie was all about. Before the threat of desegregation, parental interest in educational matters was minimal. But everyone in South Boston knew whether its football or hockey teams were winning—as they usually did.[30]

Sports consumed the entire neighborhood, with athletic leagues from midget hockey to adult softball in profusion. But "the main thing was football," especially the annual Thanksgiving Day game with Italian East Boston, where one of the city's major ethnic and territorial rivalries could be played out on the gridiron. Even a schoolgirl athlete who played basketball and softball found her greatest thrill in becoming a cheerleader—"all the girls tried out for cheerleading." No incipient feminism here. And Southie athletes wore their letter sweaters long past their school days, emblems of their best memories.[31] In 1973 the Thanksgiving contest determined the district title, but in 1974 there was no game between the schools. Instead, two football clubs, the South Boston "Chippewas" and the East Boston "Fittons," played a game whose halftime festivities were turned into an antibusing rally, with the proceeds of the game going to the antibusing cause.[32]

The presence of many poor and working-class families in Southie contributed to the emphasis on public schools, which in turn fed the obsession with sports, which accounted in part for the weakness of parochial schools. Educational opportunity and social mobility had little to do with what Southie High symbolized to its constituents. The relative lack of alternatives for Southie residents in the form of parochial schools or suburban refuges mattered little where Southie High was concerned because they did not wish to give it up. What was being torn away from them, they felt, had much to do with identity, turf, loyalty, and community relationships. The militants thus decided that if the school was no longer theirs, it would not be anyone else's, and for three years a sort of scorched earth policy turned the building into a wasteland.

Once ROAR determined to allow no peace in the school, the pattern of incidents became clear: whenever the numbers of students present would climb during periods of calm, new disruptions would send attendance figures plummeting. Early on many students stopped by the South Boston Information Center after school to file reports, as well as for counseling and coaching. During 1974–75 the SBIC had ROAR members directly in the school, including as an aid Warren Zaniboni, chief of the "South Boston Marshals" and sometime Hicks bodyguard. (Ironically, Zaniboni was keeping his two daughters out of school.) When white students staged walkouts, one white girl told her teacher, "the white kids have to go, or they'll get beaten up." In 1972 white football players told of "getting a bad name," presumably because they were allowing blacks on the team (in order to have a team) and were leading students back into school after boycotts. In November 1975 Headmaster Reid testified in court that most student demands, black and white, were prepared with the assistance of adults.[33]

The court inadvertently contributed to trouble by mandating that white and black students meet separately, without supervision, to elect representatives to biracial councils. The white students would meet, refuse to participate on the councils, and then stage antibusing rallies. The worst of these occurred December 6, 1974, with SBIC adults in the auditorium, five days before the Faith stabbing.[34]

Attendance went up somewhat during year two, but still fell far below projections. Some Southie students continued to see themselves, as WEEI Radio said in April 1976, as "freedom fighters," and to see every hall skirmish as part of a larger political battle. Most kids, said a state trooper who served at Southie, "didn't even know why they were fighting half the time; they just felt they were supposed to."[35]

Garrity's two Boston University experts, Dentler and Scott, had advised the judge that any school—and Southie High in particular—could be "*turned around overnight*" (italics mine) with a new reform administration. But the situation did not improve after Judge Garrity put the school in receivership, removed Reid, and recruited to replace him the progressive Jerome Winegar from Minnesota (the chant "Go Home, Jerome" now entered Southie's repertoire). As federal and state money poured in for new programs, the turbulence continued. Indeed, there was actually less integration in the school in year three than in year one. Soon the new headmaster was saying that he would need "six to seven years" to change things. The most commonly heard comment from students of both complexions, meanwhile, was "I hate this school." One Southie senior boy said "If anyone asks me if I've ever 'done time,' I'll tell them, 'Yeah, *I've* done time.'" On May 31, 1977, nine buses carrying a total of 115 black students pulled up, an average of 12 per bus. Malloy observed: "School opens for the personnel: 35 troopers, 55 transitional and security aides, 120 teachers and administrators, 3 secretaries, kitchen staff, as well as peripheral personnel." Winegar summed up the third year: "Anyone who thought this place could change in a year was dreaming."[36]

Eventually, as expert Dentler put it, the high school was "taken away" from those it had served for generations. To those who "lost" the school, desegregation seemed "almost like punishment." Said state representative Michael Flaherty of the court order, "*We're being punished for what we are.*" (Italics mine.) Flaherty meant that Southie was the type of place viewed as an anachronism by the technocrats, bureaucrats, and developers. South Boston's basic flaw, its popular Senator Billy Bulger averred in 1973, was to be "too successful in providing what neighborhoods should provide," and this true neighborhood based on family and personal ties stood in the way of "the concepts of homogenization of lifestyle pursued by our planners, social scientists and engineers."[37]

South Bostonians believed they were being punished also because they were seen as racists. The unrestrained expression of bigotry in South Boston cannot be denied: the racist graffiti repeatedly painted on the high school, the obscene racist chants of mobs, the stonings and beatings of blacks who strayed into Southie, the harassment of the few blacks or Hispanics who still lived there by the early 1970s, the ugly incidents perpetrated against interracial groups taking part in the St. Patrick's Day parades of 1964 and 1965, and the insensitivity to blacks' situation in society measured in polls during these years and expressed often in the *South Boston Tribune*.[38] Hostility to blacks had been escalating for at least a decade before 1974, and Southie's leaders tended to be more tolerant of the haters and moral pygmies in their midst than those in other neighborhoods.

Yet racism explains only part of the reaction. South Bostonians often pointed to the fact that blacks before busing had come often into Southie without incident. Adrienne Weston, an independent, tough woman originally from the West Indies, was the only black teacher at Southie High in 1973. As Phase 1 began, she feared for her life, but during 1973–74 she said "it was good to teach here. The students did their work and no one called me 'nigger.'" Of the mobs outside the school, she commented, "Those people out there are crazy, because they don't like this being shoved down their throats."[39]

Many South Bostonians who did not hate blacks as such, feared poor black youths and black neighborhoods as sources of crime and violence. This fear was real, not just a cover for "purely" racial feelings. However exaggerated the perception, many whites, not only South Bostonians, saw black Roxbury as crime infested, and some who had lived on its borders or fled from districts engulfed by the ghetto had been mugged or terrorized by poor black youths. One parent told Ione Malloy that his boy was scheduled to be bused to Roxbury the following year: "I worked nine years in Roxbury as a street cleaner, and I'll never let him go there."[40]

Police, firefighters, cab drivers, and public service workers, of which there were so many in Southie, often had seen the worst side of ghetto culture. The images also were fed by economic competition and the vulnerability of Southie men in the police, fire, and public works departments who might lose a promotion to affirmative action or might see a relative fail to join the department "family."[41]

Irish Catholics' perceptions of the unrestrained sexuality of ghetto culture further intensified fears of blacks. Many whites associated ghetto blacks with promiscuity, teenage pregnancy, single-parent families, and prostitution. Irish Catholics, for a variety of reasons, have tended to be puritanical in sexual matters and have cloaked "sins of the flesh" with an aura of taboo. Desegregation raised the specter of friendships and even sexual intercourse between Southie's white daughters and black males, about whose sexual prowess Boston's white men believed old myths and made nervous jokes. This fear seldom found direct expression, but as William A. Henry III pointed out, was often subtly played upon. Henry argued that no one addressed sexual fears more explicitly than Southie's own Louise Hicks, who "almost invariably spoke of 'this terrible, terrible, forcible busing.' The customary term of opprobrium was, of course, 'forced' busing. That language carried a political message of helpless rage. Hicks's inventive choice of word called to mind instead the charge of 'forcible rape.' Busing was not just a symbolic rape of a parent's control. It might, Hicks was telling us, lead to an actual rape as some high school girl, however pure of heart, by her very unattainable beauty incited the purportedly uncontrollable sexuality of young black men."[42]

The sexual theme arose implicitly in the epithet of "nigger lover" that fell on even the police and teachers who were just doing their jobs. One policeman in front of Southie confronted an old woman yelling obscenities who taunted him by saying that she hoped that when he got home he found his wife "in bed with a nigger."[43]

An anonymous flyer distributed by the South Boston Liberation Army to high school students also addressed the issue directly: "We do not expect you to hate blacks. We do not ask you to fight blacks, but we *demand* that white girls keep away from black students and aides. *We seek revenge on anyone that violates this rule.* Names of the guilty will be publicized. They and their families will be driven out of South Boston. Because of Forced Busing, blacks are the enemy. When Forced Busing stops perhaps things will be different. But until then anyone disgracing South Boston will be dealt with severely. *Do not be a white nigger.*" To be a "white nigger" was to fall into the ranks of an underclass. Indeed, blacks constituted for insecure whites a lower caste, bearing the stigma of a ghetto culture that marked them as depraved and dangerous. Not all South Bostonians saw all blacks this way, and only a few saw all blacks in these terms all of the time. But the worst, most obsessive fears of some resonated along lines of race, class, and culture to permeate Southie's resistance.[44]

Defended Neighborhoods: Charlestown

Like South Boston, Charlestown's high school occupied a central place in the Town's geography and emotions. It too sat on a hill, next to a historic monument to revolutionary patriotism, an antiquated and dilapidated anachronism that was the focus of a community pride which to many outsiders also seemed a throwback to another era. It too seemed a place where time had stood still.

Charlestown qualified perhaps even more as an urban village, with fifteen to seventeen thousand persons packed into one square mile of a hilly peninsula. Over the years Italians and others had moved in and intermarried with the predominant Irish Catholics, so that everybody was related to everybody else. Thus loyalty to "Our Town" transcended anything necessarily Irish or Catholic. Although excluded from Phase 1, Townies served notice early that the advent of busing there would be no cakewalk. Warned one Townie on the eve of Phase 2: "Charlestown's resistance to busing this fall will make South Boston look as peaceful as Vatican City."[45]

Treated partly as a dumping-ground for institutions unwanted elsewhere, Charlestown had been closed in by ugly steel and concrete bridges and highways built mainly for the convenience of others, and a noisy, dirty elevated railway had been thrust through its heart. In the 1930s bulldozers made way for a large housing project, over the screams of many of those displaced, and by the 1960s the project had deteriorated into a cauldron of social disorganization. In the 1970s it would provide militant antibusing leaders and many young street warriors. Despite its vaunted solidarity, however, a split in Charlestown clearly emerged between poor and middle-class antibusers.[46] In this way Charlestown's antibusing struggle recapitulated a fight a decade earlier against urban renewal that had divided the Town in similar fashion.

In the early 1960s the Boston Housing Authority (BHA; later the Boston Redevelopment Authority, BRA) and master planner Ed Logue saw Charlestown as a dilapidated urban sore spot, ripe for rehabilitation. The planners turned to Charlestown fresh from their demolition of Boston's West End, a physically run-down but socially stable, mostly Italian neighborhood that the BHA had stigmatized as a "slum" and transformed into a high-rise citadel of upper-income luxury apartments. Most uprooted West Enders, meanwhile, shifted for themselves, carrying in their baggage a set of unmet "rehousing" promises. The Townies had watched urban renewal in the West End, and they greeted Logue and the BRA with a resistance that in major ways anticipated the protest against desegregation.

To counter the BRA, fearful Townies organized Self-Help Organization Charlestown (SHOC). In its first year, SHOC negotiated with the BRA while in typical Townie fashion it organized teen dances, bake sales, rubbish drives, and lot cleanups, and issued a monthly newsletter. But soon the BRA sought to bypass SHOC by organizing a federation with which to negotiate that would include the monsignors of Charlestown's three parishes, the Knights of Columbus, labor leaders, and ultimately fifty-seven local groups, some with few members, as a way to minimize the role of SHOC. In response, SHOC became "fanatically" antirenewal.[47]

Thus, when Logue called for a hearing on January 7, 1963, SHOC took to the streets with sound trucks to mobilize its supporters to defend against the BRA and "destruction." The objectors made a shambles of Logue's meeting, but Charlestown was by no means united: some favored the BRA plan, some wanted rehabilitation of existing buildings but no destruction and rebuilding, while others opposed any change whatever. Already, too, in a pattern strikingly similar to what would appear during "the busing," middle-class leaders of the moderate federation were deriding SHOC leaders as "nobodies" and sneering that no SHOC representatives lived on the tops of Breed's or Bunker Hills, both "respectable" quarters of the town.[48]

During the next two years the BRA built support for urban renewal and came back with inducements: only 10 percent of Charlestown's houses would be removed, full information would be guaranteed, and the hated El—the elevated railway that since 1903 had turned Charlestown's Main Street into a wasteland—would be torn down. On March 14, 1965, some twenty-eight hundred citizens jammed into the town's armory with policemen lining the walls for another hearing. The meeting went smoothly for an hour as proponents had their say. But when opponents started talking, the temperature rose dramatically. Already the clergy had been told they were being used and supporters had been called "Judases" when one opponent unleashed bedlam by shouting: "I don't have to do it. I don't have to do it. It's my home and that's what I'm fighting for. You can stick the money up your ass."[49] One of the priests then called for a vote, and as bedlam reigned Logue stood on a table and made a count that he claimed supported renewal by three to one, and which provided him with a mandate to take to the city council.

Although the promoters of urban renewal ultimately won, the Townies may have succeeded in winning significant concessions from the city and in getting a plan as "benign" as possible at the time.[50] The controversy unquestionably unfolded a remarkable dress rehearsal of the busing battle and fueled many Townies' distrust of planners, technocrats, and liberal reformers.

Desegregation, however, unleashed violence in a way that urban renewal had not. Opposition to busing was much more intense, in part because race was involved. In the early 1970s, too, a national economic downturn hit Charlestown particularly hard, with the closing of the historic Charlestown navy yard. Now, too, the housing project reflected urban malaise. In 1973, 68 percent of the project's families had no father and 80 percent were on some kind of public relief. Many of the families were refugees from "urban renewal" elsewhere in the city. The project people, moreover, burned with resentment against other Townies, especially the hilltoppers, whom they knew looked down on them as "riffraff" and "project rats."[51] And it was the housing project's residents who were affected the most by the court order because as those with the least resources they were least able to escape.

When antibusing activities began in Charlestown, however, the rowdy elements were not in evidence. In 1973 a middle-class group organized a chapter of the Massachusetts Citizens Against Forced Busing, which included the publishers and editor of the *Charlestown Patriot* and mothers from lace-curtain households. By fall 1974, however, new impulses broke through and on September 25, three hundred Townies organized the Charlestown branch of ROAR, christened it Powder Keg, and elected as head Pat Russell, a mother from the project. When asked about the chapter's name, Russell replied, "because we have a short fuse."[52]

In September 1975, when busing finally came to Charlestown, a massive police presence forestalled a "Second Battle of Bunker Hill" but also angered many Townies and stiffened their backs. Mothers' prayer marches and confrontations with the police, protest demonstrations, and chaos in the high school continued through the year. As in Southie, ROAR was "calling the shots" in the high school, though here too the black students gradually fought back. In April 1976, the celebrated spearing with an American flag of black lawyer Theodore Landsmark on City Hall Plaza was perpetrated by a Charlestown youth who with friends had joined Southie youngsters for a protest march.[53]

Despite the similarities with Southie, explicit racism was less freely expressed in Charlestown. The *Patriot* and moderate leaders urged that Charlestown not disfigure itself with obscene graffiti. These remonstrations were often ignored, but that they were made at all suggests the Town's different style. The Town's pragmatism could be seen in the politicking of Maurice Gillen, a thirty-five-year-old meter reader with Boston Edison. Nonviolent and no racist, Moe Gillen was a quintessential Townie, born there, married to one, and residing nested among his and his wife's relatives. He fervently opposed busing as the offspring of addle-headed planners and ivory tower experts, and his wife was a founding member of Powder Keg. But Gillen believed it was foolish not to try to broker as mild a plan of desegregation as possible, and he helped organize a broad-based task force, including the state representative, members of the clergy, parents, and several militants, to negotiate with the court.

Although stunned by the original masters' plan, which made their high school into a magnet for technical training and required heavy busing in and out, Gillen hung in and steered a wary course among Charlestown's bristling factions. Eventually, his committee won concessions, most notably the high school's being continued as a district school, though the level of busing remained high. When Gillen accepted Judge Garrity's invitation to serve on the Citywide Coordinating Committee, four militant members of his group resigned in protest. But the coalition had held together long enough for moderates to play a significant role.[54]

Although moderates were harassed less than in Southie, militants frustrated initial attempts to elect biracial councils, while some Townie parents experienced enough pressure to make them change their minds about independent action. Terry Wrenn, wife of an elevator mechanic and mother of five, with four children in parochial schools in 1975, attended a meeting of the court's citywide council. Wrenn distrusted the top ROAR leaders as well as the school committee ("For years they knew busing was coming and they sat on their ass. I voted for those idiots"). She also fiercely opposed busing, but when screaming neighbors called on the phone to berate her for attending the meeting, "I came off the thing, and that's not like me." In fact, Wrenn received calls just because she had been seen talking to a reporter: "They said they thought it wasn't too good an idea to talk to the press."[55]

During 1975–76, too, the level of violence in Charlestown rose, some of it apparently having little to do with busing. Robberies, car thefts, purse snatchings, and random vandalism proliferated. Antibusing vandalism climaxed in February 1976 when project youths set up barricades in the streets and battled police with rocks and bottles nightly for almost a week. Rocks crashed through a picture window at the branch library and a butcher store was looted. The police often seemed to be surrogate targets for "niggers."[56]

As middle-class moderates withdrew from both the resistance and the schools Powder Keg meanwhile had spawned a splinter group called the Defense Fund, dominated by men, whose purpose was to raise money for the legal defense of young Townies arrested at the high school or in the streets. One Defense Fund member wrote to the *Patriot* that "we're tired of marching, praying, demonstrating."[57]

Racism as surely contributed to neighborhood defense in Charlestown as in Southie, as did fear of black ghetto culture. Racial violence in Charlestown during these years was often virulent, from rock throwings, to beatings, to the shooting of a black football player. But a powerful class dynamic was also at work among the powerless who felt they were trapped as others were not. "How can it be the law of the land, as we are told," wrote one Charlestown mother to Judge Garrity, "when you can move less than 1 mile away and be out from under this law?"[58]

Finally, the parallels with the antirenewal fight serve as an important reminder that more was involved in antibusing than racial hostility or even class resentment. The forces behind urban renewal (substitute "busing"), wrote one opponent, are "detrimental to our town" but are very strong politically, not just in city government and among financial groups who live in wealthy suburbs but also in universities: "For them there is something undemocratic and un-Democratic and un-American about people if they are not thoroughly mixed, moving and manageable by the government and economic forces."[59]

The Italians: East Boston and the North End

Whites of Italian ancestry lived throughout Boston, including Southie and Charlestown. They were most concentrated, however, in East Boston, a heavily three-decker, working-class neighborhood of just over thirty-eight thousand in 1970 that lay across Boston harbor and that was connected to the city by two tunnels. "Eastie's" geography, social character, and intensely hostile response to the threat of busing certainly qualified it as a defended neighborhood. Its geography and perhaps its reputation also seem to have caused it ultimately to be left out of Phases 1 and 2.

But during the mid-1970s an enormous amount of antibusing energy poured out of East Boston, led predominantly by Elvira "Pixie" Palladino, who won election to the school committee in 1975. Throughout the Northeast, of course, Italian-Americans participated prominently in white backlash movements and "produced white-hope saviors like Frank Rizzo in Philadelphia, Tough Tony Imperiale in Newark, and Mario Procaccino in New York City."[60]

For a time the antibusing imperative managed to bridge over the longstanding rivalry between Italian East Boston and Irish South Boston. Joining Eastie in this alliance to a lesser degree was the Italian North End, a picturesque corner of the city best known for its markets, restaurants, and festivals.

As Irish Catholic culture clashed with African-American black ghetto culture (or, usually, with images of that culture), so too did the Italian-American ethos with its emphasis on family honor and *ben educato*, that is, proper raising and correct bearing. Italian concepts of "good education" did not tend to stress an Anglo-Protestant achievement ethic geared to economic mobility or moving away from one's roots. Italians tended not, thusly, to pursue formal education as did, for example, Jews earlier and African-Americans later. Indeed, East Boston produced one of the lowest proportions in the city of high school graduates, and probably no more than 10 percent of Italians went on to accredited colleges. Italian parents did stress that their children learn not to dishonor the family.[61]

The importance of avoiding shame to Italians can be seen vividly in the fact that in 1970 only 7 percent of families in East Boston were receiving Aid to Families with Dependent Children (a mere 3 percent in the North End), even though almost a quarter of the families in these districts had family incomes of under $3,000 per year. Italians, of course, tended to avoid both divorce and welfare. Meanwhile, they perceived black families as unstable and dependent on welfare. This perception had much to do with the threat posed by desegregation, particularly the prospect of having children bused into black neighborhoods.[62]

A quiet neighborhood up to the 1960s, East Boston too had been roused by a populist movement marshaled to defend against powerful outside forces. The defense of East Boston turf had been going on well before 1974, not against desegregation but against the Massachusetts Port Authority (MPA) and nearby, expanding Logan Airport. The community had been fighting battles against airport noise, air pollution, and truck traffic, and already had lost three parks comprising seventy acres of recreational space as well as over one thousand units of housing. In September 1968 some six hundred heavy trucks a day began pounding through Maverick Street, "an old, densely populated street lined with homes," to and from the airport. This sparked a spontaneous protest, and grandmothers and housewives with baby carriages barricaded the street. State police cleared the roadblock, but by early October the governor and mayor announced the trucks would use an alternate route.[63]

East Bostonians then joined a new organization—The Greater Boston Coalition (GBC)—to lobby to stop highway expansion. Massport renewed its efforts in East Boston in February 1969, but after an April "surprise attack" by the MPA on one tree-lined street, residents pulled down a construction fence and their state representative, George DiLorenzo, got himself arrested. That night 250 residents met and cheered every mention of civil disobedience. The latter soon took the form of activists using their cars to slow traffic to a crawl on arteries leading to the congested airport. While the GBC eventually won its struggle to arrest highway construction, Eastie's wars with Logan continued into the 1970s.[64]

The veterans of wars with Massport and highways did not move over wholesale into antibusing. One of them, for example, Monsignor Mimie B. Pitaro, initially led a fight against the patronage-ridden administration of the federal poverty program in East Boston. His devotion to the neighborhood and enthusiasm in the struggle against Massport led local citizens to elect him to the state legislature in 1970, the first Catholic priest ever so honored in the state's history. But Pitaro refused to vote against the Racial Imbalance Act, which led to his defeat for reelection in 1972.[65]

Busing created a deep split in East Boston. Some of Pitaro's former allies worked to implement the court orders or distanced themselves from militant antibusers. Some were antibusing and the Massport-highway wars had toughened them: "Anyone who is still living here after the loss of Wood Island Park, noise of Logan Airport, and the smells from the oil tanks and large trucks," wrote one mother to Judge Garrity, "is never going [to move or to bus]. As a life-long resident you will not tell me what to do with my children." Already East Bostonians had joined demonstrations against the Racial Imbalance Act and the district had voted heavily for hard-liners on the school committee. After Garrity's decision, a ROAR chapter sprang up led by Palladino; her militants established an information center and began to plan for alternative schools.[66]

A small group of moderates also functioned. East Bostonians for Quality Education (EBQUE) announced its intention to work for peaceful implementation. Evelyn D. Morash, a member of the liberal Board of Education and a leader of EBQUE, of course was harassed: she received threatening phone calls and windows in her home were broken. A nephew of Palladino's and the son of Charlestown antibuser Tom Johnson were actually arrested for making obscene phone calls, but nothing came of it. Yet EBQUE fought back, sending around leaflets to smooth Phase 2 arguing that "busing will not go away." EBQUE, however, hardly reflected local sentiment. In January 1975 an antibusing HSA meeting and bake sale attracted some three hundred parents, while an EBQUE meeting mustered about three dozen persons, many of whom were clergy, teachers, and other professionals, with parents of school children accounting for only half a dozen.[67]

Yet neither did Palladino's ROAR completely reflect community attitudes. As early as December 1974 a group of twenty-five activists left the ROAR Information Center. The defectors said that while they thoroughly disliked the court order, they wanted some "middle ground" way of coping with what was now an irreversible situation. These moderates advocated a "foster parent" plan to insure the safe passage of black children into East Boston. They remained opposed, however, to sending their own children out.

One defector, Anthony Cestrone, who had been Palladino's right-hand man in the center, said: "I helped Pixie when she asked because I thought she was a sweet girl doing something for a good cause. But the more ROAR and Information Center meetings I attended, I saw they were really against blacks, and I don't want to be part of a racist organization." Like Pixie's group, these antibusers would continue petitioning and lobbying for a constitutional amendment, but they saw East Boston differently from Palladino. "Pixie," one mother said, "would like to think East Boston is as fired up as Southie, but it isn't true."[68]

Ironically, many observers outside of East Boston perceived it as potentially explosive—primarily because of stereotypes held regarding the predominantly Italian population. A state trooper at Southie High remarked casually regarding Eastie: "Over there they'll use bullets." That organized crime was associated in the popular mind with Italians, and that in fact it had been most entrenched and lethal in the North End and East Boston, certainly fostered this impression. Yet, ironically, the North End itself was low key about busing. A small antibusing group, North End Voices for Equal Rights (NEVER), participated in some ROAR demonstrations but opposed violence and even boycotts. The North End's relative restraint could be traced in part to having most of its children already in parochial schools, and because Phase 1 affected it primarily by busing in some 250 mostly Chinese students. The Chinese regard for ancestry and family and their well-known work ethic eased their acceptance by the Italians.[69]

Perhaps the oft-made threat of East Bostonians "to plug up the two holes" (i.e., the tunnels) and the perception of Mediterranean volatility influenced the judge and his experts in excluding East Boston from desegregation. The judge had received a flurry of letters from East Boston parents in the fall of 1974, most of which stated in no uncertain terms their writers' intentions not to put their children on buses going out of East Boston.[70] Though it is unlikely that these warnings influenced the implacable judge, the perception existed throughout the city that Eastie's geography, the tunnels, and the Latin temper (actual or imputed) had combined to win East Boston a reprieve.

Semisuburbia: Hyde Park

If you will offer something better than my neighborhood school, I would gladly accept.

No way will my family climb down the ladder. We are going up not down, no matter what you order. —Mr. and Mrs. R. D., Hyde Park, to Judge Garrity, Oct. 16, 1974

The basic fact of life for the residents of Canarsie was the precariousness of their hold on middle-class status, the recency of their arrival in that exalted position, and the intense fear that it might be taken from them. —Jonathan Rieder, Canarsie

Buses can take a rider a long way from downtown Boston to neighborhoods that seem almost suburban but are still part of the city. Hyde Park is such a place, not isolated or cohesive enough to qualify, strictly speaking, as a defended neighborhood, yet ardently antibusing and conscious of turf. With a population of about thirty-eight thousand (overwhelmingly white, though a few blacks could be found in the schools) in 1970, Hyde Park resists clear-cut classification, a hybrid best characterized as semisuburban. Working-class families of Irish, Italian, and other backgrounds, moving up from housing projects or low-rent districts, found in Hyde Park affordable housing and a within-city version of the suburbs. For many, it meant having arrived.[71]

Hyde Park parents thus often reacted to the court order with intense resentment born of the fear that it would take away from them all that they had gained. Thomas O'Connell, a father of seven and owner of a two-story house that he had built himself, had spent fourteen years in public housing. Similarly, Joseph LoPiccolo, a welfare investigator for the state, had enrolled his daughter in a private school rather than have her bused. On school's opening day in 1974 he watched the buses come in and said bitterly: "I worked three jobs just to be near this school and this church. Now it's all being taken away from me."[72]

Proximity to suburbs that were excluded from busing fueled this strong strain of resentment. "When I bought my home I had three things in mind," one father wrote to Judge Garrity, "namely the church, the school, and the shopping center. . . . [My children] will never be bused against my wishes. . . . If you are so concerned about the so called minority, as a beginner you might consider building some low income housing out in Wellesley and the rest of suburbia. You people are the real villains who have discriminated against the minority for years and years."[73]

Antibusing organization was strong, and in August 1974 some eight hundred parents gathered at a municipal building and voted to hold a two-week boycott of schools. Both the MCAFB and ROAR were active, the latter structured Southie-style with a pyramid network of phone callers. Leaders of Hyde Park's ROAR worked prominently in the citywide organization and marshaled troops for demonstrations. Different factions, however, coexisted easily in Hyde Park, and local groups tried everything from lobbying and legal appeals to alternative schools and boycotts.[74]

In overcrowded Hyde Park High School the pattern resembled that in the defended neighborhoods. Although mobs did not gather routinely and clash with police, violence erupted inside throughout the school year. After the mid-October stabbing of a white by a black, fifty to sixty police officers were stationed inside. The police presence and the installation of metal detectors caused white attendance to rise, but after the December vacation fighting, riots, arrests, and police invasions continued to the end of the year. Although trouble did not reach levels as high as at Southie or Charlestown, incidents continued.[75]

In some ways what surprises about Hyde Park, given the level of rage, was that violence was not worse. No signed letter threatened Judge Garrity with more menace than one sent by a Hyde Park resident who called the judge a "no good bastard" and hoped "to hell someone picks you off and bombs or fires your house in Wellesley." Yet some tried to comply with the court order and, despite their strong convictions of its injustice and their fears of black crime, even participated in biracial councils.[76]

Between 1970 and 1980, as some black families moved in, residential white flight increased. The white population fell from over thirty-eight thousand to about thirty-two thousand while the black population went from .4 to 7 percent of the total. Tensions rose and in 1982 journalists described some blocks as hostile "racial frontier[s]." The high school by then was 85 percent black.[77] Thus, like their suburban cousins, most semisuburban white Hyde Parkers simply escaped from the schools.

West Roxbury

During 1986 a movement arose in the black neighborhood of Roxbury to secede from the city. In a referendum on the issue the vote went strongly against establishing a new municipality, which would have been named "Mandela" after the South African black nationalist. A joke went around Boston at the time, to the effect that if the referendum passed, then in West Roxbury a secession movement would develop, with the new city to be named "Botha."

The subject of racism in West Roxbury has its less funny side. In 1982 a black woman and her young son drove to a West Roxbury home to buy used furniture. Stopping to ask directions, the thirty-two-year-old city planner encountered white youths who told her she was in West Roxbury not Roxbury, and "they told me if I bought the house 'they'd kill me.'" That night the house was painted with obscenities and slogans such as "Keep West Roxbury White."[78]

Such a story gives West Roxbury the flavor of a defended neighborhood. Was there as much racism in West Roxbury as in Southie? Perhaps, but West Roxbury expressed its opposition to desegregation in ways very different from Southie. Of course Southie had its moderates and West Roxbury its militants, and in comparing them one uses ideal types. But West Roxbury's antibusing movement was predominantly moderate, middle class, and individualistic.

One of the first "streetcar suburbs," West Roxbury was about as suburban as a Bostonian could get in the city. For the upwardly mobile it was, said Alan Lupo in 1974, "one of the last outposts. . . . a big sprawling ward at the southern tip of the city. . . . There are probably some Yankees left . . . and certainly some Protestants, there is an increasing number of Jews forced out of the neighborhoods to the north. But . . . West Roxbury is a largely Catholic community, whose members number politicians, well-paid appointed officials, civil servants, police, firemen, realtors, small business proprietors, doctors, and those blue-collar guys who will mortgage their grandmothers to live there."[79]

West Roxbury's population increased in the decade before 1970 more than any other part of the city. Its median family income ranked second while its portion of residents completing high school ranked first. Employees of the state, federal, or city governments, or utilities headed 60 percent of the households. The neighborhood was far from uniformly middle class, but of a population of over thirty-one thousand, only seventy-seven were black.[80]

In a 1975 poll the neighborhood ranked high in "outrage" over busing, and close to 80 percent agreed with the statement that forced busing violated constitutional rights (just 6 percent behind Southie).[81] On one issue, however, West Roxbury parted company with the most militant neighborhoods: was it more important that order be maintained as Phase 2 was carried out, or was it more important that protest continue even if some violence happened to take place? Southie had the most who would continue to protest at the risk of violence, 26 percent (61 percent opted for peace), East Boston was second with 18 percent, Charlestown was third with 16 percent, and further down West Roxbury-Roslindale tied for sixth place with only 11 percent, while 81 percent there chose peace, only 7 percent less than in Roxbury. "The lace curtain Irish," said one councillor, "are very, very opposed to the court order, but they are not marchers or demonstrators." Thus, West Roxburyites could join antibusing militants in other neighborhoods in establishing a private, alternative school (West Roxbury Academy), but mob scenes outside the high school were not to be.[82]

West Roxbury's middle-class parents had long shown intense involvement in the schools. Local HSAs vibrated with concern for education well before they became geared up for antibusing.[83] In the spring of 1973 many residents joined the throngs that marched on the state house seeking repeal of the Racial Imbalance Act. In 1974 ten buses took demonstrators from the Robert Gould Shaw School, and the total participating from West Roxbury-Roslindale was estimated at two thousand. Meanwhile, some local activists moved on into Massachusetts Citizens Against Forced Busing.[84]

But despite the anger that seethed also in West Roxbury, most neighborhood leaders emphasized order and safety. Some militants did advocate boycotts, and K. Marie Clarke, a West Roxbury resident and head of the city HSA, was pressured into calling one. But she limited it to one day and urged that parents keep their children home or take them to church. The *Transcript* opposed boycotts, and boycott advocates, indeed, seem to have been on the defensive in West Roxbury, where most parents would not keep children home unless the schools were demonstrably unsafe. This attitude prevailed in part because many possessed the resources to transfer their children elsewhere.[85]

ROAR members lived throughout West Roxbury and Roslindale, and a local branch of ROAR came into being in October 1974 as the Tri-Neighborhood Association (TNA). The group held a dance and then a Sunday afternoon rally at Billings Field on November 3, where three thousand turned out to listen to speeches from leading antibusers. The enthusiasm resplendent at sunny Billings Field, however, faded with the winter snows. Though activists and the *Transcript* boosted the ROAR-sponsored March on Washington in March 1975, antibusing was waning.[86]

As it did the TNA became dominated more by militants close to Hicks. In April 1975 they engaged in the picketing of a building site for a new high school because, said Janet Palmariello of the information center, it would not be a district school—only 200 of its 1,250 seats would be reserved for West Roxbury students. On April 24, joined by ROAR activists from Charlestown and East Boston, Palmariello led protesters in preventing trucks from using the main entrance to the site. The next morning police arrested her, the district court quickly released her, and the picketing continued.

But civil disobedience was not West Roxbury's dominant style. The number of picketers reached only as high as fifty, and not all were from West Roxbury. Indeed, a letter from the information center to the *Transcript* sarcastically began by saying that the demonstration once more gave West Roxbury residents "an occasion . . . to exemplify their now well recognized apathy."[87] Moderation outweighed militancy in West Roxbury, and common ground existed there, if anywhere, for a middle-course solution to desegregation such as that embodied in the unrevised masters' plan. Strong support existed also for the position worked out by attorneys for the Boston HSA. They conceded that the Boston School Committee had been guilty of discrimination in the twenty-two schools for which plaintiffs and the court had provided evidence. They pleaded, however, that desegregation remedies be limited to the schools to which segregative practices had been applied. In Boston, in 1975, that too was a moderate position.[88]

Once the court rejected the masters' plan, however, the dominant reaction in West Roxbury to busing, according to state representative Michael Connolly, was "to get out from under. Either move out of the city or take their children out of the public schools."[89] A West Roxbury lawyer wrote to Garrity that he and his wife had grown up in West Roxbury and after his attending Harvard Law School they had decided not to move to the suburbs despite "some of the difficulties and unfashionableness of living in the city." They hoped to send their children to the same schools they had attended. Now, their community activities allowed them to see that many worried parents were making plans to move out or place their children in private schools. They too were contemplating moving, especially because of the hazards threatening their nine-year-old daughter. At her Roslindale school, he had learned, a young black girl had been beaten by other black girls for associating with white children. His daughter, in an adjacent class, "is being constantly threatened physically (struck *at least* once in the face) and tormented and verbally abused by a group of black girls—all for reasons unknown. Many people have advised me that I would be further jeopardizing her physical safety if I tried . . . to have the school principal and teachers to admonish the black girls."[90]

Far from being militant, this parent had hoped for a plan "which can be embraced by both blacks and whites." He could have added, as did another West Roxbury parent of similar views writing to the judge: "I share with you the dream that this City can have children learning and living together in friendship. However, how is this possible if there are not enough white youngsters in the public schools[?]"[91]

In September 1975 local officials were talking of a "mass exodus," particularly by parents of elementary school children. By 1977 the publisher of the *Transcript*, James G. Colbert, described the impact of white flight on the Randall G. Morris School. Ten years ago it was one of the best in the city. Now it was "just another mediocre elementary school with severe disciplinary problems." School officials claimed that its racial composition was 58 percent black, 40 percent white, and 2 percent other, but this was misleading because it included two classes of all-white kindergarten children. Many white parents sent their children there for kindergarten only, then sent them elsewhere to avoid their being bused. Subtracting kindergarten, there were only 35 white children to be integrated with 137 black in grades one to five. Thus, one first grade classroom, for example, contained 15 black children and 1 white. Another had 13 black and 2 white. And so it went in other grades. "Under the guidelines laid down by Judge Garrity all the regular classes at the Randall Morris School from grades 1 through grade 5 are illegally segregated by needless and wasteful busing."[92]

Colbert was no rabble-rouser. Indeed, he was an establishment type, closely tied to the city's power structure. A Boston Latin and Harvard graduate, as a reporter and columnist for various local papers he became a good friend of the late mayor, John B. Hynes, who appointed him to the Boston Redevelopment Authority in 1957. He remained on it for over twenty years, unabashedly "a champion of special interest" and a wielder of power through his columns on local politics. A member of the Tri-Neighborhood Association at its inception, he chaired its committee on alternative schools. Yet Colbert also backed Mayor Kevin White during these troubled years, giving him credit for his efforts to insure safety.[93] Colbert typified, in short, the middle-class perspectives of his neighborhood.

Perhaps more representative of West Roxbury parents was K. Marie Clarke, a registered nurse who won election as president of the Boston HSA in the late spring of 1975. Clarke had grown up in Dorchester, attended public schools and then a Catholic high school. Active in local affairs since at least 1970, in 1975 she had one son at MIT, a daughter at Boston Latin, and another son at the Robert Gould Shaw middle school. Clarke had begun lobbying against the imbalance act through her HSA activities, primarily by serving concerned parents as "a provider of information." She marched once to the State House but otherwise asserted emphatically, "I'm no demonstrator." Indeed, she distanced herself from ROAR and clearly had great disdain for South Boston methods. It angered her that the South Boston HSA was run by adults who did not have children in the schools and was essentially an arm of the South Boston Information Center. Clarke was a legalist who concentrated on court appeals. She participated in making TV spots appealing for peace, and with some ambivalence agreed to serve on Garrity's Citywide Coordinating Committee, which she believed unrepresentative of Boston parents.[94]

Clarke regarded the Racial Imbalance Act and the court order as inequitable and punitive of Boston. It was "ludicrous" that the "lily-white suburbs," whose legislators had set the standard for Boston, were unaffected: "In five minutes I can go to Dedham, Needham, or Newton. . . . I can walk to Dedham." She resented charges of racism against those who opposed the court order, particularly coming from suburbanites and the *Globe*. She had no objection to black students coming into West Roxbury but did fear sending her children into black neighborhoods. The suburbs, in any case, should have been involved in a metropolitan plan of desegregation.[95]

While serving on the legal committee of the Boston HSA, Clarke worked closely with an antibusing black parent from Roxbury, Liza Tinsley. One winter day she and Tinsley met at Clarke's home on business while Tinsley's children waited outside in her car. Some white youths came along and began to throw snowballs and ice at the car, shouting "Niggers get out of here!" Clarke heard the noise: "I went out and I was wild." She issued an immediate press release describing the incident and praising Tinsley as an opponent of forced busing and "a faithful friend and ally, never hesitating to attend court hearings in defiance of the NAACP and others. Racism is ugly at best! How sad that some of the youths in this community who should publicly applaud this black woman, can do nothing better than attempt to assault her children. Burned out of her home in her own community, must she also suffer harassment in ours?"[96] Though Clarke typified the dominant strain of moderation in West Roxbury, she did not represent all of her neighborhood any more than James Kelly represented all of South Boston. But viewed from a distance, the contrasts between the two districts are striking.

Concern for the quality of education in West Roxbury preceded the busing agitation and made for a greater willingness to cooperate with implementation, despite distaste for the court orders. The defended neighborhoods would not participate in the biracial councils (though later ROAR switched tactics and elected its own people to the councils). As a Charlestown mother said, "Do they think we can't see through that? It's just a trick to get you to go along with that damned busing. We won't have any part of their election over here." In five white neighborhoods, over a third of the residents saw the councils as "just a gimmick set up by the court to try to get people to cooperate," with 45 to 47 percent thinking thusly in Southie, Eastie, and Charlestown. Even in Roxbury 33 percent shared that perspective. But in West Roxbury-Roslindale only 24 percent dismissed the councils as a trick.[97]

In West Roxbury, with its middle-class emphasis on upward mobility, concern for the Latin schools was particularly intense. More West Roxbury parents thought in terms of sending their children on to college, of course, so preparation at all levels was important, and choice of schools a weighty family decision.

Marie Clarke believed wholly in individual choice, and she opposed the court order in part because it deprived her of the crucial choice of her childrens' schools. But antibusing protest or compliance also involved individual choices. "If you don't believe you can send your kids to school safely, don't interfere with the rights of others [to send theirs]." In South Boston, militants did impose on the rights of others.

Antibusing was much more individualistic in West Roxbury, and parents reacted more to the impact of busing on their families than on the neighborhood as a whole. Consequently, West Roxbury was pluralist and tolerant by comparison with Southie. Irish Catholic and working-class impulses fused in the latter to present a visage to the outside world of clannishness, cohesiveness, and strong distrust of outsiders. There was actually more division in Southie than the world was permitted to see. As one West Roxbury ROAR activist said, "We in West Roxbury were as opposed to busing as Southie . . . but they have Southie pride. They will hide a lot of things to save their pride." Southie put more emphasis on "sticking together."[98]

Lacking the strong sense of turf and community identity of Southie, many West Roxburyites were as alienated, in fact, by Southie tactics as they were by liberal and suburban probusers. White flight developed quickly in West Roxbury because middle-class parents would tolerate neither their children being out of school nor in threatening situations. They possessed the resources to flee; it was not their style to stay and fight through direct action or collective protest. That was Southie's style, and many fought against the court order through choice, or because they had, as many observers put it, "no alternatives."

Some West Roxbury antibusers defined themselves by distancing themselves from Southie. Southie-bashing may have allowed them, in fact, to feel better about themselves and to assuage guilt. Feeling pangs of guilt often enraged antibusers since they believed with their heads that they had no reason to feel guilt in their hearts. This triggered great anger at those who might be judging them. In the middle-class antibusing precincts Southie provoked embarrassment but also provided a measure of relief in promoting self-satisfaction for responsible and moral antibusing activity.

The question asked earlier: "Was there as much racism in West Roxbury as in Southie?" is the wrong question. And the fact that West Roxbury/Roslindale also scored lower than Southie and East Boston on poll questions that revealed "insensitivity to blacks"[99] is also not particularly important here. For one thing, it is possible that middle-class types in suburban settings do much better at hiding their real feelings from pollsters. But the essential differences between West Roxbury and Southie should not be seen in any case exclusively in moral terms. West Roxburyites possessed not only the inclination but the resources to escape from busing, by moving out of the city or placing their children in private schools, or in nearby suburban refuges. Too many in South Boston lacked resources and safe retreats, and Southie also lacked the refuge a well-developed parochial school system could provide.

7

The Antibusers
Children of the 1960s

In a strange inversion, images of the 1960s pervade Boston's anti-busing protest of the 1970s. But something jars and does not fit. The housewives, blue-collar ethnics, and middle Americans shouting slogans, marching, and chanting in the 1970s are the wrong people. A short time before, blacks, long-haired college youth, native Americans, countercul-ture freaks, feminist women, gays, and the oppressed-minority-of-the-week were filling the streets and television screens of the nation. What now was "Middle America," or slices of it, doing out there head to head with helmeted riot police? Were these the people whom Richard Nixon had called the "silent majority," now angrily demonstrating and carrying on like yippies and peaceniks?

In profound ways the antibusers were heirs of the protesters of the 1960s, even as they reacted against them and their values. While the antiwar radicals had sometimes burned American flags, antibusing dem-onstrations were often festooned with hundreds of hand-held Stars and Stripes. Yet in a massive irony not lost on many of the participants at the time, the antiestablishment protests of the 1960s shaped and influenced the antibusing movement.

The greatest irony, of course, was that the immediate model for all the protesters of the 1960s and 1970s was the black civil rights movement, whose tactics ran back to boycotts and freedom rides in the 1940s, and back further to labor union strikes and sit-ins of the 1930s. By the early 1970s, a protest style that in the context of the Vietnam War and the civil rights movement had been the property primarily of southern blacks and then of middle-class white youth now became appropriated by the white working class, lower-middle-class ethnics, and middle-class respectables. The 1970s demonstrators, in short, completed the democratization of the sixties forms of protest that the mass media, particularly television, had communicated and popularized throughout the country.

It was not just antibusers who imitated sixties-style protests, as twenty thousand construction workers showed in June 1972 when they marched on the State House to protest cutbacks in city projects and highway building. When Governor Sargent tried to speak to the hard hats, he was drowned out by chants, jeers, and obscenities. The workers were a color-ful lot, sporting green, white, red, or gold hard hats, and mostly peace-ful, though at times their brushes with police became tense. "What are the pigs [police] going to do?" asked one young worker, in a phrase redolent of sixties argot.[1] But the antibusers, so different from their predecessors in the streets, carried the analogue much further.

The well-known episode of September 9, 1974, when Senator Ted Kennedy was driven from City Hall Plaza by a ROAR crowd of several thousand, has been seen, rightly, as symbolic of the white backlash that transformed Kennedy Democrats into antiliberals who voted for George Wallace and Richard Nixon. The rage against Kennedy reached such a torrent because of the feeling, especially among Irish Catholics, that Ken-nedy, one of theirs, had betrayed them. The incident also illustrated both the similarities and differences between the antibusers and their 1960s predecessors.[2]

The crowd first turned their backs on Kennedy, then chased him from the plaza to the safety of the Federal Building. This same crowd, which pursued the senator until the glass panes of the doors behind him shat-tered at their onrush, had sung, moments before, holding American flags, "God Bless America." As Kennedy fled, they shouted "Pig, Pig." "Pig"? The epithet came right out of the sixties, when it had been in the mouths of blacks hectoring cops or flower children taunting armed Na-tional Guardsmen. In clashes with the police over the next two years, antibusers would use the term again, which now came often from the mouths of blue-collar ethnics who had been one of the original targets of the name in the 1960s. "God Bless America," on the other hand, harkened back to another world, to relatively placid urban villages and tree-lined semisuburban precincts of the 1950s when the sunshine of post–World War II affluence and national confidence was not darkened by rapid social change and cultural disorientation.

What is most striking about the antibusers, however, and what has not been sufficiently appreciated by earlier accounts, is the extent to which they not only resembled but deliberately sought to imitate the methods and strategies of the 1960s civil rights and antiwar movements. ROAR had come into existence in 1974, just after the federal court ordered desegregation and extensive busing. But already the crowds marching on the State House to lobby against the Racial Imbalance Act had begun to look like their predecessors. If they had been on their way to Schaefer (now Sullivan) Stadium, observed one reporter, "you would have said they were football fans." But Patriots' fans would not have been carrying a huge placard bearing a Nazi swastika and reading "STATE BOARD OF EDUCATION." Nor would so many sports fans have been wearing buttons proclaiming a political or social message. As in the 1960s, "buttons," as one South Bostonian remembered, "were big," and one felt great pressure to wear them. As the actual start of desegregation grew near, antibusing rallies frequently broke into chants of "No! No! We Won't go!" echoing the draft resisters who protested the Vietnam War. Soon the antibusers got the chant exactly as it had been earlier, "Hell, no! We won't go!"[3] The resemblances existed at more than the rhetorical level. The school boycotts of the antibusers extended the more limited boycotts called by blacks and liberals in the early 1960s. The white boycotts lasted for weeks rather than days and affected many more persons, in and out of the antibusing enclaves.

The establishment of alternative schools by antibusing parents who refused to send their children at all to public schools also mirrored the founding of "freedom schools" earlier by civil rights groups. Here, too, antibusing efforts were more extensive. These institutions also resembled, of course, the all-white academies that flourished throughout the South in the 1950s and 1960s following the *Brown* decision.[4]

Yet the Boston antibusers themselves tended to see their efforts as parallel to the alternative black schools created in Roxbury in 1969. "The same feelings of impotence and frustration," said *Globe* education writer Muriel Cohen, "mark the campaign by white parents to create alternative schools." Mary Binda, a thirty-eight-year-old mother of three, was a founder of South Boston Heights Academy (which by January 1976 enrolled some 450 students). She recalled taking the subway from Southie to Harvard Square, walking into the Harvard Graduate School of Education Library, and asking for a book about alternative schools. Someone at the circulation desk brought her a volume describing a black freedom school of the 1960s. She also wrote letters seeking information from persons across the country who had created "underground schools."[5]

Mothers' prayer marches, recitation of the rosary, three-day prayer vigils, and the like—all by antibusers—had not been modes of the young radicals in the 1960s. But adults participating in civil rights protests in the South in the 1950s and 1960s, and even in Boston in the 1960s, had conducted similar events. Some of the Charlestown mothers of 1975 recalled prayer marches held during World War II for their men in the armed forces. Pat Russell, leader of Powder Keg, the local ROAR chapter, used a more proximate reference point as she led a mothers' march: "If Martin Luther King could do it, so can the women of Charlestown." Soon after, the women sat down in the street and sang briefly, "We Shall Overcome." They did seem more comfortable singing "We Are the Girls From Charlestown" or "The Battle Hymn of the Republic," or, better yet, striking up the football cheer, "Here We Go Charlestown! Here We Go!" As they walked up to a wall of police, however, the women were reciting Hail Marys and Our Fathers. As they passed a fire station on one of their marches the firemen clanged their bell in support while a postman standing on a corner cheered, "Right on, girls, right on!" Other slogans differed greatly from those of the sixties, but the defacing of public buildings with graffiti was a hallmark of the 1960s as it was of the 1970s.[6]

Antibusers also held sleep-ins and sit-ins. In July 1975, thirty-four demonstrators led by Louise Hicks staged a sleep-in at Mayor White's suite at the Sheraton Boston Hotel during the national conference of mayors. Sit-ins were even more common, such as the one in December 1975 staged by fifty ROAR demonstrators led by James Kelly at the offices of the state's congressmen at the Federal Building.[7] In the 1960s antiwar protesters lay down in front of troop trains and politicians' cars. In September 1974 antibusers lay down in front of *Boston Globe* delivery trucks to protest what they saw as the paper's probusing bias. On other occasions, too, antibusers got down under car wheels or otherwise blocked vehicles with their bodies.[8]

Antibusers complained of harassment by the FBI, although they experienced little of the attention intelligence agencies lavished on radicals in the 1960s. Their complaints, though, echoed the radicals' and blacks', as did the appearance of antibusing leaders before the U.S. Commission on Civil Rights in June 1975 where several refused to testify or lashed back at the commission. John Kerrigan's outlandish rhetoric there recalled the high jinks of rebel youth before congressional committees and courts.[9]

The scene could have been a college campus in 1968, with police arresting demonstrators and carrying off many who passively resisted. Instead, in October 1975 there were some fifty antibusers holding a "prayer protest" within one hundred yards of South Boston High (violating the judge's orders regarding assemblies near the school), and some were lifted by their elbows and carried into a police wagon.[10]

Perhaps the most obvious imitation of civil rights protests was ROAR's grandly conceived March on Washington. On March 18, 1975, over twelve hundred Boston-area faithful left by bus for a twelve-hour trip to the nation's capital. Not all who went were ROAR militants—some were average citizens opposed to the court orders. But all were in for a grand disappointment. In Washington they marched through a drenching rain along the same route—from the Washington Monument to the Capitol—that civil rights and antiwar throngs had traveled during the past decade. But joined by only a few sympathizers from Maryland, they numbered just fifteen hundred. Virtually ignored at the Capitol steps, they warmed themselves by belting out "God Bless America." A Washington policeman commented: "The water and mud at the Monument were like the Poor People's March back in the '60s. Only the people have changed."[11]

Antibusers frequently made indirect references to "other groups . . . who have demonstrated and demanded and got everything they wanted." Often antibusers thought explicitly in terms of the civil rights movement. Charlestown's Alice McGoff joined Powder Keg because she believed in direct-action tactics. If opponents of the court order were going to get anywhere "they would have to learn something from the civil rights activists and anti-war demonstrators of the sixties. They would have to take a leaf out of Martin Luther King's book." She hoped the march on Washington would be "precisely the kind of dignified but forceful demonstration that would win them recognition. ROAR was developing into a white NAACP." While marching in the rain, however, McGoff feared that "she looked even worse than the hippie demonstrators who'd filled this same avenue through the sixties with their long hair and Vietcong flags. She'd dismissed them as a bunch of nuts. Who would have thought she'd be out here herself a few years later with mascara streaking her face like Apache war paint?"[12]

Antibusers frequently quoted Martin Luther King's axiom that any bad law is the same as no law, as did an anonymous flyer distributed in South Boston, signed by "Patricia Henry":

> The Rev. Martin Luther King, Jr., rose to fame fundamentally because he taught his followers to resort to civil disobedience, that is, to refuse to honor or obey laws they considered to be unfair, unreasonable, etc.
>
> For this, his birthday has now been made into a State Holiday by our respected leaders. And many of our leading liberals in Washington are working to make it into a national holiday.
>
> This amounts to giving official and legal sanction to the philosophy of civil disobedience.
>
> Very well, then. The people of South Boston, Hyde Park and similar communities would be quite justified in resorting to civil disobedience in September of 1974.[13]

As it had earlier, civil disobedience sometimes slid over into uncivil behavior interfering with others' rights of free speech and assembly. Small groups of ROAR militants often pursued extremist tactics, disrupting meetings of moderates who were trying to get their children through school safely and productively, or harassing those they identified as the enemy. In one incident, a ROAR squadron mobbed Senator Ted Kennedy as he left a Quincy high school, jostling him, trying to jab him with small flags, slashing the tires of his car, and placing small children under its wheels, forcing Kennedy to flee with a police escort to a subway station. Some ROAR men in Southie and Charlestown almost welcomed invasions of their turf by members of the radical splinter group, the Progressive Labor Party (PLP). The PLP's Committee Against Racism believed in physical confrontation, and the South Boston bravos gladly gave it to them whenever they could, with fists, brass knuckles, baseball bats, chains, and other weapons. (Whenever the police intervened, they usually arrested the CAR members.) Antibusing streetfighters, however, more frequently clashed with police.

Though evidence never materialized of a bomb plot to blow up the bridges going into South Boston (as alleged by the FBI), antibusing terrorists did use fire bombs, and terrorism was being deliberately used, as the Mayor's Committee on Violence said on June 23, 1976, "as a political weapon. The smashing of store windows, the defacing of public landmarks, the destruction of historic shrines are examples of the stepped-up pace of violence in this city."[14] While reminiscent of the radical Weather-

Clashing Symbols, September 1974: South Boston antibusing protester wears long hair and peace symbol while holding a racist effigy of a black. UPI. Courtesy of Bettmann Archives.

men's "Days of Rage" in the sixties, such acts also signaled that the extremist antibusers shared with splinter groups of the 1960s a deep frustration at their sense of powerlessness and an angry alienation from mainstream America. Along with frustration and alienation, typically, went obsession: "I didn't smile or laugh for three consecutive years," said South Boston Information Center leader James Kelly. "I was obsessed with busing, the injustice, the stupidity." The antibusing violence, according to Kelly, "took on a life of its own," and political leaders could not control it.[15]

Perhaps the supreme irony in the parallels between the 1960s and the 1970s lay in the antibusers' cry of "police brutality." This complaint had been heard earlier, of course, almost exclusively from the black ghetto, and then from white campus protesters. In the beginning, the thought of such a development was humorous. In September 1974 Deputy Mayor Robert Kiley explained to two police superintendents that Mayor White wanted tough police action in Southie: "He thinks one thing they'll understand is firmness," adding, joking, "he feels they won't go to the ACLU [American Civil Liberties Union] in Southie." To which one police official replied, "Yeah, not too many to our internal complaints bureau from Southie." Kiley, laughing, added, "No brutality complaints."[16]

That perception quickly changed. After the TPF raid on the Rabbit Inn in October 1974, protests of police brutality arose throughout the city. Antibusers especially hated and feared the TPF, who dressed in menacing gear and were trained to act ferociously to intimidate crowds and control mobs. Pat Russell of Charlestown called them "the most brutal men I've ever seen," and after a Southie mob clashed with them following the Faith stabbing, William J. Foley, former city council president and heretofore a friend of the police, said: "That goddamn TPF is a collection of sadists."[17]

Though policemen profited greatly from busing in overtime pay, it was also for them an agonizing ordeal. The Boston force, one of the largest and oldest in the nation, with few minority members, itself hated busing. An estimated 60 percent possessed ties with South Boston by origin, residence, or kinship, and the police union, the Boston Police Patrolmen's Association (BPPA), was vehemently antibusing. Indeed, the BPPA voted funds to help finance legal challenges to the court order, voiced opposition through its journal *Pax Centurion*, took a full-page antibusing ad in a ROAR publication, and initially threatened obstruction of the judge's orders by claiming they were vague and open to selective enforcement.[18]

Despite all this and their lack of sympathy for blacks, the police and antibusers inevitably collided. "It was difficult for many of the guys to identify with the kids in Harvard Square during the riots [in the 1960s]," said one TPF officer. "But these people in South Boston are like us, with homes and families and all. . . . Let me say this, though, after the third or fourth rock comes flying, you tend to forget about the righteousness of their cause."[19] Still, the confrontations were unnatural. The TPF had come into existence in the 1960s to control black riots and antiwar protests. Carting off long-haired hippies, young radicals, and blacks had not been difficult. Now, the protesters were from their own social stratum and mostly shared their cultural attitudes and values.

The ironies were not lost on some of the participants. Robert Kiley described to Mayor White and other staff members a meeting he had with antibusing leaders about a planned demonstration. "They agreed there would be no wholesale arrests of women if it could be avoided. And no dogs. The thing that cracks me up is this is like dealing with Mel King in 1969."[20]

Out of the Kitchen

The antibusers' affinities with challenging movements of the 1960s are all the more striking, of course, because many antibusers had disdained the causes of the 1960s. The white backlash, as noted earlier, had formed part of a general reaction against unwelcome social and cultural change. This included a hostile response to what many, especially working- and middle-class urban ethnics, saw as bra-burning and man-hating "women's libbers." The new feminism, like so much else in the 1960s, owed an enormous debt of inspiration to the black freedom movement. Women active in the struggle to lift blacks out of second-class citizenship came to see parallels in which blacks' oppression mirrored their own condition. Spreading out from caucuses in the civil rights and antiwar movements, "consciousness raising" among women (and gradually among men) pervaded the country. "Of all the social movements of the 1960s," according to historian William Chafe, "the one that retained the most strength in the 1970s was the struggle for women's liberation and women's rights."[21] Since the type of women who tended to be feminists also tended to be prodesegregation and to live elsewhere than in the desegregating neighborhoods, it was perhaps inevitable that the women's movement and the antibusers would collide.

In Boston their most publicized clash came in April 1975 when about fifty ROAR women showed up at a rally at Faneuil Hall for the Equal Rights Amendment (ERA) sponsored by the Governor's Commission on the Status of Women. The one hundred or so ERA backers never got started, as the ROAR group shouted anti-ERA slogans and would not allow anyone to speak. Elaine Noble, the nation's first elected openly lesbian state legislator, was taunted with chants of "We like men!" Pixie Palladino stood up and began reading a statement claiming that the ERA women did not represent Boston mothers and that a forum should be provided for antibusing women. When a well-heeled suburban lady told Pixie "you are our guest, and if you don't behave, I'll have to ask you to leave," Pixie thundered back, "No! You're *our* guests, this is *our* City Hall [*sic*]. No bunch of ladies from the suburbs is going to kick the women of Boston out of their own City Hall." This incident, plus occasional statements from antibusers opposing the ERA, seems to establish a clear-cut case for hostility between the women's and antibusing movements.[22] Yet interviews with antibusing women and other evidence suggest a more complex relationship.

Antibusing women admittedly lacked interest in the women's movement, and when they thought about it were likely to regard it as dominated by affluent suburbanites or flighty radicals interested in frivolous issues and with whom they had nothing in common.[23] "The ladies in question," the *East Boston Regional Review* said of antibusers, "did not wear designer clothes. They did not swim at the country club nor sponsor charity balls nor write in their leisure time for the Sunday *Globe*. . . . Daughters of archtypal Blue collar 'ethnic' neighborhoods all, with (to media ears) foreign-sounding names, these women were an ungainly sight to the kind of opinion-forming suburban people who rarely if ever meet women with seven, eight, nine, more children, who must work for a living, who dwell in three-decker flats, and whose closest pass to 'the finer things in life' was the rare three-week vacation fought for and saved over years and years."[24]

Yet women did dominate antibusing at a time of enormous change for women. By 1970 half of American women, according to a Gallup poll, agreed they were victims of discrimination; four years later, two-thirds agreed. During these years, also, women continued to enter the work force and, unlike the 1950s when women over thirty-five tended to be the job takers, the greatest increase occurred among younger women of childbearing age. In the 1970s traditionally "masculine" professions made room for women—the proportion of women entering law schools, for example, went up 500 percent. Antibusing mothers were not likely to be going to law school (though Louise Hicks had done so in the 1950s), of course, but other changes unavoidably engulfed them as well. In the 1950s, for example, over 70 percent of all U.S. families consisted of a working father and a stay-at-home mother. By 1980, only 15 percent were in that condition.[25]

Most importantly, opinion surveys showed that while many women still thought the women's movement "too extreme," the same women in most cases "endorsed feminist positions on day-care centers, repeal of abortion laws, equal career opportunities for women, and a greater sharing of household tasks."[26] Unquestionably, many antibusing women experienced these changes and sometimes benefited from them even as they decried feminism itself.

The prominence of women in antibusing leadership and activity to a great degree simply reflected traditional working-class culture. Women and children in many ways, as Suttles has pointed out, define neighborhoods. It is mothers and children who often must walk to and from schools or stores and whose activities map out a zone of security. Many antibusing women also were continuing involvement in schools that they would have pursued even without desegregation. Mothers had typically been more involved in schools and had assumed more responsibility for parenting (though that too was changing in the 1970s), and "parental rights" were the principal rights antibusers sought to reclaim. Irish-American women in particular had "dominated family life and . . . enjoyed a greater degree of independence relative to women in other cultures." The Irish immigrant and working-class heritage had reinforced a tendency to matriarchy, with most men working long hours at physical labor and too many falling prey to an early death or alcoholism. The large families of Irish Catholics also fostered strong personalities in mothers, as well as sayings reflecting that heritage: "Girls grow up, but a boy is a boy all his life."[27]

If some antibusing women were just extending what had already been socially approved behavior, others, however, were nudging up to and across the boundaries of convention. The intensity of antibusing commitment usually meant that women were at home far less: husbands, housework, and children got neglected, or husbands took up the slack. Several antibusing women conceded that they saw antibusing activity place a debilitating strain on many marriages. According to ROAR activist Phyl-

Message for Guard: Massachusetts National Guardsmen receive antibusing
message in South Boston, September 1975. AP. Courtesy of Wide World Photos.

lis Igoe of Roslindale, for some already shaky marriages the stress of
activism provided the coup de grace. "It just so happened," said Igoe,
[that] many people we met split."[28]

In some cases antibusing extended previous community involvement
but to degrees they hardly anticipated. It also brought unexpected influence and positions of leadership. In Gail Sheehy's book *Pathfinders*, the
chapter on Bingo Doyle is a portrait of Charlestown's Maurice Gillen,
whose antibusing activism became a turning point in his life. Sheehy
could have found scores of Boston women for whom antibusing represented a similar transition.[29]

Sometimes husbands drew lines. K. Marie Clarke of West Roxbury told of one woman, asked to speak in public, who declined because her spouse made it clear that he would not tolerate her participation carried that far. Other women did drop out because of domestic pressure. Clarke spoke appreciatively of receiving "passive encouragement from my husband. At one point . . . I know, he was extremely unhappy with my activities, but . . . well, he told me that he would have to be a little more flexible and give a little bit on it." Clarke then went on to make this astonishing admission: "I always felt if I took care of the children, and was there when he needed me, and we had a home, he had his meals, most of the time. [Interviewer: You prepared all the meals?] Yes, most of them. My husband does not cook. . . . If I'm not going to be home, I would always leave spaghetti sauce and meatballs made in the refrigerator, so that all they'd have to do was boil the macaroni; or I'd leave a beef stew." This from a woman who held a job and headed the Boston Home and School Association and put in long hours on its legal committee. Neither Clarke nor her husband regarded her as a "feminist" (her daughters' boyfriends did). But her life did change, she declared, and she experienced a sense of empowerment she had not thought possible. For many other women, antibusing did launch them, in the words of a moderate whose work for peaceful implementation dramatically changed her life, "out of the kitchen."[30]

The Media and the Antibusers

They were heroes and martyrs—we were racists. —James Kelly

April 1976 was a violent month in Boston. The most notorious incident, though not the most lethal, occurred when a black lawyer on his way to a meeting at City Hall happened to cross the path of a demonstration of some 150 antibusing youths from South Boston and Charlestown. As a stunned mayor watched the scene from his office high above, the youths attacked the black man, Theodore Landsmark, and one of them tried to use the staff of a large American flag as a spear, striking Landsmark a blow across the face. The photograph of that bitterly ironic moment won a Pulitzer prize.

Normally, antibusing demonstrators carried many replicas of the Stars and Stripes at their rallies and marches. And they sang patriotic songs such as "America the Beautiful" or most often "God Bless America." When a November 1974 rally of three thousand in West Roxbury closed with the Pledge of Allegiance and the singing of "God Bless America," the crowd was accompanied over loudspeakers by a Kate Smith recording, whose booming voice during World War II had become linked ineluctably with that music and with wartime good feelings of unity. It expressed the quintessence of patriotic feeling, hope, and all that was good about the country. The war for many meant a time during which their Americanism had been cemented and the isolation of ethnic tribalism softened. The display of patriotism thus came naturally to these Middle Americans. But it also sprang from more immediate and conscious sources. Their measuring of themselves against antiwar and black separatist protesters of the 1960s was as obvious as it was deliberate.

The comparison sprang from the conviction (which underlay "Patricia Henry's" dripping sarcasm) that they were good Americans, good citizens, and not troublemakers like those who had preceded them in the streets. They were not asking government for anything except to leave them alone. The easy display of their patriotism arose in part from the desire to prove, especially to the media, that they were better Americans than the antiwar hippies and radical blacks that the media had seemed to lionize.

The most important way in which the antibusers in their own minds did not manage to replicate the civil rights and antiwar movements was in relation to the media. This is an enormously complex question, because it ultimately involves how in fact the media did portray the civil rights, antiwar, and other protest movements of the 1960s, as well as antibusing. Various studies, particularly a recent book by Todd Gitlin, *The Whole World Is Watching: Mass Media in the Making and Unmaking of the New Left*, have shown that the impacts of the media on the protests of the 1960s were not at all uniformly benign. Indeed, the incongruity that Gitlin himself felt, as a participant, between his experience of the antiwar New Left and the media's portrayal of it, finds a powerful echo in the complaints of antibusers.[31]

For the purposes of this discussion two points are clear: firstly, antibusers believed that the "liberals" who ran the media had presented the civil rights movement in a favorable light. This judgment was summed up by militant antibuser James Kelly's comparison several years later: "They were heroes and martyrs—we were racists." Secondly, it is generally accepted that in the early years of the civil rights movement in the South the presence of *Life* photographers, radio microphones, and above all television cameras played an enormously beneficial role in dramatizing the brutality of the caste system that white southerners imposed by force on southern blacks. As Gitlin put it, "television brought . . . images of repression—those unblinkable cattle prods, those police dogs of Birmingham—to the living rooms of Northern liberals, and helped mobilize them into the financial base of the movement and the political base for its achievements (and its limits) in national politics. For isolated civil rights workers in dangerous areas of the Deep South in the early sixties, attention in the national press was a form of protection against local sheriffs."[32]

By the late 1960s, the media had entered into a symbiotic relationship with antiwar and other protesters. To a significant degree, attention in the nation's airwaves could not only dramatize a cause and provide invaluable "free advertising," it could also confer legitimacy or, conversely, illegitimacy on a movement. The mass media indeed are able to "certify" movements and individuals or to "decertify" them.[33]

The antibusers campaigned hard to dramatize their plight and to gain legitimacy for their cause. It was a campaign they came to believe they never won and never could win. The liberals who in their view controlled the media would never anoint them, as it were, with victim status, never allow them to be draped in a mantle of morality. Instead, the antibusers saw themselves portrayed as bigots and racists. This created tidal waves of frustration and rage among militants as well as many moderates.

The importance of the media in the antibusers' calculations is underlined by the movement's storefront headquarters being labelled information centers. The South Boston Information Center made its appearance in September 1974 partly in response to "misinformation" coming out of City Hall and partly because of the "media blackout" and "unfair reporting," especially by the *Boston Globe*. The center's job was to purvey "what's really happening" regarding busing and, presumably, win the battle for public opinion.[34]

But what really rankled the antibusers was their perception of a double standard on the part of the media. "How come when Negroes have a civil rights march people pay attention," asked one Southie father, "but when we do nobody stirs? Don't we have civil rights?" This lament became especially bitter during the rain-soaked march on Washington, which drew minimal media coverage. Avi Nelson, a local radio talk-show host and antibuser, complained, "If 50 anti-war demonstrators had marched to the Capitol a few years ago, they [TV networks] would have been there."[35]

Both antibusing leaders and the rank and file, like much of the merely semiattentive American population, had been taught to be media-wise by simply watching television and recognizing its impact on events. Mayor Kevin White, analyzing the first days of September 1974 at South Boston High, observed: "When the audience [i.e., newsmen, TV cameras] clears, things quiet down. Nobody wants to get hit [by police] for nothing. Only for the tubes." Indeed, two young boys in South Boston shortly afterward were overheard discussing the morning's demonstrations and one said to his friends: "I don't know if they [protesters] can make the noon news, but it'll be on the 6 o'clock and the 11 o'clock." In Charlestown a *Globe* reporter asked a youth if he would answer a few questions, and got the reply, "I'm sorry, but I've already talked to the Associated Press and the *Los Angeles Times*. I'm not talking to anyone else."[36]

The first major outbreak of school violence perpetrated by blacks at English High in October somehow had been anticipated by the media. The first teachers to leave the building saw TV camera crews waiting out front and suspected a set-up. Both the police and the Mayor's Committee on Violence worried about the relationship between media coverage of demonstrations and the excitation of violence, while sometimes newspaper and television commentators themselves suggested a causal link while covering the coverage.[37]

The expectation of violent resistance to the beginning of desegregation in Charlestown brought hordes of media ready for "another Southie." The Townies reacted with ambivalence, "performing" for the media to dramatize their cause and gain coverage that would depict them as victims, while also feeling that the media were making things worse and exploiting them. A September 18 Mothers' march that began with "Our Fathers" ended with curses against reporters. Pat Russell grabbed a megaphone and yelled, "We want all media to leave our town. We don't want them and we don't like them." A group of teenagers more harshly warned photographers and camera crews, "no pictures, you bloodsuckers."[38]

For the three years during which resistance to desegregation flared in Boston, the antibusers complained of both the quality and quantity of the coverage they received—perpetually slanted, they believed, to make them look bad and to favor their enemies. "It was one-sided," Richard Laws recalled grimly, "always one-sided."[39] Sometimes their complaints seemed contradictory. On the one hand, they faulted the media (particularly national) for emphasizing violence and for making them appear to be prejudiced and savage. On the other hand, they cried out that the media (particularly local) were not presenting an accurate picture of how bad things were in the schools. What all media were not doing, they felt, was showing that the presence of blacks in the schools was a major source of trouble. "Why is it that it is always the whites who are pictured as the aggressors," asked columnist Dick Sinnott, "and the blacks so shy, almost demure?"[40] The antibusers believed black students' aggression against white students to be extensive, and they wanted the media to tell this part of the story to show that desegregation was not working.

Though this desire was unrealistic, the antibusers had a point. Many of them knew from personal experience that blacks often were the aggressors, especially outside of Southie, Charlestown, and Hyde Park, but that side of the story was in fact downplayed by the media, except in local newspapers such as the *Transcript*. Ione Malloy's account of the ordeal of black and white students in South Boston High shows that the media barely scratched the surface of just how bad conditions could be, whatever the cause. News reports of the school, agreed one state policeman, especially those in the *Globe*, bore little relation to the "macabre horror show" inside.[41]

Antibusers across the city charged that a media conspiracy existed to underplay desegregation-related violence. In October 1974 Dick Sinnott wrote that the conviction among Boston parents that school news was being "managed, manipulated, distorted," and bad news suppressed, had grown into a roar of anger. "The Watergate coverup wouldn't make a good puddle in the tidal wave of discontent, distrust and suspicion of the Boston media sweeping this old town."[42]

Views of the media's role varied widely throughout Boston, but many moderates and even some black leaders and white radicals joined in raising the claim of a media conspiracy. NAACP head Thomas Atkins told the U.S. Commission on Civil Rights that the media had served the city poorly by giving "sugar-coated coverage." Maureen Costello of Roslindale, a leader of MCAFB, agreed, and she also complained of the national media's branding of Boston protesters as racist. Senator William Bulger of South Boston went further, charging that although forced busing was a failure, the media insisted otherwise. "A victory for the NAACP must be salvaged, no matter how great the distortion of reality. My constituents live under Orwellian conditions, saturated by an Orwellian media, watching the segregation of their public schools in the name of integration."[43] Bostonians of every party tended to agree most with the

Mounted Patrol Moves In: Police push back crowd outside South Boston High School following the stabbing of a white student by a black student inside the school. AP. Courtesy of Wide World Photos.

notion that they had been made to look bad, but the heart of the antibusers' complaints was that they were depicted unfavorably, that the workings of desegregation were distorted, and that black violence was ignored.

The truth was that during the summer of 1974 the Boston media had agreed to downplay violence. Thus coverage of the first day of school in local papers, for example, contrasted dramatically with that in the *New York Times*. The *Times* and other outside sources subsequently faulted the locals for not presenting all of the story. City journalists countered that national reporting tended to be sensational. Most ironic, however, was the fact that the local media's plans to cover desegregation had been made in open meetings and their intentions announced to the public. The Boston news outlets did downplay violence in the fall, justifying their actions by arguing that most of the city's schools were desegregating relatively peacefully, and that the few trouble-spots should not dominate the news.[44]

While antibusers criticized all media for their desegregation coverage, the *Boston Globe* aroused their greatest outrage. Moderates and militants alike saw *Globe* editors and reporters as advocating a social policy with which they did not want to live, since most of them lived in the suburbs. Those who lived in the city, if they had school-age children, did not send them to public schools. Indeed, of the paper's top twenty editors, all but two did reside outside of Boston, as did most reporters.[45] Antibusers loved Billy Bulger's crack that to telephone the *Globe's* "urban team" after 5 P.M. you had to dial "1" first.

The alienation from the *Globe*, as J. Anthony Lukas pointed out, had been building for at least a decade. Its coverage of racial issues "had been skewed toward the black community," while it often showed condescension to the Irish working class. Chief editor Thomas Winship once had referred privately to the antibusing majority on the school committee as "those f—heads." At the same time, the paper's liberal position on related issues such as the youth culture, women's lib, birth control, abortion, gay rights, and pornography also created a backlash against it in the neighborhoods.

During 1974–75 militant antibusers picketed the *Globe*, lay down in front of its delivery trucks, and often denounced its news coverage and editorial statements. ROAR also organized a boycott that contributed, with other causes such as a price hike, to a circulation drop of about fifteen thousand and the loss of an estimated seven thousand readers. The publishers and editors received threats against their safety, frequent bomb threats came into the *Globe* building, shots were fired into it on several nights from passing cars on Morrissey Boulevard bordering South Boston, company trucks had their tires slashed, and antibusers for months "went around and stole the *Globe*, depositing them in Boston Harbor."[46]

Yet the *Globe's* sports page kept the paper popular in the antibusing neighborhoods, and the antibusers found themselves prisoners of the *Globe's* hold on Boston's consciousness. As one astute observer of the Boston scene put it, "The antibusers' focus on the *Globe* was entirely rational. If it [an event] wasn't mentioned in the *Globe*, it didn't happen."[47]

Aware of the anger seething against it in the precincts where it had once been popular, the *Globe's* editors did not stop backing desegregation but did try to make amends by opening its columns occasionally to antibusing leaders and by scrupulously covering ROAR activities. Indeed, many thought the *Globe* gave ROAR too much attention and exaggerated its importance. A moderate antibusing parent like Emily DeCesare of Roslindale regretted that "the majority of people that felt the way we did around here, most of us parents, were never depicted in the news."[48]

The *Globe* and the media represented the most influential sector of what antibusers saw as a liberal establishment arrayed against them. The antibusers targeted both media and establishment in such actions as a June 1975 ROAR motorcade of 250 flag-bedecked cars carrying one thousand demonstrators to the South Natick home of John I. Taylor, president of Affiliated Publications, the *Globe's* parent company. The picketers protested *Globe* coverage of desegregation as well as Taylor's membership on the board of directors of United Way, an establishment operation run by liberals that ROAR said was giving money to promote acceptance of busing.[49] In the antibusers' view, the liberal elite's values had permeated the media, the Democratic party, and the church, as well as the state and national governments. Ultimately it was the liberals who were denying legitimacy to their protests and who insured that they continued to be stigmatized as racists.

Antibusers measured their outsider status in many ways. Many recalled bitterly how in 1970, after Nixon's Cambodian invasion and the killings of students at Kent State University, Governor Francis Sargent had ordered the state house flag flown at half-mast. This incident, remembered in one version or another, had provoked antibusers and continued to haunt them. In 1973, one Roslindale mother lobbying at the capitol vented her anger at the governor "who always comes out when there's a peace demonstration." When Judge Garrity decided in the spring of 1975 to look into the antibusers' "alternative schools," West Roxbury antibusers exploded: "Thinking back to 1968 when the Freedom Schools were being instituted to provide quality education for black youngsters, were they prevented from doing so? an emphatic NO! and yet these schools were racially identifiable."

Dick Sinnot frequently hammered at the double standard that the media had applied to antiwar and black protesters in contrast to antibusers. After two Hicks lieutenants, Rita Graul and Virginia Sheehy, were summoned into court by Judge Garrity to be questioned about their possible knowledge of disruptions in the schools, Sinnott praised the two as heroines. In the sixties when the colleges and streets were swollen with dissent, he said, both were home caring for their families and neighborhood, not burning flags. Both had children who had served in the armed forces, but a court order had now changed their lives, leading to a summons and the necessity of their standing on constitutional guarantees of freedom of speech. "But instead of praise and support from the same liberals who would have canonized the Berrigans and Fondas and Rubins and Hoffmans and draft evaders, Rita Graul and Virginia Sheehy receive only ridicule and taunts."[50]

ROAR

The antibusers' anger with the media, liberals, and the establishment connected also to a widespread distrust of politicians and alienation from politics. Boston's political culture already possessed a high degree of cynicism regarding politics and the uses of public life. In the 1950s political scientists had discerned an "alienated voter" as the peculiar feature of City elections. The sense of politics as a game in which the players are motivated primarily by self-interest and patronage created a mentality that was streetwise and highly vulnerable to disenchantment at the same time.[51]

This was particularly so for most rank and file ROAR members and the true believers who carried the organization at the precinct level. Several ROAR leaders, notably Hicks and her lieutenants, were intensely political, and their pursuit of their own interests would eventually contribute to the fracturing of ROAR and the collapse of the antibusing movement. But the mass of infantry resisted being tied to the fortunes of particular political leaders, and once many antibusers discovered that some leaders had been pursuing politics as usual, their sense of disillusionment deepened.

For about a year after its inception in the spring of 1974, ROAR displayed all the features of a typical social movement trying to change public policy. It gave its members hope, something to do to try to bring about change, and allowed them to ease somewhat their rage at not being heard by giving them a place to vent—literally to shout—their views of busing. "Shouting," one ex-member observed, was almost "routine" at ROAR meetings. ROAR also provided a sense of community,

Street Sitters: Antibusing demonstrators outside Charlestown High School blocking buses, September 1976. AP. Courtesy of Wide World Photos.

with meetings bubbling with conviviality, singing, and socializing. And in the fall of 1974 ROAR members exulted over a major political victory and show of strength at the ballot box.

The issue was the referendum on reorganization of the school committee that Mayor White had brought forward to eliminate the at-large elected committee and to replace it with one appointed by the mayor. ROAR made this into a test of its own strength and argued that a vote against reorganization was a vote against forced busing. In November, White's plan lost by a twenty thousand vote margin, which ROAR leaders then claimed as their core strength citywide as they crowed about having "kicked Kevin White's ass."[52]

In many ways not apparent at the time, this would be the high point of ROAR's success, and certainly of its unity. In 1975 ROAR began to wane, although it revived in May with Judge Garrity's rejection of the masters' plan and his orders for increased busing in Phase 2. Similarly, in December the judge's placement of South Boston High in receivership gave Southie's militants a shot in the arm. But ROAR's aggressive style, its association in the minds of many with disruption if not violence, and its demand for total conformity meant an inevitable withering of its influence. In addition, the task of keeping Boston's ethnically Balkanized neighborhoods united and taming the ambitions of their ever-hungry politicians was insurmountable.[53]

For a time ROAR succeeded in bridging the political chasm separating Italian and Irish Americans.[54] And for a time Southie's always full crop of aspiring politicians had held their ambitions in check. Early on a barely concealed rivalry had been present between grand dame Hicks and the rising Raymond Flynn. Flynn's mayoral ambitions were well known by early 1975, and Hicks and her people, who dominated ROAR's inner circle, would brook no one (other than Hicks) using antibusing as a stepping-stone, though Flynn was probably just testing the waters at this early stage of his career. In any case, as the 1975 mayoral campaign developed Mayor White's principal opponent, Senator Joseph Timilty, attracted the votes of many antibusers, but Hicks and ROAR remained ostensibly neutral.[55]

In reality, Hicks and White had cut a secret deal as early as June 1974, and it was the clever use of patronage by White, and the subsequent explosion of the Eastie-Southie rivalry, that not only neutralized antibusing politically but also broke it apart and finished it as a significant political force. Six days after Judge Garrity's decision, Hicks went to City Hall for a secret meeting with White and agreed to keep ROAR neutral in electoral politics. Realizing she would not be able to beat White for mayor, Hicks promised also to support him in the council whenever possible. In exchange, White would funnel patronage to her supporters. In the fall of 1975, for example, Hicks's son received a $17,000 a year job with the Boston Arena Authority, rumored to be a "no show job," and his name was kept off the payroll until the following March. Several Hicks lieutenants also quietly received city jobs. By June 1975 the odor of the fix was in the air—as one Southie housewife told a reporter for the *Real Paper*: "I don't like it. . . . Rita Graul and Virginia Sheehy weren't even there [at a South Boston meeting with Mayor White], and they're supposed to be the leadership in South Boston—they're never around when there's any opposition to Mayor White, and I think they're working hard to have him elected again. Every place you turn, somebody's selling out. Everything points to it. If I could put my finger on it, I'd stand up and screech."[56] For Mayor White, a few low-paying jobs on the public teat paid handsome dividends, neutralizing a volatile force threatening him politically and ultimately contributing to calming resistance to desegregation.

When the ROAR rupture came, ideology and political differences provided the ostensible causes. Pixie Palladino of East Boston, allied with John Kerrigan and "Dapper" O'Neil in the background, emerged as spokesman for the hard-core ROAR militants and anti-White elements. Several issues brought the feud to a head. After the Hicks-dominated executive board accused Palladino of disloyalty, she counterattacked by criticizing Hicks for going to Washington to testify for a bill sponsored by Senator Henry Jackson that would give special funds to school systems under court orders to desegregate. Palladino argued that acceptance of the money meant acquiescence to federal interference and to busing. Let busing bankrupt the city if need be, urged Palladino. In addition, Hicks's faction supported Jackson in the upcoming presidential primary, while Palladino's group preferred Alabama governor George Wallace. When Jackson appeared in Charlestown on a campaign stop, Palladino's shock troops shouted him down. Then in mid-February 1976, Palladino attacked Hicks at an open ROAR meeting on the issue of federal funds. The next Sunday the eighteen member executive board met and ousted Palladino and her allies. On March 10 Palladino, Kerrigan, O'Neil and several hundred militant antibusers met at the city council chambers and established "United ROAR," an organization separate from the Hicksite ROAR Incorporated. Though Lukas and other writers have given the impression that the Palladino-Kerrigan group was more prone to violence, the Hicksites of course had friends in the South Boston Marshalls and the terrorist underground in Southie. While Palladino and Kerrigan expressed themselves more frequently in public in crudely racist fashion, the sources of the split sprang not from strategic, tactical, or stylistic differences but from patronage and political rivalries based on personalities, neighborhood, kinship, and ethnicity.[57]

Authority and the Antibusers

In the ROAR breakup, ironies folded upon ironies. After Palladino's ouster, Rita Graul justified the action by pointing to the purged East Bostonians having engaged in "disruptive actions." Because of yelling and disorder, "we were not allowed to conduct a meeting. We couldn't get a vote. It was disastrous and I was ashamed to be associated with these . . . people."[58] The same tactics by which ROAR had disrupted meetings of Judge Garrity's biracial councils and other groups were now being turned inward on ROAR itself. The politics of incivility, to which certain 1960s protesters also had resorted and found to boomerang on themselves, engulfed ROAR in similar fashion.

One legacy of the 1960s has been a huge jump in the amount of rudeness present in American public life. "Young people" of the New Left and the counterculture pioneered in removing inhibitions and barriers to behavior once regarded as unthinkable. But far more than the rise of rudeness, the breakdown of authority—respect for, confidence in, obedience to—preceded and paralleled the antibusing movement, shaping its style and tactics.

The prestige of authority has varied throughout American history and has inspired much commentary through the years, from Puritan preachers to contemporary philosophers. In the early 1970s, scholars and journalists alike newly discovered the topic at the same time that a consensus again had emerged that authority had declined. The mood was captured by a 1975 title, *The Twilight of Authority*.[59]

The causes of this particular declination were vastly more complex than the antics of protesters in the 1960s, which constituted but one of several motors and symptoms of change. The scale of society and government, and especially the growth of distant, impersonal government contributed heavily, as did the actions of government leaders, beginning with President Lyndon B. Johnson's deceptions of the public and Congress in creating a United States war in Vietnam and climaxing with the resignation of Richard Nixon from the presidency following revelation of a variety of illegal activities conducted in the White House. The pardon of Richard Nixon by Gerald Ford, the unelected president, one

South Boston High School, December 11, 1974: Police Superintendent Joe
Jordan stands by overturned police car. Thomas E. Landers Photo. Courtesy
of *Boston Globe*.

month after Ford took office (just as the court order went into effect in
Boston), as well as ongoing disclosures of wrongdoing by government
intelligence agencies, further fed the mood of disillusionment and led to
an across-the-board decline of trust in public institutions during the decade from 1965 to 1975. When Mayor White made his equivocal appeal
for obedience to the law in Boston in September 1974, he referred to
"the traumatic events of the past several months in Washington," which
had shown that "we are a government of laws, and not of men."[60]
White's point was well taken, but unfortunately the Watergate scandal
also suggested a general climate of disregard for law—and if all the
president's men had broken laws with seeming ease, why should ordi-

nary citizens continue to revere the so-called majesty of the law? Why, indeed, should they not challenge or disregard laws that they regarded as bad and unjust?

Demographic trends over which no one had any control also did their part. The youth culture's slogan "never trust anyone over thirty" was coined just as the median age of the population reached its lowest point in the twentieth century and was appropriately a shibboleth of the baby-boom generation born just after World War II. The cohorts coming of age in the late 1960s questioned accepted verities of American life as no generation had since the shock of the Great Depression of the 1930s. The work ethic, marriage, family life, even the "bitch goddess" of American culture, success, came under fire. Nothing was sacred. As the divorce rate climbed in the 1970s the typical nuclear family of two parents and two children went the way of the Edsel.[61]

The Catholic church followed other institutions in losing the powerful grip it once had on its members' beliefs and behavior. From 1970 to 1978 attendance in Greater Boston had declined from 75 to 55 percent, but more vital from the standpoint of desegregation was parishioners' galloping disregard for priests' authority. Many Catholics had been alienated by the Catholic clergymen's participation in the civil rights, antiwar, and other liberal causes. Lukas described the mothers' marches in Charlestown during 1975–76, during which the women frequently beseeched priests to join them in the streets and to pray with them, not for them. On one occasion, as the marchers went by a rectory and saw a priest looking out a window one of them shouted, "See, we don't need you anymore. We deal with God directly."[62]

The kind of communities that had been unlikely to organize any kind of protest as late as the 1950s discovered a decade later a willingness among some of their residents to organize, to protest in the streets, and to fight for their interests.[63] Repercussions from the 1960s were felt very quickly in Boston in neighborhoods of the "silent majority" and of the hitherto passively obedient working class. The "Maverick Street" ruckus in East Boston in 1968 had provided a sharp contrast to what had been the normal disposition of an Italian-American working-class neighborhood. Those who had shaken their heads at rebelliousness a short time before were saying, "Maybe we should do like the blacks do." Indeed, one group of mothers and children blocking the big trucks on their way to Logan Airport sang "We Shall Overcome." Though East Bostonians retained reservations about demonstrations, one housewife explained their actions thusly: "Legally, we couldn't get anywhere. The only way we could get anywhere was to demonstrate. If you write a letter, they put it on a desk, and there it sits." A grandmother who sat in the street to block the trucks shouted defiantly: "Let them arrest me. People have already taken too much. They're fed up to here. The riot won't be in Roxbury, but here."[64]

In the 1960s protests against highways had united members of neighborhoods as diverse as East Boston, Roxbury, and Cambridge, blue-collar ethnics and cosmopolites. Similarly, fights over urban renewal in Charlestown, Brighton, and the South End, in addition to the legacy of the West End's demolition, had fed the distrust of authority in general and of experts, bureaucrats, developers, and social engineers in particular. Some of these "renewal" battles enlisted blacks, social workers, and sympathetic professionals (as in the South End) who would end up on the other side (i.e., prodesegregation) in the busing wars. But the overall impact was to erode further the legitimacy of the powers that be, to create suspicion of programs sold as beneficial to the common good, and to fragment the city's constituent elements into combatants in a struggle that has been called "street-fighting pluralism."[65]

In a 1980 novel, *Firewatch*, Allan Dennis Burke depicted a Boston high school turned into a hellhole in its second year of desegregation. Cynicism, hatred, and spasmodic violence routinely crush the spirits of all involved; the students are preoccupied with grievances and racial fighting, and teachers regard the students and themselves with contempt. The main character, a security officer, reflects the other teachers' slavery to the patronage system run by the school committee in which merit hardly counts while political connections and bribes are the road to better jobs and pay. The system was obviously in place before desegregation, but racial turmoil seems to have released all inhibitions on self-interest and corruption.

Firewatch seems to be very much about the absence of any moral center, of any legitimate authority residing outside or inside any of its characters. The removal of many traditional restraints engendered by the 1960s, though hardly mentioned, are powerfully implicit as the context in which action proceeds. At one point, for example, at a meeting of the faculty after the school has been rent by its worst riot one teacher cries out:

Too many kids in this school are getting away with murder. . . .
That's the problem. We all know. Sure as I'm standing here we all
know every kid arrested today'll be on the streets tomorrow. Not one
of those kids'll spend a single day in jail or pay a penny in fines. Its a
joke to them. And we sit and take it. We got used to havin' things this
way. Kids showing up for class stoned. Teachers assaulted. Cussed
out. We got teachers on the faculty think it's normal for a school to be
like this. They've never known anything else. Well it's not normal and
it's about time we did something to stop it.[66]

The transition described here had taken place only recently. American
schools, as Diane Ravitch has pointed out, enjoyed a long period of
stability after the limiting of immigration in the 1920s. The Depression
contributed by suppressing the birth rate and the schools did not begin to
experience major disturbances until new patterns of internal migration
began to take effect in big cities after World War II.[67]

Teachers' authority, under challenge in the 1950s, declined in the
1960s. During desegregation it was discovered that conditions in the
schools were not as many citizens remembered them. When in 1975, for
example, Police Commissioner Robert diGrazia criticized teachers for
"abdicating their roles as disciplinarians," he indicated that he was out
of touch. Similarly, Judge Garrity made two surprise visits to South Boston High and came away with sharply negative impressions, characteriz-
ing the building as more like a prison than a school. The president of the
high school's faculty senate responded angrily: "It seems as if his idea of
a high school came out of an Andy Hardy movie." During the 1960s
Boston's schools had already joined others nationwide by experiencing a
sharp rise in vandalism, as they "were broken into, robbed, and in six
instances set on fire." By 1975 high schools across the country, according
to testimony given before a U.S. Senate subcommittee, were "riddled
with violence and drugs and . . . learning is second to survival."[68]

Meanwhile, members of the baby-boom generation graduated from
college and transformed the teaching profession. A new militant union-
ism grew nationally and by 1970 reached Boston as the city experienced
its first teachers' strike ever. On March 24 some 70 percent of teachers
stayed out for the day and some three thousand marched through downtown Boston. In late April teachers picketed school headquarters at 15
Beacon Street and in front of many schools, then staged another walkout
on May 4, with about two-thirds staying out. Observers noted the arrival

of a "new breed of teacher who is less intimidated by 'headquarters' and is more willing to strike, even if it means breaking the law." Indeed, for violating a court injunction the Boston Teachers' Union (BTU) president was jailed for thirty days and the BTU was fined $4,000. The Suffolk Superior Court judge blasted the union for causing "confused and bewildered parents" and for "flouting the authority of the court in a willful affront to its power."[69]

Teachers marching and picketing became a favored media symbol of the widespread climate of defiance of authority and surely must have helped unsettle students. During the March 24 strike, in fact, students at English High ran wild, overturning desks, chairs, and lockers. But disciplinary problems with students had preceded the eruption of the new militancy from teachers.

As it had on college and university campuses, stirrings of protest began among blacks and then spread almost simultaneously to white high school students. Blacks, of course, had held boycotts and marches in 1963–64, but a new round of protests beginning in 1968 reflected the radicalization the civil rights movement underwent in the mid-1960s. Yet the first rebellion essentially continued moderates' earlier demands for better schools. Black teachers at the severely overcrowded Gibson School took a group of students out of the school with them and started their own "liberation school." The school committee immediately suspended the teachers, and as the controversy simmered, a black student at English High was suspended for wearing a dashiki. Black students there went on a rampage, which quickly spread to other schools. Teachers in Roxbury were assaulted, firemen trying to put out a brush fire behind Brighton High School were stoned, and disturbances, looting, and clashes between police and black youths lasted for days. A September 25 rally of five hundred students at Franklin Park led by adult militants demanded the right to wear African dress, recognition of black student unions, and a curriculum dealing with black history and culture.[70]

The incidents raised the temperature of race relations in Boston several years before Garrity's court order and also contributed to the white flight developing during these years from other causes. The Jeremiah Burke High School, for example, up to 1966 was an integrated all-girls school, 20–25 percent black, about 5–8 percent Chinese, and the rest white, with a substantial representation of students of Jewish, Irish, and Italian background. In April 1968 Martin Luther King, Jr.'s assassination sparked a riot and in the aftermath, said a veteran teacher, "many,

many of the white kids left the school." Then in October the English High dress code incidents provoked "a major confrontation outside the school. . . . Then all of the white students left except for the seniors who graduated the following June in '69." After that, the Burke was virtually all black.[71]

Almost simultaneously with black student disturbances, for very different reasons, white students launched their own protests. On September 25, 1968, some five hundred East Boston High School students staged a noisy march through East Boston protesting conditions at the school. The previous spring and summer parents had complained of unsanitary, messy lavatories, and a local television program had aired their grievances. The students, however, had other issues, including poor lighting, a shortage of books and typewriters, broken desks and tables, an unresponsive headmaster, and particularly the demand that boys no longer be required to wear ties. "If the kids at those other schools can wear African clothes," said one sixteen-year-old, "we shouldn't have to wear ties." But the protest was not a show of solidarity with black students. On the contrary, leaders of the march also charged that the school's twenty-three black students received special privileges such as free lunches and car fare. And some chanted along the line of march, "Two, four, six, eight, Eastie wants to segregate!"[72]

Some East Boston parents had not yet assimilated the new order of things in the youth culture. Angry fathers and mothers stormed up to parading students and hauled their offspring out of line, taking them home or back to school. One man thrashed his son on the spot. One mother, Mrs. Rose DiTomaso, who had taken her daughter home, agreed that the school needed improvement but "all this marching" was not the solution. She also believed the boys should wear ties. Her daughter Denise thought differently about the ties, and about the marching: "It's the only way anybody listens. It's the only way to get change."[73]

Student disruptions continued over the next three years, extending beyond the peak of college and university demonstrations by blacks and antiwar students. Students for a Democratic Society (SDS) and other New Left groups attempted to recruit followers at various high schools, even Southie. In early 1970 black student protests erupted again after two black English High students were accused of robbery. Again demands arose for more black teachers and counselors, black studies, an end to discrimination against black students, and more of a student role in governance.[74]

Flowers and police at South Boston High School, December 12, 1975. Photo by William Brett. Courtesy of *Boston Globe*.

The school committee, in response to "a pattern of violent incidents both within and immediately outside" the schools, in October 1970 appointed a commission to report on violence in the schools. The commission's June 1971 report, based on questionnaires answered by several thousand students, made for depressing reading. The schools were laced with racial tension, though the commission took comfort that the "hard core haters, both black and white, are in the small minority," consisting of perhaps 10–15 percent of each group. The commission also found that drugs were "used heavily by students of all ages," mainly pills and marijuana, "sometimes on school premises." Extortion existed in varying degrees, practiced especially by youngsters who needed money to finance their drug habit. Finally, the commission concluded that "the mere presence of TV cameras and equipment was almost certain in itself to cause disturbance" and indeed that some news persons "allegedly aided and abetted some students in their acts of defiance."[75]

A year later, however, black students still staged boycotts and engaged in angry chaotic exchanges with the School Committee, while white student protests continued also, focused still on curriculum, governance, physical plant, dress codes, and such demands as smoking and telephone privileges. Whites and blacks occasionally joined forces, but "racial confrontation" such as that which brought 45 policemen into Hyde Park High in October 1972 was more common.[76]

Thus, discipline in the schools had slackened badly on the eve of desegregation, with racial tension already high, absenteeism and tardiness on the rise, and substitute teachers a mainstay of the system. A Franciscan nun who taught in a middle school in the mid-1970s described the rampant abuse of free materials and the almost perpetual insolence of some students "who refuse point blank to comply with the ordinary rules of classroom discipline and behavior, and who meet all educational efforts on their behalf with disruption." Even at West Roxbury's Shaw, a school with a good reputation, the principal disclosed a "breakdown of discipline, with assaults on teachers, attempts to set fires, extortion of money by pupils, bomb scares, [and] complete lack of cooperation on the part of pupils in apprehending the culprits." Symbolic of the new era, in March 1970 a federal district court judge ruled that a seventeen-year-old boy in suburban Marlboro High School had the right to wear his hair long and the principal could not force him to cut it. The state Secondary School Principals Association unsuccessfully appealed the decision on the grounds that it encouraged students to defy authority.[77]

Indeed, many things prompted students to defy authority, and likewise their parents. Antibusing parents recognized the changes taking place, and some of them stood four square against them. No doubt family responses to youth's new assertiveness varied widely within the ranks of militants, moderates, and the minority favoring desegregation. But most probably found themselves accommodating the new order.

Perhaps the most supreme irony of all, a "joke of history" the philosopher Hegel would have called it, was the incongruity of parental adjustment in the context of what the antibusers saw as the worst imposition on their natural rights. The alienated right most complained of was that of choosing where to send their children to school, ultimately, the right of parental control over their own children. But witness the scene as described by Lukas in Alice McGoff's household in Charlestown on the first day of Phase 2. McGoff had enrolled her three youngest in Catholic schools in nearby suburbs. Her oldest three were assigned to Charlestown High. Although antibusing leaders had called for a one week boycott and many of the McGoffs' friends were not going to go, Alice left the decision up to her kids. " 'I hope you won't go,' she said. 'It'll show the judge we mean business. *But I won't stop you. You're old enough to make up your own minds.*' " (Italics mine.) Of course, McGoff was a widow and lacked a father's presence to help enforce parental authority. That night, ailing in bed, she was unable to prevent her boys from going out into the violent streets. But the core issue of parental control surely takes on an ironic and poignant coloration in this example of domestic relations that no doubt reached well beyond the McGoff household.[78]

One year earlier, reporter Alan Lupo had stood at the communications center in City Hall known as "The Bunker" as city officials tensely awaited the first reports on day one. A policeman turned to him:"You wonder if there wasn't a better way of doing this. You hope it will go well, but I doubt it. People resent being told. Twenty years ago you could tell people to do something, but not anymore."[79]

8

Reactionary Populism

All of our nation's history since the American Revolution is studded with social movements that combined contradictory elements. Antibusing offers another case of a typical American hybrid, a populist movement with reactionary tendencies. "Reactionary populism" describes the whole of a movement that included the organized and unorganized, militants and moderates, terrorists as well as middle-class reformists respectful of democratic norms of civility. But the mix of populism and reaction varied greatly within the ranks of antibusing leaders, factions, neighborhoods, families, and individuals.

The populist character of Boston antibusing arose from the location of antibusing in the lower and middle ranks of society, from its mobilization of ordinary citizens into new avenues of participation, and from those moderate, mostly middle-class or stable working-class antibusers who were in fact reformist, egalitarian, and antielite. Militant antibusing did not challenge established structures of political or economic power, but it did spring from the bottom half of the population and exuded fierce class resentments and antielitism. Its focus on "judicial tyranny" was largely circumstantial, and not something about which citizens ordinarily felt much anxiety. Yet antibusing at all levels drew upon a widespread sense of injustice, unfairness, and deprivation of rights, which did activate ordinary people to unprecedented degrees in the 1970s.

Despite its limitations antibusing possessed many affinities with the "new citizens' revolts" of the 1970s that were directed against big business or impersonal, bureaucratic government. In a book cataloging and describing these grassroots instances of "democracy in action," movements of "neighborhood defense" figured prominently. The protests reflected, according to Harry C. Boyte, the desire of Americans on many fronts "to regain some measure of power over a world seemingly out of

172

control." Many community groups formed, as in Boston, in reaction against highway building, urban renewal, and other social engineering programs that rode roughshod over neighborhoods and ordinary people.[1]

Yet antibusers mounted no significant challenges to the axis of power in Boston that runs from corporate boardrooms in tall skyscrapers to the City Hall offices of the mayor, council, assessors, Redevelopment Authority, and other political-bureaucratic agents. The boycotts of the hated *Globe*, and of Jordan Marsh and Filene's, had not much effect. These mostly rhetorical initiatives and the withholding of contributions from United Way, as well as from Cardinal Medeiros's charities, hardly constituted economic radicalism.[2]

Nor did antibusers raise questions about the city's tax structure and its enormous reliance on property taxes; or about Boston's extraordinary amount of tax-free real estate, both private—churches, universities, hospitals, museums, and other cultural institutions—and governmental. With a tax rate of $174.70 per thousand of value, Boston spent in the early 1970s $839 per pupil, while upscale Brookline, with a tax rate of $63.50, spent $1,280 per pupil. All of the nation's forty-eight most populous cities except Boston had sources of revenue other than the property tax, but bankers and businessmen on several occasions raised big money to defeat a statewide graduated income tax. Despite their frequent fulminations about the rich who escaped busing, antibusing pols never demanded new taxes on corporations or banks to pay for improved schools.[3] Given school department waste, however, or its creation of one of the most administrator-laden school systems in the Western world, one can understand why no popular clamor existed for increasing school funding. Yet ROAR and its allies said little about the bloated school bureaucracy, and of course some of the most blatant patronage jobbers on the school committee were its most vocal antibusers. At the grassroots level, many parents were outraged by the school department's entrenched ineptitude, nepotism, buddyism, and cynicism, but ROAR and antibusing politicos made no fuss and asked for no changes.

ROAR also offered no genuine, consistent support for metropolitan desegregation—neither did the NAACP and its white allies. Yet antibusers of all kinds complained repeatedly of the injustice of the suburbs being left out of the judge's orders, and some urged expansion of METCO. But ROAR spoke out of both sides of its mouth on this issue, sending emissaries and propaganda to the suburbs to agitate suburban fears that they would be the next to be forced to bus.[4] Although the judge and plaintiffs were not disposed to move toward metropolitan remedies, ROAR made no serious attempt to address suburban exclusion constructively.

In toting up what ROAR did not do, it is important to note also that it eschewed right-wing extremists of the lunatic fringe who rushed to Boston in the fall of 1974 to capitalize on turmoil. These included a self-styled "Imperial Wizard" of the Ku Klux Klan who had no discernible following and similar ragtag elements of the American Nazi Party who entered South Boston peddling antiblack and anti-Semitic poison. The Wizard, David Duke (now a Louisiana state representative), who during the 1970s seemed always assured of media coverage despite police reports that he represented hardly anyone, walked the streets of Southie one September day, visiting bars and accosting whoever would listen. Most adults were wary and he failed to get a hall for a meeting, but younger persons got excited and by nightfall an impromptu rally of five to six hundred gathered at Dorchester Heights. There were lots of beer bottles and the garbage man gave the mostly young crowd what it wanted: unrestrained racist rhetoric. After the mob was fired up, many went off to the high school to skirmish with police. But when the Klansmen tried gathering in recruits at $3 a head the crowd's enthusiasm dampened, and it quickly dwindled.

Stripped of all the "nigger" baiting, the Klansman's message to Southie was that it needed to organize, not pursue violence. One Southie kid commented: "I think the guy is obviously a nut, but we don't have nothin' else. I guess we'll try it his way. We need organization." Southie was in fact already organized, so the Klan left Boston having contributed but a momentary titillation to Boston's agony. In contrast to the Klan, the Nazis were run out of town. South Bostonians actually demonstrated against the Nazis, and when the latter tried to open a storefront in Southie, it was picketed and soon closed.[5]

The ultra-right, paranoid John Birch Society, however, did better at attracting antibusers, some of whom turned to it for its simplistic explanation of how communist conspirators in high places were at the root of racial trouble. The Birchers made scattered converts throughout the city, but they too ran into resistance. In Charlestown a faction of Powder Keg leaders acquired a Birch film from a Boston policeman and showed it to an antibusing meeting in January 1975, but most of those present reacted with horror. Some, ironically, thought it must be a "communist film." Most Charlestown antibusers simply recoiled from such rabid hate mongering.[6]

The Boston Irish tradition had always harbored xenophobic, ethnocentric, and antiliberal strains. Even when the Boston Irish were giving big electoral majorities to Franklin Roosevelt's New Deal and toasting the rogue progressivism of James Michael Curley, part of whose appeal was a Robin Hood image of robbing from the rich to give to the poor, some still inclined to intolerance and reaction. In 1936 the isolationist, right-wing Liberty party, which equated the New Deal with communism, had run stronger in Boston than any other city, perhaps because its vice presidential candidate was a local Irish Democrat who had been district attorney for Suffolk County. The strain of antiliberalism carried through into the 1940s. Norman Mailer captured it in his classic novel of World War II, *The Naked and the Dead*, in his portrait of Gallagher, the working-class fascist from South Boston.[7]

Though their assimilation and upward mobility increased after World War II, the Boston Irish nevertheless remained insecure and defensive in their relations to other groups, whether below or above them on the social ladder. In the 1950s, of course, a new and more virulent form of anti-Communism appeared with Joe McCarthy, the Irish Catholic from Wisconsin, one of whose sometime recruits was Robert Kennedy, the Irish Catholic from Massachusetts. Shortly afterward, however, Robert's brother John, a veteran of World War II, was making an appeal based on the nationalizing and generous impulses of wartime unity.

John Kennedy was actually a rather conservative President, yet his short presidency (1961–63) ushered in an era of change, in part because of the impact of Kennedy's youthful, progressive image, and in part because of some of Kennedy's actions and rhetoric, high among which must rank his moral appeals on behalf of civil rights legislation. Obviously, many Bostonians rejected these appeals, yet others responded to Kennedy's leadership in this area and even in the 1970s continued in the New Deal-New Frontier tradition of pluralist toleration and cooperation. The Boston Home and School Association, for example, continued to work for moderate reform even as it opposed Garrity's court orders of 1974–75.

The association represented thousands of parents across the city and deliberately stressed the fact that it was "multi-racial and ethnically integrated," especially that it had black members and at times in the past had been led by blacks. In December 1974 Judge Garrity made the association, at its request, an intervener in the federal suit. Garrity never accepted the association's position, developed by its lawyer Thayer Freemont-Smith, that the court's remedy should not be systemwide but rather applied to the specific schools in which unconstitutional action had occurred. But the Boston HSA sought to advise the court and school officials on many other matters as well, including Latin School admission policies, discipline codes, safety on buses, student assignments, vocational schools, curriculum, and, after 1976, school closings.[8]

In contrast to ROAR and some local chapters captured by ROAR, the association urged parents to participate in biracial councils, indeed, to take part in any activity by which they could exert some leverage. And the HSA even criticized the excess of administrators in the school system, opposing in 1977, for example, the addition of vocational educational administrators to the central office "in a system," it said in court, "which is already top-heavy with administrators." Despite the media's association of it with antibusing militants, the Boston HSA was constructively opposed to the court orders, reformist, and according to corporation counsel Herbert Gleason, a liberal associate of Mayor White, "a responsible group."[9]

J. Anthony Lukas recently emphasized the class basis of the antibusing protest: "The federal court orders of 1974 and 1975," said Lukas, ". . . assured that the burden of integration would fall disproportionately on the poor of both races. One need not proceed from a Marxist perspective—as I do not," he added, "to observe that class is America's dirty little secret, pervasive and persistent, yet rarely confronted in public policy."[10]

From the beginning the liberal establishment has dismissed this point of view and regarded class as subordinate to race and morality. Tom Winship, *Globe* editor during the 1960s and 1970s, continued to articulate the moralist approach in a reply to Lukas: "I think he's overemphasized the class-over-race thesis. From where I sat for 25 years, if I wasn't looking at racism, I don't know what I was looking at. Racism of the rawest sense." Similarly, Robert Dentler, the architect of Phase 2 and now the principal public defender of the court's actions, scornfully discounted the class context and pointed to racism as the most important cause of violence in Boston.[11]

Lukas was hardly the first to call attention to "America's dirty little secret." Winship, despite his own views, gave free rein to several *Globe* columnists, as well as various commentators including teachers, politicians, priests, and antibusing leaders who from the beginning pointed to socioeconomic inequities involved in Garrity's orders. In October 1974 the noted pro-integration psychologist Robert Coles had dropped a bombshell in the *Globe* by writing that it was a "scandal" that busing "should be imposed like this on working-class people exclusively. It should cross these [class] lines and people in the suburbs should share in it." In December the well-known priest, sociologist, and novelist Andrew Greeley declared in the *Boston Pilot* that "it cries to heaven for vengeance that this form of punishment—and that is what it is—should be imposed on the poor and not on the well-to-do. If there is to be busing, let it be imposed on all social classes, not on those who are most ill-equipped to bear its burden." The next year New Yorker Jimmy Breslin came to town to cover busing and described it as "a Battle Royal for the poor," a fight between "two groups of people who are poor and doomed and who have been thrown in the ring with each other."[12] Meanwhile, emphasis on the class dimensions of the busing controversy increasingly found its way into scholarly books and articles.[13]

Bostonians did not need to go to libraries to get the message. Every Boston political leader who appeared before the United States Commission on Civil Rights in June 1975 argued the inequity of busing for the city's poor, from moderates such as Mayor White and school committee-woman Sullivan to hard-liners such as Kerrigan and Hicks. The message was delivered clearly by City Council President Gerald O'Leary, who began by emphatically denying that racism was behind opposition to the court order. Responding to a commission statement quoting Horace Mann about "our" bringing about unity in the schools, O'Leary asked: "Who are the 'we'? The affluent, well-to-do, or the poor? . . . Is it those least able to bear the burden who are asked to do it? When they refuse, when they stand to be counted, social theorists who live in comfortable suburban towns call them racists." Whatever the motives of those who made these points, there was much truth to them, as there was to John Kerrigan's stark summation that "the real issue is that those who can escape, escape."[14]

The most telling laments of economic injustice came from neighborhood activists and isolated and ordinary citizens. In South Boston a father whom psychologist Thomas J. Cottle called "Clarence McDonough" poured out his rage on learning that his boy had been assigned to Roxbury. "They went and did it to me," he said bitterly, "those goddamn sons of bitches."

> I told you they would. I told you there'd be no running from them. You lead your life perfect as a pane of glass, go to church, work 40 hours a week at the same job—year in, year out—keep your complaints to yourself, and they still do it to you. They're forcing that boy to go to school miles from here in a dangerous area.
>
> . . . someone's got to tell me how this Garrity guy, this big-deal judge gets all this power to push people around, right the hell out of their neighborhood, while everybody else in the world comes out of it free and equal.

"Who do they pick on?" McDonough raged on. "The rich? He picks on people right here, this street."[15]

Many letters written to Judge Garrity by worried or anxious parents asked him if he would bus his children to Roxbury, and most agreed with the answer provided by a Dorchester father: "No, you have enough money for your kids to go to a private school." A West Roxbury mother wrote similarly to Garrity suggesting that he ask himself: "Would I want my children to be subject to this unjust law, if I was a working class citizen of Boston, not a Federal Judge, that could send his children to any school of *his choice*." "You live in suburbia," wrote an East Boston mother. "I would love to live there too and have my children go to school there, but I can't because I can't afford a nice house like you have. It would be wonderful if children from South Boston, Hyde Park, Roxbury, East Boston, and the rest of the City could go to the nice suburban (or any private) schools like your kids did, and the children of Senator Kennedy and Senator Brooke and Governor Sargent—but the fact is they cannot. And, they cannot because the majority of the people who live in the City do not have the money to live in the suburban areas."[16]

Suburban exclusion from the judge's orders, of course, mightily fed the sense of economic injustice. In the 1970s the pseudopopulist Kerrigan, as Hicks had earlier, hammered away at the hypocrisy of the "lily white" suburbs. He relished taunting the suburbs with proposals to expand METCO enormously or to open suburbia to low-income housing and specifically nonwhites.[17] Though most of this was done for effect, it reflected in part the class resentment of many Bostonians.

"Suburban liberals," in particular, constituted the principal enemy of

the antibusers. The judge and other representatives of the federal government, the TV newspeople, and the *Globe* editors, along with many
Globe reporters who lived outside Boston, all were linked by suburban
residence, liberal views, and support of busing.[18] In 1973 Dick Sinnott
pointed out that the seven justices of the Massachusetts Supreme Judicial Court, the lawyers arguing for racial balance, and most of the State
Board of Education, who were deciding Boston's fate, were people "WHO
DON'T LIVE HERE, WHO WON'T LIVE HERE." Similarly, a Roslindale leader
of a local petition drive against the Racial Imbalance Act observed acidly
that "the well-fixed private school liberals with good jobs and big houses
in snob-zoned localities are summoning the public school workingman
to face the moral crisis of our time."[19]

However cynically some antibusers may have played with it, the resentment generated by suburban exemption ran deep and wide through
white Boston. Ironically, the suburbs hardly ranked as enlightened bastions of prodesegregation opinion. True, most white liberals advocating
desegregation did live outside of Boston, and significantly the overwhelming majority of letters to Judge Garrity backing him (a small percentage of those received) came from the suburbs or points west. The
suburbs, however, sheltered much diversity of opinion. After September
1974 antibusing groups sprang up in several suburbs, while some towns
had refused to open their schools to METCO. These included nearby,
working-class Somerville as well as retreats like Winchester (where, it is
said, affluent Irishmen go between retirement and death). Winchester,
after years of debate, rejected METCO participation in a referendum
only to have the school committee vote in early 1975 to bus in black
students. This evoked noisy protests, circulation of recall petitions, and
the painting of racist slogans on the driveway and car of one committee
member.[20] Such incidents only reinforced the Boston antibusers' notion
that they were being picked on and their belief that the desire to avoid
blacks was widespread in all sectors of white society. Militants sometimes told reporters: "Sure we're racists—isn't everybody?"

La Pasionaria of East Boston: Resentment Politics

*Ladies in baseball jackets, with anxious faces and "Charlestown" and
"Eastie" embroidered on their backs were cheering. . . . Pixie looked ra-
diant as a bride, svelte as a commentator. Wearing her silver top over
sleek pants, her long hair dropping danceably to her shoulders, she was*

already beginning to change. A new look, a vast world of confidence sep-
arating her from that fatigues-and-boots past. . . . She was proving that
even the ethnics of Boston can come a long way, baby, if only they are
given the opening to prove it. —East Boston Regional Review

By their nature populist movements have often launched men and
women from relative obscurity into prominence. Most of the city's
antibusing spokespersons were either established office holders or striv-
ing politicians who rode antibusing into office. Elvira "Pixie" Palladino
seemed more of a natural phenomenon, exploding on the scene from the
ranks of angry mothers who often came boiling out of the neighborhoods, cast up by the hot fury of grassroots upheaval. With her disdain
for middle-class proprieties and her fiercely aggressive working-class,
ethnic style, she embodied the fears and aspirations—and above all the
resentments—of the antibusing multitudes in as unfiltered a fashion as
any other antibusing leader.

Her grandparents were immigrants, part of the early twentieth-cen-
tury stream of *contadini* from southern Italy, her father a steady worker
in a rubber shoe factory. After graduation from East Boston High
School, Elvira Nastri worked for five years as a stitcher in a clothing
factory before marrying Nunzio Palladino, also an assembly-line worker.
In the 1960s, as her two children entered the same public schools which
she had attended, Pixie joined the local home and school association,
headed a Brownie troop, and managed one of the first girls' ice hockey
teams in the area. By 1966 her HSA activity had carried her into the
ranks of Louise Hicks's cadres opposing the Racial Imbalance Act, and
she trekked with them each year to the State House to testify against the
bill.

She enlisted in another front line of neighborhood defense when the
Boston Redevelopment Authority proposed Infill Housing, a plan to
place low-income housing units on small sites scattered throughout the
city. To block the possibility of blacks and other minorities coming in,
Palladino worked with the "SAVE EAST BOSTON" group. In 1971 Palladino's neighbors elected her president of the Cheverus-Bradley-Guild
HSA, and before long she was the best known of Eastie's antibusers. As
the campaign for repeal of the imbalance act intensified, so did Pixie's
commitment and anger at those responsible for it—blacks, liberals, suburbanites, and especially upper-class politicians. Her tough, street-talk-

ing, macho manner could be balanced with humor and even flirtatious charm. Pixie, however, could say just about anything to anybody at any time or place, damn the consequences. Italians in Canarsie, according to Jonathan Rieder, "embodied the hard, rowdy side of backlash because history gave them resources of symbolic and physical toughness, because their social standing left them vulnerable to competition from minorities, and because their values bred hostility to the permissive currents of modern culture."[21]

Palladino often trod roughly on black sensibilities, and on one occasion, in the middle of a "peace" meeting at City Hall in the fall of 1974, she shouted and pointed her finger at Melnea Cass, the gentle, grand old black lady of Boston civil rights. Critics loved to tell of how she spat on a priest—Monsignor Mimie Pitaro. Pixie's defenders explained that she had made instead an Italian "kiss of death" sign (it could have been a southern Italian gesture). It might well have been Palladino, too, who stood up in the gallery of the State House on the day Pitaro voted for the Racial Imbalance Act and yelled, "Sleep well, you creep." Feared and disdained by her enemies, Palladino was admired by antibusers for "having guts" and for being "not scared of anybody." "Pride in guts," said Rieder, "marked the exuberance of the plebeian who had launched a strike against powerful interests."[22]

There were many shouters and screamers among frustrated antibusers, but few were as focused as Palladino, especially in the presence of TV cameras. Representing East Boston on ROAR's executive board (with her twin sister Rosamond "Trixie" Tutela, in whose house she lived), Pixie often spoke up as the point person for demonstrating mothers. When John Kerrigan decided to move on from the school committee, he urged his friend Pixie to run for his seat on the committee.

Even before gearing up for a political campaign, Palladino had gained more visibility by her dogged and virulent harassment of Senator Edward Kennedy. Since the September 9, 1974 episode on City Hall Plaza when the ROAR crowd had humiliated him, Kennedy's visits to Boston had been attended by antibusing demonstrators determined to embarrass him further. Pixie ranked first among his tormentors, hounding him like a banshee. In February 1975, at a hearing on air passenger fares in the Federal Building, Palladino led a shouting outburst that featured such declamations as "We never took a plane in our lives and we can't afford it. What about forced busing?" The worst incident came in April in

Quincy when Palladino's shock troops forced Kennedy to flee under police escort to an MBTA station where the pursuing mob threw stones at the train.[23]

Palladino campaigned essentially as a one-issue candidate. Like her mentor Kerrigan, she found the *Globe* a useful foil and ran against the media even while benefiting from its coverage. With a classic Italian-American working-class concern for early job security (and not college education), Palladino tried to diversify her appeal by stressing improved vocational schooling to insure high school graduates good jobs. But her platform was basically a fundamentalist revival of Hicks's stands back in the 1960s. Frightened and frustrated white Bostonians knew where Pixie stood.[24]

To her antimedia posture Pixie added populist and class themes, portraying herself as a champion of "the little people" who was looked down on by the liberal establishment. When critics wondered if someone with only a high school education should serve on the school committee, Palladino struck back at the "class snobbery that questions my qualifications." In good populist style, too, she inveighed against politicians and represented herself as nonpolitical. After her election she recoiled from being labeled a "school committeewoman," saying "I'm a wife and a mother and I worked hard for my title as homemaker."[25]

Of course Pixie's family had already benefited from the patronage line that ran from City Hall through Louise Hicks: her husband now had a city job, and Kerrigan had found her daughter a job in the School Department. But Pixie motivated squadrons of women to go out and work for her on election day, not just in Italian Eastie but also in Irish Southie. They urged voters to pull the lever for "Hixie and Pixie" because they believed that the East Boston scrapper was one of their own.[26]

Thus did Palladino become the first East Bostonian and the second Italian-American elected to the at-large school committee, no small feat in a citywide election in which Irish names usually dominated. Her exultations over her victory as a triumph of "little people" contained much truth.[27] Palladino's rise to the school committee seems inconceivable, however, without the powerful dynamic of the antibusing anger raging through the city.

In some ways she did not fit the mold of the conventional backlash candidate. Unlike Hicks, Pixie exuded no aura of conformity to religious pieties. She admitted, for example, that her Catholic devotion consisted of infrequent attendance only on major holy days and ceremonial occasions. She departed from the church's teaching on birth control as well as abortion, and she thought the Vietnam War was a bad cause—another example, as she saw it, of the government having too much power over the lives of its citizens. While Pixie was no feminist, she nevertheless was highly unusual among Italian-American working-class women who, even of the middle class, had been among the least likely to venture "out of the kitchen" and into political activism. Palladino and her sister enjoyed the advantage of acquiescent husbands and households that in their families had been organized traditionally around dominant women. (Nunzio, who "gives her a hand with the vacuuming," would have preferred things otherwise, but "we sat down and talked," he said. "She knew what she was getting herself in for, and I didn't complain.")[28]

Election to office brought some polish to Pixie's rough edges, but not a complete severance from the roughhouse tactics of political incivility. When in February 1976 two hundred ROAR rowdies invaded a meeting of the City Coordinating Committee at English High, forcing chair Arthur Gartland to end the proceedings before they began, a satisfied Pixie stood smiling on the stage as the CCC people stalked out.[29]

Palladino was a second generation antibusing leader, one created by the movement itself. Though her ties to politicians were closer than they seemed, and she too played political footsie with Mayor White, she transmitted a successful antipolitical appeal in 1975 and personified better than any other antibusing leader the essence of reactionary populism.

Her pugnacious style was pure backlash. She could be as crude and insensitive to blacks as Kerrigan or "Dapper" O'Neil, though unlike them she sometimes denied that she was prejudiced. What came through most strongly from Pixie Palladino's wide-ranging array of furious resentments, however, was a ferocious anger toward upper-class types such as Kennedy and Garrity and those she scornfully called "the beautiful people." The Kennedys, she said, like upper-class Yankees, look down on *"people of color like me."*[30] (Italics mine.) In other words, these class and status enemies regarded working-class Italians like Palladino, in her mind, as an inferior caste, like the blacks. Society's pecking order of status groups clearly put blacks and Italians like herself near the bottom. The fancy Irish and the high-toned WASPS found it fashionable to patronize the blacks, but the Italians were simply a negligible lower caste to be ignored and avoided. Underneath the guts and the bravado, it seems, lurked a deep social insecurity and sense of vulnerability typical of those on the margins of respectability.

Fear of Blacks

I was borned [sic] in Roxbury on Blue Hill Avenue 40 years ago. A person would either happen to be insane or want to commit suicide to travel in that area today. I moved to Mission Hill . . . when I started High School. To me, that was God's little acre until the projects, two (2) behind the church and one (1) in Jamaica Plain, became non-white. When I was living there, there was no such thing as locked doors or being afraid to walk the streets at night. . . . Now the priests are warning the old people not to come to daily mass because of rampant crime . . . i.e., muggings, stabbings, etc. My parents still live in fear with double and triple locks on their doors. —J. P. K. to Judge Garrity

Two years earlier, this letter writer told Judge Garrity, his brother had been knifed by two blacks who tried to rob him while in his car stopped at a traffic light. The brother died a year later. "What the real problem is [*sic*] a tremendous clash in cultures, economics, etc." Not all white Bostonians victimized by black crime, or feeling vulnerable to it, were able to muster that degree of dispassionate analysis.[31]

In the 1960s Louise Hicks had become the darling of fearful whites who admired her for standing up to black civil rights leaders' demands. Hicks's firmness contrasted with the permissive toadying of white liberal leaders. A Pixie Palladino exuded not only the Hicks posture of "standing up to them" but, in addition, conveyed even more. In a situation in which, in the words of an astute school administrator, "the average white person is scared shitless of blacks," Pixie came across as an intimidator. And to whites who felt fearful and intimidated, this was profoundly satisfying.

Fear of black crime would have existed in Boston without an antibusing movement, but the long-running controversy over the schools made everything worse: fear, actual crime by blacks against whites, white retaliation, or, in some cases, preemptive strikes, white terrorism, and white perceptions of black lawlessness and amoralism. In 1974 the antibusing movement circulated police statistics showing that black areas of the city were much less safe than white, and that fall Hicks, Bulger, and Representative Michael Flaherty of South Boston issued a statement regarding Roxbury, "A Declaration of Clarification," that became a lightning rod of contention. It outraged blacks and liberals by asserting that "there are at least one hundred black people walking around in the black community who have killed white people during the last two years." Crime within Roxbury was such that "no responsible, clear-thinking person . . . would send his child there." The South Boston leaders called on black leaders to find means to end "the routine violence which ravages the black community. Any well-informed white suburban woman does not pass through that community alone even by automobile. Repairmen, utilities workers, taxi-drivers, doctors, firemen all have refused at one time or another to do what Judge Garrity demands of our children on an everyday basis."[32]

The antibusers had hold of part of the truth. Blacks did commit violent crimes (e.g., aggravated assault, rape) disproportionately. But most of those crimes were black on black. White perceptions of robbery and burglary, however, were squarely on the mark. Most of these crimes did involve blacks on whites, because whites tended to have more valuables and blacks could steal in white areas bordering black and then disappear into the ghetto.[33] Whites believed that such crimes happened rarely if ever in white bastions such as Southie or Charlestown, which is not to say that tough white districts did not suffer from their own crime problems. But whites tended to think of white enclaves as safe, and their patterns of life seemed to contrast starkly with the disorder they saw prevailing in black areas.[34]

Fear of black crime ran through many of the letters written to Judge Garrity during 1974–77, particularly in those sent by many elderly persons. They told of being mugged, beaten, hospitalized, or of witnessing beatings, and also of the sad process of neighborhood change. "They (the colored people) made a hell-hole of Mission Hill so let them stay there." They wrote of the even sadder mutation of acquiring hatred and prejudice: "I liked them at first but when I saw their savagery I had no use for them." Some merely vented their fears but others told of personal experiences, not perceptions, but lived realities.[35]

The national economic downturn of the early 1970s and the rise in unemployment and drug use made street crime worse. And since the 1960s, the middle classes generally had seen the legal system and courts growing permissive and "coddling criminals." In 1973 white perceptions of black crime had intensified considerably in Boston because of two particularly brutal murders committed by black teenagers. In October, twenty-four-year-old Rene Wagler, living in Roxbury in a women's integrated collective, had run out of gas a few blocks from her apartment. Returning along Blue Hill Avenue shortly after 9 P.M. with a two-gallon can of gas, six young blacks set on her, dragged her into a vacant lot, doused her with the gasoline, and set her ablaze. Four hours later, with virtually no skin surface left, she died at Boston City Hospital. Two days earlier, ABC-TV had shown the film "Fuzz," which included scenes of white delinquents on the Boston waterfront torching homeless tramps for kicks.

Two days later, Louis Barba, a sixty-five-year-old retired contractor and lifelong Boston resident, was fishing at the Pleasure Bay Pond behind the Columbia Point housing project. A large gang of black youths began to stone him, then stabbed him to death with his own fishing knife. Shortly after, a twenty-year-old white cab driver, working to raise college tuition, was found stabbed to death in a vacant lot in Roxbury. These murders shocked white Bostonians just as the decade-long desegregation controversy approached a climax. To make matters worse, black leaders expressed no regrets but rather anger at the disparity they saw in the attention given by the police and media to white and black deaths.[36]

The Wagler-Barba murders formed part of the background of the Southie "Declaration" on black crime. Three black teenagers were arrested in the Barba case, none in the Wagler. At a meeting in Southie in December 1974, as parents voiced a long litany of concerns, one asked: "What about the white woman who was burned to death in Roxbury? The murderers haven't been caught yet. How do we know they aren't right here with our kids?"[37]

In Charlestown white youths reacted immediately to the Wagler murder by attacking the few blacks who lived there. Black aggression against whites in Charlestown was as rare as white aggression in Roxbury—it did not happen. Yet Alice McGoff's daughter Lisa revealed to Lukas the nightmarish fears that haunted her in anticipation of black students' arrival in Charlestown. Rumors ran about that blacks would come riding into town shooting anyone they saw. "A few kids went down to the bridges to serve as lookouts, and for nearly a week many project families . . . slept with baseball bats by their beds." No carloads of blacks showed up, but Lisa and most of her friends believed that "when the buses came, the black kids would step off armed to the teeth and ready to rumble. She believed that most black boys were out to molest and rape white girls, that black girls would attack white girls in the ladies' room, and that blacks of both sexes carried knives, razors, scissors, stickpins, and other weapons."[38]

Ironically, the worst fears of white parents for their children who would be bused to schools in the ghetto probably were the most exaggerated. Many of those schools, due to the efforts of their staff, black parents, and young black social workers, proved to be among the safest in the city. In January 1975, white parents connected with the Massachusetts Experimental School, whose children commuted to Roxbury from several neighborhoods, issued a statement declaring that their children had been attending schools in Roxbury for five years and more, and that the whites had been safe and "welcomed in the community and in its schools." The Experimental School parents said they were distressed by all the talk about the dangers of sending white children into black areas: "These stories are frightening and we know they are not true."[39]

The schools in which white children seem to have had the most trouble with blacks appear to have been those on the borders of black and white neighborhoods or those which had been white but, because of white flight, rapidly became preponderantly black. It appears that black children often entered mostly white schools feeling insecure, and as such places "tipped" rapidly, the blacks then went on the offensive. Conversely, black parents sending their children into white bastions had just as much reason to be afraid. In Southie and Charlestown, for example, blacks were subjected to deliberate harassment. Inevitably, the blacks fought back and sometimes it was in a more potentially deadly fashion. Only whites, after all, were stabbed or hit with heavy metal objects such as a padlock or shop hammer. These incidents led antibusing whites to feel justified in their claims about black violence. In Canarsie a major source of opposition to busing "lay in the apprehensions of white parents about exposing their children to tough lower-class kids. While racism and hysteria inflated those fears, the nervousness was based on a realistic grasp of the greater proficiency of lower-class children in violence."[40]

Fear of Change: The Reactionary as Conservative

If the major newspapers and local television stations played down black aggressions in the schools, as antibusers claimed, one journalist in Boston, Dick Sinnott, did persistently call attention to black attacks on whites. Sinnott unflaggingly criticized busing, liberals, the media, and the suburbs, and was perhaps the most popular print spokesman of the antibusing legions. His column appeared regularly in the *Transcript*, serving West Roxbury, Roslindale, and Jamaica Plain, the *South Boston Tribune*, *Charlestown Patriot*, *Dorchester Argus-Citizen*, and a dozen other neighborhood weeklies, including the *Post-Gazette*, which circulated widely in the suburbs. Sinnott also came to be a fixture for several years on local television news shows as one of the few media representatives of the antibusing position.[41]

Sinnott's education and career had led in conservative directions. After attending various business colleges, with a stint at the University of Wisconsin Naval Training School, he spent eleven years as a reporter for the Associated Press, and in 1959 he became press secretary to Mayor John Collins. In 1969 Kevin White appointed him city censor and chief of the licensing division. In his last four years as a reporter, Sinnott had served as New England entertainment editor and thus knew show business. It seemed fitting that the man who served as the city's moral watchdog, holding the gates against obscenity and pornography, also expressed so effectively the reaction of white neighborhoods against Boston's desegregation. The connection between the general backlash against the social and cultural changes of the 1960s and the specific white backlash against black militance that Hicks had embodied in the 1960s found perhaps its fullest articulation in the 1970s with Sinnott.

In 1974 Sinnott lived in Hyde Park and had four sons in the public schools. Two of them were in Boston Latin, but he pulled out the youngest two and sent them to Catholic schools. Though Sinnott had grown up in Dorchester, his roots ran straight back into the antibusing heartland: his father boasted of his Townie origins while his mother hailed from Southie.

Sinnott once described his readers as "mostly 40 or older. Bostonians who were affected by the Depression and who fought in or vividly remember World War Two, and/or the Korean War. They remember FDR and Alfred Landon and Wendell Wilkie and Harry Truman, they liked Ike and they used to boo when Herbert Hoover's face appeared on the Pathe news."[42]

For these people black militancy, affirmative action, and forced busing were part of an entire syndrome of social malaise rampant since the 1960s. On a broad range of issues Sinnott voiced the anxieties of the vulnerable lower-middle and middle classes: excessive rights for criminals, insufficient protection for victims, restoration of the death penalty, opposition to gun control, abortion, and pornography. It was not so much Sinnott's ideological consistency that mattered to his readers, however, but rather his ability to articulate their frustration, anxieties, and anger. As one older West Roxbury couple wrote to him, "When we read your column, it is like hearing an echo of our thoughts."[43]

Sinnott persistently opposed the Racial Imbalance Act and court orders of 1974–75. After 1974 he frequently championed ROAR, though he also boasted of his independence of any group and even complained of receiving hate mail from South Boston because he was not militant enough for some diehards.[44] In fact, Sinnott never advocated boycotts, for example, nor did he ever defend unruly demonstrations or violence. On the other hand his rhetoric was often strong, and he sometimes implied that the antibusers might be justified in engaging in civil disobedience or disruptive protest.

Reaction against the 1960s ran through Sinnott's columns like a compulsive refrain. Sometimes implicit, more often it came through in explicit contrasts between the "decent," middle-class Bostonians and the protesters of the 1960s who trashed property and violated laws almost with impunity. In his most widely read column written soon after Garrity's June 1974 decision, Sinnott tried to respond to the calls, letters, and pleas of those he encountered every day asking what they should do. In a grim, sardonic tone, Sinnott said he thought that most of us, with great reluctance, would comply with the law. "After all, we are law'n order persons, now aren't we?" And it was the law, he continued, "a rotten law" that "we will spend every day, every night, every moment fighting to repeal."

The middle-class "law'n order" people deserved better, said Sinnott. They were the backbone of the country, "the ones who enlisted in the Army and the Navy and the Marines on December 8th, yes 8th 1941. We're the poor sunavabees who pay our taxes and sweat tuitions, sweat mortgages and car payments and the cost of groceries and fuel, get no hand outs, give our blood, take our turn in line, volunteer for charities, and work two jobs, sometimes three." But our government was treating us with utter contempt, shipping our children here and there to satisfy the whims of social experimenters, none of whom live in the city—"and you, you are a cipher." "Praise Angela Davis! Hurrah for Ellsberg! Feel sorry for poor Patricia Hearst! But the poor, battered, bruised white Bostonians. Forget them."[45] Sinnott's readers loved it, and the *Transcript* reprinted the column five weeks later, as did other publications, notably the police union's *Pax Centurion*.

Sinnott rarely let slip a chance to bash "suburban liberals" and "the media" who, from their "safe sanctuaries" outside Boston, indulged themselves in telling us "what 'racists' we are, what 'bigots' we are because we object to forced busing. And they go home to their Newtons, their Wellesleys, their Marbleheads, their Braintrees—their rinso white communities—where a select few minority kids come out and spend six hours in their schools but are forbidden to live there."[46] Yet Sinnott never showed any interest in metropolitan plans of desegregation, in part because he believed that they never had a chance.

Sinnott epitomized what happened to the Democratic party rank and file in the 1960s and 1970s. He had grown up in an Irish Catholic household in which "FDR was next to the Pope." But backlash against the Democratic party's identification with blacks, minorities, and protesters in the 1960s had carried Sinnott into the ranks of those conservative Democrats who had begun voting for Republican presidential candidates by 1968. The imposition of busing on Boston in the 1970s, which he regarded as one of the most misguided policies of liberal social engineering, cemented his defection from liberalism and the national Democratic party.

Powerlessness and Voice

We're voicing our opinions for once. It should be heard. —Donna Glynn, April 4, 1973, Roslindale housewife

We have had no voice in this decision. —Stella Brown, Sept. 9, 1974, Charlestown activist

The people of this city feel in their hearts that they have no effective voice or spokesman before your court. —Rep. Raymond Flynn to Judge Garrity, Oct. 16, 1974

We can no longer be lambs, but lions who come forward to have our voices heard. —Louise Hicks, Mar. 26, 1975

There is frustration on several levels . . . unemployment, the economic crunch, Vietnam, Watergate, poverty, a feeling that they have no voice in their own destiny. —Rev. Robert J. Boyle, Sept. 20, 1975

The antibusers' complaints that they lacked "voice" tapped into attitudes as powerful as any other in motivating protest and generating widespread discontent. Having no voice meant that they were essentially powerless; not being heard was the condition of those who were being unjustly imposed on by a too-powerful government and what they saw as the arbitrary whims of an appointed federal judge. It meant, as Sinnott said, that they were "the outcasts of the 70s."[47]

Thus, the name of the principal antibusing organization, Restore Our Alienated Rights, symbolized the attempt to find a voice that would be heard by "the system." The seemingly perpetual motorcades, originating mostly in South Boston but drawing out frustrated and angry parents from every neighborhood, in their own way signified the same effort to create enough sound or noise that would somehow crash through the walls raised against them. The motorcades invariably went their way honking, blasting on their horns in endless cacophony. One Roslindale activist told me of banging her horn so loudly and often that it broke off. Hyde Park leader Richard Laws recounted the story of a friend's young daughter who was with her family in a funeral procession and wanted to know why all the cars were not honking their horns, because she had been in so many motorcades "night after night after night" with horns blaring away. Thus did those who felt voiceless "sound off" and vent their frustration.[48]

The sense of powerlessness felt by antibusers was observed repeatedly by reporters and public officials. Mike Barnicle of the *Globe* described a Hyde Park housewife in 1973 who joined the April demonstration and tried unsuccessfully to talk with Mayor White. "Rita Rushton," he said, "is no hater. She isn't a bigot. She isn't a racist. She worries about the five kids she's got in this city's public schools and another one in college. She worries about a husband who works hard to pay the mortgage and keep the groceries on the table. And Rita Rushton walked out of Kevin White's office feeling just as powerless and as alienated as she had when she woke up five hours earlier."[49]

Often when ordinary people participate in some kind of public action in a departure from habitual inattention, their sense of efficacy increases. For many citizens moved to antibusing protest, however, this boost never came. Constance Maffei, a Roslindale moderate, in September 1974 decided to sign a public letter opposing school boycotts, but did so with a "very hopeless feeling." "There's a general depressed feeling here," she said, "that we don't count anymore." An official at Charlestown's Kennedy Family Service Center had urged many to "take part in this busing situation" as a way to defuse anger and potential violence, but he observed that after many persons took part "they realized they were powerless to act. Whatever potential for violence there is reflects this degree of powerlessness."[50]

Perhaps the most eloquent testimony to the feeling of powerlessness was a letter to Judge Garrity from a distraught parent who never used the word. The man simply told in meticulous detail, in capital letters, of an assault on his son by three black youths in a lavatory at Madison Park High School resulting in the fifteen-year-old white youth running home with an injured left eye. The father told of his visits to hospital, school, police station, federal building downtown, and elsewhere, of lack of redress, and of his request for a transfer. Denied, he would keep the boy home. The father said he represented no group and had written on his own. His letter constituted a hymn of rage, resulting from an inability to do anything, or even to get anyone to listen.[51]

In a similar vein an older couple wrote to the judge about receiving a busing assignment for their only son. They described a life of good citizenship as volunteers helping with the elderly, charities, and the like, while in recent years noticing "a slow erosion of . . . freedoms along with a decline in the morale and morals of the people. We now realize we should have spent our time opposing this federal government. . . . We feel the federal government has gotten too much power, but we feel powerless to fight it. When we received this student notification our spirits were almost broken. We shall not obey this dictate, but rather, we shall move away."[52]

Antibusing leaders had been warning of the dangers of a too powerful government for years. "If under a court order a child can be forcibly taken from his parents into unfamiliar, often hostile neighborhoods," said Louise Hicks, "then we shall have opened a pandora's box of new, unlimited government powers." Many of the angrier letter writers to Judge Garrity accused him of acting in the mode of a Hitler or Stalin. Others complained of judicial "tyranny" or expressed their bewilderment and rage at one man having so much power and acting like a "dictator." "My goals?" fumed Peg Smith of Charlestown: "I want my freedom back. They took my freedom. They tell me where my kids have to go to school. This is like living in Russia. Next they'll tell you where to shop."[53]

Antibusers somehow managed to play humorously with the theme of big government as various flyers—most probably produced at the SBIC —testify. One, "A WHITE CHRISTMAS?????," began: "We have been informed that a 'White Christmas' would be in violation of Title 2 of the

Civil Rights Act of 1974" and that "All Christmas trees must have 23% Colored Lights and must be placed throughout the tree and not segregated in back." Another told of a man going into his neighborhood tavern to get a beer and being told he had been "reassigned" to a bar in Chinatown.[54]

Political Consequences

Since 1964 one politician at the national level had been campaigning for the Democratic presidential nomination with appeals to just this syndrome of powerlessness and frustration with big government, along with tapping into the reaction to the black push for equal opportunity. George C. Wallace, the Alabama governor who had raised a ruckus with his vow to "stand in the schoolhouse door" to prevent the integration of the state university, had entered Democratic primaries that year and shocked liberals and political observers by scoring heavily in several border and northern states. In addition to symbolizing resistance to black demands, Wallace sounded the theme that "power has passed from the people to the government."

In 1968 he ran as a third-party candidate and garnered 13 percent of the vote nationally, attracting both Democrats and Republicans. Yet in Boston Wallace ran behind his national average at only 5.9 percent. Even in the two South Boston wards, he managed only 9.7 and 9.2 percent, his best showings in the city. Wallace ran best, however, in areas where antibusing or racial tensions were building. Crippled by an assassin's bullet in 1972, he watched helplessly as Nixon pursued a "Southern strategy" and established himself as an antibusing candidate, thereby winning over many potential Wallace supporters, especially from the Democrats. But the pugnacious, bantamlike Wallace was back in 1976, campaigning again in the Democratic primaries. He had little chance of winning the party's nomination, but this was the candidate who habitually exhorted the resentful or alienated to "send them a message."

Wallace supporters' leading attribute, according to a detailed study of them, was that they felt powerless. In responding to Wallace, "they are demanding that the system operate in a legitimate fashion, rewarding effort and faithfulness, distributing goods and services equitably. . . . there is only so much to go around, and governmental response to civil rights demands means that one's 'share' has to be jealously guarded, as blacks are perceived as getting more than what rightfully belongs to them." Compared to Humphrey and Nixon voters in 1968, Wallace voters also tended to be the most antiblack on all measures of racial attitudes. At the same time, Wallace backers did not differ much from Nixon and Humphrey voters on most demographic measures, landing "solidly in the middle," while issues relating to powerlessness distinguished Wallace voters best.[55]

In 1976 Wallace came to South Boston as the champion, as Sinnott might have said, of the enlisted man. He campaigned mostly in and around Boston, speaking not only of antibusing but also of the "survival of the middle class," speaking to cheering crowds of antibusers and to the discontented. Wallace's crowds relished his bashing of "exotic liberals" and "ultra elitists," while he tapped deep discontent over a troubled economy and impersonal government. "He can appeal to people who feel they've been cheated and put upon," said one reporter, "because he feels that way too." His attraction was not just racist, another journalist agreed, but expressed a traditional antigovernment syndrome. "He is anti-media, anti-Establishment, anti-urban, anti-authoritarian, anti-intellectual and anti-foreign," said the *Globe's* David B. Wilson, "and he plays those themes on the heartstrings of the earth's rejected."[56]

Wallace faced weighty competition for the antibusing vote from Senator Henry "Scoop" Jackson of Washington state, a well-known conservative Democrat and advocate of military might and toughness toward the Soviet Union who also staked out a strong position opposing busing for racial balance. Jackson, however, had sponsored a bill to provide federal aid to districts undergoing desegregation and that incurred the wrath of the irreconcilables. In a primary with five Democratic candidates representing a cross section of the political spectrum, Jackson carried the state with 23 percent of the vote, while Wallace came in third with 17 percent (Morris Udall was second with 18 percent, Jimmy Carter fourth with 14 percent). In Boston, however, where the liberal wards tend not to turn out well in primaries, Wallace won almost 29 percent of the city's vote. To no one's surprise, the Alabaman ran extremely well in South Boston, winning over 68 and 61 percent in the two Southie wards. He rang up 44 percent in Charlestown, and also did well in East Boston, Hyde Park, Dorchester, and West Roxbury. Together Wallace and Jackson, two firm antibusers, won over 80 percent in Southie's Ward 6. Citywide they combined for a hair less than 50 percent of the total.[57] The Wallace tally was very much a protest vote. A CBS/*New York Times* poll revealed that less than half of Wallace voters believed he could win the presidency, and nearly two-thirds refused to name a second Democratic choice, far more than among those who voted for any other candidate.[58]

The sense of alienation to which Wallace appealed reflected itself during these years also in a rising unwillingness of voters to make choices in local elections. In 1975 Mayor White, for example, squeezed out a narrow victory (52 percent), as discontent with candidates and with city government generally, along with many antibusers' refusal to vote, caused an astounding rise in the number of blank ballots. But the trend had been under way for years. "Neither of the above" in effect rose from 2,764 in 1967, to 6,066 in 1971, to almost 10,000 in 1975.[59]

Voter apathy would remain a chronic problem in most cities, but by the election of 1977 the antibusing fury had finally run its course in Boston city elections. As recently as 1975 every candidate for local office had needed to recite a pledge of allegiance to antibusing. But in 1977 school committee moderate Kathleen Sullivan became the leading vote getter. Pixie Palladino was narrowly defeated for reelection, while the first black in 75 years was elected to the committee. John Kerrigan was soundly defeated in a bid for a second Council term, and most astoundingly, Louise Hicks finished just out of the running in the council race. A political era virtually ended.

In a relatively high turnout for an off-year election Palladino missed reelection by less than one hundred votes and was replaced on the committee by John O'Bryant, a black who had first run in 1975 and who became the first black to serve on the school committee since 1901 and the first ever to do so by a citywide election. O'Bryant had drawn upon a solid base of black and liberal votes, bullet voting in the black precincts, and the blessing of Mayor White and his organization. He may have benefited too from the Irishness of his name (seasoned political observers believed that some who voted for him did not know he was black).[60]

Kerrigan's demise had been expected after revelations that he had maintained a Waltham woman on the city payroll as his legislative aide for fifteen months at $300 a week whose principal responsibility had been addressing Christmas cards. More surprising had been the erasure of Louise Hicks, who just two years before had still been the city's top vote getter in the council race. Hicks could still place fourth in the September preliminary without campaigning, but in November suddenly

Hicks was tenth and off the council by a mere 128 votes. For years she had told people there would be no busing. "Well," said one councillor, "of course there is busing and she has no other issue." As Hicks's star fell, that of her young South Boston rival rose. Ray Flynn, former state representative, made a strong second place showing in the council race, but no longer because of antibusing. Instead, he had identified himself with antiabortion and as a hard worker and had projected a "more reasoned opposition" to the court orders.[61]

The election had been enlivened by a referendum to change the mode of electing the council and school committee from at-large to a combination district and at-large. Each would elect nine members from districts equal in population and four at-large members. A state legislator from Brighton, William Galvin, had proposed this change—Brighton having sent none of its residents to the council for over two decades. The plan had the backing of most liberals, the *Globe*, blacks, most candidates for office in 1977, and twenty-eight of the thirty-five members of Boston's delegation to the legislature. The city's leading antibusing officeholders opposed it and in the referendum vote, majorities against the plan rolled in from South Boston, East Boston, Charlestown, Hyde Park, and, as before, West Roxbury. The Galvin plan failed, however, even as some of its most prominent opponents lost at the polls.[62]

So 1977 did mark the point at which the "school bus as an easy vehicle to office has apparently run out of gas." Kathleen Sullivan had been the lone moderate arguing that while she disagreed with the court orders, the school committee had a responsibility to carry out the law. Hard-line majorities, however, had forced Judge Garrity to assume ever increasing responsibility for running the schools. Now, all committee electees agreed with Sullivan's position. The handwriting had been on the wall all during the campaign, as no candidates had promoted themselves solely as antibusing. And while the district plan lost, the neighborhoods were already restless over the White administration's emphasis on downtown development, seemingly at their expense. Several neighborhood activists either won or ran very well in the election. Busing would probably never be accepted by a majority of Bostonians, said one reporter, "but inevitability has set in. People are beginning to realize there are things the City Council can and should do. Haranguing U.S. District Judge W. Arthur Garrity, Jr., while city streets remain unplowed is not one of them."[63]

The political fallout from the desegregation controversy hardly ended with the subsiding of the obsession with antibusing in local elections. The discontent that Wallace had exploited continued to percolate in presidential elections and to bedevil the national Democratic party. Though Boston lagged behind the rest of the nation in turning away from the Democrats, its vote over the period 1960 to 1984 still traced the collapse of the Democrats, as well as the decline in turnout that has marked modern politics. In 1968 Boston still voted heavily Democratic and Richard Nixon was still unpopular (table 8.1). Even in 1972 Nixon, now an incumbent president with a weak Democratic challenger (McGovern), managed to win only a third of Boston's vote. But in 1976 Gerald Ford, an accidental president with limited appeal, won over 35 percent. The 1976 vote clearly registered the dissatisfaction with the Democratic party caused by the desegregation controversy.

The two Reagan elections also highlighted the backlash of 1976. As early as 1975 the former Hollywood actor and California governor's campaign for the Republican nomination began to attract attention among Boston's antibusers, who loved his antigovernment rhetoric and of course his opposition to busing.[64] Reagan's 1984 vote in Boston of 36.2 percent actually surpassed Ford's, but that reflected the general approval accorded Reagan and his landslide win that year. More significant was his poor running the first time in 1980, falling behind Ford's 1976 showing in votes and percent.

By 1984 Boston remained comfortably Democratic, but the Democratic vote had fallen by eleven points since 1960. Only three wards of twenty-two actually ended up in the Republican column: 6 and 7, the two South Boston wards (with part of Dorchester in 7), and 20, West Roxbury (with part of Roslindale) (tables 8.2–8.4). In 1976 South Boston went Republican, and the other wards that voted more Republican than the city average included most of the hard-core antibusing areas. By 1984 the Democratic percentage in wards 6 and 7 had dropped by 46.9 and 44.4 points, respectively, since 1960.

The change came later in West Roxbury—a slight plurality for Reagan in 1980 and then a small majority in 1984 (51.4 percent), for an overall drop of 18.7 points since 1960. While Irish Catholics generally remained a Democratic group, they were far less Democratic than earlier, particularly in Boston. The tug of disaffection could be powerful: one moderate antibuser of West Roxbury who had been "normally Democratic," a backer of progressive Michael Dukakis for governor and liberal enough to vote for George McGovern in 1972 because of his opposition to the

Table 8.1. Boston Presidential Voting, 1960–1984

	Democratic party	%	Republican party	%	Third party	%	Other parties	Total
1960	218,422	74.4	74,086	25.2			923	293,431
1964	220,007	86.1	34,583	13.5			898	255,488
1968	171,250	75.3	41,562	18.3	13,363	5.9	1,332	227,507
1972	139,598	66.2	70,298	33.3			1,043	210,939
1976	115,805	60.4	67,604	35.3			8,242	191,651
1980	95,133	53.3	58,656	32.9	22,577	12.6	2,127	178,492
1984	131,745	63.4	75,311	36.2			743	207,799

Table 8.2. Ward Six, South Boston Presidential Voting, 1960–1984

	Democratic party	%	Republican party	%	Third party	%	Other parties	Total
1960	8,659	88.1	1,160				11	9,830
1964	7,446	90.1	808				14	8,268
1968	5,731	77.9	886	12	718	9.7	20	7,355
1972	4,261	61.4	2,652				30	6,943
1976	2,733	40.6	3,735	55.4			273	6,737
1980	2,224	37.5	3,169	53.4	472	7.9	65	5,930
1984	2,821	39.2	4,291	59.6			27	7,199

Table 8.3. Ward Seven, South Boston Presidential Voting, 1960–1984

	Democratic party	%	Republican party	%	Third party	%	Other parties	Total
1960	11,111	87.5	1,572				17	12,700
1964	9,971	89.4	1,161				16	11,148
1968	7,676	78.9	1,135		898	9.2	18	9,725
1972	6,077	64.8	3,258				35	9,370
1976	3,933	45.4	4,410	50.9			328	8,666
1980	3,507	44.4	3,713	47.1	579	7.3	92	7,891
1984	3,863	43.1	5,070	56.5			34	8,967

Table 8.4. Ward Twenty, West Roxbury Presidential Voting, 1960–1984

	Democratic party	%	Republican party	%	Third party	%	Other parties	Total
1960	15,279	67.1	7,407	32.5			91	22,777
1964	17,036	79.4	4,338	20.2			81	21,455
1968	15,155	67.8	5,663	25.3	1,444	6.5	94	22,356
1972	12,265	56.3	9,429	43.3			82	21,776
1976	10,780	51.3	9,511	45.3			713	21,004
1980	8,540	41.7	9,267	45.3	2,457	12	196	20,460
1984	10,225	48.4	10,875	51.4			45	21,145

Vietnam War, voted for Ford in 1976 and even Reagan in 1980.[65] Thus, while Democrats suffered their heaviest losses in working-class wards, significant erosion took place in middle-class areas. While Boston remained a Democratic city because of the big cushion of anti-Republican votes with which it began, in the rest of the nation these kinds of changes spelled disaster for Democrats in presidential elections for most of the period after 1964.

In the 1980s the populist manifestations of antibusing could take a variety of forms. In 1983 Ray Flynn became the first South Bostonian elected mayor based on a campaign solidly rooted in the neighborhoods and a coalition that included progressive populists attracted by Flynn's substantial commitment to fairness. The preliminary election had been a contest between Flynn, longtime black activist Mel King, whose "Rainbow Coalition" offered an even broader democratic appeal than Flynn's, and David Finnegan, former school committee member and talk show host with heavy backing from businessmen and developers. The final was a Flynn-King runoff, a campaign notably free of racial tension, marked by cordial competition between the two men. Flynn won, carrying 80 percent of the white vote.[66]

Critics have argued that Flynn's populism was flawed by narrow concentration on economic problems shared by poor blacks and whites and a failure to acknowledge institutional racism. Yet Flynn immediately served notice that his administration would not tolerate attacks on blacks and that he would reach out to minorities. Soon he had compiled a better record in hiring minorities than Kevin White, whom angry whites had derided as "Mayor Black." In 1987 Flynn committed his administration, before the election, to desegregate public housing, beginning in South Boston. This sensibly held off federal action against Boston and the loss of substantial state and federal funds. Though Flynn won reelection easily, his Southie neighbors gave him "the back of the hand" —they were the only wards he lost—and soon angry whites were shouting racial epithets at Flynn. Yet during 1988 and 1989, token public housing desegregation moved forward, slowly but without incident, in Southie and Charlestown.[67]

The limits to democratic populism imposed by the context in which former antibusers lived and worked is perhaps best shown by the case of Dan and Nancy Yotts, former firebrands of the South Boston Information Center. Like Ray Flynn, the Yotts's embraced rent control, affordable housing, and jobs, but also did not stop at questioning "who was making the money when triple-deckers were refurbished and turned into condominiums, and who was displaced."

In 1985 Dan, allied to Flynn, had become executive director of the South Boston Community Development Corporation. He made enemies by opposing development of the billion dollar Fan Pier, projected for thirty acres between Southie and downtown, which Dan said would be good for businessmen but not for Southie because it would bring in heavy traffic and drive out low-income people. Alan Lupo noted that some politicians who had opposed busing "were now leading the charge" for the Fan Pier, which "threatened Southie's working stiff population more than busing ever had." Nancy too stepped on toes, particularly those of saloonkeepers and their political allies, when she won a fight to revoke the liquor license of the Lithuanian Club, which she argued had become a gathering spot for drug dealers. After Nancy said that "the drugs are coming right out of the gin mills," the Yotts's home had eggs thrown at it and windows broken.

In 1987 life in their cherished South Boston became unbearable after Dan spoke his views candidly in an interview with the *Boston Ledger*. He described Southie as a "feudal" system controlled by the two Bulger brothers, Senator Bill ruling most legitimate aspects, while brother James J. "Whitey" Bulger, a known underworld boss, oversaw most illegal activities. It was hard, said one reporter, to find anyone "who categorically disagrees with that oversimplified analysis." But few would say so publicly. Dan also said that some public housing residents should be evicted because their income levels were too high, and that, yes, the projects should be desegregated. With this came nasty phone calls and then, after coming home from church one Sunday morning and finding their car tires slashed, the Yotts's decided to leave.[68]

Perhaps more representative of those who persisted in South Boston was James Kelly, formerly of the SBIC and ROAR, who won election to the city council as a district candidate in 1983. Kelly's antibusing fervor remained undiminished, as did his opposition to anything smacking of affirmative action. Some black leaders regarded him as an unreconstructed racist, a belief rekindled in 1988 by Kelly's taking the lead against the desegregation of public housing under the familiar banner of "freedom of choice." Yet Kelly's "fight" now was emphatically not in the streets but in the courts and through the media, and there were no incidents when the first black family moved in.

Even Kelly's severest critics conceded that he worked extremely hard in responding to people's everyday needs in his district. "Constituency service," said Kelly, "is not philosophical." This self-described "union-oriented Reagan Democrat" could take surprising positions, advocating the cause of midwives at Boston City Hospital, for example, or joining a fellow councillor, a gay, in promoting a human rights ordinance.[69]

Kelly had changed in other ways too. Although Kelly cultivated a populist reputation as a champion of the "little people," he favored commercial and industrial development, saying it could be controlled and that new housing would just bring in more "outsiders." Critics pointed out that Kelly had not supported rent control nor placing limits on conversions of three-deckers into condominiums. They charged that many "little people" were being driven out of triple-deckers (and seeking public housing) because of real estate interests from whom Kelly had received more contributions than any other councillor during the past year.[70] Thus the legacy of antibusing in the 1980s seemed as contradictory as the movement itself was in the 1970s. That is in keeping with the nature of reactionary populism.

9

Battlegrounds

*All persons entering the main building on L-Street must pass
through metal detectors as a condition to entering the building. Students and others must surrender items listed in the laws of Massachusetts, Chapter 269 . . . not exclusive of the following: firearms of any
kind; any knives; razors, or other objects sharpened into blades;
clubs; athletic equipment, such as baseball bats, hockey sticks; um-
brellas, karate sticks; moon chucks, or rods of any kind; pipes, brass
knuckles, and other metal objects; screwdrivers, wrenches, hammers,
or other metal tools; chains; whips; ropes, or any combination of objects fashioned into such; combs and picks with metal teeth; rattails;
scissors; metal nail files; hat pins; mace and other chemicals such as
spray paint and spray deodorant; bottles and cans; alcohol; illegal
drugs; fireworks. Possession of any of the above may result in suspension. —South Boston High School Weapons Policy, 1975*

In the end, it was a war nobody won. The antibusing movement failed
in that Judge Garrity's decision withstood all the appeals mounted
against it in the courts and streets. Not for eleven years did Garrity
withdraw and turn immediate responsibility for the schools back to the
school committee. Yet as one ROAR activist claimed later, with only
partial inaccuracy: "We never gave up. We won. We prevented it for
eight years [after 1965]. . . . *His* [Garrity's] *program was never a success.*"[1] (Italics mine.) Indeed, the resistance resulted, particularly if white
flight is counted as one expression of antibusing, in schools that by the
1980s were more highly segregated by race than before. They also were
more lopsided than ever—debilitatingly so—in the lower-class composition of their students.

Garrity and his advisers did try heroically to improve the Boston
schools, and in some cases succeeded. The "quality education" they pro-

moted often meant curriculum changes and inculcation of values that one would find prevailing in middle-class schools. Ironically, their constituency became less middle class all the time, and frequently working-class parents simply did not want fancy curricula.[2] Though desegregation was far from a universal disaster and many schools and students enjoyed good experiences over the next decade, no one looking at the schools in the 1980s could avoid asking if the results on balance justified the costs, not only the dollars spent but the social and psychic costs, especially the pain and disruption caused to thousands of families, white and black.

The antibusing militants' warnings of "resegregation" proved all too accurate, but of course they had labored mightily to make it so. Though many factors contributed to white flight, the opponents' prophecies had been self-fulfilling. Both moderate and militant antibusers predicted white flight and resegregation. Many moderates tried to stem the tide. The militants' actions often promoted it, and with grim satisfaction they blamed white flight on the judge, blacks, and busing.

"That's what the whole anti-busing movement is based on," said one young mother, "a situation is set up which seems to prove the things they want you to believe." She offered in example the case of her child's school where the black kids who were bused in left fifteen minutes early. The principal thus made only white kids stay and clean up. This caused resentment against the blacks. "They were only little kids and they didn't say, gee, the teacher should find a better system that's fair. What they'd say was those lucky black kids get out of work." Worse, a rumor spread that black children were defecating in the sinks. She thought, "that's crazy, that can't possibly happen." It turned out that plumbing problems in the school were causing waste back-ups in the sinks. But some whites in and out of the school spread the story because it fit their "preconceived ideas that black kids are animals or some other ridiculous thing."[3]

The principal battlegrounds, of course, were the neighborhood high schools of South Boston, Charlestown, and Hyde Park. These schools became symbols of defiance in which the antibusers tried to prove their point that busing could not work. On these testing fields militants combated desegregation with orchestrated campaigns of turmoil, which prevented the establishment of peace and order, let alone education, within their tense classrooms. Their corridors bristled with fear and aggression and became the front lines of collision between blacks and whites, where children and teenagers carried out the trench warfare launched by the anger of alienated, recalcitrant adults. Having "lost" these schools to desegregation, the militants' first response was to make them not worth having because of the trouble that came with them. Eventually, they would not be worth having—at least as examples of successful desegregation—because not enough whites stayed to create racial balance.

The contested schools constituted only a minority of all schools, as probusers tirelessly observed. Yet the troubles in those arenas spread out like ripples in a pond, adding to the climate of violence and to the many independent chains of attack and retaliation excited among whites and blacks across the city.

From the very start hot debates raged over how well desegregation worked. Everyone agreed that three high schools were notoriously troublesome, as were several middle schools. Although student suspensions had fallen during the second year, assaults on teachers had increased threefold. But the index regarding assaults was laughable and a result of laxer standards, since some students who had assaulted teachers were not even suspended. Of course, many schools and children were unaffected by the violence and hatred. During the first two years, some schools at all levels desegregated peacefully and provided adequate educations, while others successfully combined desegregation and improved education. Student witnesses before the United States Commission on Civil Rights in June 1975 gave upbeat reports on the first year at the Jeremiah E. Burke High School, during which, one black girl testified, "as the year progressed, we talked and we got to understanding, and we found, like, a common ground."

A year later the mayor's task force on violence reported that 150 of 165 schools appeared to be functioning smoothly, a fact which the panel urged be given greater publicity. Yet the mayor's committee also observed a significant lack of communication between white and black students in most schools, and when the Commission on Civil Rights later that summer issued its report—also claiming that desegregation overall was successful—political leaders across the city, including Mayor White, criticized it as inaccurate and misleading.[4]

Evidence that desegregation and education proceeded successfully in many pockets of peace across the city came from reactions to the court's proposals to close schools in 1977 and 1979. Ironically, the reasons the court targeted schools for closing often bore a relation to their success, as many tended to be older, underenrolled elementary schools. Consequently, they enjoyed stable populations that were usually integrated. The parents involved with these schools, serving in HSAs or on the court's Racial Ethnic Parents Councils (REPC), along with faculty, staff, and neighborhood groups, rallied to their support with pleas that they remain open, praising not only their educational value but also their racial harmony. In 1977, even in South Boston, for example, the HSA officials of the Oliver Hazard Perry School described it as having good, safe education and a stable enrollment of 33 percent black, 10 percent Hispanic, and 57 percent white, while "running well with no racial problems, no incidents, and no suspensions for 1976–77."[5]

But white flight made debates over the effectiveness of desegregation pointless. Just because they anticipated trouble, many white parents went to extraordinary lengths to protect their children, sending sons or daughters to live with relatives as far away as Ohio and Florida. Some parents simply feared violence without necessarily expecting that blacks or whites would be responsible. Given the fear and tension abroad, this was often a reasonable expectation. Some white parents feared blacks, specifically poor, ghetto blacks, and they feared neighborhoods they saw as "high crime" areas. Other whites feared blacks in ways that were wholly unreasonable and let themselves be governed by self-justifying racist fantasies.[6]

White parents also withdrew their children from the system after negative encounters with blacks. It is impossible to estimate what part of white flight resulted from such direct experiences, but they did contribute and also must have had a ripple effect. Some of these stories appeared in the newspapers, though not enough to suit the antibusers.

Many parents, and a few students, also wrote to Judge Garrity telling him of assaults or harassment: the fifteen-year-old junior on her own attending classes at Roslindale and South Boston who found it difficult to pay attention because of constant tension, who did not regard herself as prejudiced, and who found it trying "when I'm told (in exact words) 'I'm gonna' kick your ass, bitch,' when I'm just minding my own business" and racially motivated harassment kept on; the Roslindale father who described the Philbrick School as racially imbalanced with more blacks than whites, with blacks given preferred treatment ("let's keep peace") while white children were unsafe going to restrooms and in the school yard, with blacks not allowing whites to participate in games, white children ganged up on, in his view the "school totally taken over by blacks"; the Hyde Park antibusers and parents who lamented the racial attack on seven "of the outstanding 10th graders" at Rogers Hyde Park Annex who had now left the school; the West Roxbury mother of a fourteen-year-old boy beaten by two blacks wanting a quarter, the day after he missed school because the bus did not show up, "no explanation, therefore no school"; the Hyde Park mother whose daughter's bus was stoned by blacks and who now suffered from nightmares and other emotional upsets; the West Roxbury parent whose five children had already attended the Shaw School, now majority black, whose sixth, an eleven-year-old, had known many anxious mornings and had now been assaulted twice; the Dorchester father whose boy was attending Dorchester High, which instead of being 52 percent white was 65 percent black, and which would soon be 70 to 80 percent black, where a black "in jest" pulled a knife on his son and was told to put it away by a black aide, where his son and two others had their pockets emptied by blacks during a fire drill; and the Boston father whose daughter came home needing three stitches in the back of her head.[7]

Several parents repeated the theme that "it's common knowledge that the lavatories in some of these schools are manned by young toughs who demand money from kids that have to use them." "I don't care what color my kid is sitting next to," wrote one Roslindale mother, "as long as he gets the education. . . . I'm willing to work at living together in peace and harmony but *I don't want my kids hurt* in the process."[8]

White parents often complained too of the "foul language" to which desegregation exposed their children. One Hyde Park mother wrote to Judge Garrity sarcastically thanking him for her daughter's quick maturing: "If it were not for busing she would not learn such phrases and words (to mention a few) as FUCK YOU, YOUR MOTHER SUCKS, YOU HAVE A BLACK CUNT/DICK." The mother had tried to keep her daughter relatively innocent, "But I guess nine years is quite old enough."[9]

In a 1977 Thomas Fleming novel set in Albany but very much about Boston, the liberal, Anglo-Protestant wife of a pragmatic Irish mayor tries to soothe fears over busing in a blue-collar, ethnic neighborhood. In an auditorium filled with a crowd of Irish, Italian, and Polish parents, one angry mother demands:

"How are the kids gonna learn when half the class is a bunch of ignorant niggers?"

"Now, now, let's have a little order here," Marie McKenna [the mayor's wife] said.

"Please don't use that word—I think it's very important to start using the right words in this argument. Black Americans, Afro-
Americans."

"They call us honkies," Helen Karpinski said. "My husband's on
the cops. . . . He gets called a honky bastard every day."

"There are stupid people—I mean angry people, people saying the
wrong things—on both sides. But we should set an example, I think."

"Why?" Helen Karpinski said. "My kids don't use the kinda language their kids use. One word, the worst you ever heard in the English language, in their mouths all the time. A word that accuses people of—of rapin' their mothuhs. I don't want my kids goin' to school
with people that use that kind of language. I'll take forty, fifty, sixty in
a class rather than expose them to that kind of language."[10]

As important in stimulating white flight as negative encounters with
blacks was the silent, corrosive resistance of a large part of the school
administration.[11] In their brief for desegregation, *Schools on Trial*, Garrity's experts Robert Dentler and Marvin Scott charged that "the school
committee and its agents" resisted desegregation continuously from
1974 through 1980 by providing faulty student enrollment data; by not
building new facilities or repairing and maintaining old; by opposing
school closings and maintaining thousands of excess seats; by allowing
the school transportation system to be plagued by corruption and mis-
management; and by simply evading the requirements of the court in
constituting schools and hiring teachers.[12] Some of these actions promoted white flight, some did not. Particularly harmful was the corruption endemic in the bus companies, which was probably worse during
these years and which especially outraged parents.

Even more damaging to implementation and education was the continual reassignment of pupils during the first three years of desegregation, which, together with curriculum changes, made for a chaotic lack
of continuity in students' lives. The judge and his advisers extended the
turmoil of year one by creating a new plan for Phase 2. By early 1976,
however, the judge recognized the need for stability and in issuing a plan
for the fall of 1976 called it "2B" to signal that he was responding to a
widespread parental and teacher demand for continuity.[13] Yet in both the
spring of 1976 and 1977 letters flooded into Garrity's office (and calls
and letters into school administration offices) regarding assignments.
The protests often came from women and men who were the back-

bone of the school system, active in HSAs, or the court's REPCs. A sad letter came to Garrity that summer by way of Dentler, to whom it originally had been sent, from a previously committed foot soldier in the struggle for desegregation: "I am getting out of the Boston School situation. We were promised that this Phase would be only a dotting of the i's, a crossing of the t's. But the turmoil goes on—kindergarten, transfers of Bi-lingual Students." Admittedly there now was more quality education than in years. "But it goes on and on. The litigation has taken on a life of its own. I have abandoned my plan to try to induce White parents to return to the Boston Schools. Why should they? At least at St. Mary's of Brookline their stomach is not constantly churning."[14]

In the mid-1970s two views of white flight existed in Boston. One, held by leading probusers and Garrity's closest advisers, denied that significant white flight was taking place. Thomas Atkins of the NAACP, Martin Walsh, a former Jesuit priest in charge of the Justice Department's Office of Community Relations and a Garrity confidant, and court experts Dentler and Scott all minimized the degree of white flight. As late as the fall of 1976 Dentler denied any white flight. Questioned by reporters just as he was about to board a plane at Logan Airport, Dentler joked that the only flight he knew about was an airplane leaving Boston. These men pointed to the academic studies of their choice, such as those by Harvard's Thomas F. Pettigrew or Boston University's Christine H. Rossell, that found in comparative studies of cities undergoing desegregation that court-ordered busing had "little or no effect" on white flight.[15]

A second, more widespread view prevailed among the parents and politicians of Boston and, it should be added, most outside journalists. Estimates of white student flight for the first year commonly ranged from eight to ten thousand.[16] Later it became apparent that most of the larger estimates were inflated because the school system had initially provided inflated figures of white student enrollments for the point at which desegregation began. Despite this, and taking into account the fact of a long-standing decline in white enrollment in the schools that began before desegregation and was due to other causes, white students exited the system after 1974 at far higher rates than previously and the loss attributable to busing, while hard to measure precisely, had to be substantial. By 1978, as Rossell pointed out, most studies of white flight now showed that in the first year of implementation rates of white departure increased substantially. The debate would seem to have ended completely when in the 1980s even Dentler and Scott finally admitted that in 1975 they did not foresee the scale of white flight and were tempted to downplay its importance in public, that it in fact "reached a high velocity in 1975," and that white flight could account for at least half of the total white loss from the schools during 1974 to 1980.[17]

A systematic study of students who fled into Catholic schools during the first two years of busing has conservatively estimated the number to be no less than two thousand—some estimates have ranged considerably higher. In any case it is now generally accepted that substantial numbers went into parochial schools despite Cardinal Medeiros's directives to Catholic schools not to exploit busing and not to accept students whose transfers would aggravate racial imbalance. Virginia Sheehy complained of church pressure "which makes you feel immoral. It's the law, they say. . . . I tell them I never read a commandment saying, 'Thou Shalt Bus Thy Child.' It's not the law. It's an interpretation of the law. Some people have moved already. Some have their kids in parochial schools, despite what you read in the papers. Someone has a friend or knows a sister. You know, there's politics in the church too."

Certain urban and suburban schools became known as havens for whites seeking refuge from busing. In the novel *Firewatch*, the following conversation takes place between a school guidance counselor and a priest. The latter has just admitted that enrollment in Catholic schools has increased.

> "But that's unofficial. His Eminence would rather we didn't profit from desegregation."
> "But you have profited?"
> "As a good soldier who follows orders, I have to say we don't fill our schools at the expense of the desegregation plan. On the other hand, as the pastor of these people. . . . Well, it's very hard to turn away mothers who come to you with tears in their eyes, literally. 'My son's the only white in his class. He's been beat up. My daughter—' Well, the stories get worse. How true are they? I don't know. But just the fact that people tell such stories, I often feel obligated to make room in our classes."[18]

No doubt the causes of white flight will continue to be debated, but there is no debate about the composition of the Boston schools in the 1980s and little about their lack of quality. In 1973 roughly 60 percent of the students in the public schools had been white. By 1980 the percentage had dropped to 35, by 1987 it was 26, and many of them were concentrated in certain elementary schools, Boston Latin or East Boston, that had experienced minimal busing. More importantly, the socioeconomic level of the school population, low before the court orders, had also fallen steadily: by 1985 a staggering 93 percent of Boston's students came from families with incomes low enough to get free or reduced price lunches; 60 percent of school families made less than $15,000 per year. By 1988 nearly 40 percent of the system's ninth graders were dropping out before graduation, while 43 of the system's 120 schools did so poorly that they qualified for special state aid because of low student scores. Middle-class blacks who lived in the city tended to send their kids to private schools as well. During the eleven years of supervision by Judge Garrity and Professor Dentler, the white and black middle classes, some already with fragile commitments to the public schools, had abandoned them in droves.[19]

Despite this massive liability, many good things had happened: some downtown businesses and higher educational institutions had forged closer links with the schools, at least for a time; new coalitions of parents and teachers had formed; more minority teachers, principals, and administrators had been hired; and some schools functioned more effectively than before.[20] But the indices of social decay, unfortunately common elsewhere in urban America in the 1980s, were too painful to be ignored.

In 1979 it was estimated that on any given day in the city an average of 14,000 students were not in school. During 1981 to 1985 over two-fifths of the students entering high school dropped out; most of the girls exiting did so because of pregnancy. About 12,000 kids (of 58,000 in 1987) had some sort of special needs; 2,500 were on court probation; one parents' group estimated that 46 percent "need remediation and probably cannot read their textbooks with understanding"; though Boston students constituted only 7 percent of all pupils in Massachusetts, they accounted for 19 percent of all children on Aid to Families with Dependent Children; and during 1986–87 school officials confiscated two hundred knives and forty-eight guns from students.[21] The list could run on. These were not just Boston but national urban problems as well. But the sad and apparently ineluctable effects of massive segregation by class were all too obvious.

By the 1980s, in fact, resegregation and dismal conditions had led some black parents of school children to plead for a lifting of the student assignment system. In 1982 a *Globe* poll found rampant disappointment among black parents, with four out of five favoring open enrollment over the current court-ordered assignments. Blacks favoring the court plan had fallen from about half in 1974 to 14 percent in 1982. The original fourteen plaintiffs from the 1972 NAACP suit had dwindled to only three with children in school, all of whom shared blacks' general unhappiness, while two of them also now preferred freedom of choice. Thomas Atkins, now at the NAACP national office in New York, opposed this shift, but the plaintiffs' lawyers on the scene, Robert Pressman and Larry Johnson, a black, in September 1982 filed a motion with the court asking for a "freedom of choice desegregation plan."[22]

The gargantuan irony of this was not lost on anyone familiar with the Boston saga. "Freedom of choice" had been a shibboleth of the anti-busers. After eight years of court-ordered desegregation, 80 percent of black parents and the remaining black plaintiffs were asking for the same thing. Not for another six years would the courts and school committee, prodded by Mayor Flynn, act to set in motion the process needed to change the system.

If the schools in which blacks found their children in the 1980s prompted disillusionment, the societal setting of those schools hardly struck them as the promised land. In the late 1970s racial violence in Boston's streets had persisted, with incidents involving whites attacking blacks running abnormally high. In housing projects across the city whites waged campaigns of terror to drive out black families. Violence ebbed and flowed in the schools as well, with the fall of 1979 bringing stonings of buses at Southie, the shooting and paralyzing of a black football player at Charlestown, the stabbing of a white East Boston student with a hunting knife, and many other incidents in and out of the schools. Parts of the city were still off-limits to blacks, while whites hardly ventured into Roxbury or black sections of Dorchester.[23]

Finally, in the 1980s racial violence began to subside, and the 1983 election campaign set a new tone of civility in race relations. In 1983, too, Boston changed to a mixed electoral system of at-large and district representation, and several blacks won election to the school committee and council. Soon, the city had a black school superintendent.[24] Yet for most of Boston's black population, life in Boston often looked the same or seemed worse. No change had registered in the index of residential segregation between 1970 and 1980. In 1980 blacks were twice as likely to be unemployed than whites; in 1985 four times as likely. "By every negative social indicator," observed Alan Lupo, "poor housing, school dropout rates, high infant mortality, low income, unemployment, jail sentences—blacks were outpacing whites in Boston."

Although a black now sat in the rarified chambers of a club of elite business executives known as "The Vault," blacks' progress in corporate Boston was difficult to measure. By 1985 the number of black workers in city and state jobs had risen dramatically in the last three years, but even though the economy was booming the percentage in private companies actually had dropped. The Vault itself had instituted a program to recruit minority members to entry-level management positions, but John Larkin Thompson, President of Blue Cross and Vault director, acknowledged that the program had not yielded significant results. Even the improved climate that Flynn had fostered seemed to be at least partly a media creation. In 1987 a *Globe* poll found that blacks were decidedly less upbeat than whites in perceiving better relations in the city. More importantly, a 1989 study by the Federal Reserve Bank found that black neighborhoods suffered from a racially skewed pattern of lending by banks, thrifts, and mortgage companies.[25]

Lack of progress for most blacks in Boston was hardly unusual but resembled the national pattern over the past twenty years: the emergence of a small but significant black middle class and continuing discrimination against and submergence of a large black underclass, which was increasingly ravaged by drugs and crime. The Boston scene may have had perhaps fewer bright spots than cities with larger black populations, but the incongruities of Boston seemed all the more striking because of all the costs incurred in the attempt to reform the schools, enhance equality of opportunity, and, as a by-product of course, change society.[26]

In December 1982 Judge Garrity took the first steps to remove himself from the Boston schools, whose functioning he had guided in detail since 1975. Having issued some four hundred orders during that period, he now turned monitoring of compliance over to the State Board of Education for the next two years, reserving the right to reenter the case should school officials or the city demonstrate noncompliance. Almost three years later, in September 1985, Garrity issued his "final" orders, giving the schools back to the school committee and retaining only standby jurisdiction over student assignments, faculty composition, the condition of school buildings, parental involvement, and vocational education.[27]

Long before Garrity withdrew, popular verdicts on busing had been coming in. Locally, calls to scrap busing from those who had previously supported or accepted it had mounted during the early 1980s. The *Boston Herald*, never enthusiastic, often suggested that something else be tried. In December 1982 it grudgingly conceded that Garrity had succeeded in breaking down barriers of segregation and improving education but that forced busing had little positive effect on either of those two accomplishments. The progressive journalist Alan Lupo, writing in the *Phoenix* in 1983, labelled busing "an effort at tinkering, and tinkering solves very little." The next year visitors to South Boston High School found that racial tension there was no longer news: rates of disturbance and suspension had fallen into the middle range of Boston's schools. The 30 percent white contingent was the highest proportion of whites in any neighborhood school, and at least it co-existed with blacks (42 percent), Hispanics (15 percent), Asians (12 percent), and native Americans (1 percent). But "the problems of racial tension in America have not been solved at the school," where students came and went from their separate neighborhoods and whose families' median incomes were the lowest of any high school in the Boston metropolitan area. By 1986 Hyde Park High School was 82 percent black, "basically a black school." One black parent wondered: "What good is putting a black child in a white school if the educational standards don't stay high?"[28]

Judge Garrity and his experts bore large responsibility for the outcome, a responsibility, however, that too many tend to forget was shaped by the reckless, self-serving actions of school committee members over many years. Garrity's decision finding the school committee guilty of discriminatory practices was made inevitable by the flagrantly racial practices of committee majorities over a decade. When the state courts earlier had forced development of a desegregation plan by the state board, the committee refused to modify it in any way. After taking fourteen months to craft a purist's decision that would stand the scrutiny of higher courts, Garrity had little time to think about the consequences of the specific remedy he ordered to be visited upon thousands of people. Garrity found it irresistible to adopt a plan already ordered by the state court, thereby bringing together the authority of state and nation. Unfortunately, the populace acted on by this joint authority failed to be impressed, if they did not miss the point altogether. Garrity would have been wiser to consider deleting the part of the plan that paired the high schools of South Boston and Roxbury.

If not dropped altogether, why could this pairing not have been postponed a year, allowing the rest of the city to desegregate without being influenced by the certain explosion that was bound to erupt from Southie? Why could not seniors have been allowed to graduate from the schools they had attended already? Why did the South Boston-Roxbury students need to make three major changes in three years? "What suburbs," asked Southie teacher Ione Malloy, "would tolerate their children going to three different schools in three years?" Why did two areas of the city with the highest rates of unemployment, areas among those with "mortality rates far higher than in regions the Federal government routinely declares 'natural disaster areas' following some calamity of nature," areas which scientists had dubbed "death zones," need to be thrown together to discharge the national commitment to desegregation? The judge did not see, as one Hyde Park mother observed, that the children "are only going from one ghetto to another."[29]

During the years 1974–77, the Roxbury-South Boston pairing was counterproductive, making desegregation overall look worse and function less well than it would have otherwise. A principal author of the state plan, Charles Glenn, later admitted the pairing was a mistake, and no less an ardent supporter of the court than *Globe* editor Thomas Winship called it, in retrospect, "a dirty trick" and "an unfair burden on both neighborhoods."[30] No one responsible for imposing busing thought that the protests would last as long as they did. Once the troubles at Southie High became prolonged, however, the court ignored suggestions that it be closed and moved to a neutral site, so Southie militants possessed for as long as they wanted a stage on which to dramatize that busing would not work.[31]

Garrity's revision of the masters' plan for Phase 2 owed nothing to the school committee and its years of wrongdoing before 1974. The revised plan, devised by the court's experts, again launched massive reassignments and again the world of Boston's public school parents and children was turned upside down. The judge's choice here symbolized to his critics his reliance on a small circle of advisers who were nonresidents of Boston and widely perceived as cosmopolitan outsiders. Besides Dentler and Scott, Garrity relied heavily on the ex-Jesuit priest, Martin Walsh, who came to Boston in November 1974 to head the U.S. Justice Department's Community Relations Service. Like Garrity, Walsh lived in suburban Wellesley, which did not endear him to neighborhood leaders, some of whom saw him as "bumbling, incoherent and sanctimonious." Like Garrity, Walsh was perceived as "out of town, and out-of-touch."[32]

Judge Garrity has also been criticized for not taking firm enough measures with antibusers, particularly with regard to boycotting and violence. Of course the mayor, police, and municipal judges also bore responsibility for the high level of disruption in Boston, and high levels of unemployment also contributed to the intensity of protest in working-class neighborhoods. Denver, a relatively affluent city, desegregated its schools at the same time as Boston without violence or outbursts of racial hatred. U.S. District Judge William E. Doyle ordered gradual integration there, but when antibusers called a boycott, Doyle issued a series of restraining orders that effectively squelched the boycotts. In Boston, Corporation Counsel Herbert P. Gleason, a supporter of desegregation, wondered about Garrity's reluctance to do so: "I am not the only one bewildered by his [Garrity's] willingness to issue orders requiring people to do things that are more disturbing to their lives than anything that has ever happened to them . . . at the same time he is extremely reluctant to issue orders which could limit people in conduct far less significant to them, which is calculated to interfere with the execution of the other orders he has issued."[33]

Garrity watchers were perplexed also by his forging of an alliance with school superintendent Marion J. Fahey during 1975–76. The year before the school committee had voted not to renew the contract of Superintendent William J. Leary, whom the committee perceived as having shown too much independence in implementing desegregation. Fahey's promotion was regarded as engineered by John Kerrigan, whose interest in patronage jobbing was well known. But Fahey soon began to cultivate the judge and Garrity went out of his way to praise Fahey, who brought in a safety plan creating two hundred new jobs, including fifty-three new administrative posts. Shortly after, moderate school committee member Kathleen Sullivan stood up in Garrity's courtroom to say that the judge's confidence in Fahey was misplaced. She called the safety plan a "patronage grabbag" and asserted that the jobs generated would go largely to cronies of Kerrigan.[34]

In September 1976, four distinguished panelists led by Illinois's superintendent of education, Joseph M. Cronin, delivered a report on the school system, which they had been asked to prepare by the Mayor's Committee on Violence. The panel's

> most negative and depressing finding so far was [that] the patronage method of making appointments still pervades the Boston school system. Friends neighbors and relatives of School Committee members

ask for and get special consideration for jobs. Who you know often counts more than what you know. . . . Job and employment questions pervade and poison the entire operation. . . . The result is low morale and cynicism by teachers and parents and substandard performances by many midmanagers in the system. An excellent person or good performance at a school or department is often unobserved or lost or even punished.

All this held true, said the panel, for the most recently elected committee, which continued to inculcate "going along with the system" and to engage in ticket selling for dinners to give committee members "times." The panel criticized Superintendent Fahey for demoting several able administrators while nominating for promotion several "of questionable competence." The panel conceded that the quality of her nominations had recently improved.[35]

Given Boston's political culture, if busing created patronage bonanzas for school administrators, it naturally became a golden opportunity for other city employees to profit from its implementation. The blame for this, of course, hardly rests with Judge Garrity and his advisers. Primary responsibility lay especially with the school committee, which, for example, made contracts with bus companies run by cronies and riddled with inefficiency and fraud. From 1974 to 1977 a pattern prevailed of "overpayments, haphazard administration and legal problems that . . . triggered court suits involving millions of dollars" and every major bus company hired by the city. Most owners of the bus companies, ironically, lived in the suburbs outside Boston. But some hard-line committee members may not have minded these problems, since they may have wanted to run up big bills. Kerrigan allegedly said in December 1975 that "the only way we will beat desegregation is to bankrupt the city."[36]

Police overtime was the most expensive part of desegregation: in the first year, for example, desegregation's total cost was $21.2 million, with police overtime accounting for $13.3 million. Policemen often experienced severe stress on busing duty, but many welcomed the fat paychecks that enabled them to buy cars and other big ticket items. One officer named a new fishing boat "Phase I" and was looking ahead to acquiring a summer cottage that would be called "Phase II." Police overtime was a true windfall, but some other city employees and several elected officials simply took advantage of chaos to steal something.[37]

The attitude of the judge's advisers toward these tangible costs sometimes seemed insensitive. Robert Dentler and Marvin Scott were costing a minimum of $56,000 a year, submitting bills that the judge ordered the city to pay without review. Dentler, not known for his humility, seemed arrogant to many and often struck a high moral pose toward his critics. Martin Walsh, when told that the first four years of desegregation had cost the city $77.1 million, loftily replied: "You can't put a dollar value on correcting constitutional wrongs. Correcting the wrongs of the past has no price tag."[38]

Most of all, antibusing protest might have been dampened by Judge Garrity's taking stronger measures with the recalcitrant majority of the school committee in 1974–75. They certainly gave him every reason to hold them in contempt of court, but at the moment of truth Garrity demurred. The committee's flouting of the court's authority could only have added to the disrespect for the law in Boston in 1975. Kerrigan and his crew won their bluff—they certainly had no desire to go to jail or even to pay fines. Jail would have cost them dearly, and the real possibility of disbarment for Kerrigan could have induced him to jump through hoops for the judge.[39]

In the final analysis the court's responsibility for perpetuating the antibusing movement will always be less than that of the antibusing political entrepreneurs who promised "never" and then exhorted their frustrated followers "to stick together and fight." Moreover, Judge Garrity occupied an unusual position as virtually the only "scapegoat" for a legally necessary and highly unpopular social policy. By scapegoat I mean in this case less one who is sinless or a sacrificial offering than one who functions primarily as a "heat taker." In the past quarter-century elected officials increasingly have succeeded in channeling tough issues away from the political arena and into the courts. Politicians do this primarily because it is in their interest to avoid taking clear positions on controversial issues, which often spells the difference between surviving or failing politically. Since judges are usually immune to the electoral process, they function for executives and legislators as convenient heat takers.[40] Judge Garrity ended up taking much abuse that should have been directed at the school committee or others. In desegregation, implementation depends heavily on other leaders being willing "to get out front," to risk political capital, and "to be a focus for opposition and a rallying point for convincing the public."[41] It was relevant, at this deeper level of symbolism, that so many of the hostile cards and letters sent to Garrity during 1974–77 called him "you old goat."

In Boston, Judge Garrity stood almost alone as a heat taker. The *Globe* could be said to have "gotten out front" on busing, and anti-busers hated it, of course, but its owners, publishers, and editors did not come to personify desegregation. Cardinal Medeiros's statements in support of busing caused many of his flock to react with dismay, protest, and even vilification of His Eminence. But Medeiros, the first non-Irish prelate of Boston in the twentieth century, was already resented on that account by many of his clergy and parishioners. Despite several attempts to exercise moral leadership, he was effectively neutralized by the bitter divisions among his clergy and flock. An embarrassing contretemps with South Boston suggested his unwillingness to put himself into an even worse position. When asked by a reporter why he did not go to South Boston and calm the people, he replied that the people there had tuned him out, many did not go to mass, and they no longer listened to him. *"Why should I go to South Boston and get stoned?"* (Italics mine.) In the ensuing flap, Medeiros apologized and said Mass in Southie, but his initial, unguarded statement illustrated dramatically his desire to be made into no more of a scapegoat than he already was.[42]

The most artful evader of heat was the mayor. Kevin White, of course, faced an election in 1975, and as a result "he never acknowledged the legitimacy of the court order" and even implied that school boycotting was legal (it is against state law and can result in criminal prosecution). White saw himself as brokering the situation, and he did take the lead in providing safety and controlling violence. But he did not do enough on behalf of implementation, according to his critics. Yet White's middle course along a taut high-wire contributed more to minimizing violence than most other major actors, and he certainly had a far higher profile than the new governor elected in 1974, Michael Dukakis, who had none at all.[43]

The actions of the mayor and judge are relatively easy to observe and assess. Less obvious was the role of some of the most powerful men in Boston, namely the heads of Boston's banks, insurance companies, and top corporations, in short, Boston's economic elite. The course of desegregation had much to do with the fact that these men overwhelmingly lived outside the city in the suburbs. Consequently, this entire power sector, which often wielded crucial influence in southern cities in making desegregation peaceful, had little stake in or impact on the outcome in Boston.

In 1975 Robert J. Lamphere, vice president of the John Hancock Insurance Company, told the United States Commission on Civil Rights that he saw the role of business leaders as "supplemental": "I don't think we frankly see ourselves as one of the major actors in this situation." The executive director of the Boston Chamber of Commerce, William F. Chouinard, was more to the point. He estimated that of the 1,660 firms in the greater Boston Chamber, at least 90 percent of the chief executives lived in the suburbs. Chouinard said that "it's very, very difficult for members of the business community to argue effectively with people who live in the city that their kids should be brought from one end of town to the other, when in fact most of them live in suburbia, and for whom this problem is something which they just simply read about."[44]

Diane Ravitch, the historian of New York City's "school wars" from 1805 to 1973, described a succession of struggles between different religious, cultural, and racial groups, coinciding roughly with each new wave of immigration into the city. "Each school war is characterized by the combat of principle against principle," she wrote, "of one set of rights against another, of the strongly held interests of one group against those of another. For these reasons, none of these issues is ever permanently settled." In a vein similar to that of Ravitch, J. Anthony Lukas has interpreted the Boston controversy as one between two competing goods or values, community and equality.[45]

Principles and values were indeed at stake in the streets of Boston, but (as Ravitch and Lukas also were aware) so too was control of a patronage system, jobs, and of preferred paths of educational mobility. These struggles pitted black against white. The Irish had wrested control of city government and the schools from the Yankees by mobilizing more votes. They shared those resources with rivals such as the Italians insofar as their competitors also won elections or proved their political influence. Along came the blacks without many votes but with demands for resource reallocation. The Irish and their white allies from other groups were not about to grant to the blacks any moral leverage or to agree to change the rules of the game from the interest group conflict that had prevailed for over a century.

While the controversy was between blacks and whites, it also was in several ways a clash between whites and whites over different versions of community itself and over whose lifestyle should prevail. The school desegregation ordered by Judge Garrity was at one level an attempt by mobile professionals and elites to impose their liberal, cosmopolitan, middle-class values on working- and lower-middle-class people who embraced the values of localism and personalism. The residents of defended neighborhoods certainly saw desegregation in part as an attempt by elite outsiders to change them and their way of life. Even Bostonians who lived in sections that were less turf-conscious than the tribal neighborhoods nevertheless recognized that they too were living in places that, for a variety of reasons not all of which they understood, were the designated battlegrounds of racial justice.[46]

10

Race, Class, and Justice

*After reading 'The Best and the Brightest' by David Halberstam, a
story of what went on in Viet Nam, I am convinced busing is the Viet
Nam of the seventies, and you, sir, are Lyndon B. Johnson.
May you have a Clark Clifford on your staff.*
—*Mrs. J.P.F. to Judge Garrity*

While Boston's antibusing resistance uniquely generated protracted
conflict, it is easy to lose sight of the frustrations that civil rights groups
experienced in other northern cities.[1] In San Francisco and Chicago, for
example, efforts to gain integrated schools by African-Americans in the
1960s led to quite parallel events in both cities: superintendents' denials
that segregation existed, alarms that forced busing would destroy the
neighborhood school, and black protests or boycotts.

In Chicago, official immobility gave way to time-consuming studies
and to limited attempts at student transfers, which provoked bitter white
protest. By the time the federal department of Health, Education and
Welfare was willing to induce a plan of magnet schools and voluntary
busing (1975–77), the white school population had fallen to under 25
percent. In San Francisco, white officials moved quickly to endorse integration in the abstract, but antibusing neighborhood groups delayed
concrete action until a federal court decision brought about busing in
1971. Chinese and Hispanics joined whites in protesting and boycotting the desegregation plan, and white flight rapidly resegregated many
schools. Soon black parents too were expressing a preference for neighborhood schools. By 1978 less than 17 percent of students were white.
A second NAACP suit finally produced a 1982 plan to enrich black
schools, but by then funds to finance school improvement dried up.[2]

Boston, Chicago, and San Francisco all formed part of a national
pattern that produced a vast de facto resegregation of public schools,

222

both north and south. This ghettoization was one of both race and class and was accompanied by "hard times" for public schools as their financial resources, morale, and credibility all declined sharply.[3]

During the 1970s, as the nation's white majority had turned massively against busing, blacks in some areas also had retreated deliberately from busing. Events in Atlanta in 1973 were particularly significant in promoting a retreat that cut across racial and political lines. As white flight drained the schools of white students, the local NAACP abandoned racial balance, leaving most schools segregated, in exchange for a hefty share of administrative control (50 percent), including the superintendency. Elsewhere in the South, the "Atlanta Compromise" led both liberal judges and local NAACPS—usually in defiance of the national NAACP as in Atlanta—to agree to revisions in busing plans. San Francisco's blacks pursued a similar strategy, and in Detroit, Mayor Coleman Young, a black, opposed the imposition of massive busing on a system that was already 74 percent black.[4] By the 1970s, therefore, some black leaders with unimpeachable civil rights credentials had concluded that "continued emphasis on racial balance remedies was a suicidal strategy for the civil rights movement."[5]

Though the retreat from busing owed most to the stark numbers involved in white movement to the suburbs, the Boston saga also contributed forcefully to the reassessment just described. Boston became a potent, nearly universal symbol of what not to do.[6] Boston's currency as a negative symbol extended even into the realm of scholarship. Many analysts of desegregation law and judicial practices saw Garrity's involvement with the details of routine school operation (such as ordering school supplies or basketballs) as excessive. Many social scientists, moreover, had moved to the position already widespread among the public that the costs of desegregation were not worth it.

Still, busing had its staunch academic advocates who did not at all join the trend to relax pressure for busing. They argued that voluntary programs had rarely worked, that trade-offs for "separate but equal" could not be trusted, that separate black schools usually inhibited black social mobility, and that some busing programs, such as that in Charlotte-Mecklenburg, North Carolina, were outstanding successes. Defenders of busing had argued from the beginning that fears of busing had been exaggerated and that the more information people had about busing, the more they accepted it. By 1981, in fact, some polls began to show support for busing among those families that had actually experienced it. One probusing scholar argued that the "costs outweigh the benefits" attitude now constituted a "new mythology" regarding desegregation.[7]

In their sensitive study of desegregation in Nashville, Tennessee, Richard A. Pride and J. David Woodward took note of this position and countered that granting it were true, "the new mythology had a firm grip on Nashville." They found that "the general public, parents and teachers [white and black] were convinced that the costs of busing were high and the benefits incidental." Even a majority of black parents believed that busing damaged achievement, and Nashville's blacks divided sharply over the issue.[8]

Pride and Woodward conceded that many social science studies found that busing often had positive effects, including enhancing black achievement while not diminishing white. But if a city could not be persuaded otherwise and "contrary attitudes" prevailed, "then busing has failed in terms of attitudes or social change."[9] For many advocates of busing, however, neither the cost-benefit calculus nor the opinion of those affected by busing matters. "For those of us who feel school desegregation is a matter of 'simple justice,' it can be deemed effective if there are any positive impacts at all. . . . there are some policies which have such great intrinsic value that the costs are not highly relevant."[10]

Since the costs of busing have been distributed with great unevenness through society, however, this attitude ignores the highly relevant matter—relevant to successful implementation and to standards of justice in our society—of who bears the costs of busing. In Boston, as has been seen above, this was indeed important. In Nashville, according to Pride and Woodward, the burden of busing fell most heavily on blacks. Blacks opposed most of all the closing of Pearl High School, an all-black facility that was the first comprehensive high school for blacks in Tennessee, designed by black architects, constructed by black contractors, and with a heritage of black student accomplishment and pride. This kind of loss for black communities occurred across the South.

There has been far too little attention paid in the desegregation literature to the fact that during the desegregation of the South the number of black principals, administrators, and teachers declined drastically, removing most of a generation of role models from those positions. Too little has been written of the closing of the counterparts of Pearl High in other communities, south and north. In Boston, for example, the principal of a good elementary school in Roxbury that was racially imbalanced but had a high enrollment because of its popularity with parents, wrote to Judge Garrity to prevent his school being closed. "I strongly believe," he said, "that the burden of desegregation has been too long placed on the back of the Roxbury and Jamaica Plain communities."[11]

If there is anything to the analogy that sees busing as "the Viet Nam of the seventies," it lies in the fact that once again poor blacks and lower-class whites were the foot soldiers for a war initiated and pursued by liberal elites, and most of the affluent and college educated were exempt.

If Boston was unique, then, primarily because of the extremity of opposition incurred, why did things go so badly in Boston? In the long view the answers run deep into Boston's history, to the mid-nineteenth century when peculiar group dynamics among Yankee Protestants, lower-class Irish Catholic immigrants, and a small black population exacerbated an already hostile relationship between the two low-status groups. While most native Protestants mingled with neither group, Yankee reformers treated the blacks with a paternalist benevolence, however distant, and regarded the Catholic Irish with fear, disdain, or contempt. The two pariah groups shared competition for jobs at the bottom as well as symbolic status as the "niggers" of Anglo-Protestant society, which was enough for the Irish to adopt an unforgiving attitude toward the African-Americans. When the black ghetto of poverty would develop in the mid-twentieth century, it added images of black behavior that were anathema to Irish-American culture.

The native Protestants' highly developed sense of caste and class, of course, had much to do with society's pecking order and the havoc that subordinate groups wrought on one another, but this was not, as the conventional wisdom would have it, a matter of "the Irish doing to the blacks what the Yankees once did to the Irish." The Irish were clashing with the city's "colored" before the Civil War, and during that conflict it was the Irish North End that erupted in violent riots against the draft (and against hated "black abolitionists"), riots put down only with force and bloodshed.

In the long view the answer runs back partly to the halting of Boston's annexation of the near suburbs in the 1870s, a pivotal event that brought Boston into the mid-twentieth century as one of the smallest cities in the nation in relation to its metropolitan area. This legacy, together with the nation's exemption of suburbs from participating in solutions to racial problems (culminating in *Milliken v. Bradley*), made any school desegregation plan applied only to Boston highly biased in terms of class.

The historic givens also included the development after 1900 of a political culture dominated by Irish Catholics, in which the political hegemony of the former minority was not matched by a sense of economic or social security. Boston's politics also featured intense group rivalry characterized by what one political scientist has termed "street fighting pluralism," in which to the victorious interest or ethnic group went the spoils of office. The politics of Irish-dominated cities have been prone especially to an ethos of patronage that is personalist and particular. In the 1970s the political culture of Boston nurtured the belief that busing could be stopped by the normal operation of the open and behind the scenes workings of politics, that busing could be "fixed" like a traffic ticket.

For generations, too, the Catholic church had preached that parents' rights over their childrens' education superseded the power of the state to intervene in the education of children. And finally, over the long run, neighborhoods had survived in Boston that were urban villages defined by ethnicity, religion, class, race, and place, threats to which could mobilize intense resistance transcending any inner divisions. Those neighborhoods, moreover, in the quarter century before school desegregation began, had suffered a variety of losses, incursions, and betrayals at the hands of social planners offering "progress." In some cases, indeed, neighborhood defense had incited populist revolt against the outsiders and their local collaborators, protests which anticipated the antibusing movements in style and inner substance.

The answer to why things went so badly in Boston runs more nearly into Boston's post-World War II history, to the population shift from 1950 to 1970, which led to a rapid rate of increase in the African-American population, an expanding ghetto, and deterioration of housing and of schools in black neighborhoods. (Although bankers, realtors, and the federal government influenced most the development of residential ghettos, the racial policies of school committees also played a role.) Simultaneously, whites migrated to the suburbs, so that by 1970 Boston's population of some 600,000 was ringed by a "suburban noose" consisting of over a million and a half persons, more than 98 percent white in racial composition (the 2 percent nonwhite was a generous estimate and included persons in prisons and military bases).

Jobs as well as population flowed out to the suburbs, particularly with the rapid buildup of electronics and high-tech industries in the so-called golden circle of Route 128. As tens of thousands of jobs came into being, old and new blacks of Boston were screened from access to them by lack of mass transport and their inability to move into suburbs.

The central city population, but especially the public school constituency, was in general less affluent than the suburban, in part because of the outflow of affluent whites with children, and in part because of the extensive Catholic parochial school system, which also tended to siphon off families with greater resources or higher aspirations and concern for the quality of education. The white depopulation of Mattapan, a Jewish neighborhood, by the misuse of a well-intentioned program of residential integration, contributed further to removing moderate, middle-class elements from the public school arena.

Most immediately, the answer to why things went so badly in Boston runs to the decade before 1974, during which controversy over schools was almost continuous and Boston's racial climate was poisoned, especially by local political leaders who were entrepreneurs of the white backlash. These riders of the whirlwind ensured that when desegregation came, it would come by federal court order. Even then, they refused, with impunity as it turned out, every opportunity to mitigate the drawbacks of the plan created by agents of the State Board of Education, which was the only one available to the judge.

Unfortunately Judge Garrity, who spent fourteen months constructing an airtight diagnosis of the segregative actions engaged in by the Boston School Committee from 1963 to 1972, gave no attention to this plan and its obvious strategic and political deficiencies, especially its pairing of the leading ghetto high school with that of South Boston, the center of resistance to student transfers over the past decade, and the neighborhood most notorious in the city for its hostility to blacks. Moderates found it difficult to rally to this plan, and the judge next appointed a team of masters to design a new plan. They created a plan with less busing but more racial imbalance, which in the superheated atmosphere of Boston in 1975 generated a minimum of opposition and some support. But Judge Garrity rejected key features of his own masters' plan, and ordered his two academic experts to deliver a revised plan. The Phase 2 school assignments necessitated increased busing, reassigned students once again, and on balance stimulated further white flight.

Meanwhile, some school officials, following the lead of the school committee majority, did what they could to stymie implementation, while others, along with officials in other city departments, did what they could to profit from the chaos. The police and city judges were also in sympathy with the antibusers, so penalties for disturbing the peace were light, unless antibusing violence was directed at the police, which, in South Boston and Charlestown, often was the case.

Judge Garrity's judicial personality made him reluctant to interfere, as he saw it, with First Amendment rights to freedom of speech, so that school boycotters and perpetrators of violence were given wide leeway. Even more importantly, Judge Garrity allowed the school committee majority, led by Kerrigan, to defy the court's authority without penalty. By not proceeding against the politicians, Garrity left them in "visible power positions" where they continued to control patronage and have influence. That, of course, meant that they continued to receive what they regarded as their main benefit from serving on the committee.[12] Like some students of the 1960s who had broken laws and demanded (and won) amnesty, the committee majority had engaged in cost-free civil disobedience.

The turmoil of the 1960s, too, had contributed in a major way to the climate in which antibusing protest took place, to the decline of respect for authority and of public civility. The tactics of civil disobedience, guerrilla theater, and jousting with police had spread by the 1970s to former members of the "silent majority."

Desegregation has been instituted fairly peaceably in cities in which diverse leaders have shown a united front in support of it. In Boston, the mayor campaigned for peace but distanced himself from the court orders, the cardinal was neutralized by passionate divisions in his church, Governor Dukakis was invisible, and so was the city's economic and status elite, which lived in the suburbs.

In contrast, southern elites, which did not always promote desegregation, often did so because they tended to live in their cities and had stronger incentives to work for racial peace. In Greensboro, North Carolina, when school desegregation finally came after a long period of agitation by a black civil rights movement, the local elite moved to ensure a peaceful transition. According to William H. Chafe, "Although a classic 'power elite' may not have existed in Greensboro, the swiftness and effectiveness with which change finally occurred in 1970 and 1971 illustrates the ability of political and economic leaders to act decisively when it is in their interest to do so."[13] But Boston's economic leaders constituted an absent elite and lacked both incentives and the leverage to exert a comparable influence.

The absent elite and the middle classes who had moved to the suburbs might have been involved, of course, if Judge Garrity had been able to impose a metropolitan plan that transcended the boundaries between city and suburb. Garrity's June 1974 decision had left open the possibility of suburban participation, beyond the existing METCO program, in part because the U.S. Supreme Court was still deciding *Milliken v. Bradley*. This was the Detroit case in which a U.S. district court judge had imposed a city-county desegregation plan because there existed too few white students in the Detroit public schools to bring about any meaningful desegregation. But less than a month later, the Supreme Court overruled the Detroit opinion and in effect erected a *cordon sanitaire* between city and suburb, ensuring that affluent whites (and blacks) could escape desegregation by suburban residence. In a sharply dissenting opinion, Justice Thurgood Marshall accused the majority of catering to a "perceived public mood" and said that by excluding suburban whites from school desegregation the Court had ensured that urban school remedies for segregation would increasingly pit poor whites against poor blacks. "The *Milliken* principles," as Gary Orfield put it, "when applied to old cities, embody a social policy that whites with the least income, status, and power must bear the entire burden of desegregation, while those who can afford upper income housing in segregated suburbs may be completely insulated."[14]

Even without *Milliken*, it is not clear what might have happened, since the idea had never gained much of a foothold in Boston. Back in the mid-1960s, Boston Redevelopment Authority director Edward Logue had criticized plans to deal with Boston's segregated schools solely within city limits as "unimaginative and cowardly." In 1966, testifying before the Commission on Civil Rights, Logue impiously criticized the Kiernan Commission report for limiting its redistricting plans "to the relatively low income, the Italian, Irish, and Jewish neighborhoods which border the ghetto." The adjacent suburban town of Brookline, Logue observed, was not included, because the Kiernan panel did not consider achieving racial balance "as a burden to be shared beyond the corporate limits of the city." The federal government, said Logue, had much to do with suburbanization and Boston's population loss. He deplored the fact "that communities outside of Boston, with some of the finest school systems in America and with insignificant numbers of nonwhite children, are not required to help." He proposed to begin by shipping eight thou-sand black children from Boston into twenty-five or more suburbs and keeping children in the primary grades in their neighborhood schools. Trying to solve the problem with a "sole city solution," he concluded, "is a dead duck in our day."[15]

Both the State Board of Education and the school committee, other-wise at loggerheads, denounced Logue's suggestions, as did some of the local media. Logue soon left Boston, but metropolitan proposals cropped up now and then in bills introduced by Boston legislators or suggestions from antibusers, though the motivation behind most of these proposals was to deflect attention from Boston or to give suburban legislators second thoughts about the Racial Imbalance Act. Mayor White advo-cated metropolitanism at times, but no influentials consistently pro-moted it, and the black plaintiffs and their white liberal allies were di-vided on the matter, with none of them enthusiastic.[16]

The white civil rights lawyers arguing the desegregation case also tended to shy away from metropolitan approaches because they too ap-preciated the legal difficulties involved, and because they knew that dis-criminatory practices had been so flagrant in Boston and that the remedy under law and recent Supreme Court decisions was obvious. At one hand was an ironclad case that would survive any appeals—on the other hand was a high-risk path of uncertain result at best.

Still, the lack of support for a metropolitan approach in Boston was surprising. Few other cities had depended for so long or so heavily on metropolitan models for solving urban problems: metro parks and other recreation facilities, water supply, sewers, zoos, and a separate metro police force. Boston's unique geography alone provided a compelling case.

Ironically, on an individual level most black civil rights leaders with school children in fact showed their preference for a highly individual-ized "metropolitan solution" by placing their children in METCO and having them bused out of Boston into predominantly white suburban schools. Some observers have described METCO as a form of black community control of schools, but nothing could be further from the truth. The Operation Exodus program might be so described as a rough form of community control: in 1965–66 Exodus parents themselves ar-ranged transport for their children from overcrowded ghetto schools to underutilized, majority white schools elsewhere in the city. But METCO removed many of the best black students from Boston's public schools, skimming away children whose parents tended to be middle-class strivers, more concerned about their children's education and willing to fight for school quality. METCO less resembled community control than it did a private school system for blacks, analogous perhaps to the Catholic parochial schools, to which some black middle-class parents in fact sometimes compared it. METCO indeed was a classic privatist solution to a general social problem—the inferior education of black children—that addressed it by setting up a funnel through which only a few could pass to a better education and increased life opportunities. Even the lucky few, as Mel King said later, sometimes suffered because of the psychological stress of their situation. King added that METCO also distracted energy from deeper problems and reinforced the sense that only white schools could be quality schools. But the truly sad thing about it was the way in which it impoverished further the stepchild of education in the Massachusetts commonwealth, the Boston public schools, and that it fed the impulse to deal with the effects of racial discrimination on an individual rather than group basis. One can understand why METCO waiting lists have been crowded, because, whatever the disadvantages for blacks, the benefits far outweighed the alternative. Yet METCO, when judged by a utilitarian standard of social justice, is not community control but rather a form of "black flight."[17]

Despite the criticism of King and others, METCO still enjoys sacred-cow status in Boston. In 1989 the Boston Teachers' Union caused a flap when it considered a resolution calling for METCO students to return to the city's schools. METCO administrators were quick to express outrage, and the president of the Black Educators Alliance of Massachusetts asked "Why didn't they [the BTU] say anything about white students in private and parochial schools?" Why, indeed? But then, are private and parochial schools funded by the state? METCO is.[18] It is supremely ironic that a publicly funded program has exaggerated the separation of classes and concentrated further the poor in central city schools.

METCO, in good privatist, capitalist fashion, wholly ignores the question of "who is left behind?"[19] The answer, of course, is the great majority of urban blacks, or those whom William Julius Wilson has called "the truly disadvantaged." Wilson is one of the few scholars who has called attention to the effect on black urban ghettos of the exodus from them of the black middle and stable working class. This flight increases the "social isolation" of the ghetto underclass, whose joblessness creates an even greater need for institutions formerly sustained by those who flee, for job network systems, and for mainstream role models whose very presence "help keep alive the perception that education is meaningful, that steady employment is a viable alternative to welfare, and that family stability is the norm, not the exception."[20]

The failure to consider a metropolitan solution in Boston formed part of a nationwide pattern of what amounted to, in effect, piecemeal desegregation, not thoroughgoing desegregation affecting all sectors and all classes. Some radical critics of desegregation had made this point all along. Recently, Jennifer Hochschild has argued that school desegregation has been incomplete and floundering not only because most white Americans do not want it, but also because it is intended by elite decisionmakers to be incomplete. Elites make choices, according to Hochschild, that result in a little desegregation for nonelites but avoid subjecting society to fair and universal integration.

If pushed too far desegregation would undermine "the hidden but pervasive class structure" and would attack not only the precarious position of poor whites—as it usually does now—but also the privileges of rich whites. "Full and complete desegregation would call into question parents' rights to send their children to private schools, teachers' seniority rights, the sanctity of city/suburb school district lines, and local financing and control of schools, to mention only a few sacred cows. Not only the poor but also rich whites would have to give up precious components of their class position for desegregation to be complete."[21]

Other critics of school desegregation take the argument further. Daniel Monti has described St. Louis's desegregation as providing a "semblance of justice," while in reality reinforcing the social order. In Monti's view school protests and the institutional response are analogous to "ritualized rebellions" that blow off steam but accomplish little change in society. Derrick Bell makes the compelling point that practically all the reforms resulting from civil rights litigation invariably promote the interests of the white majority. Perhaps the best known example of this is the *Brown* decision, whose practical impact was delayed years and decades, while it immediately benefited the United State's image in the midst of the Cold War.[22]

So desegregation does not get pushed very far—instead, we get a little, but not too much. Virtually no scholar looking at Boston and lacking any personal interest in defense of the desegregation process there has failed to see that the lower classes did the desegregating, the middle classes did the fleeing, either immediately or after a short trial (some stayed because their children traveled on insulated or relatively "safe" tracks to the sixth grade and then escaped into the six-year Latin schools), while the affluent were exempt from the start.

One consequence of the some, not-too-much desegregation that tends to be imposed on the lower classes is that the white working class screams and acts out its frustration in public. Neighborhood militants and racists are catapulted into influence and to the forefront of media attention, while an aura of shame begins to infect the atmosphere. This allows the rest of society, particularly middle-class liberals, to feel morally superior to the "racists" in South Boston. It's not a new dynamic, but an old story hanging from an enduring hoary myth. I am referring to the distorting lenses of what I call the "redneck myth," which served elite defenders of southern segregation so well for so long. One historian of the South recently dubbed this the "grit thesis," namely, the persisting myth perpetrated by and convenient to the upper classes that racial extremism and especially violence is caused by the lower classes and runs against the wishes of the elite. The grit thesis was never true except in fragments. The upper class had no more sympathy for blacks than the lower class, but expressed racism in a very different style. Upper-class racism was not overtly violent but operated in more subtle forms by manipulating social institutions: "Ownership of the land, control of money and credit, of schools and courts, and domination of the marketplace can be just as violent, if not, indeed, more violent than guns, whips, and bombs."[23]

The soft style or "civility" of upper-class southern racism was one of the principle themes of William H. Chafe's elegant study of the modern civil rights movement in Greensboro, North Carolina. Chafe, too, deflated the traditional view that the upper crust would treat blacks better but were prevented from doing so by redneck resistance. "Some affluent whites did promote racial justice, helping to guarantee that Greensboro's atmosphere would at least be 'civil.' . . . But the primary resistance to significant racial breakthrough also came from white leaders of the upper class." Elite whites, in fact, exploited the threat of redneck rebellion and exaggerated the strength of the Ku Klux Klan, but the crucial role was played by those "who held power in the first place. They, not the poor whites, were in charge."[24]

When racial strife moved north, the myth adapted and became the urban redneck myth. It continues to provide the comforting reassurance that the lower classes of American society are primarily responsible for racism, both overt and institutional. Though the myth is embattled, it has powerfully shaped popular and academic perceptions of northern opposition to busing. The urban rednecks are recognizable not only by their brutish public manners, of course, but also by their lifestyles. These symbolic stand-ins for southern rednecks are of course "ethnics," usually Catholic, who live in neighborhoods that cosmopolitan journalists and intellectuals regard as provincial backwaters of prejudice and ignorance. Even some scholars who have written sympathetically of such enclaves have tended to treat them in a condescending fashion and at a minimum share with hostile critics a conviction that they are anachronisms incompatible with modern life. People who live in urban villages are given high marks for enjoying a degree of community found rarely now in American society, but their communities tend to be described as shabby, out-of-date, out-of-step relics from the past that are inevitably doomed by progress. It is a short step from assuming that these places will no longer exist to the assumption that they should no longer exist. Need it be said that this is not the way residents of such locales see themselves?

When liberals encounter urban ethnics challenging such approved targets as urban renewal, developers, pollution, or corporations, they applaud such manifestations of popular democracy proceeding from what they regard as so unlikely a source. In the late 1960s, for example, a coalition of neighborhood groups and professional allies joined forces to oppose a highway building program that was running amok in several neighborhoods. The antihighway coalition staged demonstrations that much resembled the antibusing protests that would soon follow. Like the antibusers, they came on passionately, with raised voices, and expressed distrust and alienation not only because they saw their neighborhoods being ruined but also because of the way decisions were being made. The coalition's lobbying eventually reached both mayor and governor, and the highways stopped. A liberal bureaucrat praised the coalition's "negative" participation: "If we value participation, and if most citizen participation is reactive to perceived threats, we should be anything but contemptuous of 'negative' participation. On the contrary . . . it constitutes the very heart of modern democracy. Most initiative in each sector of policy belongs to men who work full time within it. The system's democratic aspect lies in its mechanisms for enabling aroused 'amateurs' to constrain them."[25] The antibusers, "aroused amateurs" to be sure, can be described at least as "negative" participators, even if one is not willing to see their movement as a case of participatory democracy, 1970s style.

The antibusing movement drew heavily from the clannish, cohesive networks of ethnic and working-class neighborhoods. These can function as a source both of populist insurgency and of reaction, but liberals and progressives have difficulty appreciating populism when it emanates from blue-collar ethnics who live in urban villages, so the populist character of antibusing has not been much recognized.[26]

The political consequences of the rise of reactionary populism and of the divisions between localist ethnics and cosmopolitan liberals have been far-reaching. As seen in chapter 8, the national Democratic party suffered significant losses in Boston's white neighborhoods. Despite Jimmy Carter's victory in 1976 it was already clear that the major political casualty of the social and cultural shockwaves let loose was the national Democratic party, particularly the historic New Deal coalition forged by Franklin D. Roosevelt during the Great Depression. Though the Democrats have managed to dominate the Congress and state governments for most of the recent period, from 1968 to 1988 they have lost five of six presidential elections.

Many causes contributed to the undoing of the New Deal coalition, including the embourgeoisment of much of the working class, the decline of labor unions, the Vietnam War, and the rise of so-called social issues. But the factor of race and the white reaction to the black struggle for equal citizenship and equal opportunity, first in the South, then in the North, probably constituted over the long run the most powerful solvent of the New Deal coalition.

In the 1930s the New Deal had established a commanding presence among the voters. Even during the two Eisenhower elections in the 1950s, when the nation chose a popular war hero as president, a majority of the electorate remained Democratic in party loyalty. But the disintegration had begun, and eventually party loyalty itself would fade in a new era of ticket-splitting and voter independence. When Truman and the Democratic platform supported a moderate civil rights program in 1948, southern Dixiecrats revolted. Not widespread enough to defeat Truman, the rebellion was a harbinger of the dissolution of the "Solid South." By 1964, even as President Lyndon Johnson of Texas trounced Republican challenger Barry Goldwater of Arizona, a majority of white southerners voted for Goldwater, who had voted against the Civil Rights

Act of 1964. The Democratic party increasingly became identified with black civil rights demands and affirmative action for blacks and other minorities—not to mention the protest movements of the 1960s. The debate over the Vietnam War, too, was waged principally within the Democratic party.

Many white northerners, especially blue-collar workers, urban ethnics, Catholics, and union members, who had been Democratic stalwarts, felt threatened in the 1960s by a broad array of social and cultural changes. Many came to see gains for blacks and other minorities as somehow a diminution of their status and rights. The white backlash thrived on a sense of politics as a zero-sum game in which the redressing of wrongs for blacks came to be perceived as a loss for those whites most socially and geographically proximate to blacks. These fearful whites began to respond to the appeals of conservative politicians who argued that the civil rights revolution had gone far enough and who presented themselves as champions of stability and traditional values. Increasingly, the core of the old Democratic coalition in both the South and North supported conservative or reactionary politicians, from Wallace to Nixon to Reagan, who postured as populist defenders of the little man. "Reagan," said Wilson Cary McWilliams, "usurped the Democrats' role as spokesman for many of America's outsiders."[27] To paraphrase McWilliams: Reagan and his fellow pseudopopulists have usurped the Democrats' traditional role as spokespersons for America's white outsiders.

Some antibusing activists became wholly fused into right-wing, conservative politics. In the 1980s the antibusing newspaper, the *South Boston Marshal* was ardently pro-Reagan, stridently anti-Soviet and for a big military build up, anti-gun control, anti-nuclear freeze, and of course antiliberal and against racial quotas or any kind of preferences given to minorities. But more important were the Democrats who remained so in state and local politics, but who in the 1980s became known as "Reagan Democrats" because of their hostility to what they regarded as the misguided liberalism of national Democrats. Senator Bill Bulger of South Boston remained Democratic, but his (and other antibusing politicians') exhortations to "get off our backs . . . [and] leave our children alone" found an echo in Reagan's slogan of 1980, "to get the government off the backs of the people."[28]

If reactionary populism, with all of its contradictions, continues to be misunderstood as it has been, particularly by liberals and progressives, then conservative politicians—whose trickle down economic policies consistently favor corporations and the wealthy—will continue to reap votes among the very "little people" whose social well-being is made so precarious by those same policies. Boston antibusing was not a democratic social movement and surely did not "seek a transformation of power relations." Organized antibusing particularly did not "transcend barriers of parochialism, defensiveness and powerlessness."[29]

Yet antibusing nevertheless shared many affinities with the "new citizens revolts" of the 1970s directed against big business or impersonal government. Most ironically, both militant and moderate antibusers shared the heritage of the 1960s, had learned from and been socialized by the civil rights, antiwar, and other protests. The antibusers flourished in a climate in which protest had become common and raucous, and they were affected and shaped by the rapid decline of respect for authority, particularly government authority, in the late 1960s and early 1970s. Given their perception of the media's impact on the protests of the 1960s, the antibusers sought most to emulate the civil rights protesters of the 1960s, but they failed in their attempt to be portrayed by the media as heroes and martyrs, and even failed at gaining status in the public eye as victims.

For the opponents of busing the threat to their neighborhoods and lifestyles constituted a trampling on their freedom. The authors of perhaps the most widely discussed book on the condition of American values in the 1980s, *Habits of the Heart*, concluded not surprisingly that freedom "is perhaps the most resonant, deeply held American value. . . . Yet freedom turns out to mean being left alone by others, not having other people's values, ideas, or styles of life forced upon one, being free of arbitrary authority in work, family, and political life."[30] For many antibusers who were not racists and not prejudiced, the court orders amounted to having other people's values forced on them, a situation made all the more unpalatable by the evident fact that the others did not need to abide by those same values.

Of course freedom is a matter of degree. We trade some of it, in effect, for social order, comity, civility, and sometimes for social justice. If everybody were left alone, we would never come close to achieving integration or equity, so obviously everyone, not just some, and particularly not the lower classes and poor, must give up some of that freedom.

To understand reactionary populism we must recognize the role of class and its consequences in the formation of public policy, particularly policies designed to alleviate racial injustice.[31] If class is ignored, as it was in Boston and consistently tends to be in dealing with desegregation, then those policies have little chance of success.

Class and race (and ethnicity and class and race) have been entangled for a long time in the course of American history. Disentangling them is often a slow, painful process, painful in that the truth is often difficult to confront.[32] That racism has distorted much of American history and continues to flourish is all too obvious. The commitment to uproot and eradicate racism needs continual renewal. But policies designed to defeat racism that do not consider the class structure and that institute or perpetuate unequal class participation in state mandated integration will continue to meet with resentment and resistance.

Policies pursued in fulfillment of equal rights, equal opportunity, and integration must be fair and universal, and elites (Democratic or Republican, liberal or conservative) must ensure that any potential costs of any policy designed to meet those commitments will not be borne by only a part of the citizenry. The school desegregation experience shows that partial remedies lead to failure. What has worked best are plans with clear legal requirements consistently enforced by the courts and by administrative agencies supported by local officials, and plans that do not leave out sectors of the population, allowing easy escape over (in this regard) artificial political boundaries.[33]

Metropolitan school desegregation plans, specifically, have worked best. White flight, with or without court orders, has been hindered by the "degree to which the school district encompassed the housing market area and thus made flight impractical." Yet a leading scholar of metro plans has concluded that their stability has been ignored by the media and policymakers.[34]

Bridging the "Berlin Walls" of the suburbs, however, will not be easy.[35] The protection accorded to the affluent is simply assumed in American society, as if it is part of the natural order. Of course, a maze of deliberate discriminatory laws and economic practices makes it so. Massachusetts suburbs are characterized by racial and class exclusion, despite the passage in 1969 of a state law designed to make suburban towns do their share of providing low-income housing, by giving the state power to remove local obstacles to subsidized housing. By 1989 Massachusetts shared with California the distinction of having the most expensive housing in the country, but only 28 of the Bay State's 351 communities had met the law's goal of having 10 percent of their housing stock "affordable"; 95 towns had yet to build any subsidized housing at all. Affluent suburbs in the Boston vicinity, it was well known, went to great lengths to avoid subsidized housing. The marketplace and suburban governments work together effectively to keep poor families, and of course minorities, out of suburbs.[36]

Finally, it follows logically that any private schools existing in any metropolitan area undergoing school desegregation must be regarded as potential recruits in any plan involving massive transfers of students. The decisions and investments that many public school parents make regarding housing and schooling are no different in kind from those undertaken by private school families. Perhaps no single measure would do more to focus the attention of business, media, and governmental elites on what is really going on in public schools. In the design of desegregation policy, Congress, state legislatures, and the courts must begin anew by questioning the presumed right of private schools to exist independently of desegregation laws that mandate obedience to what are proclaimed to be universal laws to all citizens.

Until policies are designed that are practical and universal, and that does not necessarily mean large scale, then white resistance will continue to flourish against partial applications, targeted at less affluent whites who are presumed to be less racially tolerant and virtuous than their more affluent cousins. It will take great political skill and sensitivity to put together a political coalition that will pursue both racial and economic justice. But the record shows that it is difficult to achieve one without the other.

Appendix

Table A.1. Percentage Approving of Boycotts by Neighborhood

South Boston	58
Charlestown	45
East Boston	42
West Roxbury/Roslindale	36
Dorchester/Mattapan	35
Hyde Park	31
Jamaica Plain	26
Central Boston	16
Roxbury	13

Table A.2. Neighborhood Desire for Continued Protest

In the next year or two the federal court order to bus can be stopped and done away with.

	Percent agreeing
East Boston	46
Charlestown	43
Hyde Park	41
South Boston	39

Table A.2. *continued*

West Roxbury/Roslindale	37
Dorchester/Mattapan	29
Jamaica Plain	28
Central Boston	21
Roxbury	19

The people of Boston should continue to fight Phase 2.

	Percent agreeing	Percent difference
South Boston	59	+20
East Boston	56	+10
Charlestown	53	+20
West Roxbury/Roslindale	48	+11
Hyde Park	42	+1
Dorchester/Mattapan	36	+7
Jamaica Plain	31	+3
Central Boston	24	+3
Roxbury	17	−2

Table A.3. Neighborhood Acceptance of Busing's Inevitability

	Busing is now inevitable. Percent agreeing	Should cooperate. Percent agreeing	Percent difference
East Boston	49	36	−13
Hyde Park	52	47	−5
Charlestown	54	37	−17
South Boston	56	32	−24
West Roxbury/ Roslindale	59	48	−11

Table A.3. *continued*

	Busing is now inevitable. Percent agreeing	Should cooperate. Percent agreeing	Percent difference
Jamaica Plain	59	62	+ 3
Dorchester/			
Mattapan	66	53	− 13
Roxbury	70	73	+ 3
Central Boston	72	66	− 7

Source: All appendix tables adapted from *Boston Herald*, Aug. 15, 1975, p. 16.

Notes

Preface

1. David T. Wellman, *Portraits of White Racism* (Cambridge: Cambridge University Press, 1977), pp. xviii, 35, 41.

2. Harold Cruse, *Plural but Equal: A Cultural Study of Blacks and Minorities and America's Plural Society* (New York: William Morrow and Co., 1987), p. 383.

3. Upper-class whites, as portrayed in Tom Wolfe's popular novel *Bonfire of the Vanities* (New York: Farrar, Strauss, and Giroux, 1987), travel through the black ghetto reluctantly and only at high speed. Wolfe spins his tale of contemporary New York from the explosive consequences that result when a Wall Street bond broker gets lost while driving through The Bronx, and the panic that ensues when he and his mistress realize they might be trapped in "the jungle."

4. J. G. to Judge W. Arthur Garrity, Nov. 30, 1975, Letters to Judge Garrity (hereafter GL). Judge Garrity received hundreds of letters during the 1970s from Bostonians and from all over the country. He was kind enough to let me read them, on condition that their authors' full names not be given here, only their inititals. As of this writing, they are still in his possession at his office in Boston. (The letter quoted at the beginning of the preface, from Mrs. R. C., is in this collection.)

5. V. B., South Boston, to Judge Garrity, Jan. 12, 1975, GL.

6. T. F., Brighton, to Judge Garrity, May 28, 1975, GL.

7. Pamela Bullard and Judith Stoia, *The Hardest Lesson: Personal Accounts of a School Desegregation Crisis* (Boston: Little, Brown and Co., 1980), pp. 64, 67, 71. I have tried to show inner conflicts similar to those besetting ethnic working-class persons of Boston as described in Richard Sennett and Jonathan Cobb, *The Hidden Injuries of Class* (New York: Vintage Books, 1972).

Chapter One

1. U.S. Commission on Civil Rights, *Desegregating the Boston Public Schools: A Crisis in Civic Responsibility* (Washington, D.C.: GPO, 1976), p. xix.

245

2. Robert Kiley, interview with author, July 8, 1983. Kiley was deputy mayor for Public Safety during 1974–75. In the fall of 1974, twenty-five other northern cities, including Los Angeles, Denver, Detroit, Indianapolis, and San Francisco, were under similar orders. Steve Curwood, "Unique Case: Outcry Set City Apart," *Boston Globe* (hereafter *Globe*), Sept. 4, 1985. See also, Albert S. Foley, "Mobile Alabama: The Demise of State Sanctioned Resistance," in Susan L. Greenblatt and Charles V. Willie, eds., *Community Politics and Educational Change: Ten School Systems under Court Order* (New York: Longmans, 1981), pp. 319, 322.

3. Like Frances Fox Piven and Richard A. Cloward, I do not equate protest "movements" with "movement organizations." *Poor People's Movements: Why They Succeed, How They Fail* (New York: Pantheon Books, 1977), p. 5.

4. J. Anthony Lukas, *Common Ground: A Turbulent Decade in the Lives of Three American Families* (New York: Alfred A. Knopf, 1985).

5. Jonathan Rieder, *Canarsie: The Jews and Italians of Brooklyn against Liberalism* (Cambridge, Mass.: Harvard University Press, 1985), p. 172.

6. Further irony arose from the linkages between the American civil rights movement and the fight for Irish Catholic freedom in Northern Ireland, which had both violent and peaceful elements. Many Catholics of Northern Ireland, in their struggle against the Protestant Irish and England, had adopted the tactics of passive disobedience and protest from American blacks. There existed some sympathy for the overseas Catholics in the working-class neighborhoods that became so staunchly antibusing. Thus inspiration for antibusing protest methods had originated in the black churches of the southern United States and had come to Boston directly from the South and indirectly from the South through Ireland. I am indebted to Dr. Thomas N. Brown for calling my attention to this point.

7. Robert N. Bellah, Richard Madsen, William M. Sullivan, Ann Swidler, and Steven M. Tipton, *Habits of the Heart: Individualism and Commitment in American Life* (Berkeley: University of California Press, 1985), p. 279; Mark Crispin Miller, "Prime Time: Deride and Conquer," in Todd Gitlin, ed., *Watching Television* (New York: Pantheon Books, 1987), pp. 183–228.

8. Richard D. Alba, *Italian Americans: Into the Twilight of Ethnicity* (Englewood Cliffs, N.J.: Prentice-Hall, 1985), pp. 171, 173. Michael Novak, *The Rise of the Unmeltable Ethnics: Politics and Culture in the Seventies* (New York: Macmillan Co., 1971); Richard Polenberg, *One Nation Divisible: Class, Race, and Ethnicity in the United States Since 1938* (New York: Penguin Books, 1980), esp. pp. 231–50; Thomas J. Archdeacon, *Becoming American: An Ethnic History* (New York: The Free Press, 1983), p. xviii.

9. The term "ideological ethnicity" is from Howard F. Stein and Robert F. Hill, *The Ethnic Imperative: Examining the New White Ethnic Movement* (University Park: Pennsylvania State University Press, 1977), p. 2. Barbara Miller Solomon, *Ancestors and Immigrants: A Changing New England Tradition* (Cambridge, Mass.: Harvard University Press, 1956); Oscar Handlin, *Boston's Immigrants: A Study in Acculturation* (New York: Atheneum, 1968).

10. This view of the HSA is from Peter Schrag, *Village School Downtown* (Boston: Beacon Press, 1967), pp. 138–39, 141.

11. The complexity of that story has been disclosed already in several books dealing with Boston desegregation, notably by Lukas in *Common Ground*. Lukas depicted antibusing leader Louise Hicks, for example, not as a racist but as a politician responding to and manipulating her constituents. Sensitive to the class and cultural dimensions of the reaction against busing, Lukas has also developed the theme that the working-class Irish were angriest not at blacks or Yankees but at Irish leaders who betrayed them and who were representatives of the "two toilet Irishmen" in the suburbs who had made it. See J. Anthony Lukas, "All in the Family: The Dilemmas of Busing and the Conflict of Values," in Ronald P. Formisano and Constance K. Burns, eds., *Boston, 1700–1980: The Evolution of Urban Politics* (Westport, Conn.: Greenwood Press, 1984), pp. 241–57.

Earlier, another journalist turned historian, Alan Lupo, saw ethnic and working-class parochialism as laced with racist elements, but he also recognized that "the real issue was less the separation of races than the separation of classes. . . . For one class lived in Boston and some older communities nearby, and quite another class lived in most of the suburbs." *Liberty's Chosen Home: The Politics of Violence in Boston* (Boston: Little, Brown and Co., 1977), pp. 148–52, 159.

Both Lupo and Lukas realized that Boston's urban renewal programs of the 1950s and 1960s had benefited downtown developers and politicians but had created bitter reservoirs of distrust and alienation in the neighborhoods that preceded, paralleled, and fed the frustration over court-ordered busing. A 1984 book by a social anthropologist put the economic development of Boston at center stage and interpreted opposition to busing "as a protest against the social and economic dislocation experienced by lower-income whites in the creation of the New Boston." Whites displaced by post-industrial structural change then vented their frustration into racial antagonism and antibusing. J. Brian Sheehan, *The Boston School Integration Dispute: Social Change and Legal Maneuvers* (New York: Columbia University Press, 1984), pp. 2, 181–83.

Richard H. Buell, Jr., with Richard A. Brisbin, Jr., *School Desegregation and Defended Neighborhoods: The Boston Controversy* (Lexington, Mass.: D. C. Heath and Co., 1982), also downplayed racism.

D. Garth Taylor, *Public Opinion & Collective Action* (Chicago: University of Chicago Press, 1986), presented data taken from five surveys between 1973 and 1975 showing that the majority of those opposed to busing in Boston did not believe in white supremacy or the separation of races. Taylor maintained that a nonracist majority was moved to protest by a sense of injustice, a perception fed by suburban exclusion, and the ability of those with money to escape participation. Taylor did find that 18 percent of the city's whites opposed even voluntary desegregation, believed in blacks' social inequality, and saw segregation as legal (pp. 55–63, 197).

The only book-length account to emphasize racism is Jon Hillson, *The Battle of Boston* (New York: Pathfinder Press, 1977), which held rather implausibly that the Democratic party's political machine undergirded antibusing protest by encouraging and manipulating working- and middle-class white racists.

12. William A. Henry, III, "Uncommon Ground," *Boston Magazine*, Oct.

1986, p. 206: "There was a belief that somehow if we do all the right things, [that] we do all the time to affect the executive . . . or the legislative branch of government, we are going to be all set." Peter Meade, interview with Gail P. Eagan, Jan. 15, 1987, in Gail P. Eagan, "The Role of the Press in the Development of an Urban Controversy: The *Boston Globe* and the Desegregation of the Boston Public School System, 1974–76," Senior Honors Thesis, Holy Cross College, May 15, 1987, Appendix 7. A teacher at South Boston High (1971–77) observed that to the students there government meant "Boston politics where you could get that summer job because your mother had worked in someone's campaign or, better yet, get that life-time appointment because you had been a loyal supporter of a certain politician." Mary G. Colvario, "Recollections of South Boston High School before and during Its First Year of Desegregation," May 1, 1978, typescript, p. 19. Mrs. Colvario kindly provided me with a copy of this text.

13. Terry Nichols Clark, "The Irish Ethic and the Spirit of Patronage," *Ethnicity* 4 (December 1975): 305–59.

14. Judge W. Arthur Garrity, Jr., interview with author, July 1, 1986; see note 8; see also Arthur L. Stinchcombe and D. Garth Taylor, "On Democracy and School Integration," in Walter G. Stephan and Joe R. Feagin, eds., *School Desegregation: Past, Present, and Future* (New York: Plenum Press, 1980), pp. 157–86, and John Stack, "Ethnicity, Racism, and Busing in Boston: The Boston Irish and School Desegregation," *Ethnicity* 6 (1979): 21–28.

15. Regarding the impact of suburbanization on New York City, see Ira Katznelson, *City Trenches: Urban Politics and the Patterning of Class in the United States* (Chicago: University of Chicago Press, 1982), pp. 95–98.

16. Thomas F. Pettigrew, "Racial Change and Social Policy," *Annals of the American Academy of Political and Social Science* 441 (January 1979): 121.

17. Stewart and Pettigrew quoted in Joe R. Feagin, "School Desegregation: A Political-Economic Perspective," in Stephan and Feagin, *School Desegregation*, p. 45; Norman C. Amaker, "Milliken v. Bradley: The Meaning of the Constitution in School Desegregation Cases," in U.S. Commission on Civil Rights, *Milliken v. Bradley: The Implications for Metropolitan Desegregation* (Washington, D.C.: GPO, 1974), pp. 9–11. For the political context, see George R. Metcalf, *From Little Rock to Boston: The History of School Desegregation* (Westport, Conn.: Greenwood Press, 1983), pp. 162–92.

18. U.S. Commission on Civil Rights, *Route 128: Boston's Road to Segregation,* January 1975, Washington, D.C. (this was actually a report of the Massachusetts Advisory Committee to the Massachusetts Commission Against Discrimination); Michael Ryan, " 'Route 128' to Take Buses to Suburbs?" *Boston Phoenix* (hereafter *Phoenix*), Jan. 21, 1975, pp. 11, 14; Pettigrew, "Racial Change and Social Policy," 121; Forest M. Cason, "Residential Segregation, School Desegregation: The Boston Case," seminar paper, Clark University, April 1975.

19. Studies of white flight during desegregation show that whites with higher incomes and occupations are the first to leave. See, e.g., Richard A. Pride and J.

David Woodward, *The Burden of Desegregation: The Politics of Desegregation in Nashville, Tennessee* (Nashville: University of Tennessee Press, 1985). In 1970 whites in Boston constituted one-fifth of those in the metropolitan area and were far less affluent than the four-fifths outside (U.S. Commission on Civil Rights, *Route 128*, p. 32).

20. Sam B. Warner, *Streetcar Suburbs: The Process of Growth in Boston, 1870–1900* (New York: Atheneum, 1972), pp. 163–64; Matthew Edel, Elliot D. Sclar, and Daniel Luria, *Shaky Palaces: Home Ownership and Social Mobility in Boston's Suburbanization* (New York: Columbia University Press, 1984), pp. 241, 242; Frank Levy, *Northern Schools and Civil Rights: The Racial Imbalance Act of Massachusetts* (Chicago: Markham, 1971), p. 31.

21. Peter S. Canellos, "A Lingering Urban Folly," *Boston Sunday Globe*, Dec. 11, 1988, sec. A, pp. 21, 24; Lukas, *Common Ground*, pp. 211–12; Congressional hearings in 1971 dealt with the "redlining" of Mattapan, *Globe*, Sept. 14–16, 1971; Stephen B. Young, "Jewish Attitudes toward Busing in Boston," seminar paper, Clark University, May 5, 1976.

22. In the nation generally the existence of private or parochial schools has impeded effective desegregation. Gary Orfield, *Must We Bus? Segregated Schools and National Policy* (Washington, D.C.: Brookings Institute, 1978), pp. 59–61.

23. John H. Mollenkopf, *The Contested City* (Princeton, N.J.: Princeton University Press, 1983), pp. 140–44; Schrag, *Village School Downtown*, pp. 28–29. On the historic relative lack of mobility of Irish Catholics, see Stephan Thernstrom, *The Other Bostonians: Poverty and Progress in the American Metropolis* (Cambridge, Mass.: Harvard University Press, 1973), pp.168–75, 250.

24. *Globe*, Dec. 8, 1971, p. 3, and Apr. 23, 1972, p. 22; Al Larkin, "Plan Would Lower Passing Police Grade," *Globe*, Apr. 11, 1972, p. 24; William F. Doherty, "Judge Tells Police: Hire Blacks Who Failed Test," *Globe*, Mar. 28, 1973, p. 3; "What Wyzanski Really Said About Police Exams," *Globe*, Apr. 10, 1973, p. 15; Joseph Harvey, "State Court Overrules Wyzanski," *Globe*, May 11, 1973, p. 6; Anne Kirchheimer, "11 Women Join Hub Police Force, Start Walking Their New Beats," *Globe*, Aug. 29, 1972, p. 3; Tom Riley, Jr., "U.S. Sues Boston Fire Department," *Boston Herald* (hereafter *Herald*), Jan. 25, 1973, p. 1; Nick King, "Firefighters Hiring Rule Allowed to Stand," *Globe*, Apr. 15, 1975, p. 2. In 1987 Mayor Flynn appointed as fire chief a South Bostonian whose father had been chief and whose two sons were firefighters. Thomas H. O'Connor, *South Boston: My Home Town: The History of an Ethnic Neighborhood* (Boston: Quinlan Press, 1988), p. 236.

25. *Herald*, Nov. 4, 1975; *Globe*, Nov. 3, 4, 1975; Robert Ward and Jerome Sullivan, "Officer Hurt; Construction Workers Picket Hub Phone Office," *Globe*, Mar. 19, 1976, afternoon edition.

26. Gary McMillan and Robert J. Auglin, "2000 Workers Demonstrate at City Hall Plaza," *Globe*, May 8, 1976, pp. 1, 4, morning edition; Joe Henry, "Hostile 'Hard Hats' Demonstrate in City Hall," *Herald*, May 8, 1976; *Boston Sunday Herald*, May 9, 1976. See also, Jerry Taylor, "Group Damages Equipment, Library Construction Halted," *Globe*, Apr. 13, 1976, morning edition; *Globe*,

Mar. 19, 22, and May 7, 1976, afternoon edition; *Herald*, Apr. 22, 1976; and Luix Overbea, "Why Construction Workers, 'Third World' Group at Odds," *Christian Science Monitor*, May 11, 1976.

Regarding the history of racism in craft unions, see Gary McMillan, "In Craft Unions, 'Brotherhood' Not for All," *Globe*, Apr. 27, 1983, pp. 1, 18. In contrast, a business agent for Ironworkers Local 7 recently said: "I think it's no secret that 10 years ago the building trades were a real tight group. But right now we have fathers who can't get their sons in." Bruce Butterfield, "Labor's Affirmative Action Pledge," *Globe*, Nov. 22, 1988, p. 39. See also, James Green, "The Making of Mel King's Rainbow Coalition: Political Changes in Boston, 1963–1983," in James Jennings and Mel King, eds., *From Access to Power: Black Politics in Boston* (Cambridge, Mass.: Schenkman Books, 1986), pp. 99–135, especially for developments after 1977.

27. Sheehan, *The Boston School Integration Dispute*, p. 182. A similar argument is made by Christine Rossell, "The Mayor's Role in School Desegregation Implementation," *Urban Education* 12 (October 1977): 257, 259.

28. Mayor's Committee on Violence, June 23, 1976, to Mayor Kevin White, p. 16.

29. *Globe*, Sept. 4, 1985, p. 35; Loretta McLaughlin, "Poverty—Not Busing—Called Biggest Evil for Pupils," *Globe*, Mar. 25, 1976.

30. Jean Marie Mulvaney, interview with author, June 23, 1983.

31. The stress on racism in recent years has moved away from what has been labeled "old-fashioned racism"—that is, overt hatred of blacks—and focuses now on "modern racism"—a more sophisticated, indirect, and symbolic form of racism that has adapted to the post-civil rights movement milieu. David O. Sears, Carl P. Hensler, and Leslie K. Spear, "Whites' Opposition to 'Busing': Self-Interest or Symbolic Politics?" *American Political Science Review* 73 (June 1979): 369–84; John B. McConahy, "Self-Interest versus Racial Attitudes as Correlates of Anti-busing Attitudes in Louisville: Is It the Buses or the Blacks?" *Journal of Politics* 44 (1982): 696–717.

32. Jonathan Kelly, "The Politics of School Busing," *Public Opinion Quarterly* 38 (Spring 1974): 23–39; Everett F. Cataldo, Michael W. Giles, and Douglas S. Gatlin, *School Desegregation Policy: Compliance, Avoidance, and the Metropolitan Remedy* (Lexington, Mass.: D. C. Heath and Co., 1978); Michael W. Giles and Douglas S. Gatlin, "Mass-Level Compliance with Public Policy: The Case of Desegregation," *Journal of Politics* 42 (August 1980): 722–46; M. Stephan Weatherford, "The Politics of School Busing: Contextual Effects and Community Polarization," *Journal of Politics* 42 (August 1980): 747–65; McKee J. McClendon and Fred P. Postello, "White Opposition: To Busing or to Desegregation?" *Social Science Quarterly* 63 (March 1982): 70–82; Frank Brown and Waithira Mugai, "Court-Ordered School Desegregation: One Community's Attitude," *Journal of Black Studies* 13 (March 1983): 355–68; Lawrence Bobo, "Whites' Opposition to Busing: Symbolic Racism or Realistic Group Conflict?" *Journal of Personality and Social Psychology* 45 (1983): 1196–1210.

33. McKee J. McClendon, "Racism, Rational Choice, and White Opposition to Racial Change: A Case Study of Busing," *Public Opinion Quarterly* 49

(1985): 216. Studies focusing on Boston include Stinchcombe and Taylor, "On Democracy and School Integration"; Bert Useem, "Solidarity Model, Breakdown Model, and the Boston Anti-Busing Movement," *American Sociological Review* 45 (June 1980): 357–69; Christine Rossell, "School Desegregation and Community Social Change," *Law and Contemporary Problems* 42 (Summer 1978): 133–83; Thomas M. Begley and Henry Alker, "Anti-Busing Protest: Attitudes and Actions," *Social Psychology Quarterly* 45 (1982): 187–97.

34. Harold Cruse, *Plural but Equal: A Critical Study of Blacks and Minorities and America's Plural Society* (New York: William Morrow Co., 1987), p. 20; Howard Schuman, Charlotte Steeh, and Lawrence Bobo, *Racial Attitudes in America: Trends and Interpretations* (Cambridge, Mass.: Harvard University Press, 1985), pp. 77, 84–87, 93–96; Gary Orfield, *Public School Desegregation in the United States, 1968–1980* (Washington, D.C.: Joint Center for Political Studies, 1983), p. 4.

35. Pettigrew, "Racial Change and Social Policy," 119.

36. Diane Ravitch, *The Troubled Crusade: American Education, 1945–1980* (New York: Basic Books, 1983), p. 145; for the process of change, pp. 114–81.

37. James T. Hannon, "The Catholic Church and School Desegregation in Boston," Master's thesis, University of Wisconsin, Madison, 1980, p. 17; see also pp. 18, 20–23; Taylor, *Public Opinion & Collective Action*, p. 104.

38. David M. Tucker, *Arkansas: A People and Their Reputation* (Memphis: Memphis State University Press, 1985), pp. 92–96; David Wallace, "Orval Faubus: The Central Figure at Little Rock Central High School," *Arkansas Historical Quarterly* 39 (Winter 1980): 314–29.

39. This account of New Orleans is based on Morton Inger, *Politics and Reality in an American City: The New Orleans School Crisis of 1960* (New York: Center for Urban Education, 1970).

Chapter Two

1. Walter Muir Whitehill, *Boston in the Age of John Fitzgerald Kennedy* (Norman: University of Oklahoma Press, 1966), pp. 56–57; "Busing . . . Irish vs. Blacks, Blacks," Alan Lupo File of materials related to Boston desegregation, in his possession (hereafter Lupo File).

2. Jennifer L. Hochschild, *The New American Dilemma: Liberal Democracy and School Desegregation* (New Haven: Yale University Press, 1984), p. 144; see also, pp. 92–145; Robert L. Crain, with Morton Inger, Gerald A. McWorter, and James J. Vanecko, *The Politics of School Desegregation: Comparative Case Studies* (Chicago: Aldine Publishing Co., 1968), pp. 191–92.

3. Byron Rushing, "Black Schools in White Boston, 1800–1860," in James W. Fraser, Henry L. Allen, and Sam Barnes, eds., *From Common School to Magnet School: Selected Essays in the History of Boston Schools* (Boston: Trustees of the Public Library of the City of Boston, 1979), p. 27; Leonard W. Levy and Douglas L. Jones, eds., *Jim Crow in Boston: The Origins of Separate But Equal Doctrine* (New York: DaCapo Press, 1974), pp. 261–62; Carlton Maybee, "A Negro Boy-

cott to Integrate Boston Schools," *New England Quarterly* 41 (September 1968): 358; Carter Goodwin Woodson, *The Education of the Negro Prior to 1861* (New York: Arno Press, 1968), pp. 95, 320–25; *Boston Pilot*, Oct. 6, 1855; Ronald P. Formisano, *The Transformation of Political Culture: Massachusetts Parties, 1790s–1840s* (New York: Oxford University Press, 1983), pp. 331–33.

4. Richard Kluger, *Simple Justice: The History of Brown v. Board of Education* (New York: Alfred A. Knopf, 1975); Numan V. Bartley, *The Rise of Massive Resistance: Race and Politics in the South during the 1950s* (Baton Rouge: Louisiana State University Press, 1969). "To its most devoted adherents, the *Brown* decree promised a kind of secular salvation." David L. Kirp, *Just Schools: The Idea of Racial Equality in American Education* (Berkeley: University of California Press, 1982), p. 7.

5. For firsthand accounts by participants, see Howell Raines, ed., *My Soul Is Rested: Movement Days in the Deep South Remembered* (New York: Penguin Books, 1983).

6. Stephan Thernstrom, *The Other Bostonians: Poverty and Progress in the American Metropolis, 1880–1970* (Cambridge, Mass.: Harvard University Press, 1973), pp. 197–202; Daniel Golden and Donald Lowry, "Boston and the Postwar Racial Strain: Blacks and Whites in Boston: 1945–1982," *Boston Globe* (hereafter *Globe*), Sept. 27, 1982, p. 18.

7. Mel King, *Chain of Change: Struggles for Black Community Development* (Boston: South End Press, 1981), pp. 24, 13; see also pp. 9–11, 34, 270–71; Harvard Center for Law and Education (hereafter HCLE), "A Study of the Massachusetts Racial Imbalance Act" Publication no. 6019, February 1972, p. 14; U.S. Commission on Civil Rights, *Hearing Held in Boston, Ma., Oct. 4–5, 1966*, (Washington, D.C.: GPO, 1967), pp. 51–52, 147, 154; Thomas Simmons, interview with author, June 5, 1984. Otto and Muriel Snowden, social workers who struggled early to prevent deterioration in Roxbury and who also wanted better schools, established Freedom House in 1949. In the early 1960s they were focused on urban renewal. Snowden and Snowden, "Citizen Participation," *Journal of Housing* 8 (1963): 435–39.

8. In contrast to the view expressed here, a recent book proposed that integration "was essentially a strategy designed to further the interests of the Afro-American elite, who used it as a device to manipulate blue-collar workers and poor people arriving from the South." The black elite received its cues from a white ruling class interested in maintaining its hegemony. J. Brian Sheehan, *The Boston School Integration Dispute: Social Change and Legal Maneuvers* (New York: Columbia University Press, 1984), pp. 48–71, 267–74. Sheehan's own account provides evidence contradicting his thesis, e.g., the efforts of the traditional black elite as early as 1950 to improve education for black children (p. 52). The motives of middle-class black parents and professionals in seeking better schools enjoyed an existence independent of the designs of the white power structure, as revealed, e.g., in testimony before the U.S. Commission on Civil Rights in 1966. *Hearing*, pp. 297–314, passim. Upwardly mobile, middle-class blacks of the type moving into the Mattapan district were particularly interested in racially balanced schools; see Charles M. Sullivan, with Sandra Farrow, Kath-

ryn N. Hatch, Richard A. Cohen, and Alan Keyes, eds., "Five Ethnic Groups in Boston: Blacks, Irish, Italians, Greeks, and Puerto Ricans," A joint report by Action for Boston Community Development and United Community Services of Metropolitan Boston, June 1972, pp. 121, 126.

9. Joe R. Feagin, "School Desegregation: A Political-Economic Perspective," in Walter G. Stephan and Joe R. Feagin, eds., *School Desegregation: Past, Present and Future* (New York: Plenum Press, 1980), pp. 31, 32; see also, Stanley Lieberson, *A Piece of the Pie: Black and White Immigrants Since 1880* (Berkeley: University of California Press, 1980). There is an extensive literature on this subject. I have found useful: Christopher Jencks, "Busing—The Supreme Court Goes North," in Nicolaus Mills, ed., *The Great School Bus Controversy* (New York: Teacher's College Press, 1973), pp. 22–23; Diane Ravitch, *The Great School Wars: New York City, 1805–1973* (New York: Basic Books, 1974), pp. 233–47; and "Busing," *Ramparts*, Dec. 1974–Jan. 1975.

10. Ravitch, *The Great School Wars*, pp. 251–54, 258–60, 267, 269, 271, 273.

11. HCLE, "Racial Imbalance Act," pp. 13, 15; Edgar J. Driscoll, Jr., "Frederick J. Gillis, 95, Educator, Retired Superintendant in Boston," *Globe*, Dec. 27, 1988, p. 55; Emmett H. Buell, Jr., with Richard A. Brisbin, Jr., *School Desegregation and Defended Neighborhoods: The Boston Controversy* (Lexington, Mass.: D. C. Heath and Co., 1982), p. 62; King, *Chain of Change*, p. 31; Noel Day, "The Freedom Movement in Boston," *Integrated Education* (December–January 1964–1965): 11–12.

12. Peggy Lamson, "The White Northerner's Choice: Mrs. Hicks of Boston," *Atlantic Monthly*, June 1966, pp. 58–62; Howard John Chislett, " 'Nothing Will Stop Us': The Climax of Racial Segregation in the Boston Public Schools, 1963–1974," Ed.D., Teachers' College, Columbia University, 1979, pp. 109–10.

13. The national NAACP had just announced on May 18 a drive against school segregation based on housing patterns. This came two days after New York State's education commissioner had declared de facto segregation as illegal as de jure. Sheehan, *The Boston School Integration Dispute*, pp. 54–55, 62–63. See also, J. Anthony Lukas, *Common Ground: A Turbulent Decade in the Lives of Three American Families* (New York: Alfred A. Knopf, 1985), p. 124.

14. Lukas, *Common Ground*, p. 124. Sheehan gave an extensive account of the June 11 hearing, *The Boston School Integration Dispute*, pp. 58–63. Ruth Batson, Chairman Education Committee, Boston branch [NAACP], "Statement to the Boston School Committee, June 11, 1963," K. Marie Clarke Papers (hereafter Clarke Papers; this collection of materials is currently stored at Mrs. Clarke's home in West Roxbury).

15. Lamson, "Mrs. Hicks of Boston," pp. 60–61; Sheehan, *The Boston School Integration Dispute*, pp. 66–67; Chislett, " 'Nothing Will Stop Us,' " pp. 133, 114–15; Dave O'Brian, "Conversation: Arthur Gartland: Why Busing Had to Be," *Boston Phoenix* (hereafter *Phoenix*), Dec. 2, 1975, p. 6. School committee member Joseph Lee expressed the committee's exasperation with the NAACP: "They won't come to meetings when asked, and when they do, they walk out before the meeting gets going. We don't demand they admit 'de facto *integration*'

in the schools before we agree to talk . . . [but] they insist we accept their verdict before the trial starts!" Joseph Lee to Owen B. Kiernan, Commissioner of Education, Aug. 17, 1963, in folder, "Joseph Lee 1965–66," Board of Equal Educational Opportunity, Massachusetts Department of Education, Quincy, Massachusetts.

16. Lukas, *Common Ground*, p. 128. For national events see Allen J. Matusow, *The Unravelling of America: A History of Liberalism in the 1960s* (New York: Harper and Row, 1984), pp. 85–92.

17. Buell and Brisbin, *Defended Neighborhoods*, pp. 61, 62; Lamson, "Mrs. Hicks of Boston," p. 59; Lukas, *Common Ground*, p. 119.

18. Lamson, "Mrs. Hicks of Boston," p. 59.

19. Ira Mothner, "Boston's Louise Day Hicks: Storm Center of the Busing Battle," *Look*, Feb. 22, 1966, p. 77. Peter Schrag, *Village School Downtown* (Boston: Beacon Press, 1967), pp. 19–20.

20. Lamson, "Mrs. Hicks of Boston," p. 61; Crain et al., *Politics of School Desegregation*, pp. 44, 49; King, *Chain of Change*, pp. 35–36.

21. Buell and Brisbin, *Defended Neighborhoods*, p. 64.

22. See ibid., pp. 64–66, for a good description of the 1963 election and Hicks's vote, including a comparison of her support in each ward in 1961 and 1963.

23. For general accounts, see William L. O'Neill, *Coming Apart: An Informal History of America in the 1960s* (New York: Quadrangle Books, 1971), pp. 170, 172–75; Godfrey Hodgson, *America in Our Time: From World War II to Nixon: What Happened and Why* (New York: Vintage Books, 1978), pp. 219–20.

24. Hodgson, *America in Our Time*, pp. 214–15, 267; Jody Carlson, *George C. Wallace and the Politics of Powerlessness: The Wallace Campaigns for the Presidency, 1964–1976* (New Brunswick, N.J.: Transaction Books, 1981), pp. 30, 33, 37–41.

25. Sheehan, *The Boston School Integration Dispute*, p. 71; Ravitch, *The Great School Wars*, p. 276; King, *Chain of Change*, pp. 37–38.

26. King, *Chain of Change*, pp. 34, 37; Chislett, " 'Nothing Will Stop Us,' " pp. 121–22.

27. Alan Lupo, *Liberty's Chosen Home: The Politics of Violence in Boston* (Boston: Little, Brown and Co., 1977), p. 147.

28. Jonathan Kozol, *Death at an Early Age: The Destruction of the Hearts and Minds of Negro Children in the Boston Public Schools* (New York: Bantam Books, 1968), p. 123. During the sit-in at the Federal Building, the U.S. district attorney received the protesters sympathetically: " 'I respect your point of view,' he told them. 'I have let Washington know of your presence here. If I get a reply, I will let you know immediately.' He shook hands before going back to his office." The district attorney was W. Arthur Garrity, Jr. The story appeared in Chuck Fager, "Boston to Selma and Back—the March to Racial Justice," *Boston Sunday Globe*, Mar. 16, 1975, sec. A, pp. 1–2.

29. Fager, "Boston to Selma and Back," pp. 1–2; Kozol, *Death at an Early Age*, pp. 123, 125; Schrag, *Village School Downtown*, p. 103; Sheehan, *The*

Boston School Integration Dispute, p. 83; for King's visit, see Lukas, *Common Ground*, pp. 17–18.

30. In 1972 the state commissioner of education, Thomas J. Curtin, said that the Massachusetts board had gained national recognition in 1963 by issuing a pioneering statement regarding racial imbalance, and that in 1965 the board "again awakened the national conscience with its publication of *Because It Is Right—Educationally*." Thomas J. Curtin, "Because It Is *Still* Right," a statement by the commissioner of education, Commonwealth of Massachusetts, 1972.

31. Massachusetts State Board of Education, *Because It Is Right—Educationally*, part 2, pp. 73–76. Report of the Advisory Committee on Racial Imbalance and Education, April 1965.

32. Ironically, the black historical perspective could also be used for devastating criticism of melting-pot ideology, e.g., Harold Cruse, *The Crisis of the Negro Intellectual: From Its Origins to the Present* (New York: William Morrow and Co., 1967).

33. Richard Polenberg, *One Nation Divisible: Class, Race, and Ethnicity in the United States since 1938* (New York: Penguin Books, 1980), pp. 202–27, 243–48. Books such as Michael Novak, *The Rise of the Unmeltable Ethnics: Politics and Culture in the Seventies* (New York: Macmillan Co., 1971), asserted the defiant mood of the new ethnicity.

34. See HCLE, "Racial Imbalance Act," pp. 37, 39–53, for a detailed account of the legislative maneuvering. For the views of civil rights leaders and several members of the Kiernan Commission, see the letters in the folder "Ad Hoc Committee on Racial Imbalance," Board of Equal Educational Opportunity, Massachusetts State Department of Education, Quincy. In recent years, criticism of the Racial Imbalance Act has come from whites and blacks, radicals and conservatives; see Sheehan, *The Boston School Integration Dispute*, p. 80; King, *Chain of Change*, pp. 42–43; George V. Higgins, *Style versus Substance: Boston's Kevin White & The Politics of Illusion* (New York: Macmillan Co., 1985), pp. 78–79.

35. In 1963 Representative Royal Bolling had introduced a fourteen-word bill to ban state aid to communities with racially imbalanced schools. That same year the New York commissioner of education and Board of Regents declared all schools over 50 percent Negro to be racially imbalanced and failing to provide equal education. Ravitch, *The Great School Wars*, p. 268, pointed out that New York City's schools were changing so fast that this standard soon became unrealistic.

36. Frank Levy, *Northern Schools and Civil Rights: The Racial Imbalance Act of Massachusetts* (Chicago: Markham Publishing Co., 1971), p. 12; see also, pp. 4–5, 143, 161–63. Eventually the state assumed an overwhelming share of the cost of relieving racial imbalance in Boston.

37. Joining Hicks were William O'Connor, a business administration instructor and former teacher, and the eccentric veteran Joseph Lee, descendant of a prestigious Yankee family. Only committeeman Arthur Gartland, a liberal businessman and civic leader, took a consistently pro-integration position. Unpredictable was Thomas S. Eisenstadt, a young, ambitious attorney first elected with

Hicks in 1961. Eventually winning election as sheriff of Suffolk County in 1969, Eisenstadt's rivalry with Hicks often shaped his positions, as when he suprised everyone by joining Gartland in approving the Kiernan report. HCLE, "Racial Imbalance Act," pp. 16, 17, 36.

38. Buell and Brisbin, *Defended Neighborhoods*, pp. 68–69; Lamson, "Mrs. Hicks of Boston," p. 62; Crain et al., *Politics of School Desegregation*, p. 46.

39. Robert L. Levey, "Busing—A Non-Word with Racial Emphasis," *Boston Sunday Globe*, June 6, 1965.

40. *Globe*, Aug. 13, 19, Sept. 3, 9, 1965; Robert Healy column, Nov. 1, 1965; Robert L. Levey, "Suddenly, Busing Looms Larger as Answer to Racial Imbalance," *Globe*, Dec. 16, 1965; HCLE, "Racial Imbalance Act," pp. 30–31; U.S. Commission on Civil Rights *Hearing, 1966*, p. 127; *Boston Herald* (hereafter *Herald*), Sept. 5, 1965.

41. *Globe*, Sept. 11, 14, 1965; Robert Coles, "Busing in Boston," *Boston Sunday Globe*, Oct. 17, 1965; *Globe*, Sept. 19, 1966, morning edition; Schrag, *Village School Downtown*, pp. 122–23; *New York Times*, Oct. 17, 1966; U.S. Commission on Civil Rights, *Hearing, 1966*, pp. 128, 129.

42. *Globe*, Sept. 9, 1965, afternoon edition; *Globe*, Sept. 14, 1965, morning edition. Harassment by the school committee apparently gave the black parents greater motivation. U.S. Commission on Civil Rights, *Hearing, 1966*, pp. 129–30.

43. On the origins of METCO: Schrag, *Village School Downtown*, pp. 134–35; U.S. Commission on Civil Rights, *Hearing, 1966*, pp. 142–82; regarding funding, HCLE, "Racial Imbalance Act," pp. 114, 260–61. In December 1982 METCO bused 3,271 students to thirty-four towns at a cost of $8.6 million, had about 5,000 on its waiting list, and had long since achieved establishment status. Its executive director, Jean M. McGuire, a black, was serving her first term on the Boston School Committee. *Globe*, Dec. 4, 1982, p. 8; see also *Boston Sunday Globe*, May 28, 1972 and *Globe*, Aug. 28, 1974, afternoon edition.

44. Schrag, *Village School Downtown*, p. 15; also, pp. 16–17; Mothner, "Boston's Louise Day Hicks," p. 77.

45. J. Michael Ross, Thomas Crawford, and Thomas Pettigrew, "Negro Neighbors—Banned in Boston," *Trans-action* 3 (September–October 1966): 14.

46. Ibid., 13, 16–17. "Half of the pro-Hicks group owned their own home, compared to 37 percent of her partial supporters, and 29 percent of her critics" (p. 16).

47. Ibid., 15–16; Buell and Brisbin, *Defended Neighborhoods*, p. 74; Mothner, "Boston's Louise Day Hicks," pp. 77, 78.

48. Crain et al., *Politics of School Desegregation*, p. 39.

49. "Report on the Schools of Boston" quoted in Massachusetts State Board of Education, *Because It Is Right*, p. 24. For a substitute teacher's description of a "slum school, broken windows and all," see William A. Koelsch, "Progress Book 1962–63 Teaching," p. 5, property of William A. Koelsch.

50. Kozol, *Death at an Early Age*, pp. 51, 54, 55. For attitudes of black parents to ghetto schools, see U.S. Commission on Civil Rights, *Hearing, 1966*, pp. 20–182; King, *Chain of Change*, p. 44.

51. Lukas, *Common Ground*, p. 28, gave the views of Alice McGoff of Charlestown comparing the Irish and black experiences.

52. During the decade after 1963, committee members moved on to such posts as city councillor, Congressperson, sheriff of Suffolk County, register of probate, governor's councillor, and ran for mayor, district attorney, Congress, and other offices. David Harmon and Jason W. Chin, "The Politics of the Boston School Committee in the School Desegregation Controversy," seminar paper, Clark University, April 1976.

53. Lukas, *Common Ground*, pp. 122–23; Robert A. Dentler and Marvin B. Scott, *Schools on Trial: An Inside Account of the Boston Case* (Cambridge, Mass.: Abt Books, 1981), p. 188. Regarding black political weakness, see Mel King, "Three Stages of Black Politics in Boston, 1950–1980," in James Jennings and Mel King, eds., *From Access to Power: Black Politics in Boston* (Cambridge, Mass.: Schenkman Books, 1986), p. 24, and Thomas Simmons, interview with author, June 5, 1984.

54. William V. Shannon, *The American Irish: A Political and Social Portrait* (New York: Macmillan Co., 1963), pp. 183, 184–187; Schrag, *Village School Downtown*, p. 33.

55. Senator William Bulger, interview with Clark University students, Spring 1975; Bulger expressed substantially the same views in "Boston's Orwellian Nightmare," *Globe*, Feb. 10, 1975.

56. Sheehan, *The Boston School Integration Dispute*, p. 60; Schrag, *Village School Downtown*, p. 22.

57. Alan Dennis Burke, *Firewatch* (Boston: Little, Brown and Co., 1980), pp. 328–29.

Chapter Three

1. Harvard Center for Law and Education (hereafter HCLE), "A Study of the Massachusetts Racial Imbalance Act" Publication no. 6109, February 1972; Department of Health, Education and Welfare. Office of Civil Rights, Northeast Region. *Distribution of Students by Racial and Ethnic Composition of Schools, 1970–1976*, (Washington, D.C.: GPO, 1978), p. 211.

2. *Boston Sunday Globe*, Dec. 26, 1965; Emmett H. Buell, Jr., with Richard A. Brisbin, *School Desegregation and Defended Neighborhoods: The Boston Controversy* (Lexington, Mass.: D. C. Heath and Co., 1982), pp. 74–75; Wendy Bauman, "Busing Chronology [1849–1975]," *Boston Globe* Library, typescript; *Boston Herald* (hereafter *Herald*), June 28, 1966; HCLE, "Racial Imbalance Act," pp. 169–82; *The Boston School Decision* (Boston: Paperback Booksmith, 1974), which is the full text of Judge W. Arthur Garrity's decision in *Morgan v. Hennigan*.

3. HCLE, "Racial Imbalance Act," p. 190; Buell and Brisbin, *Defended Neighborhoods*, p. 76; Bauman, "Busing Chronology," pp. 11–15.

4. HCLE, "Racial Imbalance Act," p. 191, n. 105.

5. Peter Schrag, *Village School Downtown* (Boston: Beacon Press, 1967), pp.

125–26. For criticism of the school committee plans as "little more than empty gestures," see editorial, *Herald*, June 30, 1966.

6. *Herald*, May 24, 1966; *Boston Globe* (hereafter *Globe*), Oct. 29, 1966, morning edition. *Boston Sunday Globe*, Jan. 29, 1967. Bertram G. Waters, "'Voluntary' Key Word in School Bus Dispute," *Globe*, Jan. 29, 1967. During 1969–70 the annual ritual of board approval was interrupted while representatives of Model Cities tried to negotiate a proposal that would put black and white children together in part-time learning situations. This idea eventually led nowhere. HCLE, "Racial Imbalance Act," pp. 190–212; Buell and Brisbin, *Defended Neighborhoods*, p. 76; Bauman, "Busing Chronology," pp. 14–19.

7. Buell and Brisbin, *Defended Neighborhoods*, pp. 79, 80. See also Lukas, *Common Ground*, pp. 134, 135, and J. Brian Sheehan, *The Boston School Integration Dispute: Social Change and Legal Maneuvers* (New York: Columbia University Press, 1984), p. 56, who characterized Hicks's supporters as outsiders in the new Boston. Elliott Friedman placed Hicks in the "anti" tradition earlier personified by James M. Curley: "Anti a lot of things: blue-ribbon committees, closed employment doors, the self-righteousness of the privileged, the arrogance of the establishment, anti-Yankee, a feeling that the Irish are still on their knees. . . . These people look at Mrs. Hicks, and say she's got the courage to stand up to the papers, to the establishment, to the whole system, and that's the basis of her support." *Globe*, May 7, 1967, quoted in George V. Higgins, *Style versus Substance: Boston's Kevin White & The Politics of Illusion* (New York: Macmillan Co., 1985), p. 82.

8. Higgins, *Style versus Substance*, pp. 72–73, 76. For an example of condescension toward Hicks and her supporters by one of the liberal national media, see "Backlash in Boston—And Across the U.S." *Newsweek*, Nov. 16, 1967, p. 29.

9. Higgins, *Style versus Substance*, p. 101. James Jennings, "Urban Machinism and the Black Voter: The Kevin White Years," in James Jennings and Mel King, eds., *From Access to Power: Black Politics in Boston* (Schenkman Books, 1986), p. 70. Alice McGoff of Charlestown, one of J. Anthony Lukas's representative antibusers in *Common Ground: A Turbulent Decade in the Lives of Three American Families* (New York: Alfred A. Knopf, 1985), voted for Hicks repeatedly for school committee and city council, but not for mayor, because she thought Kevin White was better qualified (p. 453); Buell and Brisbin, *Defended Neighborhoods*, pp. 81–84.

10. In Boston, too, a new toughness arose as Herbert Hambleton became deputy superintendant in charge of the Educational Planning Center, which was responsible for racial balance planning. Hambleton abruptly cut down on meetings between the board and school system representatives and declared himself a staunch defender of the neighborhood school. HCLE, "Racial Imbalance Act," pp. 116–17, 143, 212–21, 330–31; Memorandum from Commissioner [Neil V. Sullivan] to J. Harold Flannery, Dec. 1, 1971, Files, Bureau of Equal Educational Opportunity, Massachusetts State Department of Education, Quincy, Massachusetts (hereafter BEEO Files); William Crowley, interview by telephone with au-

thor, July 11, 1984; *Globe*, Mar. 15, 1969, morning edition; *Boston Sunday Globe*, Mar. 30, 1969.

11. Charles L. Glenn, interview with author, July 2, 1985; Charles Leslie Glenn, untitled sermon, Dec. 12, 1977, photocopy, BEEO Files. In a recent book, Glenn embraced Lukas's description of him in *Common Ground* as "implacable" on school desegregation, "with a 'passionate zeal on racial issues.' " Charles Leslie Glenn, Jr., *The Myth of the Common School* (Amherst: University of Massachusetts Press, 1988), p. x.

12. Buell and Brisbin, *Defended Neighborhoods*, p. 76; J. Michael Ross and William M. Berg, *"I Respectfully Disagree with the Judge's Order"*: *The Boston School Desegregation Controversy* (Washington, D.C.: University Press of America, 1981), pp. 74–75; *Globe*, Jan. 14, Aug. 5, 1969, Feb. 2, 1970, morning edition; *Globe*, Jan. 24, 28, 1969, afternoon edition.

13. HCLE, "Racial Imbalance Act," p. 221. Glenn and his allies were working intensely behind the scenes to get the board to stand firm on "the Boston Imbalance Showdown." Strategy and internal bureaucratic politics are described in Glenn's personal journal kept during these months. "First Journal—Charles Glenn, Confidential, I, beginning Aug. 2–5 [1971]," BEEO Files [pp. 8, 11, 12, 14].

14. HCLE, "Racial Imbalance Act," p. 223; Hambleton quoted on pp. 230–31; see also *Globe*, Apr. 18, June 12, 1971, morning edition; Nina McCain, "Busing in Boston Is Easier Said Than Done," *Boston Sunday Globe*, Sept. 12, 1971.

15. *Globe*, Sept. 8, 1971, morning edition. In early September Lee parents also picketed the homes of the three school committee members who had voted to cooperate with the board. HCLE, "Racial Imbalance Act," p. 250.

16. *Globe*, Sept. 9, 10, 13, 1971, afternoon edition; *Globe*, Sept. 10, 16, 1971, morning edition.

17. McCain, "Busing," *Boston Sunday Globe*, Sept. 12, 1971.

18. *Globe*, Sept. 22, 23, 1971; Buell and Brisbin, *Defended Neighborhoods*, p. 77; Ross and Berg, *"I Respectfully Disagree,"* pp. 79–80. Craven claimed he had been given wrong data by the school department's Educational Planning Center; Craven, running for city council, came in tenth. HCLE, "Racial Imbalance Act," p. 250.

19. Ross and Berg, *"I Respectfully Disagree,"* p. 80; Buell and Brisbin, *Defended Neighborhoods*, p. 78. Ironically, the committee was enjoying some success in other schools. The new William Monroe Trotter School, a "magnet" school designed to be attractive enough to pull white students into a Roxbury neighborhood, had opened peacefully with about 53.5 percent black and 46.5 percent white children. The new Marshall School also opened with about seven hundred white and three hundred black students, while school officials also claimed that the new Haley and Hennigan schools were balanced. McCain, "Busing," *Boston Sunday Globe*, Sept. 12, 1971; a few white parents actually chose the Lee school, *Globe*, Sept. 23, 1971.

20. HCLE, "Racial Imbalance Act," pp. 223, 307, 308; *Globe*, Sept. 23, 1971,

afternoon edition. Commissioner Sullivan allegedly charged that racism was at the heart of the protest. The Human Rights Commission of the Boston archdiocese criticized Father Burke, whom Mrs. Hicks defended to wild applause. *Globe*, Sept. 13, 1971, morning and afternoon editions.

21. *Boston Sunday Globe*, Aug. 27, 1971; *Globe*, Sept. 23, 1971, afternoon edition. The authors of the HCLE study, in contrast, criticized the board for settling for "far too little" in August 1971, for being too attentive to the politics of the situation from 1967 to 1971, and for inadequate enforcement. "Racial Imbalance Act," pp. 324, 327, 329, 330–38. The fullest account of the Lee school controversy is in HCLE, "Racial Imbalance Act," pp. 221–46.

22. Glenn discussed "our changing strategy in fighting off efforts to destroy the RIA." Charles Glenn, personal journal, A-400 Journal, April 1972, p. 9, BEEO Files.

23. *Globe*, Dec. 2, 1971, pp. 1, 26, May 29, 1974, p. 22; Ross and Berg, "*I Respectfully Disagree*," pp. 77–82; Buell and Brisbin, *Defended Neighborhoods*, p. 78; HCLE, "Racial Imbalance Act," pp. 256–57; U.S. Commission on Civil Rights, *Hearing Held in Boston, Massachusetts, June 16–20, 1975*, (Washington, D.C.: GPO, 1978), pp. 474–75.

24. J. Harold Flannery, interview with author, Jan. 12, 1984; Ferne Arfin, "Blacks Sue to Integrate Schools," *Herald*, Mar. 16, 1972, p. 1; Lukas, *Common Ground*, pp. 218–19. The *Globe* said flatly that "the School Committee has now changed school segregation 'by fact' into school segregation 'by Law,'" and that the state board "will now take an almost watertight case to court." *Globe*, Sept. 23, 1971, afternoon edition. Regarding the pivotal nature of the Lee school episode from the Department of Education's viewpoint, see Charles Glenn personal journal, A-400 Journal, April 1972, BEEO Files.

25. Joseph M. Cronin and Richard M. Hailer, *Organizing an Urban School System for Diversity: A Study of the Boston School Department. Summary Report* (Cambridge, Mass.: McBer and Co., 1970); *Herald*, Oct. 4, 1970, sec. A, p. 9; *Globe*, July 20, 1971, p. 1; *Herald*, July 21, 1971, p. 1, Sept. 21, p. 1, Oct. 5, p. 1, Oct. 11, p. 3; *Globe*, Dec. 12, 1971, sec. 3, p. 25. In 1969 the Massachusetts Advisory Council on Education made similar recommendations, see Legislative Research Council, Commonwealth of Massachusetts, Report Relative to School Committees and Feasible Alternatives. House Doc. no. 5071. From 1944 on the Finance Commission made repeated suggestions that the school committee be abolished. Boston Finance Commission, "Report of a Survey of the Public Schools of Boston Conducted under the Auspices of the Finance Commission of the City of Boston" (Boston, 1944).

26. Tyke Patriquin, "The Boston School Committee Elections of 1971 and 1973," Clark University, May 1986; HCLE, "Racial Imbalance Act," pp. 300, 309–10, 312, 313; *Globe*, Sept. 23, 1971, pp. 1, 4.

27. Tom Sheehan, "John Kerrigan's War with the Media Maggots," *Boston Phoenix* (hereafter *Phoenix*), May 17, 1977, pp. 23, 26, 27; *Globe*, Jan. 8, 1974, p. 5, Nov. 10, 1977, p. 30; Michael Ryan, "Kerrigan: Held in—and Full of—Contempt," *Phoenix*, Jan. 7, 1975, pp. 12, 13; *Globe*, Jan. 20, 1975, morning edition; for the definition of a conservative, see *Globe*, Apr. 20, 1974; for *Globe*

criticism, see *Globe*, Nov. 1, 1971; quotation regarding felons, etc., *West Roxbury Transcript* (hereafter *Transcript*), Aug. 15, 1973, p. 6; Kerrigan's letter to Common Cause quoted in Dick Sinnott column, *South Boston Tribune*, Oct. 4, 1973, pp. 1, 10; U.S. Commission on Civil Rights, *Hearing, 1975*, pp. 453–54, 470, 472. For Kerrigan and Hicks's victory celebration, see *Globe*, Sept. 26, 1973, p. 1. Kerrigan often accused the *Globe* of trying "to get" him. *Globe*, Sept. 25, 1969, p. 1, Jan. 13, 1969, p. 1.

28. Joe Klein, "The Faster They Fall: John Kerrigan's Broken Promise," *Real Paper*, Sept. 25, 1974, p. 5.

29. Tom Sheehan, "Busing and the Tale of Two Schools," *Phoenix*, Sept. 10, 1974, p. 16; Howard Husock, "Conversation: Thomas Pettigrew on Busing Resistance," *Phoenix*, Sept. 28, 1976, p. 12. Schrag, *Village School Downtown*, pp. 138–41. Emily DiCesare, interview with author, June 1, 1984. For other indications of the overlap of the HSAs and antibusing from 1972 to 1974, see Sheehan, *Boston School Integration Dispute*, pp. 188, 239–40; *Globe*, Mar. 14, 1974; *Transcript*, Apr. 17, 1974, p. 36. In 1971 a few HSA chapters distributed flyers to students urging parents to attend a Faneuil Hall protest meeting. The South Boston flyers asked parents to sign a petition calling for removal of state education commissioner Sullivan. *Globe*, Oct. 2, 1971, morning edition; Boston Home and School Association memorandum, Oct. 1971; *Globe*, Oct. 5, 1971, morning edition; *South Boston Tribune*, Mar. 16, 1972, p. 1; *Phoenix*, Sept. 10, 1974, p. 6.

30. *Globe*, Apr. 24, 1972, morning edition; Charles Glenn, A-400 Journal, April 1972, p. 15; flyer, "REDISTRICTING ALERT ACT NOW NOT SEPTEMBER" with letter of Lauretta Proctor, Concerned Parents Coalition, Mar. 11, 1972, to Massachusetts State Board of Education, BEEO Files. See also, Dave O'Brian, "The Shifting Sands of Politics," *Phoenix*, July 16, 1974, p. 3.

31. Court proceedings described in Sheehan, *Boston School Integration Dispute*, pp. 88–89.

32. Joseph Rosenbloom, "They Came in Buses," *Globe*, Mar. 2, 1973, p. 12, morning edtion; Dick Sinnott column, *Transcript*, Feb. 21, 1973, p. 2. Several antibusing organizations are named in, *Transcript*, Apr. 25, 1973, pp. 4, 5, May 30, p. 6, Aug. 8, p. 4; O'Brian, "Shifting Sands," *Phoenix*, July 16, 1974, p. 3; Sheehan, *Boston School Integration Dispute*, pp. 88–90. Local organizations included: Boston Parents Association—South Boston, Roslindale Concerned Citizens League, West Roxbury Friends of the Neighborhood School, and A Local Group for Repeal of the Racial Imbalance Law.

33. *Transcript*, Mar. 7, 1973, p. 1; *Globe*, March 22, 28, 29, 1973, morning edition; *Globe*, Mar. 27, 28, and July 3, 1973, afternoon edition; "Report and Recommendations of Louis L. Jaffee, Esq., Appointed by the State Board of Education to Hold a Hearing Ordered by the Supreme Judicial Court in a Case Shortly Titled: The Boston School Committee v. The State Department of Education. May 28, 1973," vol. I, pp. 7, 8, 9–13 passim. The hearings and report fill eighteen bound volumes of typescript at the Massachusetts State Board of Education, Quincy, Massachusetts (hereafter Jaffee Hearings).

34. *Globe*, Apr. 4, 1973, pp. 1, 3, morning edition; *Transcript*, May 9, 1973,

p. 1. During this period the board received 443 letters of protest against busing and redistricting, many of which were mimeographed form letters signed by parents; another 38 letters elaborated the writers' positions. Dorothy Osborn to Professor Louis Jaffee, May 17, 1973, memo regarding correspondence received concerning racial balance plan, BEEO Files. The letters apparently were not saved.

· 35. *The New Yorker*, Mar. 11, 1972, pp. 27, 28; Jody Carlson, *George C. Wallace and the Politics of Powerlessness: The Wallace Campaigns for the Presidency, 1964–1976* (New Brunswick, N.J.: Transaction Books, 1981), p. 145; Buell and Brisbin, *Defended Neighborhoods*, pp. 15–18; David L. Kirp, *Just Schools: The Idea of Racial Equality in American Education* (Berkeley: University of California Press, 1982), p. 296.

36. *Globe*, Apr. 24, 27, 1973, morning edition; *Globe*, Apr. 26, May 2, 1973, afternoon edition; *Herald*, Apr. 27, 1973; Muriel Cohen, "Boston Told to Implement Race Balance Plan in 1974," *Globe*, June 25, 1973, pp. 1, 24, afternoon edition.

37. Ross and Berg, "*I Respectfully Disagree*," pp. 84–85, 88–89. The House and Senate also approved Flynn's home rule petition requiring local approval for school district changes, which Sargent also vetoed. "Passage of School Redistricting Bill Advocated by Rep. Flynn," *South Boston Tribune*, Sept. 27, 1973, p. 2; see also, *South Boston Tribune*, Oct. 18, Nov. 1, 15, 1973.

38. *Transcript*, Aug. 15, 1973, p. 1; O'Neil quoted in *Phoenix*, July 16, 1974, p. 18. Election results: *Globe*, Sept. 26, 1973, p. 76, Nov. 7, 1973, afternoon edition; *Transcript*, Nov. 7, 1973, pp. 1, 2. Sullivan statement, *Transcript*, Sept. 19, 1973, p. 6. See also, *Transcript*, Sept. 26, pp. 1, 2, Oct. 31, p. 1; *South Boston Tribune*, Nov. 1, 15, 1973.

39. Ross and Berg, "*I Respectfully Disagree*," pp. 88–89, 99–100; Hicks quoted on p. 100.

40. *Transcript*, Jan. 16, 1974, p. 15. Flynn quoted in Ross and Berg, "*I Respectfully Disagree*," pp. 112–13. When a reporter asked Flynn if he meant the group was willing to risk going to jail, he softened his position. Kerrigan quoted in Ross and Berg, ibid., p. 114, and *Globe*, Feb. 13, 1974. Regarding the angry mood in Hyde Park where residents were planning to fight the imbalance law, and if they lost to send their children to parochial school or keep them home, see *Globe*, Mar. 4, 1974, morning edition.

41. Ross and Berg, "*I Respectfully Disagree*," pp. 114, 119–20; *Globe*, Mar. 16, 28, 1974; *Transcript*, Mar. 6, 1974, p. 3.

42. Ross and Berg, "*I Respectfully Disagree*," p. 123. *U.S. News and World Report*, March 11, 1974; *Globe*, March 24, 1974.

43. Ross and Berg, "*I Respectfully Disagree*," pp. 124–26. The next day the legislative committee heard from supporters of the Racial Imbalance Act in a much briefer and quieter session.

44. *Herald*, Apr. 29, 1974; Ross and Berg, "*I Respectfully Disagree*," pp. 126–27; Cornelius Dalton column, *Herald*, May 26, 1974; Dave O'Brian, "Back on the Bus with Boston School Reform," *Phoenix*, Apr. 23, 1974, pp. 8, 22. Only one of Boston's twenty-two wards, Ward 12 (Roxbury), gave a yes vote (104 no,

242 yes). South Boston's two wards voted 2,398 to 30 and 2,958 to 53 against; Hyde Park voted 5,813 to 158 against, and Roslindale-West Roxbury 5,159 to 166 against. *Globe*, May 22, 1974, morning edition.

45. *Globe*, May 14, 1974, morning edition; 1971 survey reported in HCLE, "Racial Imbalance Act," p. 301. Youngsters mirrored adult opinion, although not quite so decidedly against busing, as a study of violence in the schools done for the school committee revealed. A questionnaire sent to 25,000 students included several questions about busing. With about 5,700–5,900 replying to each question ("yes," "sometimes," "no"), the answers on busing were decidedly against. "White students should be bused to black schools" elicited the most negatives: 5,757 replies, 910 "yes," 777 "sometimes," and 4,070 "no." Student survey reported in [William L. Phipps, S. J. Messina et al.], Commission on Violence Report on the Boston Public Schools to the Boston School Committee, June 1971.

46. Ross and Berg, "*I Respectfully Disagree*," p. 127; *Herald*, Apr. 29, 1974.

47. U.S. Commission on Civil Rights, *Hearing, 1975*, testimonies of Robert Kiley, p. 39; John Coakley, p. 73; and Kathleen Sullivan, p. 455.

48. Testimony of Kevin White, U.S. Commission on Civil Rights, *Hearing, 1975*, p. 512; same story also told in Richard Knox, Thomas Oliphant, and Ray Richard, "The First Year," *Boston Sunday Globe*, May 25, 1975, sec. A, p. 6; Alan Lupo, *Liberty's Chosen Home: The Politics of Violence in Boston* (Boston: Little, Brown and Co., 1977), p. 179.

49. *Globe*, Apr. 2, 1973, p. 16; editorial, "Marching Off-Balance," *Herald*, Apr. 29, 1974.

Chapter Four

1. When the plaintiffs originally filed suit, James Hennigan was the chair of the school committee. Subsequently, when John Kerrigan became chair again, the title of the case changed to *Morgan v. Kerrigan*.

2. Judge W. Arthur Garrity, Jr., interview with author, July 1, 1986. Details of Garrity's life have been assembled from J. Anthony Lukas, *Common Ground: A Turbulent Decade in the Lives of Three American Families* (New York: Alfred A. Knopf, 1985), pp. 223–31; Andy Merton, "Boston's Least Liked Man," *Boston Magazine*, April 1975, pp. 56–59, 86–91; John Kifner, "Judge Who Advocates Busing," *New York Times*, Dec. 19, 1974; and J. Brian Sheehan, *The Boston School Integration Dispute: Social Change and Legal Maneuvers* (New York: Columbia University Press, 1984), pp. 98–100. In his interview, Garrity told me of several errors in Lukas's account, but they are not relevant here.

3. Judge W. Arthur Garrity, Jr., interviews with author, July 1, 1986 and Oct. 3, 1986.

4. "The advantages and disadvantages of the introduction of middle schools were experienced almost entirely by one of the races, the black. The advantages and disadvantages of coeducation were experienced mainly by one of the races, the white. The high schools to which black students were channeled, especially

English, changed in racial composition virtually overnight. During . . . 1967–68, black students at English accounted for 18.5% of the student body. In 1968–69, the entering class at English was 56.5% black. . . . In 1969–70, the entering class at English was 76% black and 18.5% other minority. During 1967–68, 1,600 white students attended English; in September 1969, the number of white students enrolling as freshmen at English was 15." *Morgan v. Hennigan*, 379 F Supp. 410 (D. Mass. 1974).

5. *The Boston School Decision* (Boston: Paperback Booksmith, 1974). On the "inevitability" of Garrity's findings, see Roger I. Abrams, "Not One Judge's Opinion: Morgan v. Hennigan and the Boston Schools," *Harvard Educational Review* 45 (February 1975): 5–16. Garrity's finding of discrimination in the operation of the examination schools has been criticized as unfair by Nathan Glazer, *Affirmative Discrimination: Ethnic Inequality and Public Policy* (New York: Basic Books, 1978), pp. 92–93, 95–96, 103.

6. David L. Kirp, "The Bounded Politics of School Desegregation Litigation," *Harvard Educational Review* 51 (August 1981): 397–99; David L. Kirp, *Just Schools: The Idea of Racial Equality in American Education* (Berkeley: University of California Press, 1982), p. 284; John F. Adkins, James R. McHugh, and Katherine Seay, *Desegregation: The Boston Orders and Their Origin* (Boston: Boston Bar Association Press, 1975), pp. 9–16.

7. Charles L. Glenn, review of *Schools on Trial: An Inside Account of the Boston Case*, by Robert A. Dentler and Marvin B. Scott, *Equal Education in Massachusetts: A Chronicle* 3 (December 1981): 10, 11. In 1975 a team of *Globe* reporters referred to the 1974 state plan as "the desegregation plan that almost no one now defends." Richard Knox, Thomas Oliphant, and Ray Richard, "The First Year," *Boston Sunday Globe*, May 25, 1975, sec. A, p. 2.

8. Ione Malloy, *Southie Won't Go: A Teacher's Diary of the Desegregation of South Boston High School* (Urbana: University of Illinois Press, 1986), p. 6.

9. Jackson quoted in Knox et al., "The First Year," p. 7; Charles L. Glenn, interview with author, July 2, 1985. Even Judge Garrity's staunchest defenders, Dentler and Scott, comment that the Phase 1 plan "contained a component [the pairing discussed here] that seems, in retrospect, to have been designed to feed the flames." Robert A. Dentler and Marvin B. Scott, *Schools on Trial: An Inside Account of the Boston Case* (Cambridge, Mass.: Abt Books, 1981), p. 173.

The story of the black student being hung out a window was referred to by one teacher at South Boston High (1971–77) as the "legendary story of a visiting black student being suspended from the school's flag pole," which, while testifying to hostility to blacks being present, raises doubt regarding the incident's verifiability. Mary G. Colvario, "Recollections of South Boston High School before and during Its First Year of Desegregation," May 1, 1978, typescript, p. 3. According to J. Anthony Lukas, a former colleague of Glenn's reasoned: "Charlie's patience had long since been exhausted by dealing with those bigots on the School Committee. I think he said to himself, 'We've had enough of you racists in South Boston; you're going to Roxbury; let's see how you like that.'" *Common Ground*, p. 240.

10. Fred Salvucci, interview with author, Sept. 20, 1984; Robert Kiley, inter-

view with author, July 8, 1983; Robert B. Schwartz, interview with author, June 11, 1984; John Coakley, interview with author, June 5, 1984. Coakley, a highly regarded school administrator, believed that Garrity was unintentionally and the state board intentionally punitive. The last quotation is from a letter to the editor in *East Boston Regional Review*, Feb. 26, 1975, p. 2 (vol. 6, no. 8). The Citywide Educational Coalition (CEC), a moderate group working to implement desegregation and supporting the elimination of the at-large elected school committee, said "we are stuck with a bad plan badly implemented." [Circular] letter of CEC, Oct. 25, 1974, Clyde Miller, Marilyn MacPherson et al., Clarke Papers. Peter Meade, who succeeded Kiley as deputy mayor for safety, called it "an abominable plan. . . . I think the plan was put together by a group . . . particularly into South Boston [*sic*] to punish Louise Day Hicks because she was such a symbol of . . . defiance of integration." Peter Meade, interview with Gail P. Eagan, Jan. 15, 1987, in Eagan, "The Role of the Press in the Development of an Urban Controversy: The *Boston Globe* and the Desegregation of the Boston Public School System, 1974–1976," Senior Honors Thesis, Holy Cross College, May 15, 1987, Appendix 7, p. 3.

11. *Boston Globe* (hereafter *Globe*), Sept. 27, 1974; Richard Laws, interview with author, June 27, 1984 (Laws was a Hyde Park activist first in the HSA and then in ROAR). Sheehan, *The Boston School Integration Dispute*, pp. 186–87.

12. *Boston Herald* (hereafter *Herald*), June 23, 27, 1974; Knox et al., "The First Year," pp. 4, 5.

13. Knox et al., "The First Year," p. 4; The United States Commission on Civil Rights concluded that the school department had engaged in "inadequate" planning and had taken "minimal" steps to profit from other desegregation experiences, *Desegregating the Boston Public Schools: A Crisis in Civic Responsibility* (Washington, D.C.: GPO, 1976), pp. 66, 68–69. Regarding the difficulty of hiring transitional aides or bus monitors in certain neighborhoods, see, e.g., testimony of Anne Foley, Director, Intervention Center, June 16, 1975, U.S. Commission on Civil Rights, *Hearing Held in Boston, Massachusetts, June 16–20, 1975* (Washington, D.C.: GPO, 1978), pp. 77–78.

14. Kevin H. White to Bob Schwartz, Jan. 2, 1974, interdepartmental communication, and Kelliher to Kiley, Qualey, Tivnan, O'Donnell, Schwartz, Mar. 20, 1974, both in Lupo File; Robert A. Jordan, "Task Force on Busing Faces Some Major Problems," *Globe*, July 2, 1974, afternoon edition; Alan Lupo, *Liberty's Chosen Home: The Politics of Violence in Boston* (Boston: Little, Brown and Co., 1977), pp. 167–86; *Globe*, Apr. 11, 1973; *New York Times*, Apr. 11, 1973. Kevin H. White, "Achieving Equal Education in Boston: A Position Paper by Mayor Kevin H. White, April 10, 1973"; White's adviser, Bob Schwartz, was the architect of this paper and made a copy available to me. Alan Lupo's personal files were also useful.

15. *Herald*, June 23, 1974. The *Globe*, July 24, 1974, afternoon edition, and *Globe*, July 25, 1974, morning edition stories regarding business support received few column inches. Boston businessmen also promised $50,000 to aid compliance. *Globe*, Aug. 22, 1974, afternoon edition.

16. *Globe*, June 14, 1974, morning edition; *Herald*, June 23, 1974; Mel King,

Chain of Change: Struggles for Black Community Development (Boston: South End Press, 1981), pp. 157–58.

17. Lukas, *Common Ground*, pp. 398–99. Robert Healey, *Globe* editor, maintained that the cardinal encountered more opposition from his own priests than revealed in Lukas's *Common Ground* and that some were even withholding collections. Robert Healey, interview with Gail P. Eagan, Mar. 23, 1987, in Eagan, "The Role of the Press," Appendix 5, p. 5. In testimony before the U.S Commission on Civil Rights, Cardinal Medeiros sounded hesitant and defensive, even apologetic. U.S. Commission on Civil Rights, *Hearing, 1975*, pp. 200–210, esp. 205–6.

18. Joseph Egar, Manager, Dorchester Little City Hall, to Mayor Kevin H. White, City of Boston, departmental communication, Aug. 19, 1974, in Lupo File. Meanwhile, Youth Activities Center (YAC) workers, dispatched by the city to organize student "retreats" and rap sessions to promote peace, were warned that "one thing to bear in mind at all times is that we are not out to sell busing." Paul McCaffrey to YAC workers, Aug. 11, 1974, copy of memo in Lupo File.

19. *West Roxbury Transcript* (hereafter *Transcript*), July 24, 1974, p. 3.

20. Colbert column, *Transcript*, Aug. 7, 1974, p. 3; D. Garth Taylor, *Public Opinion & Collective Action: The Boston School Desegregation Conflict* (Chicago: University of Chicago Press, 1986), p. 73; regarding Ellison, see *Globe*, Jan. 23, 1976, p. 10. A poll taken for the *Herald* in 1975 found that whereas 42 percent of strong antibusers would say that the school committee had served the interests of Boston's citizens well, only 29 percent of the moderates would do so. Conversely, more moderates (62 percent) agreed that the committee had failed the people "because it refused to comply with the Racial Imbalance Law during the past ten years which brought the court suit and court-ordered/forced busing to the city" (only 48 percent of strong antibusers agreed). *Herald*, Aug. 14, 1975.

21. *Transcript*, Sept. 4, 1974, p. 2; Lupo notes "West Roxbury protest meeting, night of Aug. 29 [1974]," Lupo File.

22. Knox et al., "The First Year," p. 8; *Globe*, Sept. 1, 1974.

23. U.S. Commission on Civil Rights, *Desegregating the Boston Public Schools*, p. xxiii; Knox et al., "The First Year," pp. 11–13; Christine Rossell, "School Desegregation and Community Social Change," *Law and Contemporary Problems* 42 (Summer 1978): 146.

24. Knox et al., "The First Year," p. 8. The crowd was filled with hard-core militants, neighborhood activists, and antibusing leaders, as evidenced by those quoted in *Herald*, Sept. 10, 1974.

25. "Daily Logs," and "Neighborhood Status Reports," Sept. 10–16, 19, 1974, Lupo File; Knox et al., "The First Year," pp. 9–10; Ken Hartnett, "An Undercurrent Keeps Boston on Edge," *Globe*, Sept. 13, 1974, morning edition; Tom Sheehan, "Desegregation Day: Southie: Ugly Crowds At the Trouble Spot," *Boston Phoenix* (hereafter *Phoenix*), Sept. 17, 1974, pp. 5, 12.

26. Knox et al., "The First Year," p. 11; Anne Kirchemer, "Busing Foe Calls Policing 'Degrading'," *Globe*, Sept. 13, 1974, morning edition; Lupo notes for Sept. 15, Lupo File.

27. Knox et al., "The First Year," p. 13; Judge W. Arthur Garrity, Jr., interview with author, July, 1, 1986.

28. *Globe*, Sept. 13, 1974; Knox et al., "The First Year," p. 11; summary of police reports, Sept. 1974, Lupo File.

29. *Globe*, Sept. 30, 1974, morning edition; Knox et al., "The First Year," p. 14; *New York Times*, Oct. 5, 1974; *Herald*, Oct. 5, 1974.

30. Flyer in Lupo File; also "On Friday Oct. 4th 1974 The South Boston Home and School Association Will Join Other Anti-Busing Organizations Throughout the Country in Observing National Boycott Day."

31. Knox et al., "The First Year," pp. 14–15, 18; *Globe*, Oct. 7, 1974, morning edition; *Transcript*, Oct. 9, 1974, p. 1; U.S. Commission on Civil Rights, *Hearing, 1975*, pp. 261–71, 195–96; regarding fights at Hyde Park High and the beating of a West Roxbury white youth, see *Transcript*, Oct. 16, 1974, pp. 1, 3.

32. Knox et al., "The First Year," p. 15; Mayor Kevin White to Hon. W. Arthur Garrity, Jr., Oct. 7, 1974, Lupo File; the "Daily Log" of incidents for the first days of October shows that violence in other sections was worse than White indicated in this letter. Even Hicks had suggested the day before that the FBI be brought in because a minority of Southie residents were "out of control." Similarly, the black Baptist ministers' conference sent telegrams to state and federal officials to call in federal troops because "our children's lives are in danger; the enemy can stone the buses that our children ride at will." *Globe*, Oct. 7, 1974, morning edition; *Herald*, Oct. 7, 1974; Rev. R. M. T. to Hon. W. Arthur Garrity, Jr., Oct. 6, 1974, Garrity Letters (hereafter GL); Garrity received several similar telegrams during this time.

33. *Globe*, Oct. 9, 1974, afternoon edition.

34. Knox et al., "The First Year," pp. 13, 14–15.

35. Ford quoted in ibid., p. 16; *Globe*, Oct. 17, 1974, morning edition; Johnnene quoted in *The Nation*, Oct. 26, 1974.

36. Numbers from "Statement of Mayor White for Possible Submission to U.S. Commission on Civil Rights, June 19, 1975," Lupo File; *Globe*, Oct. 11, 1974, morning edition. Regarding the troopers, five hundred of whom came to Boston that day, see, e.g., Colvario, "Recollections of South Boston High School," p. 59, and David W. Moran, with Richard F. Radford, *Trooper: True Stories From A Proud Tradition* (Boston: Quinlan Press, 1986), pp. 127–28.

37. *Globe*, Oct. 16, Nov. 2, 1974; *Herald*, Nov. 2, 1974; Knox et al., "The First Year," pp. 16–17; John Kifner, "Boston's Politicians Play a Large Role in the Chaos," *New York Times*, Oct. 20, 1974.

38. Ken O. Botwright, "Kerrigan Calls For Citywide Boycott of Business to Discourage Busing," *Globe*, Oct. 17, 1974, morning edition; *Globe*, Nov. 11, 1974, morning edition; Nov. 25, 1974, afternoon edition. *Boston Ledger*, Oct. 25, 1974, p. 3; *Globe*, Oct. 29, Nov. 5, 1974.

39. *New York Times*, Oct. 4, 1974; Knox et al., "The First Year," p. 14.

40. Michael Ryan, "The Sound of Fury in Southie," *Phoenix*, Dec. 17, 1974, p. 26.

41. Knox et al., "The First Year," pp. 18–19; M. L., South Boston, to Judge W.

Arthur Garrity, Dec. 11, 1974, GL.

42. Kenneth O. Botwright, "A White: 'We Stick Together,'" *Globe*, Dec. 13, 1974, afternoon edition.

43. U.S. Commission on Civil Rights, *Hearing, 1975*, pp. 342–43; Curtis Wilkie, "Hyde Park's Headmaster Hailed, Assailed on Busing," *Globe*, Mar. 10, 1975, afternoon edition; *East Boston Regional Review*, Apr. 16, 1975, p. 1; Malloy, *Southie Won't Go*, pp. 103–14.

44. *Globe*, May 5, 7, 1975; *Globe*, May 14, 1974. See also, "Boston Public School Teachers Attitude Survey," June 1977, CCC, Appendix A, p. 11.

45. *Globe*, May 20, 1975, morning edition; *Globe* editorial, Sept. 11, 1974 and *Ledger*, Oct. 25, 1974; regarding planned march, see *Herald*, May 17, 1975; also, *Herald*, Oct. 7, 13, 1974.

46. *Transcript*, Mar. 5, 1975, p. 3; *Globe*, July 4, 1975, p. 16.

47. Michael Ryan, "Steering Busing Back through the Courts," *Phoenix*, Dec. 31, 1974, p. 17; Dentler and Scott, *Schools on Trial*, p. 115.

48. *Boston Sunday Globe*, Dec. 7, 1975; Sheehan, *The Boston School Integration Dispute*, pp. 189–90; Edward F. Connolly, *A Cop's Cop* (Boston: Quinlan Press, 1985), p. 162. A year later the State Labor Council would adopt a resolution supporting a constitutional amendment to prohibit forced busing, only to have the national AFL-CIO require that it overturn the resolution.

49. *Globe*, July 12, 1974, morning edition; *Globe*, Sept. 24, 1974, afternoon edition; Adkins et al., *Desegregation*, pp. 34–35; Garrity's dealings with the school committee are covered in great detail in J. Michael Ross and William M. Berg, *"I Respectfully Disagree with the Judge's Order": The Boston School Desegregation Controversy* (Washington, D.C.: University Press of America, 1981), pp. 325–46.

50. Michael Ryan, "Kerrigan: Held in—and Full of—Contempt," *Phoenix*, Jan. 7, 1975, pp. 12, 13; Tom Sheehan, "John Kerrigan's War with the Media Maggots," *Phoenix*, May 17, 1977, p. 23.

51. Knox et al., "The First Year," p. 22.

52. Robert Schwartz, interview with author, June 11, 1984. Regarding Ellison, see James Colbert column in *Transcript*, Aug. 7, 1974, p. 3; trial reported in *Globe*, Jan. 23, 1976, p. 10. Even Louise Hicks, who had a 65 percent rating among antibusers, nevertheless had alienated 35 percent of the antibusers. *Globe*, May 5, 1975.

53. Knox et al., "The First Year," p. 22.

54. U.S. Commission on Civil Rights, *Hearing, 1975*, pp. 17–18, 29; Robert Kiley testified that when five Justice Department attorneys came into the city in mid-October, despite their obtaining only two convictions, it nevertheless had a "visible impact" on protest (p. 43).

Chapter Five

1. Charles A. Radin, "The Faiths of South Boston," *Boston Sunday Globe Magazine*, Dec. 7, 1975, p. 36. Mrs. Faith had her more militant moments,

especially in the immediate aftermath of Michael's stabbing. At a rally at Boston Common on December 15, 1974, she said: "I never heard of Judge Garrity until he made his fateful decision. He seems to have more power than any dictator who ever crawled the face of the earth. When my son was stabbed, Judge Garrity's reaction was to heap more indignities on South Boston. It is now a federal offense to utter a nasty word. . . . a federal offense to breathe. We will breathe long after he is dead. . . . With our last breath, we say to you [Garrity]— Never!" Ione Malloy, *Southie Won't Go: A Teacher's Diary of the Desegregation of South Boston High School* (Urbana: University of Illinois Press, 1986), p. 60.

2. Robert Kiley, interview with author, July 8, 1983; Tracy Amalfitano, interview with author, July 8, 1983; Ken O. Botwright, "Apathy Evident in School Council Voting," *Boston Sunday Globe*, Oct. 26, 1975; "Why Doesn't Someone Pass A Law?" *Coalition* 1 (August 1975): 1–2; Pamela Bullard, Joyce Grant, and Judith Stoia, "Ethnic Resistance to a Comprehensive Plan," in Charles V. Willie and Susan L. Greenblatt, eds., *Community Politics and Educational Change: Ten School Systems under Court Order* (New York: Longman, 1981), pp. 38, 42, 48, 58; Frank J. Harris, "The Boston Church and Desegregation," *America*, Sept. 11, 1976, pp. 113–16.

3. *Boston Globe* (hereafter *Globe*), May 7, 1975, pp. 1, 8, 9; Angelo Scaccia, interview with John Mulkern, Feb. 25, 1976. John Mulkern of Babson College conducted a number of interviews in connection with an unpublished manuscript he wrote on Boston's desegregation, which he was kind enough to place at my disposal.

4. Tracy Amalfitano, interview with author, July 8, 1983; *Christian Science Monitor*, July 8, 1975; Jane Margulis quoted in U.S. Commission on Civil Rights, *Hearing Held in Boston, Massachusetts, June 16–20, 1975* (Washington, D.C.: GPO, 1978), p. 113; *Boston Phoenix* (hereafter *Phoenix*), Aug. 5, 1975, pp. 14, 15; Bernadette Malone quoted in Robert Reinhold, "Boston is Fearful in Busing Dispute," *New York Times*, Sept. 15, 1974. Judge Garrity regarded Margulis as "more supportive than opposed." Judge Garrity, interview with author, Oct. 3, 1986.

5. *Phoenix*, Aug. 5, 1975, p. 15. Rita Tomasini later became Rita Walsh-Tomasini and a member of the school committee.

6. V. B., South Boston, to Judge Garrity, Jan. 12, 1975, Garrity Letters (hereafter GL), regarding pressures on children at South Boston High (SBH). Some of the SBH aids were closely tied to the South Boston Information Center.

7. Laura White, "Multi-Ethnic Councils Work for Peace," *Boston Herald* (hereafter *Herald*), Sept. 7, 1975, sec. 5, A2; Richard Knox, Thomas Oliphant, and Ray Richard, "The First Year," *Boston Sunday Globe*, May 25, 1975, sec. A, p. 7; U.S. Commission on Civil Rights, *Hearing, 1975*, testimony of Frank DiMaggio, teacher at SBH, June 18, 1975, p. 337; *Globe*, Aug. 14, 1975, p. 11; David Rogers, "South Boston Reacts to Phase 2 like a Seasoned Fighter," *Globe*, Aug. 30, 1975, morning edition; Tracy Amalfitano, interview with author, July 8, 1983. Regarding teachers and the high school's reopening, see Mary G. Colvario, "Recollections of South Boston High School before and during Its First Year of Desegregation," May 1, 1978, typescript, p. 52.

8. *South Boston Tribune*, Sept. 12, 1974, p. 6; Maria Karagianus, "It's Not Integration She Fights, but Roxbury Makes Her Afraid," *Globe*, Sept. 11, 1974, morning edition; Knox et al., "The First Year," pp. 20, 22; U.S. Commission on Civil Rights, *Hearing, 1975*, pp. 313–15, 303–5, 307. For another South Boston mother's positive reaction to the McCormack School, see Kathleen McDonald, July 10, 1974, letter to *South Boston Tribune*, July 18, 1974, p. 6.

9. U.S. Commission on Civil Rights, *Hearing, 1975*, pp. 301, 307, 308.

10. Emily DeCesare, interview with author, June 11, 1984.

11. Richard Laws, interview with author, June 27, 1984. Another Hyde Park parent kept her daughter home the first two days. Then as she went to school her bus was stoned, setting off physical and emotional disturbances requiring visits by a doctor. By November the daughter was being kept at home. J. T., Hyde Park, to Judge Garrity, Nov. 19, 1974, GL.

12. Undated letter from "Discouraged in Dorchester" to Judge Garrity, in January 1975 folder. Another Dorchester parent wrote of her son taking the bus to the high school every day without significant incident. But his marks were declining, and he felt so little a part of the school that he had decided not to take part in graduation "due to his alienation from the school system as well as his feeling of a lack of a good education." His mother wondered about his chances of getting into college and how he could "overcome the 'stigma' of a diploma from Dorchester High School." Mrs. W. V. P. to Judge Garrity, Feb. 28, 1975, GL.

13. *Globe*, Sept. 9, 1976, afternoon edition. For a different view of the Lee School as underenrolled and an educational success that lost none of its white students once they came, see Pamela Bullard and Judith Stoia, *The Hardest Lesson: Personal Accounts of a School Desegregation Crisis* (Boston: Little, Brown and Co., 1980), pp. 169–81. Bullard and Stoia do recognize, however, that the violent reputation of the nearby Franklin Field housing project made it impossible to get more than a handful of whites to try the Lee.

14. *Globe*, Mar. 19, 1974, morning edition. Another Dorchester mother wrote to the judge of the irony of having earlier found it necessary "to defend my reasons why I sent my children to public school and not to St. Brendan's when I was a daily churchgoer. I wanted my children to be in with all types of children, all races and creeds." But now she would resist busing. "I'll take care of Jimmy's education—and I won't move from Boston. He'll be out of Boston—and where is my business. It's a damn shame that I have become so resentful of the law." T. K. to Judge Garrity, [Sept. 1975?], GL.

15. D. M. Z., Hyde Park, to Judge Garrity, Dec. 11, 1974. A Roslindale father, a member of a Racial Ethnic Parents' Council with five children in the schools, wrote emphatically to Garrity: "I also am opposed to any form of FORCED TRANSPORTATION to achieve quality education." A. E. B. to Judge Garrity, May 17, 1975, GL.

16. Evelyn Touchette, "Looking at Both Sides of School Busing Issue," *Globe*, May 23, 1974, morning edition.

17. Scott also had arrived in Boston recently, coming from the University of Pittsburgh, where he had received his Ph.D., to be an associate dean at Boston University School of Education in 1970.

18. J. Anthony Lukas, *Common Ground: A Turbulent Decade in the Lives of Three American Families* (New York: Alfred A. Knopf, 1985), pp. 249–50; Robert A. Dentler, "Boston School Desegregation: The Fallowness of *Common Ground*," *New England Journal of Public Policy* 2 (Winter/Spring 1986): 81–102; Jacob Spiegel, Francis Keppel, Edward J. McCormack, and Charles V. Willie, "Draft of the Masters in Tallulah Morgan, et al., Versus John Kerrigan, et al., March 21, 1975, pp. 50–51, Appendix C., p. 23.

19. Judge Garrity, interview with author, Oct. 3, 1986. For an argument that the masters' plan was based on faulty data, see "Brief of Respondents Massachusetts Board of Education, et al., in Opposition to Certiorari," May 7, 1976, submitted by Francis X. Belotti, et al. Re: Kevin H. White, Mayor, vs. Tallulah Morgan, et al., John J. Kerrigan, et al., Massachusetts Board of Education, et al., Supreme Court of the United States, October term, 1975, no. 75–1441.

20. "Flynn Predicts Masters Plan Ruination of Boston," *Charlestown Patriot* (hereafter *Patriot*), Mar. 28, 1975, p. 3; Clyde H. Miller, Jr., Marilyn MacPherson, et al., Citywide Educational Coalition, Inc., to Judge W. Arthur Garrity, Jr., Feb. 3, 1975, Clarke Papers; *West Roxbury Transcript* (hereafter *Transcript*), Apr. 2, 1975, p. 4. MCAFB of Charlestown, a moderate group, "strongly" opposed the masters' plan, while moderate Maurice Gillen also opposed it, *Patriot*, Mar. 28, 1975, p. 1, Apr. 11, 1975, p. 3. See also Malloy, *Southie Won't Go*, p. 91, and Knox et al., "The First year," p. 23. The latter as well as the record of discussion in West Roxbury, Roslindale, and Jamaica Plain supports the interpretation here, *Transcript*, Mar. 26, Apr. 2, 9, 14, 1975, and passim. K. Marie Clarke recalled that ROAR tried "to rally people against" the masters' plan in West Roxbury without much success. Clarke, telephone interview with author, Jan. 7, 1988.

21. *Patriot*, Jan. 10, 1975, p. 2, from White's State of the City Address. Alan Lupo, *Liberty's Chosen Home: The Politics of Violence in Boston* (Boston: Little, Brown and Co., 1977), pp. 316–20, has the fullest account of this episode. Kevin H. White, to the Hon. W. Arthur Garrity, Apr. 10, 1975. Bob Schwartz gave me a copy of this letter. There is also a copy in the Garrity Letters; see also, Bob Schwartz, Departmental Communication, City of Boston to Mayor White, Bob Kiley, Dec. 19, 1974.

22. Knox et al., "The First Year," p. 23; Lukas, *Common Ground*, pp. 249–51; John A. Finger, Jr., to Dr. Greg Anrig, Commissioner of Education, with "Analysis of the Draft Report of the Masters with Recommendations For Modifications," Mar. 31, 1975; State Defendants' Critique of Masters' Plan, April 7, 1975. U.S. District Court, Tallulah Morgan et al. v. John Kerrigan et al., Clarke Papers; Michael S. Dukakis, Governor, to John S. Sullivan, Board of Education, Apr. 10, 1975, and William Crowley, to Board of Education, Apr. 10, 1975, Clarke Papers.

23. June 1975 WBZ-TV and Radio 103, editorial broadcast, GL. Contrast this with the transcript of a WILD radio editorial, undated, GL. *Patriot*, Apr. 25, 1975.

24. Judge Garrity, interview with author, Oct. 3, 1986.

25. Ibid.; Dentler, "Boston School Desegregation," p. 90.

26. *Boston Sunday Globe*, Aug. 1, 1976.

27. Tom Sheehan, "ROAR Gets Louder—Garrity's Ruling Fires Up the Anti-Busers," *Phoenix*, May 20, 1975.

28. U.S. Commission on Civil Rights, *Hearing, 1975*, pp. 456–57. See also, James G. Colbert, "Kathleen Sullivan Critical of Garrity," *Transcript*, May 7, 1975, p. 10. Sullivan also advocated a law that would expand the voluntary METCO program and bus only children whose parents wanted them bused to suburbs with empty seats, filling up to 10 percent of their enrollment. *Transcript*, Mar. 5, 1975, p. 8.

29. "A Boston Mother" to Judge Garrity, Aug. 24, 1975, GL.

30. Charles L. Glenn, review of *Schools on Trial: An Inside Account of the Boston Case*, by Robert A. Dentler and Marvin B. Scott, *Equal Education in Massachusetts: A Chronicle* 3 (December 1981): 10.

31. *Globe*, June 18, afternoon edition; *Globe*, June 20, 1975, morning edition.

32. *Globe*, Aug. 16, 1975, morning edition; Dave O'Brian, "Summer Incidents: Teens and Racial Tension," *Phoenix*, Aug. 5, 1975.

33. Lupo chronology, typescript, Lupo File; Robert A. Dentler and Marvin B. Scott, *Schools on Trial: An Inside Account of the Boston Case* (Cambridge, Mass.: Abt Books, 1981), pp. 196–97.

34. *Herald*, Aug. 24, 1975.

35. David Broder column, *Globe*, Sept. 3, 1975; *Herald*, Aug. 30, 1975. A spin-off from the Progressive Labor Party, CAR brought about two hundred young persons to Boston and tried to provoke confrontations with ROAR. After several clashes with antibusing toughs and police, CAR became less active by the end of October. *Phoenix*, Dec. 30, 1975, p. 7.

36. *Globe*, Sept. 8, afternoon edition; *Globe*, Sept. 13, 1975, morning edition.

37. President Ford and members of his administration heartened antibusers by renewing attacks on busing. Lukas, *Common Ground*, pp. 252–58, 271–76, described the siege of Charlestown; see also, *Globe*, Apr. 4, 1976, morning edition; Malloy, *Southie Won't Go*, pp. 144–45.

38. Kevin A. White, Mayor, press release, May 26, 1975; Lupo chronology, Jan. 6, 1975; Tom Kiley to Kirk O'Donnell (Payne, Kiley, & Thorne Inc., Consultants), memo, July 31, 1975, Lupo File. Robert A. Jordan, "Election Boycott Planned by ROAR," *Globe*, July 24, 1975; *Globe*, Sept. 24, 1975, afternoon edition.

39. *Globe*, Nov. 5, 6, 1975, p. 32; George V. Higgins, *Style versus Substance: Boston's Kevin White & the Politics of Illusion* (New York: Macmillan Co., 1985), p. 183.

40. *Boston Sunday Globe*, Nov. 2, 1975, p. 10.

41. Pamela Bullard, Joyce Grant, and Judith Stoia, "Ethnic Resistance to a Comprehensive Plan," p. 44. Another reason for militant antibusers to defeat Question 7 was because black leaders favored it as a way to get blacks on the school committee. Mel King, "Three Stages of Black Politics in Boston, 1950–1980," in James Jennings and Mel King, eds., *From Access to Power: Black Politics in Boston* (Cambridge, Mass.: Schenkman Books, 1986), pp. 30–31.

42. *Boston Ledger*, Nov. 7, 1975, p. 4; *Globe*, Nov. 5, 1975, p. 2; *Phoenix*, Sept. 16, 1975, p. 34.

Chapter Six

1. Emmett H. Buell, Jr., with Richard A. Brisbin, Jr., *School Desegregation and Defended Neighborhoods: The Boston Controversy* (Lexington, Mass.: Lexington Books, 1982), p. 7; Gerald Suttles, *The Social Construction of Communities* (Chicago: University of Chicago Press, 1972), pp. 38–39.
2. Suttles, *Social Construction of Communities*, p. 13.
3. D. Garth Taylor, *Public Opinion & Collective Action: The Boston School Desegregation Conflict* (Chicago: University of Chicago Press, 1986), pp. 9–11, 46.
4. Support for busing among whites in various national polls ranged from 7 to 28 percent depending on the wording of questions, but whatever the phrasing an overwhelming majority was opposed. David O. Sears, Carl P. Hensler, Leslie K. Speer, "Whites' Opposition to 'Busing': Self-Interest or Symbolic Politics?" *American Political Science Review* 73 (June 1979): 371; Jonathan Kelley, "The Politics of School Busing," *Public Opinion Quarterly* 38 (Spring 1974): p. 24, n. 8; Everett Carll Ladd, Jr. and Charles D. Hadley, *Transformation of the American Party System: Political Coalitions from the New Deal to the 1970s* (New York: W. W. Norton and Co., 1975), pp. 171–72.
Boston's whites followed the nation in rejecting segregation in the abstract and becoming more hospitable to interracial contacts earlier shunned. The 1973–75 survey data revealed that about 60 percent of the city's whites opposed segregation. Diane Ravitch, "Busing: The Solution That Has Failed to Solve," *New York Times*, Dec. 21, 1975, sec. 4, p. 3; Sears et al., "Whites' Opposition to 'Busing,' " p. 372; Taylor, *Public Opinion & Collective Action*, p. 57; D. Garth Taylor, Paul B. Sheatsley, and Andrew M. Greeley, "Attitudes toward Racial Integration," *Scientific American* 238 (June 1978): 42, 45.
5. *Boston Herald* (hereafter *Herald*), Aug. 16, 1975, p. 4. Of the two most consistently "liberal" neighborhoods, black Roxbury was much affected by the court order. The other, Central Boston, was the home of professionals, singles, gays, students, and families with few children or affluent enough to use private schools. There existed a striking linkage between a neighborhood's militance and the degree to which its children were affected by the court order, although South Boston reported having only 25 percent of its children in the public school system, which probably reflected Southie's withdrawal from the schools. On this point, see Ione Malloy, *Southie Won't Go: A Teacher's Diary of the Desegregation of South Boston High School* (Urbana: University of Illinois Press, 1986), pp. 113–14, 116. By fall 1975, the alternative South Boston Heights Academy enrolled 576 students in grades 1 through 12. Malloy, *Southie Won't Go*, p. 280; see also, David Rogers, "South Boston Reacts to Phase II Like a Seasoned Fighter," *Boston Globe* (hereafter *Globe*), Aug. 30, 1975, morning edition; *Her-*

ald, Aug. 14, 1975, p. 8, Aug. 15, p. 16, Aug. 16, p. 6, Aug. 22, p. 1.

6. Rep. Angelo Scaccia, interview with John Mulkern.

7. Malloy, *Southie Won't Go*, p. 4; James Connolly, city councillor, interview with Mulkern, "To get to Southie you have to cross a bridge. It is a city within a city." Rep. Kevin Fitzgerald, interview with Mulkern.

8. Taylor, *Public Opinion & Collective Action*, p. 9. South Boston was not among the neighborhoods surveyed in this study.

9. Michael Beames, *Peasants and Power: The Whiteboy Movements and Their Control in Pre-Famine Ireland* (New York: St. Martin's Press, 1983), p. 216; Monica McGoldrick, "Irish Families," in Monica McGoldrick, John K. Pearce, and Joseph Giordano, *Ethnicity & Family Therapy* (New York: The Guilford Press, 1982), p. 227; Jimmy Breslin, *Globe*, Sept. 11, 1975, morning edition; see also, Nathan Glazer and Daniel Patrick Moynihan, *Beyond the Melting Pot* (Cambridge, Mass.: MIT Press, 1964), p. 245.

10. James Kelly, interview with author, June 23, 1983. "No parent in this city should be expected to stand idly by while his parental right is being torn away from him by government. He should speak boldly . . . and endure any misunderstanding [i.e., let them say "racist"] to which he will find himself subjected." Address by Senator William M. Bulger before the Knights of Columbus Communion Breakfast, Boston, Massachusetts, April 15, 1973.

11. Malloy, *Southie Won't Go*, p. 3; Thomas H. O'Connor, *South Boston: My Home Town: The History of an Ethnic Neighborhood* (Boston: Quinlan Press, 1988), pp. 69–71, 201–2; "Insider: Facing the Facts about Busing [an interview with Thomas Pettigrew]," *Boston Phoenix* (hereafter *Phoenix*), Mar. 30, 1982. Boston's ethnic enclaves were not static ghettoes, of course, but neighborhoods "with strong clusterings of poor people from ethnic minorities." Historian Stephen Thernstrom found great in- and out-migration within the same groups from the 1880s to the 1950s. He detected more stability in recent decades. *The Other Bostonians: Poverty and Progress in the American Metropolis, 1880–1970* (Cambridge, Mass.: Harvard University Press, 1973), pp. 27, 41.

12. Dr. William Kanter, interview, April 1975, in appendix of Amy Jo Freedman and David Miles, "Busing in Boston: An Historical Inquiry Into Boston's Irish and Ethnic Communities," seminar paper, Clark University, Spring 1975; Malloy, *Southie Won't Go*, p. 3. Early in Phase 1 several of Southie's elected officials confronted black leaders at a secret meeting arranged by Mayor White. At one point a black spokesman remarked in amazement: "You really think South Boston is something special, don't you?" to which the Southie delegates responded in unison, "yes, you bet we do." Richard Knox, Thomas Oilphant, and Ray Richard, "The First Year," *Boston Sunday Globe*, May 25, 1975, sec. A, p. 17.

13. Jack Beatty, "Respect for South Boston," *New England Monthly*, September 1984, p. 38.

14. Malloy, *Southie Won't Go*, p. 242; J. Brian Sheehan, *The Boston School Integration Dispute: Social Change and Legal Maneuvers* (New York: Columbia University Press, 1984), pp. 190–91; James Kelly, interview with author, June 23, 1983. In my opinion, the Mullens rumors were scare tactics floated by

antibusing leaders who wanted the authorities to believe that the ante was going up and not worth the cost.

15. "Open Meeting on Busing, Gavin School, Monday, 8/19/74, 7:30 P.M." Copy of notes in Lupo File.

16. An "unscientific" survey of fifth and sixth graders found them either unaware of or opposed to busing. *Globe*, Apr. 3, 1973, afternoon edition; *South Boston Tribune*, Mar. 16, 1972, pp. 1, 12, Oct. 25, 1973, p. 1; *Globe*, July 2, 1974, morning edition; see also *Globe*, Mar. 29, 1973, morning edition.

17. Robert J. Rosenthal, "South Boston Center a Rallying Point for Busing Foes," *Globe*, Oct. 11, 1974; *Boston Ledger*, Oct. 25, 1974.

18. William L. Riordan, *Plunkitt of Tammany Hall* (New York: E. P. Dutton and Co., 1963), p. 35. *Globe*, July 2, 1974, morning edition; J. Anthony Lukas, *Common Ground: A Turbulent Decade in the Lives of Three American Families* (New York: Alfred A. Knopf, 1985), pp. 68–71, 79.

19. Mrs. R. C. to Judge Garrity, undated [September 1974?], GL; Jean Mulvaney, interview with author, June 23, 1983; Malloy, *Southie Won't Go*, pp. 19–20, 40, 153; Eleanor Roberts, "Reid 'Cautiously Optimistic,' " *Herald*, Sept. 7, 1975, sec. 5, A2. Peggy Coughlin testified regarding boycotting: "It's so unfair because . . . there are too many people who do not have children involved who are telling those parents [who do], 'Don't send your children.' " U.S. Commission on Civil Rights, *Hearing Held in Boston, Massachusetts, June 16–20, 1975*, (Washington, D.C.: GPO, 1978), p. 315. The police radio story is based on Jean Mulvaney, interview with author, June 23, 1983.

20. Alan Lupo, notes of interview with Bill Edgerton, Lupo File; see Lupo, *Liberty's Chosen Home: The Politics of Violence in Boston* (Boston: Little, Brown and Co., 1977), p. 189; regarding "Judas," see Jon Hillson, *The Battle of Boston* (New York: The Pathfinder Press, 1977), p. 108. Regarding moderates, see Mary G. Colvario, "Recollections of South Boston High School before and during Its First Year of Desegregation," May 1, 1978, typescript, pp. 10, 54–56.

21. Mrs. F. J. C. to Judge Garrity, Aug. 14, 1975, GL; regarding O'Sullivan, see Frank J. Harris, "The Boston Church and Desegregation," *America*, Sept. 11, 1976, pp. 113–16, and Hillson, *Battle of Boston*, p. 106; college youth quoted by Hillson, *Battle of Boston*, p. 111. David Rogers, "South Boston Reacts to Phase II like a Seasoned Fighter," *Globe*, Aug. 30, 1975, morning edition. See remarks of one South Boston mother who did not want her name used "for fear of retaliation," Loretta McLaughlin, "Poverty—Not Busing—Called Biggest Evil for Pupils," *Globe*, Mar. 25, 1976. Even the prestigious Ed McCormack, who brokered the moderate Phase 2 plan, felt the backlash of Southie obsession. "When I accepted the position as master, then many of my friends in South Boston felt I had sold them out." *Boston Sunday Globe*, Aug. 1, 1976.

22. Malloy, *Southie Won't Go*, p. 63. Similarly, one Charlestown woman regarded the protesters as "radicals and nuts." Then she witnessed police action against demonstrations on several occasions: "I couldn't believe what I saw. . . . I thought it wasn't possible to happen in this country. So I walked into the center one day. . . . I've been there ever since and . . . I'm very proud to be with them." Story of Barbara Gillette, Charlestown, J. Anthony Lukas Notes.

23. Report of Mayor's Committee on Violence to Mayor Kevin White, June 23, 1976, pp. 9–10. Typescript copy in GL; copies are also available in other forms.

24. Thomas M. Begley and Henry Alker, "Anti-Busing Protest: Attitudes and Actions," *Social Psychology Quarterly* 45 (1982): 190, 191; James Kelly, interview with author, June 23, 1983.

25. Knox et al., "The First Year," pp. 20–21; *Herald*, Dec. 21, 24, 1974; *Globe*, Dec. 24, 1974, morning edition; *South Boston Tribune*, Dec. 26, 1974, p. 4; Flyer reprinting *Tribune* editorial of Dec. 26, probably issued by SBIC. In Southie's business district at least twenty-nine stores and businesses had signs in their windows stating "We Support the South Boston School Boycott." Affidavit of Patricia Lomans, May 10, 1975, Attachment to Plaintiff's Motion For Leave to Take Deposition And For An Order to Show Cause, *Morgan v. Kerrigan*.

26. Malloy, *Southie Won't Go*, p. 247.

27. Malloy provides a close chronicle for most of the first two school years and a summary of the third. Many parents' letters to Judge Garrity of course complained of black harassment, but others simply told him of the emotional suffering of their children. For example, Mrs. M. D., South Boston, to Judge Garrity, Dec. 31, 1974, GL.

28. Dave O'Brian, "Southie High: Fix It Up or Shut It Down?" *Phoenix*, Dec. 2, 1975, p. 22. Left-wing radicals accused ROAR of directing a campaign to drive out blacks to prove desegregation would not work. *Spark*, vol. 3, no. 1, January 1976, monthly of the Party for Workers Power.

29. Malloy, *Southie Won't Go*, p. 4; George V. Higgins, *Style versus Substance: Boston's Kevin White & The Politics of Illusion* (New York: Macmillan Co., 1985), p. 44; Jim O'Sullivan testimony, June 18, 1975, U.S. Commission on Civil Rights, *Hearing, 1975*, p. 307.

30. John Kifner, "Tensions and Violence in Boston Schools Are Rooted in Traditions of White Ethnic Communities," *New York Times*, May 18, 1975; Dr. William Reid, interview, April 1975, in appendix of Freedman and Miles, "Busing in Boston"; see also Reid's testimony regarding sports, U.S. Commission on Civil Rights, *Desegregating the Boston Public Schools: A Crisis in Civic Responsibility* (Washington, D.C.: GPO, 1976), p. 84.

31. Jean Mulvaney, interview with author, June 23, 1983; Dave O'Brian, "Southie High: Fix It Up or Shut It Down?" *Phoenix*, Dec. 2, 1975, p. 7. For 1986 nostalgia for predesegregation years and bitterness for those after, see Jane DuWors, "South Boston High School—A Legacy of Happiness and Heartaches," *South Boston Marshall*, Jan. 1986, p. 7.

32. *South Boston Tribune*, Nov. 21, 1973, p. 1, Dec. 5, 1974, pp. 4–5, 7.

33. Regarding SBIC, see Malloy, *Southie Won't Go*, pp. 45, 219; see Malloy also for Reid's testimony, p. 182, quotation of girl, p. 41, and football players, p. 139; regarding Zaniboni see Malloy, p. 228, and David Gumpert, "Unwelcome Recess," *Wall Street Journal*, Apr. 4, 1975. Malloy and Reid's view of outside influence is corroborated elsewhere: David W. Moran, with Richard F. Radford, *Trooper: True Stories From A Proud Tradition* (Boston: Quinlan Press, 1986), who mentions "immense pressure from the outside" (p. 122); also, Colvario,

"Recollections of South Boston High School," pp. 32–33.

34. The faculty believed that these segregated assemblies led to escalation of tension. Malloy, *Southie Won't Go*, pp. 23–24, 46–47, 49–50.

35. WEEI radio editorial, Apr. 19, 1976 (Newsradio 59 editorial), GL; and Moran and Radford, *Trooper*, p. 131.

36. Malloy, *Southie Won't Go*, pp. 212–13, 264, 273, 275; senior quoted on p. 263.

37. Address by Senator William M. Bulger before the Knights of Columbus Communion Breakfast, Boston, Massachusetts, April 15, 1973. J. M. L. [Mrs. M. F. L.], South Boston, to Judge Garrity, n.d., GL, echoes Bulger's speech; Flaherty quoted in John Kifner, "South Boston, a 'Town' of Irishmen, Feels as if It's a Persecuted Belfast," *New York Times*, Sept. 23, 1974; Robert A. Dentler and Marvin B. Scott, *Schools on Trial: An Inside Account of the Boston Case* (Cambridge, Mass.: Abt Books, 1981), p. 182.

38. Maurice Ford, "Field Trip to South Boston," *The Nation*, Oct. 26, 1974, p. 392; O'Connor, *South Boston*, p. 219; Boston University *News*, Mar. 3, 1965; *Globe*, Mar. 18, 1965; *South Boston Tribune*, Oct. 14, 1976, p. 5. Regarding harassment of blacks at the D Street project, see "Meeting on Busing Safety, Monday, July 15, 1974, Held at South Boston Library, 10 A.M.," mimeo in Lupo File, and Burt Solomon, "Waiting Down on D Street," *Real Paper*, Oct. 2, 1974, p. 7. Regarding the harassment of black members of the Meatcutters and Butchers Union, see Hillson, *Battle of Boston*, p. 99. "It [anti-black feeling] is more prominent in South Boston than in other sections of the city. . . . Yet . . . it is not the basic cause for the resistance." City Councillor James Connolly, interview with Mulkern, p. 47. See also, "Report and Recommendations of Louis Jaffee, Esq., Appointed by the State Board of Education to Hold a Hearing Ordered by the Supreme Judicial Court in a Case Shortly Entitled: The Boston School Committee and The State Department of Education." May 28, 1973, p. 32 (on file at State Board of Education, Quincy, Mass.).

39. *Globe*, Sept. 13, 1974. A white teacher, Mary Colvario, reported that she routinely heard "nigger" used openly in classes before 1974 and some male teachers speaking of "training the chimps." "Recollections of South Boston High School," pp. 10, 17–18. However, she also told of one senior black girl who was accepted by whites and of an incident of harassment against her for which Headmaster Reid delivered a severe rebuke to a silent school assembly (p. 15). Another black teacher's experience at South Boston High was very different from Weston's. After seeking a permanent appointment in the Boston system for five years, Wayne Martin was assigned to teach history at Southie. On September 3, 1974, after his first day of teachers' meetings, he was accosted near his car by three white men. One held a pellet gun to his head, pulled the trigger, and said "Bang, you're dead." Martin felt the air pressure and presumed the gun was empty, but went home terrified and intending not to go back. David Gelber, "In the Shadow of South Boston High," *Real Paper*, Sept. 18, 1974, p. 6.

40. R. D., South Boston, to Judge Garrity, May 4, 1977, GL; Malloy, *Southie Won't Go*, p. 66.

41. O'Connor, *South Boston*, pp. 209, 211, 219, 223–24.

42. William A. Henry III, "Un-Common Ground," *Boston Magazine*, October 1986, p. 204.

43. Edward F. Connolly, *A Cop's Cop* (Boston: Quinlan Press, 1985), p. 164. At a meeting with parents after the Faith stabbing, Colvario, despite extensive preparation, was caught by surprise by the first "perhaps most telling—question from a visibly upset father, 'How old are some of these boys?' Gratefully I was given some time to consider this first point when the man continued to explain his apprehensions on seeing tall, well built black boys enter the L Street Annex where his fourteen year old daughter was enrolled in the ninth grade." Colvario, "Recollections of South Boston High School," p. 53.

44. South Boston Information Center Files, undated [1975?].

45. Dill McBride, "Charlestown Braces for Busing—Some Townies Ready for Compromise," *Christian Science Monitor*, Sept. 2, 1975, p. 7; Langley Carleton Keyes, Jr., *The Rehabilitation Planning Game: A Study in the Diversity of Neighborhood* (Cambridge, Mass.: MIT Press, 1969), pp. 91, 93. Charlestown was a "tough town," said *Globe* columnist Jeremiah Murphy, where "physical courage is the quality most admired." *Globe*, Aug. 21, 1975, morning edition.

46. Charlestown's history is treated briefly and brilliantly in Lukas, *Common Ground*, pp. 76–79; see also, Sheehan, *The Boston School Integration Dispute*, pp. 210–11; Keyes, *Rehabilitation Planning Game*, pp. 99–100; and James Gillespie Blaine, "The Birth of a Neighborhood: Nineteenth-Century Charlestown, Massachusetts," Ph.D. dissertation, University of Michigan, 1978. Regarding opposition to public housing in the 1930s, see Lupo, *Liberty's Chosen Home*, pp. 83–84. See Lukas, *Common Ground*, pp. 259, 264–65, 470–71, and Sheehan, *The Boston School Integration Dispute*, pp. 240–45, whose interpretations of the controversy differ widely, yet who nevertheless agree on the class bifurcation in Charlestown.

47. Keyes, *Rehabilitation Planning Game*, pp. 104–22; Sheehan, *The Boston School Integration Dispute*, pp. 214–20.

48. Keyes, *Rehabilitation Planning Game*, pp. 121–27.

49. Ibid., pp. 125, 133.

50. Sheehan, *The Boston School Integration Dispute*, pp. 233–38; Keyes, *Rehabilitation Planning Game*, pp. 139–41.

51. Lukas, *Common Ground*, p. 151.

52. *Charlestown Patriot* (hereafter *Patriot*), Dec. 22, 1972; Sheehan, *The Boston School Integration Dispute*, pp. 240–41; Lukas, *Common Ground*, pp. 259, 264–65, 471.

53. Joseph Alsop column, *Washington Post*, Oct. 20, 1975; Regarding Charlestown's anger at the show of force, see Roberta Delaney, Manager, Little City Hall, interview with Mulkern, Feb. 13, 1976. Regarding a 1974 attack on a black and his white friends on Bunker Hill Day, see Burt Solomon, "Charlestown Sunday: One More Battle of Bunker Hill," *Real Paper*, July 3, 1974, p. 8.

54. *Boston Advertiser*, Sept. 21, 1975; Gillen was the subject of a study by Gail Sheehy in *Pathfinders* (New York: William Morrow and Co., 1981), under the name "Bingo Doyle." In a phone interview, June 17, 1983, Gillen said, "I didn't take leadership, it came my way." *Patriot*, Mar. 28, Apr. 11, 18, 1975;

Lukas, *Common Ground*, pp. 266–69; *Globe*, Sept. 3, 1975, p. 3; Diane Dumonoski, "Charlestown—'My Town'—Braces for Busing," *Phoenix*, Sept. 2, 1975, pp. 10, 14. In June 1975, Pat Russell and Tom Johnson, Powder Keg's new top officers, refused to answer questions as reluctant witnesses before the U.S. Civil Rights Commission. *Hearing, 1975*, pp. 607–19.

55. Tom Sheehan, "No Way! Not My kids on a Bus," *Phoenix*, Sept. 16, 1975, p. 26.

56. *Herald*, June 14, 1976, p. 16; for a project kid's hatred of police and "niggers," see Pamela Bullard and Judith Stoia, *The Hardest Lesson: Personal Accounts of a School Desegregation Crisis* (Boston: Little, Brown and Co., 1980), pp. 111–26. Police reports in the *Patriot* for 1975 show that Charlestown was no longer a safe town. In January vandals even wrecked the Boys Club. *Patriot*, Jan. 17, 1975, p. 1.

57. Lukas, *Common Ground*, pp. 455–56, 470–71; Sheehan, *The Boston School Integration Dispute*, pp. 254–55. In 1976 the home of *Patriot* publisher Michael Burns became the target of an arson attack, possibly because of his denouncement of violence, but he was also chief probation officer for the Charlestown District Court. Sheehan, ibid., p. 256.

58. C. D. to Judge Garrity, May 19, 1976, GL.

59. *Patriot*, July 26, 1968, quoted in Sheehan, *The Boston School Integration Dispute*, p. 229. "For SHOC the ends justified the means, and the means employed . . . were often rough. Threatening phone calls, fabricated statistics, and pressure to get pro-renewal people fired." Keyes, *Rehabilitation Planning Game*, p. 127.

60. Jonathan Rieder, *Canarsie: The Jews and Italians of Brooklyn against Liberalism* (Cambridge, Mass.: Harvard University Press, 1985), p. 32. Patrick J. Gallo has criticized the stereotype of Italian-Americans as alienated, reactionary, and antiblack, but found these attributes related to class, residential concentration, and length of time in the country. *Ethnic Alienation: The Italian Americans* (Rutherford, N.J.: Fairleigh Dickinson University Press, 1974), pp. 198–201, 208–9.

61. Richard A. Cohen, *The Educational Experience of East Boston and the North End* (Boston: Action for Boston Community Development, 1971), p. 13. The interpretation of Italian-Americans relies on Richard Gambino, *Blood of My Blood: The Dilemma of the Italian-Americans* (Garden City, N.Y.: Anchor Press, 1975); see also Rieder, *Canarsie*, p. 35.

62. Data regarding welfare is from Cohen, *The Educational Experience of East Boston*, pp. 8–9. In East Boston and the North End, 34.1 percent of heads of families had less than an eighth grade education, compared to 21.2 percent for the city; 51 percent did not complete high school, compared to 38 percent for the city; and only 14.7 percent of family heads had attended college of any sort, compared to 31.2 percent for the city (pp. 10, 11). According to one survey, 36 percent of the Irish, compared with 62 percent of the Italians, would be "very upset" by interracial marriage. Charles M. Sullivan, with Sandra Farrow, Kathlyn N. Hatch, Richard A. Cohen, and Alan Keyes, eds., "Five Ethnic Groups in Boston: Blacks, Irish, Italians, Greeks, and Puerto Ricans," A joint report by

Action for Boston Community Development and United Community Services of Metropolitan Boston, June 1972, p. 52.

63. Kristen Kelch, " 'Eastie' On Busing: Inevitable," *Christian Science Monitor*, Feb. 4, 1975; Fred Salvucci, interview with author, Sept. 20, 1984; Alan Lupo, Frank Colcord, and Edmund P. Fowler, *Rites of Way: The Politics of Transportation in Boston and the U.S. City* (Boston: Little, Brown and Co., 1971), p. 37.

64. Lupo et al., *Rites of Way*, pp. 55–57; East Boston *Newsletter*, Sept. 18, 1970, p. 2; East Boston *Community News*, Feb. 27, 1973, p. 4; Kim Royal, "Eastie: Busing's Next Southie?" *Phoenix*, Dec. 31, 1974, p. 18.

65. Fred Salvucci, interview with author, Sept. 20, 1984; Jo-Ann M. Indelicato, "East Boston Priest Elected to Battle Airport Expansion," *Boston Sunday Herald*, Nov. 8, 1970, p. 2; Nancy Pomerene, "When Priests Become Men of the People," *Globe*, Aug. 12, 1974, p. 3.

66. A. M. I., East Boston, to Judge Garrity, Sept. 30, 1974, GL; *Globe*, Mar. 2, 1973; *Globe*, Aug. 27, 1975, morning edition.

67. *East Boston Regional Review*, Jan. 29, 1975, p. 1; Kelch, " 'Eastie' On Busing"; Kelch, " 'Eastie's' Friendliness Masks Doubt," *Christian Science Monitor*, Feb. 6, 1975; Hillson, *Battle of Boston*, pp. 112–15 regarding Morash harassment.

68. Kelch, " 'Eastie' on Busing"; Kelch, "East Boston Warning Flags Out," *Christian Science Monitor*, Feb. 2, 1975; *Globe*, Mar. 10, 1975, afternoon edition. Fred Salvucci, interview with author, Sept. 20, 1984.

69. Malloy, *Southie Won't Go*, p. 20; "Police intelligence experts reported that the people of Eastie would blow up the tunnel before they allowed busing in their community." Moran and Radford, *Trooper*, p. 121. Regarding the North End: see *Globe*, June 20, 1967, afternoon edition, *Globe*, Aug. 15, 1967, morning edition; letter to editor from NEVER in *East Boston Regional Review*, Mar. 26, 1975, p. 2; *Globe*, Sept. 5, 1975, morning edition; Cohen, *The Educational Experience of East Boston*, p. 5; see also, William M. DeMarco, *Ethnics and Enclaves: Boston's Italian North End* (Ann Arbor, Mich.: UMI Research Press, 1981).

70. Ironically, in 1977 East Boston High School administrators claimed they would expect integration to go smoothly because the school had been integrated for several years and blacks had captained sports teams and been elected to student government posts. "Statement and Plans Regarding East Boston High School," June 1, 1977, developed by the Community Superintendant for District 8, the headmaster and faculty, and Central Office staff, Clarke Papers. See also, P. J. I. to Judge Garrity, Oct. 7, 1974, GL; and Peter J. Ingeneri to John J. Kelly, memorandum, Jan. 25, 1977, Clarke Papers. At a 1971 antibusing rally at Faneuil Hall with the school committee and Hicks present, George DiLorenzo got the wildest applause of the night when he said: "All we have to do is plug up the two holes, and they can't get in or out." *Globe*, Oct. 5, 1971, morning edition. Samplings from East Boston, GL: "I have never done anything against the law and I greatly respect the law, but, as far as I am concerned, my children WILL NEVER BE BUSED." Mrs. C. T., East Boston, to Judge Garrity, Oct. 4, 1974. "I

swear I will not put my 3 children on any bus." Mrs. J. J. to Judge Garrity, [Sept.–Oct. 1974?]. "My individual liberties will not be taken from me or mine under any circumstances. I repeat, UNDER ANY CIRCUMSTANCES." E. M. D. to Judge Garrity, Oct. 11, 1974. "I will not tolerate the busing of my child out of her neighborhood school." Mr. and Mrs. W. C. to Judge Garrity, telegram, [Sept.–Oct. 1974].

71. Michael Matza and Dave O'Brian, "Report from Hyde Park: Law and Order on a Racial Frontier," *Phoenix*, Sept. 28, 1982, pp. 6–7.

72. LoPiccolo quoted in John Kifner, "Violence Mars Busing in Boston," *New York Times*, Sept. 13, 1974. O'Connell described in *Globe*, June 11, 1974, morning edition.

73. E. A. B., Hyde Park, to Judge Garrity, Dec. 31, 1974, GL; "I am deprived of the right of every other parent in the suburbs to send their child to their neighborhood schools." D. M. Z., Hyde Park, to Judge Garrity, Oct. 9, 1974, GL.

74. *Globe*, Mar. 4, June 11, Aug. 21, 22, Sept. 1, Oct. 10, 17, 1974; Tom Materazzo, Manager, Hyde Park Little City Hall to Bill Edgerton, City of Boston, Aug. 21, 1974, Departmental Communication, Lupo File; *West Roxbury Transcript* (hereafter *Transcript*), Apr. 30, 1975, p. 8; Margaret Campbell, "The Opposition of Hyde Park to Court Ordered Desegregation," seminar paper, Clark University, April 24, 1982; Richard Laws, interview with author, June 27, 1984; Bullard and Stoia, *Hardest Lesson*, pp. 139–46.

75. Connolly, *A Cop's Cop*, pp. 175–82, said that protesters outside the school seldom amounted to more than twenty or thirty; Malloy, *Southie Won't Go*, pp. 19, 70, 78, 222, 223, 227, 242; Dick Sinnott column, *Transcript*, Nov. 13, 1974, p. 2; *New York Times*, Sept. 20, 1974; *Globe*, Sept. 23, 1974; Lupo Log, Sept. 24, 1974; Knox et al., "The First Year," *Boston Sunday Globe*, May 25, 1975, sec. A, p. 17; letter of fourteen-year-old freshman at Hyde Park High, unsigned, to Judge Garrity, Jan. 23, 1976, GL; Hyde Park High School Parents Ethnic Council, "Message to Parents," *Newsletter*, January 1977, p. 2; *Herald*, Feb. 2, 1978.

76. D. A., Hyde Park, to Judge Garrity, May 11, 1975, GL; see also A. O., Hyde Park, to Judge Garrity, Oct. 16, 1974, GL. In contrast are other letters from Hyde Park, all to Judge Garrity, GL: V. C. S., Oct. 28, 1976; Mr. and Mrs. P. L., [Oct. 1974?]; and regarding cooperation in council elections, F. W. O., July 14, 1975. Rep. Angelo Scaccia, interview with Mulkern.

77. Matza and O'Brian, "Report from Hyde Park," *Phoenix*, Sept. 28, 1982, pp. 6, 7.

78. Pamela Constable, "Racial Trouble in West Roxbury," *Globe*, Aug. 18, 1982.

79. Lupo, *Liberty's Chosen Home*, p. 13.

80. Jeffrey Lambert, "West Roxbury: Reactions of a Neighborhood to the Boston Busing Crisis," seminar paper, Clark University, May, 1985; Tom Sheehan, "Busing and the Tale of Two Schools," *Phoenix*, Sept. 10, 1974, p. 3.

81. *Herald*, Aug. 14, 1975; West Roxbury-Roslindale was third in percentage outraged (26 percent; Charlestown led with 32 percent), and second in agreeing

that busing violated constitutional rights.

82. James Connolly, interview with Mulkern; *Herald*, Aug. 16, 1975, p. 4. In identifying issues that were serious problems, 79 percent in West Roxbury listed "forced busing" (compared to Eastie and Southie, 89 percent, Charlestown, 87 percent, Hyde Park, 82 percent), while 93 percent in West Roxbury targeted "crime and violence" as a serious concern—the highest score given in the survey to any of twelve problems suggested by the pollsters. *Herald*, Aug. 15, 1975, p. 16. When the *Boston Sunday Globe* ran a story on antibusing that included a photograph of a supposed recent demonstration in West Roxbury, residents were outraged because the building in the photo had been destroyed by fire in 1973 and, further, "there has been no demonstration against school busing in West Roxbury during the school year. . . . The person who took [the picture] from the Globe files to dress up a story really didn't know much about West Roxbury." *Transcript*, Oct. 2, 1974, p. 4.

83. The HSAs, the *Transcript*, and elected officials closely followed the evolution of the state desegregation plan. *Transcript*, Apr. 12, 1972, p. 4; May 17, 1972, p. 2; May 24, p. 1; Dec. 6, p. 1; Dec. 13, p. 1; Dec. 20, p. 1.

84. *Transcript*, Mar. 28, 1973, p. 5; *Globe*, Apr. 3, 1973, p. 1, Apr. 4, p. 1; *Transcript*, May 9, 1973, p. 1; Aug. 22, 1973, pp. 2, 4; Aug. 29, p. 4; Nov. 21, p. 6; Colbert column, Feb. 6, 1974; Feb. 13, pp. 1, 2; Feb. 21, p. 1; Apr. 10, p. 1; Apr. 17, p. 36; May 1, p. 1; *Globe*, June 6, 1974, afternoon edition. In February 1973 the neighborhood antipoverty agency rejected a motion, fourteen to thirteen, that it go on record to favor repeal of the Racial Imbalance Act. A month later an overflow crowd attended its next meeting and turned the vote into approval by twenty-nine to two, with five abstentions. *Transcript*, Feb. 14, 1973, p. 1; Mar. 14, p. 1. In June the *Transcript* printed a rare pro-integration letter from a Boston College professor, June 27, 1973, p. 2.

85. A joint group of Protestant-Catholic clergy paid for an advertisement pleading for nonviolence. *Transcript*, Sept. 4, 1974, p. 15; Sept. 11, p. 1; Sept. 25, p. 1; Oct. 9, p. 3; Oct. 23, p. 4.

86. *Transcript*, Oct. 30, 1974, pp. 1, 4; Nov. 6, p. 7; Nov. 13, pp. 1, 25; Dec. 18, p. 4; Dec. 25, p. 4; Jan. 8, 1975, p. 3; Jan. 29, p. 4; Feb. 26, p. 1; Mar. 12, pp. 1, 4; Mar. 26, pp. 4, 12. Antibusing leaders assumed that there were not enough enthusiasts for ROAR in any one of the three neighborhoods. Janet Palmariello, phone interviews with author, Jan. 11, 14, 1988.

87. *Transcript*, Apr. 30, 1975, pp. 1, 9; *Globe*, Apr. 25, 26, 28, 1975, morning edition.

88. The independent Citywide Educational Committee also was working for peaceful implementation in West Roxbury and urged support of the biracial councils. Letter to editor, Rev. Charles Senarkark, *Transcript*, June 11, 1975.

89. Rep. Michael Connolly, interview with Mulkern. A prediction of white flight immediately appeared on the front page of the *Transcript*, June 11, 1975.

90. M. F. D. to Judge Garrity, Oct. 23, 1974, GL. Other representative letters: R. C., West Roxbury, to Judge Garrity, May 21, 1975, and R.C. to Judge Garrity, June 2, 1975, GL; Mrs. E. E. W., West Roxbury, to Judge Garrity, May 30, 1975, GL. Perhaps most reflective of the West Roxbury ethos was a mother whose

husband was a fire lieutenant working two jobs. Five of their children had attended the Shaw School, now their eleven-year-old had been assaulted twice and they experienced "numerous mornings of nervous anxiety" to get him off to school. E. E., West Roxbury, to Judge Garrity, June 30, 1976, GL.

91. C. M. to Judge Garrity, Apr. 17, 1975, GL. In a subsequent letter M. F. D., a liberal, Dukakis Democrat, told Governor Dukakis that he had never voted for "Kerrigan and Company" and deplored their action but that Judge Garrity should not punish Boston children for the school committee's sins. M. F. D. to Governor Michael S. Dukakis, Apr. 3, 1975, Clarke Papers. M. F. D.'s thinking on busing may also be seen in his "Testimony before the Regional Hearings of the Democratic Platform Committee in Boston, Faneuil Hall, on April 26, 1976." Clarke Papers.

92. *Globe*, Sept. 6, 1975, morning edition; *Transcript*, Apr. 6, 1977.

93. Charles E. Claffey, profile of Colbert, *Globe*, Dec. 24, 1978. Colbert even took the unusual step of publishing, in late 1974, two front page interviews with NAACP leader Thomas Atkins, by then a man hated perhaps only less than Judge Garrity in the antibusing wards.

94. K. Marie Clarke, interview with author, June 27, 1984; *Transcript*, June 4, 1975, p. 1. In an order of Dec. 16, 1975, placing South Boston High School in receivership, Judge Garrity distinguished between the "South Boston *High School* Home and School Association" and the Home and School Association of South Boston, identifying the latter as part of the city alliance and the former as a group that had been expelled from the city association because it was controlled by adults other than parents of children in school. "Supplementary Findings and Conclusions On Plaintiffs' Motion Concerning South Boston High School," Dec. 16, 1975, pp. 4–5.

95. K. Marie Clarke, interview with author, June 27, 1984; her views on the Racial Imbalance Act were reported in *Transcript*, Mar. 7, 1973, p. 22, and Apr. 10, 1974, p. 1. For additional Clarke views see an interview conducted by the Neighborhood Politics Project in 1982, Clarke Papers.

96. K. Marie Clarke, phone interview with author, Jan. 20, 1988; typed copy of press release in Clarke Papers.

97. U.S. Commission on Civil Rights, *Hearing, 1975*, pp. 308, 380–81; *Boston Sunday Herald*, Aug. 17, 1975, p. 55.

98. Janet Palmariello, phone interview with author, Jan. 11, 1988; "People here [in Southie] will never admit the emotional impact on their lives. We always try to solve our problems ourselves. The last thing any of us would do would be to see a psychiatrist." Loretta McLaughlin, "Poverty—Not Busing—Called Biggest Evil for Pupils," *Globe*, Mar. 25, 1976.

99. *Herald*, Aug. 19, 1975, p. 26; Aug. 22, 1975, p. 6. "When you come right down to it there may be as much racism in West Roxbury as there is in Southie. . . . But Southie is a symbol of sorts; it's self-contained, enclosed and more vocal. Everything's closer to the surface." *Phoenix*, Sept. 10, 1974, p. 16.

Chapter Seven

1. Michael Kenney, "The Massing of the Hardhats: A Protest with Differences," *Boston Globe* (hereafter *Globe*), June 29, 1972, morning edition; "The Hard Hats March," editorial, *Globe*, June 30, 1972, afternoon edition.

2. J. Anthony Lukas, *Common Ground: A Turbulent Decade in the Lives of Three American Families* (New York: Alfred A. Knopf, 1985), pp. 259, 260–62; *Globe*, Apr. 8, 1975, morning edition.

3. Joseph Rosenbloom, "They Came in Buses," *Globe*, Mar. 2, 1973, morning edition; *Globe*, Apr. 3, 1973, afternoon edition; "Open Meeting on Busing; Gavin School, Monday, August 19, 1974, 7:30 P.M.," Lupo File; *Globe*, Oct. 5, 1974, morning edition; James S. Kunen, "Who Are These People?" *Boston Magazine*, Nov. 1974, p. 51. The author was a veteran of student protests complaining about "the expropriation of my chants." Regarding buttons, see Tracy Amalfitano, interview with author, July 8, 1983.

4. *Boston Herald* (hereafter *Herald*), Mar. 6, 1975; *Globe*, Jan. 29, May 5, July 4, Sept. 26, Nov. 11, 1975, Jan. 17, 1976. M. M. to Judge Garrity, Apr. 12, 1975, letter regarding incorporation of South Boston Heights Academy, on letterhead stationery, in GL.

5. *Globe*, Aug. 29, 1974, morning edition; also *Globe*, May 5, 1975, morning edition. Mary Binda, interview with author, June 17, 1983; *Christian Science Monitor*, Sept. 10, 1974. In 1983 the South Boston Heights Academy graduated twenty-one seniors with commencement ceremonies at the John F. Kennedy Library, *South Boston Marshall*, June 1983.

6. Russell quoted in Lukas, *Common Ground*, p. 272; postman quoted in Boston *Advertiser*, Sept. 21, 1975; description of Charlestown marches in Lukas, *Common Ground*, pp. 271–73; regarding plans for a three-day "prayer rite" in Southie, see *Herald*, Oct. 6, 1974; Dave O'Brian, "Shifting Moods: Cops and the Crowds in Charlestown," *Boston Phoenix* (hereafter *Phoenix*), Sept. 16, 1975, p. 40; *Herald*, Sept. 13, Oct. 21, 1974.

7. *Globe*, July 10, 1975, morning edition; *Globe*, Dec. 17, 1975, afternoon edition; clipping in South Boston Information Center Scrapbook, SBIC; *Boston Sunday Globe*, May 18, 1975; *Globe*, May 19, 1975, morning edition.

8. *Boston Sunday Globe*, Sept. 22, 1974; flyer, "ADULTS ONLY HUMAN BARRICADE, 7 A.M.," Oct. 4 [1974]," in Lupo File.

9. *Globe*, June 18, 20, 1975, afternoon edition.

10. *Globe*, Oct. 4, 1975, morning edition.

11. *Globe*, Mar. 20, 1975. Ken O. Botwright, "It Was a Tiring Trip But It Was a Ball," *Globe*, Mar. 19, 1975, morning edition; Dave O'Brian, "The ROAR of the Crowd: Their Cause Is Still Not Seen as a National issue," *Phoenix*, Mar. 25, 1975, p. 4.

12. Alan Lupo, *Liberty's Chosen Home: The Politics of Violence in Boston* (Boston: Little, Brown and Co., 1977), p. 17; Lucas, *Common Ground*, pp. 265, 464, 465. Charlestown's Powder Keg said that the NAACP had not liked being suppressed, but because "they feel we've been a free people for so long . . . we should like being told what to do with our children. We should like sitting in a

corner and keeping our mouths shut. Well . . . [w]hat's good for them is good enough for me. Wise up brothers and sisters for WE shall overcome." *Charlestown Patriot* (hereafter *Patriot*), Jan. 24, 1975, p. 2.

13. Flyer in Lupo File. See also U.S. Commission on Civil Rights, *Hearing Held in Boston, Massachusetts, June 16–20, 1975* (Washington D.C.: GPO, 1978), p. 390, testimony of Tom Johnson of Charlestown; Robin Reisig, "Ready or Not, He's Here [George C. Wallace]," *Real Paper*, Feb. 18, 1976, p. 20.

14. Mayor's Committee on Violence to Mayor Kevin White, June 23, 1976, p. 28; regarding attacks on CAR, see *Boston Sunday Globe*, June 8, 15, 1975; *Globe*, Oct. 4, 1975, morning edition; regarding attack on Kennedy, see Cornelius Dalton column, *Herald*, Apr. 11, 1975; regarding ROAR's breakup of a CCC meeting in February 1976, see *Globe*, Feb. 18, 1976, afternoon edition. See also, Charles L. Whipple, "Trying Too Hard to be Careful," *Globe*, July 8, 1975, morning edition, and Dick Sinnott column, *West Roxbury Transcript* (hereafter *Transcript*), May 22, 1974, p. 2.

15. James Kelly, interview with author, June 23, 1983; Robert Healey, "Who's Leading the Antibusing War?" *Globe*, Dec. 13, 1974, morning edition.

16. Lupo notes, Sept. 10, 1974, Lupo File.

17. *Christian Science Monitor*, Sept. 11, 1975; Michael Ryan, "The Sound of Fury in Southie," *Phoenix*, Dec. 17, 1974, p. 26; Rabbitt Inn incident described in Richard Knox, Thomas Oliphant, and Ray Richard, "The First Year," *Boston Sunday Globe*, May 25, 1975, sec. A, p. 14, and its aftermath in Dave O'Brian, "The Club and the Gavel—Seven Days in October," *Phoenix*, Oct. 15, 1974, pp. 4, 18, 20. For meetings in Charlestown regarding "police brutality," see *Globe*, Jan. 6, 1976. A clash between a Southie "Fathers Only" march of five hundred to one thousand and the TPF in February 1976 sparked a chorus of antibusers' complaints, while Police Commissioner di Grazia, after displaying a fearsome array of sticks, rocks, and bottles used to attack and injure his men, announced a new "get tough" policy against "hoodlums," *Globe*, Feb. 21, 1976, morning edition; Ione Malloy, *Southie Won't Go: A Teacher's Diary of the Desegregation of South Boston High School* (Urbana: University of Illinois Press, 1986), p. 228.

18. Judge Garrity called in the BPPA lawyer and told him that this evasiveness would not be tolerated and the union dropped its position. Knox et al., "The First Year," sec. A, pp. 6, 8; also, *Globe*, Sept. 5, 11, Dec. 20, 1974, morning edition, *Globe*, Sept. 5, 1974, afternoon edition; U.S. Commission on Civil Rights, *Desegregating the Boston Public Schools: A Crisis in Civic Responsibility* (Washington, D.C.: GPO, 1976), pp. 108–39. Less than 5 percent of the force's twenty-five hundred personnel were minority, testimony of Professor Raymond T. Galvin, U.S. Commission on Civil Rights, *Hearing, 1975*, p. 624.

19. Joe Klein, "Cops on the Streets: Southie Doesn't Love Them Anymore," *Real Paper*, Oct. 16, 1974, p. 6. For the trials of one Southie-bred motorcycle cop, see Pamela Bullard and Judith Stoia, *The Hardest Lesson: Personal Accounts of a School Desegregation Crisis* (Boston: Little, Brown and Co., 1980), pp. 127–38. Chester Broderick of the BPPA called suburban liberals the real enemy of the police: "They go home at six and watch Walter Cronkite. But we're around at night and see people rob, rape and loot." Burt Solomon, "Cops &

Their Union: The Thoughts of Chairman Broderick," *Real Paper*, Oct. 16, 1974, p. 7. Eventually some policemen became embarrassed and frustrated with the BPPA's strident antibusing posture, not because they disagreed over busing but feeling that "even their own union had run out on them to join the very people fighting them in the streets." Mark H. Furstenberg, "The Politics of Busing, the Pain of the Police," *Boston Sunday Globe*, May 9, 1976.

20. Lupo notes, Sept. 15, 1974, Lupo File.

21. William H. Chafe, *The Unfinished Journey: America Since World War II* (New York: Oxford University Press, 1986), p. 432.

22. Jean Dietz and Robert J. Anglin, "ROAR Women Disrupt Rights Amendment Rally," *Globe*, Apr. 10, 1975, morning edition; Lukas, *Common Ground*, pp. 269–70; Jon Hillson, *The Battle of Boston* (New York: The Pathfinder Press, 1977), pp. 132–33; *Patriot*, Mar. 7, 1975, letter of Mrs. Freda Getherall.

23. Lukas described Alice McGoff's angry resentment of the ERA suburban ladies looking down on her, even while, as a woman on her own [widowed], "she could well understand why women like her cousin Mamie had fought for the vote, equal pay for equal work, the right to a good education. But this kooky new movement that had sprung up in recent years made no sense to her at all." *Common Ground*, p. 271.

24. *East Boston Regional Review*, Nov. 19, 1975, p. 5.

25. Chafe, *Unfinished Journey*, pp. 434–36.

26. Ibid., p. 434.

27. Gerald D. Suttles, *The Social Construction of Communities* (Chicago: University of Chicago Press, 1972); Monica McGoldrick, "Irish Families," in Monica McGoldrick, John K. Pearce, and Joseph Giordano, eds., *Ethnicity & Family Therapy* (New York: The Guilford Press, 1982), p. 321; Kathleen Kilgore, "Militant Mothers: The Politicization of ROAR Women," *Real Paper*, Nov. 13, 1976, p. 6; Rita Graul, phone interview with author, June 21, 1983; Virginia Sheehy, phone interview with author, June 15, 1983; Mary Binda, interview with author, June 23, 1983; Tracy Amalfitano, interview with author, July 8, 1983; Emily DiCesare, interview with author, June 11, 1984; Diane Dumanoski, interview with author, June 17, 1983.

28. K. Marie Clarke, interview with author, June 27, 1984; Kilgore, "Militant Mothers," *Real Paper*, Nov. 13, 1976, p. 5; Phyllis Igoe and Virginia Teehan, interview with author, June 11, 1984; Dick Sinnott column, *Transcript*, June 11, 1975, p. 2; letter of C. M., Hyde Park, to Judge Garrity, Oct. 10, 1974, GL.

29. Gail Sheehy, *Pathfinders* (New York: William Morrow and Co., 1981), pp. 272–78; Maria Karaganis, "My Rights Are Being Taken Away," *Boston Sunday Globe*, Sept. 1, 1974, a portrait of Hyde Park leader Francesca (Fran) Galante Johnnene, a thirty-four-year-old divorced mother of three, who when she became president of the Chittick Home and School Association in 1969 because no one else wanted the job, "was not interested in organizing bake sales."

30. K. Marie Clarke, June 27, 1984, interview with author; Tracy Amalfitano, interview with author, July 8, 1983.

31. Todd Gitlin, *The Whole World Is Watching: Mass Media in the Making &*

Unmaking of the New Left (Berkeley: University of California Press, 1980), esp. p. 17.

32. Gitlin, *The Whole World is Watching*, p. 243.

33. Ibid, pp. 290–91.

34. *Globe*, Sept. 23, 1974, morning edition.

35. Scott Kauffer, "Is Boston a Bush-League Town?" *Boston Magazine*, Sept. 1975, p. 66; Dave O'Brian, "The ROAR of the Crowd: Their Cause Is Still Not Seen as a National Issue," *Phoenix*, Mar. 25, 1975, p. 13. "The black people are being heard, but we're not." Linda Garrity of South Boston, quoted in *Globe*, Sept. 17, 1974, morning edition. On the media's double standard, see Dick Sinnott column, *Transcript*, Dec. 18, 1974.

36. Lupo notes of meetings, Sept. 11, 16, 1974, Lupo File; also, Dave O'Brian, "Don't Quote Me," *Phoenix*, Sept. 16, 1975, p. 20.

37. Tom Sheehan, "Unexpected Trouble at English High," *Phoenix*, Oct. 15, 1974, p. 6; Tracy Amalfitano, interview with author, July 8, 1983; Mayor's Committee on Violence June 23, 1976, to Mayor Kevin White; Memorandum to News Media Personnel from Police Commissioner Robert di Grazia, Aug. 21, 1975, Lupo File; Bruce McCabe, "News Coverage Restrained," *Globe*, Sept. 9, 1975, p. 19, afternoon edition. The *Globe* saw massive media coverage of Phase 2 as a threat to safety since it would "inevitably increase the tension." *Globe*, Sept. 4, 1975, morning edition. In September 1975 the state police issued some eight hundred sets of press credentials. Edwin Diamond, "School Daze: Two Case Studies in Media Mechanics," *Phoenix*, Sept. 30, 1975, *The Media: Magazine Supplement*, p. 8.

38. Nick King, "Mothers' Protest Ends With Curses," *Globe*, Sept. 19, 1975. Dianne Dumanoski, "Charlestown—'My Town'—Braces for Busing," *Phoenix*, Sept. 2, 1975, p. 10; Dave O'Brian, "Shifting Moods: Cops and the Crowds in Charlestown," *Phoenix*, Sept. 16, 1975, p. 8; also Breslin column, *Globe*, Sept. 9, 1975, afternoon edition, regarding a black mother's frustration with the media.

39. Richard Laws, interview with author, June 27, 1984.

40. *Transcript*, Dec. 18, 1974.

41. Ione Malloy, *Southie Won't Go*, pp. 13–114; David W. Moran, with Richard F. Radford, *Trooper: True Stories From A Proud Tradition* (Boston: Quinlan Press, 1986), pp. 139, 140; also, Mary G. Colvario, "Recollections of South Boston High School before and during Its First Year of Desegregation," May 1, 1978, typescript, p. 25. The same point was made by a young woman who was a student at Southie in 1975–76. Jean Mulvaney, interview with author, June 23, 1983.

42. Sinnott in *Transcript*, Oct. 2, 1974, p. 2. This was often a prominent theme at antibusing meetings, e.g., Concerned Citizens of Roslindale, *Transcript*, Dec. 18, 1974, p. 2; Tri-Neighborhood Association, ibid., Dec. 11, 1974, p. 1. Sinnott column, ibid., Mar. 5, 1975, p. 2, quoting column of Ed Forry in *Dorchester Argus-Citizen*.

43. U.S. Commission on Civil Rights, *Hearing, 1975*, pp. 417–18; U.S. Com-

mission on Civil Rights, *Desegregating the Boston Public Schools*, p. 205; Hillson, *Battle of Boston*, p. 33; Maurice Ford, "Field Trip to South Boston," *The Nation*, Oct. 26, 1974, p. 390. Headmaster Reid of South Boston High was dismayed by national media coverage but thought the local media did a better job. Eleanor Roberts, "Reid 'Cautiously Optimistic,'" *Boston Sunday Herald*, Sept. 7, 1975, sec. 5, A2.

44. Knox et al., "The First Year," pp. A12–13; Lukas, *Common Ground*, pp. 500–503; Edwin Diamond, "Looking Back on Busing Coverage," *Phoenix*, Mar. 11, 1975. Compare with the *New York Times*, Sept. 13, 1974, "First Day of School Relatively Calm," *Globe*, Sept. 12, 1974, afternoon edition, and "A Fine Beginning," *Globe*, Sept. 13, 1974, morning edition.

45. Lukas, *Common Ground*, p. 499. In 1987 state representative Michael Flaherty recalled that the *Globe's* portrait of Southie was typified by its publishing of a photo of an obese woman with no teeth, hair in disarray, her mouth open, shouting—"an image of racist bigots." Michael Flaherty, interview with Gail P. Eagan, Apr. 16, 1987, in Gail P. Eagan, "The Role of the Press in the Development of an Urban Controversy: The *Boston Globe* and the Desegregation of the Boston Public School System, 1974–1976," Senior Honors Thesis, May 15, 1987, Holy Cross College, Appendix 4.

46. Lukas, *Common Ground*, pp. 496, 498, 503–5; for a report of ROAR blocking *Globe* trucks on a Saturday night in a driving rain, see *Boston Sunday Globe*, Sept. 22, 1974; Winship quoted in William A. Henry III, "Un-Common Ground," *Boston Magazine*, October 1986, p. 203; regarding tire slashing and thefts, see James Kelly, interview with Gail P. Eagan, Jan. 17, 1987, in Eagan, "Role of the Press," pp. 72–73.

47. Fred Salvucci, interview with author, Sept. 20, 1984; also, Eagan, "Role of the Press," pp. 60–62.

48. Column of Senator William Bulger, *Globe*, Apr. 3, 1974, morning edition; Emily DeCesare, interview with author, June 11, 1984. The principal of Liberty Academy, a newly established private school in Dorchester, believed that if she "went out and demonstrated and threw a brick through a window, I'd be in the news tomorrow." Her educational work, however, would never make the six o'clock news. Kathleen Kilgore, "Militant Mothers: The Politicization of ROAR Women," *Real Paper*, Nov. 13, 1976, p. 6.

49. *Globe*, June 9, 1975, morning edition; earlier, ROAR sent three hundred cars to the Wellesley home of William C. Mercer, president of New England Telephone Company and chair of the United Way campaign. *Patriot*, May 2, 1975, p. 11; *Herald*, Apr. 14, 1975; Lukas, *Common Ground*, pp. 350–51.

50. Bob Sales, "With Thousands Behind Her, Mrs. Glynn Has Her Say," *Globe*, Apr. 4, 1973, p. 9, morning edition; *Globe*, Mar. 28, 1974. West Roxbury Information Center statement, *Transcript*, June 11, 1975, p. 4; Sinnott quotation from *Transcript*, June 11, 1975, p. 2; Donald Lewis, "Rights Commission Ends Boston Hearing," *Globe*, June 21, 1975, morning edition. "United States District Court for the District of Massachusetts, Tallulah Morgan et al., Plaintiffs, v. John Kerrigan et al., Defendants . . . Plaintiffs' Motion for Leave to Take Depositions and for an Order to Show Cause [May 1975]," Clarke Papers.

In September 1974 several 1960s protesters against segregation and the Vietnam War divided on whether civil disobedience was a legitimate tool for antibusing parents. *Globe* Sept. 13, 1974, afternoon edition.

51. Murray Levin, *The Alienated Voter: Politics in Boston* (New York: Holt, Rinehart, and Winston, 1960); see also Robert Healy column, *Globe*, Mar. 24, 1975, morning edition.

52. Interview with Richard Laws, June 27, 1984; description of a ROAR meeting at the Officers' Club in South Boston, Malloy, *Southie Won't Go*, p. 88; ROAR songs [Dec.–Jan. 1974–75?], Flyers, South Boston Information Center Files; Knox et al., "The First Year," p. A13; Robert Schwartz, interview with author, June 11, 1984; Phyllis Igoe, interview with author, June 11, 1984; Sinnott column, *Transcript*, Nov. 13, 1974; J. Anthony Lukas, ROAR File. Regarding ROAR's influence in the city, see *Globe*, Dec. 12, 1974, afternoon edition.

53. Tom Sheehan, "ROAR Gets Louder—Garrity's Ruling Fires Up the Anti-Busers," *Phoenix*, May 20, 1975, pp. 5–6. In May, ROAR held a "National Convention" at Commonwealth Pier in South Boston, *Globe*, May 19, 1975, morning edition, and Tom Sheehan, "Little upROAR at Anti-Busing Convention," *Phoenix*, May 27, 1975, p. 35; Robin Reisig, "Is Judge Garrity Failing?" *Real Paper*, Jan. 14, 1976, p. 22.

54. The ROAR flag was similar to both the Irish and Italian national flags, with a green shamrock in the center of a middle vertical stripe of white surmounted by the initials ROAR, and two other vertical stripes of green and orange. "We had to compromise on the last color," explained a woman from South Boston. *New York Times*, Dec. 15, 1975.

55. Robert A. Jordan, "Antibusing ROAR Undecided on Who to Support against White," *Globe*, Feb. 14, 1975, afternoon edition. Also *Globe*, May 9, 1974; Flynn and Hicks campaign flyers, February 1975, Lupo File; David Rogers, "South Boston Reacts to Phase II like a Seasoned Fighter," *Globe*, Aug. 30, 1975, morning edition.

56. *Real Paper*, June 14, 1975; David Farrell, "Mrs. Hicks's Son in $17,000 City Job," *Globe*, Apr. 15, 1976; *Phoenix*, June 1, 1976, p. 6; Lukas, *Common Ground*, pp. 605–6. White reciprocated in other ways, e.g., in August 1975 the South Boston Little City Hall provided picnic refreshments and equipment for a "Southie Pride Day." Rogers, "South Boston Reacts," *Globe*, Aug. 30, 1975, morning edition. In Charlestown he made similar concessions, George V. Higgins, *Style versus Substance: Boston's Kevin White & The Politics of Illusion* (New York: Macmillan Co., 1985), pp. xii–xiii.

57. Dianne Dumanoski, "Tug of ROAR," *Phoenix*, May 25, 1976, pp. 8–9, 34, 35, 36; Lukas, *Common Ground*, pp. 453–54, 454–55; *Globe*, Mar. 9, 1976; *Boston Sunday Globe*, Mar. 7, 1976; Richard Laws, interview with author, June 27, 1984.

58. *Herald*, Mar. 15, 1975. A former ROAR member described ROAR women's participation in biracial councils: "They aren't calm meetings. They come on screaming. The women remind me of the toughest girls on the block when I was growing up, girls from large families who really knew how to handle them-

selves." Howard Husock, "Southie Anti-Busers: Using the System?" *Phoenix*, Oct. 19, 1976, p. 32.

59. Robert Nisbet, *The Twilight of Authority* (New York: Oxford University Press, 1975). John P. Diggins and Mark E. Kahn discuss the events of the 1960s and 1970s in "Authority in America: The Crisis of Legitimacy," in Diggins and Kahn, eds., *The Problem of Authority in America* (Philadelphia: Temple University Press, 1981), p. 5.

60. White quoted in *Globe*, Sept. 11, 1974, morning edition. The writer of a raging, threatening letter to Judge Garrity tacked on a postscript that is suggestive in this context: "Turn this over to the FBI—the CIA, both of which are crooked and under investigation." D. A. to Judge Garrity, May 11, 1975, GL.

61. See Jonathan Rieder, *Canarsie: The Jews and Italians of Brooklyn against Liberalism* (Cambridge, Mass.: Harvard University Press, 1985), pp. 132–67.

62. Lukas, *Common Ground*, p. 363; Lukas provides an excellent discussion of working-class reactions to the church's social activism and the decline of its authority (pp. 353, 355–58, 399).

63. See Herbert Gans, *The Urban Villagers: Group and Class in the Life of Italian-Americans* (New York: The Free Press, 1962), pp. 106–10, regarding the relative passivity of such neighorhoods earlier.

64. Alan Lupo, Frank Colcord, and Edmund P. Fowler, *Rites of Way: The Politics of Transportation in Boston and the U.S. City* (Boston: Little, Brown and Co., 1971), pp. 34, 36, 37.

65. Douglas Yates, *The Ungovernable City: The Politics of Urban Problems and Policy Making* (Cambridge, Mass.: MIT Press, 1977), pp. 34–37.

66. Alan Dennis Burke, *Firewatch* (Boston: Little, Brown, and Co., 1980), p. 130.

67. See Diane Ravitch, *The Great School Wars: New York City, 1805–1973* (New York: Basic Books, 1974), pp. 233–47 regarding interwar stability.

68. *Globe*, June 21, 1975, morning edition; John Kifner, "Boston Politics and Patronage Playing Big Role in Complex Maneuvering in the School Desegregation Fight," *New York Times*, Dec. 23, 1975, p. 26; regarding vandalism, see Joseph M. Cronin and Richard M. Haller, *Organizing an Urban School System for Diversity: A Report on the Boston Public School Department* (Boston: Boston School Committee, 1970), p. 38. David C. Martin, "U.S. High Schools Riddled With Violence, Panel Is Told," *Globe*, June 12, 1975.

69. *Globe*, Mar. 24, 1970, afternoon edition; *Globe*, May 6, 1970, afternoon edition. See also, *Transcript*, Mar. 25, 1970, p. 1; *Boston Sunday Globe*, Apr. 26, 1970; *Globe*, May 5, 15, 1970, morning edition; *Globe*, May 8, 1970, afternoon edition. From 1970 to 1975 the schools experienced a sharp enrollment decline, while the number of teachers fell a comparatively small amount. Robert A. Dentler and Marvin B. Scott, *Schools on Trial: An Inside Account of the Boston Case* (Cambridge, Mass.: Abt Books, 1981), pp. 189–90.

70. *Globe*, Sept. 26, 27, Oct. 1, 1968, morning edition; *Globe*, Sept. 24, 25, 1968, afternoon edition; Mel King, *Chain of Change: Struggles for Black Community Development* (Boston: South End Press, 1981), pp. 119–21.

71. Testimony of Joseph Day, June 16, 1975, U.S. Commission on Civil Rights, *Hearing, 1975*, p. 117.

72. Charles Tarbi, "500 Protest 'Messy' East Boston High," *Globe*, Sept. 25, 1968, afternoon edition; *Globe*, Sept. 27, 1968, morning edition.

73. Janet Riddell, "A Mother, a Daughter, and a Difference over Protest," *Globe*, Sept. 27, 1968, morning edition.

74. *Boston Sunday Globe*, Jan. 26, 1969; *Globe*, Sept. 19, 1969, afternoon edition, regarding a bearded group "demonstrating with a Viet Cong flag at Jamaica Plain High School and other schools"; Mary Binda, interview with author, June 23, 1983; King, *Chain of Change*, pp. 179–81; Lukas, *Common Ground*, p. 285.

75. "Commission on Violence Report on the Boston Public Schools," to the Boston School Committee, June 1971. The committee sent out 25,000 question-naires and received, for example, 5,668 replies regarding drug use, of which only 1,527 said no to "Drugs are used in school" (p. 8). In South Boston High drugs were not particularly prevalent from 1975 to 1979, in contrast to 1983; in the mid-1970s drug use was confined pretty much to "pot, if anything." Jean Mulvaney, interview with author, June 23, 1983.

76. *Transcript*, Mar. 10, 1971, p. 1; Robert A. Jordan, "Hub Students Win 3 Demands Before Chaos Ends Meeting," *Globe*, Mar. 3, 1971, morning edition; *Boston Sunday Globe*, Mar. 21, 1971; regarding Hyde Park, *Globe*, Oct. 4, 1971.

77. *Transcript*, Feb. 17, 1975, p. 4, and Oct. 21, 1970, p. 1. See also, *Transcript*, Mar. 4, 1970, p. 4; Mar. 25, 1970, p. 4; Nov. 4, 1970, p. 4. One youth who attended a Catholic high school in the 1970s said there was a "spillover" of trouble into his school from public schools, but also that "we were having 'race riots' just to have a day off from school." James Cawley, interview with author, June 22, 1983. Expelling students for misbehavior was once common, but by 1973 the number expelled had dropped to zero. Dentler and Scott, *Schools on Trial*, p. 67.

78. Lukas, *Common Ground*, p. 254.

79. Lupo notes, Sept. 9, 1974, Lupo File.

Chapter Eight

1. Harry C. Boyte, *The Backyard Revolution: Understanding the New Citizen Movement* (Philadelphia: Temple University Press, 1980), pp. 2–3, 18. Boyte did not discuss Boston antibusing specifically, though he did suggest that some oppo-nents of busing later made common cause with blacks in Massachusetts Fair Share, and criticized busing generally as sometimes an unhealthy government intervention in community life (p. 25). A study of citizen participation in seven cities noted that in nearly every city strong antibusing groups formed, but not support groups for desegregation. Don Davies, with Miriam Clasby, Ross Zer-chykov, and Brian Powers, *Patterns of Citizen Participation in Educational*

Decisionmaking, Vol. 1: *An Overview* (Boston: Institute for Responsive Education, 1978), pp. 73–75. See also, Sara M. Evans and Harry C. Boyte, *Free Spaces: The Sources of Democratic Change in America* (New York: Harper and Row, 1986), p. 197.

2. Regarding Boston's power structure and politicians' deference to and dependence on business executives, see Boston Urban Study Group, *Who Rules Boston? A Citizen's Guide to Reclaiming the City* (Boston: The Institute for Democratic Socialism, 1984). Ken O. Botwright, "Kerrigan Calls for Citywide Boycott of Businesses to Discourage Busing," *Boston Globe* (hereafter *Globe*), Oct. 17, 1974, morning edition.

3. Peter Schrag, *Village School Downtown* (Boston: Beacon Press, 1967), p. 46; J. Brian Sheehan, *The Boston School Integration Dispute: Social Change and Legal Maneuvers* (New York: Columbia University Press, 1984), pp. 76–78; Mark Zanger, "The Myth of Populism in the Anti-Busing Movement," *Boston Ledger*, Jan. 10, 1975, p. 5.

4. ROAR pamphlet, "A stabbing Example of Quality Education," Lukas ROAR File.

5. The essential eyewitness account is Joe Klein, "The KKK Comes to Southie," *Real Paper*, Oct. 2, 1974, pp. 5–7; Thomas H. O'Connor, *South Boston: My Home Town: The History of an Ethnic Neighborhood* (Boston: Quinlan Press, 1988), chapter 8; Edward F. Connolly, *A Cop's Cop* (Boston: Quinlan Press, 1985), p. 166; Marty Goldman, "Bnai Brith Report," Lukas ROAR File.

6. J. Anthony Lukas, *Common Ground: A Turbulent Decade in the Lives of Three American Families* (New York: Alfred A. Knopf, 1985), pp. 451–52; Phyllis Igoe and Virginia Teehan, interview with author, June 11, 1984; *Charlestown Patriot* (hereafter *Patriot*), Mar. 14, Apr. 4, 1975.

7. John F. Stack, Jr., *International Conflict in an American City: Boston's Irish, Italians, and Jews, 1935–1944* (Westport, Conn.: Greenwood Press, 1979), passim, esp. pp. 54, 151–60. Norman Mailer, *The Naked and the Dead* (New York: Holt, Rinehart and Winston, 1976), pp. 266–79.

8. Thayer Fremont-Smith to Steve Moynahan, Clerk, United States District Court, June 16, 1977; Memorandum, K. Marie Clarke, President, Annual Winter Meeting, February 8, 1976, Boston Home and School Association; Objection of Boston Home and School Association to Setting Up Racial Quotas or Other Racial Preference in Examination Schools, March 4, 1975, Tallulah Morgan et al. v. John J. Kerrigan et al.; "Boston Home and School Association's Proposals on Student Assignments For the School Year 1977–78," Morgan v. Kerrigan; "Mr. Chairman and Members of the Citywide Coordinating Council," Address to Citywide Coordinating Council, all in Clarke Papers. K. Marie Clarke, interview with Neighborhood Politics Project, 1982, transcript in Clarke Papers, and K. Marie Clarke, phone interview with author, April 11, 1988.

9. Carmen Fields and Ken O. Botwright, "Some Key ROAR Members Condemn Multi-Racial councils," *Globe*, June 28, 1975; "Comments of the Boston Home and School Association With Regard to Vocational/Occupational Education 'Proposed Amendments and Modifications for unified Plan,' " Tallulah Morgan et al. v. Kathleen Sullivan et al., September 20, 1977, Clarke Papers; K.

Marie Clarke, "For Immediate Release," Sept. 11, 1975, Clarke Papers; "Request for Position ENACTED LEGISLATION," Herbert P. Gleason, Corporation Counsel, Nov. 26, 1975, Clarke Papers. HSA leaders were described as willing to cooperate with a modified plan in Bob Schwartz to Mayor White, Bob Kiley, City of Boston Departmental Communication, Dec. 19, 1974, Lupo File.

10. "A Touch of Class," *Boston Observer*, June 1985, p. 8. Lukas expanded on this theme by asserting that the working-class Irish were most angry not at blacks but at "two toilet Irishmen" out in the suburbs who, like Garrity and Kennedy, were responsible for pushing busing on them. Blacks were "surrogates for the class enemy." Kathleen Hirsch, "Common Bond," *Boston Phoenix* (hereafter *Phoenix*), Sept. 24, 1985, sec. 2, p. 15; also J. Anthony Lukas, "Boston in Turmoil: A Matter of Class," *Yale Review* 76 (Autumn 1986): 56–61. In talking to reporters and local audiences Lukas drew attention to class inequities in desegregation much more explicitly than in the book.

11. Hirsch, "Common Bond," *Phoenix*, p. 12; Robert A. Dentler, "Boston School Desegregation: The Fallowness of *Common Ground*," *New England Journal of Public Policy* 2 (Winter/Spring 1986): 95–96, 99–100.

12. J. Robert Nelson, "Blacks and Whites and Yellow Buses," *The Christian Century*, Nov. 6, 1974, p. 1029; *Boston Pilot*, Dec. 21, 1974; Mike Barnicle, "A Lack of Dialogue, an Abundance of Frustration," *Globe*, Apr. 4, 1973, afternoon edition; Mike Barnicle, "The Have-Nots Pay the Price," *Boston Sunday Globe*, Dec. 14, 1975; Murphy, "There's Fear All Right, Fear That Parents Have Lost Control of the Destiny of Their Children," *Globe*, May 25, 1976, morning edition; Patrick F. McDonough, "Forced Busing Generates Hate and Humiliation," *Globe*, Nov. 1, 1974, afternoon edition; Michael Ansara, "What's at the End of the Bus Ride?" *Globe*, Sept. 27, 1974, morning edition; *Globe*, Sept. 29, 1975, afternoon edition; Breslin, *Globe*, Sept. 11, 1975, morning edition; *Globe*, Sept. 8, 1975, afternoon edition.

13. For example, Nathan Glazer, *Affirmative Discrimination: Ethnic Inequality and Policy* (New York: Basic Books, 1976); Joe R. Feagin, "School Desegregation: A Political-Economic Perspective," in Walter G. Stephan and Feagin, eds., *School Desegregation: Past, Present and Future* (New York: Plenum Press, 1980), pp. 25–50; Emmett H. Buell, Jr., with Richard A. Brisbin, Jr., *School Desegregation and Defended Neighborhoods: The Boston Controversy* (Lexington, Mass.: D. C. Heath and Co., 1982); *Globe*, Apr. 14, 1976, afternoon edition.

14. U.S. Commission on Civil Rights, *Hearing Held in Boston, Massachusetts, June 16–20, 1975* (Washington, D.C.: GPO, 1978), pp. 459–60, 508–9, 531–33; see also, *Globe*, June 27, 1975, morning edition; and ROAR statement "What ROAR Wants from Governor Dukakis," printed in *Boston Ledger*, Jan. 31, 1975, p. 3.

15. Thomas J. Cottle, "The Buses Come for These Two," *Boston Sunday Globe*, April 13, 1975.

16. P. P., Dorchester, to Judge Garrity, July 12, 1975, L. G., West Roxbury, to Judge Garrity, undated [in Dec. 1974 file], C. M. T., East Boston, to Judge Garrity, Oct. 4, 1974, all GL. See also, Michael F. Donlon, "Testimony before the Regional Hearings of the Democratic Platform Committee in Boston, Faneuil

Hall, on April 26, 1976," in Clarke Papers. (The families involved in busing, said Donlon, "are virtually all poor and working class families.")

17. *Boston Herald* (hereafter *Herald*), Apr. 12, 1972, p. 3; *Globe*, June 25, 1972; J. Michael Ross and William M. Berg, *"I Respectfully Disagree With the Judge's Order": The Boston School Desegregation Controversy* (Washington, D.C.: University Press of America, 1981), pp. 166, 125.

18. "A Suggested Letter From Wendell to Southie," Feb. 5, 1975, by "Thomas Paine," probably a ROAR product. This satirical flyer had Judge Garrity apologizing to South Boston and saying he was planning to move from Wellesley into an integrated section of Boston; other officials, *Globe* personnel, and TV commentators "agreed that they should earn the right to criticize you" by moving into the city from places like Marblehead, Duxbury, and Scituate.

19. *West Roxbury Transcript* (hereafter *Transcript*), Mar. 7, 1973, p. 2; William Bulger interview with Clark University students, Spring 1975; *Transcript*, Aug. 22, 1973, p. 4; David B. Wilson, "Questions Demanding Answers," *Globe*, Dec. 21, 1974, morning edition; Raymond L. Flynn to Judge Garrity, Oct. 16, 1974, GL; for Alice McGoff's views of suburban liberals, see Lukas, *Common Ground*, pp. 269, 271.

20. *Globe*, July 1, 1975.

21. Jonathan Rieder, *Carnarsie: The Jews and Italians of Brooklyn against Liberalism* (Cambridge, Mass.: Harvard University Press, 1985), p. 42. The account of Palladino's background is based on "A Pixie With a Promise," *East Boston Regional Review*, Nov. 19, 1975, p. 5. Gary Griffith, "The Pixie that Roared," *Real Paper*, Sept. 10, 1975, pp. 14, 22, 24; *Phoenix*, May 20, 1975, p. 5; election profile in *Globe*, Nov. 6, 1975; Elvira Palladino, interview with author, June 5, 1984.

22. Rieder, *Canarsie*, p. 221; David Nyhan, "Pitaro Stands to Be Counted," *Globe*, Sept. 12, 1972, p. 23; Michael Kenny, "Politician, Priest, 'All in One Job,' " *Globe*, May 21, 1972, p. A6. The encounter with Cass is recounted in Richard Knox, Thomas Oliphant, and Ray Richard, "The First Year," *Boston Sunday Globe*, May 25, 1975, sec. A, p. 18.

23. *Globe*, Feb. 15, 1975, pp. 1, 4, morning edition; Cornelius Dalton, "Protest Yes, Disruption No," *Herald*, Apr. 11, 1975.

24. *East Boston Community News*, Feb. 1, 1972, p. 1, and July 17, 1973, p. 5; Julie Aubuchon, "Pixie Palladino: A School Committee Race in Boston," paper, Clark University, May 1986, pp. 6–7.

25. *Globe*, Aug. 27, Oct. 6, 1975; Eleanor Roberts, "Pixie Palladino Takes Aim," *Boston Sunday Herald*, Feb. 22, 1976, sec. 5, p. A1. During the summer Pixie and Hyde Park activist Fran Johnenne spoke to 2,000 Citizens for Neighborhood Schools in Dallas, Texas, and brought down the house with a final shout, "With our last breath, we say NEVER." *Charlestown Patriot* (hereafter *Patriot*), Aug. 15, 1975, p. 11.

26. Griffith, "Pixie that Roared," *Real Paper*, Sept. 10, 1975, pp. 24, 26.

27. *Globe*, Nov. 5, 1975.

28. Roberts, "Pixie Palladino Takes Aim;" Griffith, "Pixie that Roared."

29. Ione Malloy, *Southie Won't Go: A Teacher's Diary of the Desegregation of*

South Boston High School (Urbana: University of Illinois Press, 1986), p. 227; Roberts, "Pixie Palladino Takes Aim."

30. Elvira Palladino, interview with author, June 5, 1984; Rieder, *Canarsie*, pp. 37, 39. Regarding Italians viewing themselves as the "new niggers," see Richard Krickus, *Pursuing the American Dream: White Ethnics and the New Populism* (Garden City, N.Y.: Anchor Books, 1976), pp. 279, 291–92.

31. J. P. K., West Roxbury, to Judge Garrity, Aug. or Sept. 1975, GL.

32. John Coakley, interview with author, June 5, 1984; West Roxbury meeting, Lupo notes, Aug. 29, Lupo File; Tom Sheehan, "ROAR Gets Louder—Garrity's Ruling Fires Up the Anti-Busers," *Phoenix*, May 20, 1975, p. 33; "A Declaration of Clarification," scrapbook clipping, South Boston Information Center.

33. Many murders of blacks received no publicity, in part because of an old police maxim expressing the quintessence of institutional racism: "If a nigger kills a white man, that's murder. If a white man kills a nigger, that's justifiable homicide. If a nigger kills a nigger, that's one less nigger." Lukas, *Common Ground*, pp. 412–13.

34. Regarding white perceptions of Roxbury: "They [whites] have a black neighbor up the street. He's okay, they say. But they paint a picture of Roxbury and North Dorchester . . . of endless violence and depravity. Some are married to cops and firefighters, and the stories brought back home are not the stories of the black guy who is trying to get a mortgage or the black kid who's going to night school." Lupo, *Liberty's Chosen Home: The Politics of Violence in Boston* (Boston: Beacon Press, 1988), p. 180. Similarly, Rieder pointed out that in Canarsie the "stable interiors . . . of righteous and respectable blacks" were not so visible," while the "evidence of the streets was jarringly accessible." *Canarsie*, p. 63.

35. C. K., Jamaica Plain, to Judge Garrity, Oct. 3, 1974, GL; M. C. to Judge Garrity, Oct. 28, 1974, GL. M. S., West Roxbury, to Judge Garrity, [Oct. 1974?], L. G., West Roxbury, to Judge Garrity, [Dec. 1974], unsigned postcard beginning "YOU SEND YOUR KIDS TO PRIVATE SCHOOL" to Judge Garrity, ca. 1974–75, all in GL.

36. Ted Morgan, "Remembering Rene," *New York Times Magazine*, Nov. 11, 1973, pp. 34–36.

37. Malloy, *Southie Won't Go*, p. 66; Lupo notes, Sept. 16, 1974, Lupo File; Sheehan, "ROAR Gets Louder," p. 33.

38. Lukas, *Common Ground*, pp. 157, 304.

39. *Boston Ledger*, Jan. 17, 1975, p. 4; Knox et al., "The First Year," p. A7; Ian Menzies, "Boston Need Not Be Ashamed," *Globe*, Sept. 18, 1974; Pamela Bullard and Judith Stoia, *The Hardest Lesson: Personal Accounts of a School Desegregation Crisis* (Boston: Little, Brown and Co., 1980), pp. 202–17.

40. Rieder, *Canarsie*, p. 72. These impressions are based on my reading of the letters to Judge Garrity, 1974–77, newspaper accounts, Malloy's diary of events in Southie, 1974–76, and Lukas's detailed, eyewitness account of Charlestown.

41. Dick Sinnott, phone interview with author, Nov. 6, 1987; *Transcript*, 1973–76. In 1972 Sinnott was president of the Boston Latin School Home and School Association.

42. *South Boston Tribune*, Aug. 22, 1974, p. 12.

43. *Transcript*, Aug. 14, 1974, p. 4; also, Apr. 11, p. 2, Apr. 18, 1973, p. 2; May 14, 1975, p. 2; letter to the editor, Nov. 7, 1973, p. 6; *South Boston Tribune*, Dec. 6, 1973, p. 14; Nov. 29, 1973, p. 7; and May 2, 1974, p. 8.

44. *South Boston Tribune*, Apr. 12, 1973.

45. *Transcript*, July 17, 1974, p. 2; reprinted Aug. 28, p. 2.

46. *Transcript*, July 24, 1974, p. 2; also June 19, p. 2; Oct. 16, p. 2; Oct. 23, 1974, p. 2; and Nov. 28, 1973.

47. Sinnott in *Transcript*, Mar. 26, 1975, p. 2; on this topic generally, see Albert O. Hirschman, *Exit, Voice and Loyalty: Responses to Decline in Firms, Organizations, and States* (Cambridge, Mass.: Harvard University Press, 1970).

48. Phyllis Igoe and Virginia Teehan, interview with author, June 11, 1984; Richard Laws, interview with author, June 27, 1984.

49. Mike Barnicle, "A Lack of Dialogue, an Abundance of Frustration," *Globe*, Apr. 4, 1973, p. 3.

50. Maffei quoted in Anne Kirchheimer, "Busing Foes Not Sure What's Next," *Globe*, Sept. 13, 1974, morning edition; Robert B. O'Brien, deputy director of the center, quoted in *Globe*, Sept. 3, 1975, p. 3; see also, *Herald*, June 14, 1976, p. 16.

51. T. K., Hyde Park, to Judge Garrity, Oct. 13, 1974, GL.

52. Mr. and Mrs. F. T. C., Dorchester, to Judge Garrity, July 14, 1975, GL.

53. Hicks speech of October 1973 quoted in *Transcript*, Oct. 31, 1973, p. 2; Smith quoted in *Globe*, Sept. 7, 1975, p. 22; GL, Sept.–Dec. 1974, passim. See also the flyer, "Redistricting Alert Act Now NOT SEPTEMBER" with letter of Lauretta Proctor, Concerned Parents Coalition to Massachusetts Board of Education, Mar. 11, 1972, Files of Bureau of Equal Educational Opportunity, Massachusetts State Board of Education, Quincy. The judge's "totalitarian attitude" is also discussed in letter to the editor, Col. John J. McCarthy, *Patriot*, Jan 10, 1975.

54. Flyers, ca. 1974, in GL.

55. Jody Carlson, *George C. Wallace and the Politics of Powerlessness: The Wallace Campaigns for the Presidency, 1964–1976* (New Brunswick: Transaction Books, 1981), pp. 6, 91, 97, 103, 111–124. See also, Krickus, *Pursuing the American Dream*, pp. 275–77.

56. Robert Weisman, "Wallace Aim: 'Send a Message,'" *Boston Ledger*, Feb. 6, 1976, p. 6; Carlson, *George C. Wallace*, pp. 205, 209; Robin Reisig, "Ready or Not, He's Here," *Real Paper*, Feb. 18, 1976, p. 22; David B. Wilson, "Wallace Waves a Magic Wand," *Globe*, Feb. 14, 1976; *Globe*, Mar. 27, 1975, afternoon edition.

57. *Herald*, Feb. 13, 1976, p. 3; Carlson, *George C. Wallace*, p. 209; *Globe*, Mar. 3, 1976, pp. 17, 18, for election returns.

58. Carlson, *George C. Wallace*, p. 209.

59. *Globe*, Oct. 30, 1975, afternoon edition; *Globe*, Nov. 6, 1975, p. 19; on ROAR's decline, *Boston Sunday Globe*, June 29, 1975.

60. *Globe*, Nov. 9, 1977, various stories, morning and afternoon editions; Gary McMillan, "Decision to Stay on Board Causing Tierney Problems," *Globe*,

Nov. 3, 1977, p. 3; Ron Hutson, "O'Bryant Never Doubted Victory," *Globe*, Nov. 9, 1977, p. 19, afternoon edition; Sheehan, *The Boston School Integration Dispute*, p. 178.

61. Walter V. Robinson, "Connolly Tops in Council," *Globe*, Nov. 9, 1977, pp. 1, 15; Robert Healey, "The Message: One Issue Is Not Enough," *Globe*, Nov. 9, 1977, p. 36; other stories in same issue.

62. Galvin plan, various stories, *Globe*, Nov. 9, 1977; Walter V. Robinson, "Candidates in Hub Favor District Plan," *Boston Sunday Globe*, Oct. 30, 1977, p. 13; Peter Cowen, "The View from Beacon Hill, Brighton, South End," *Globe*, Oct. 31, 1977, pp. 1, 6; Nick King, "Most Legislators Support District Voting," *Boston Sunday Globe*, Oct. 30, 1977, p. 12; *Globe*, Nov. 6, 1977, p. 13, and *Globe*, Nov. 7, 1977, p. 14, afternoon edition, on South Boston opposition; Robert L. Turner, "Galvin Bill Defeat Puzzles Analysts," *Globe*, Nov. 9, 1977, p. 77, contained vote by wards; Martin F. Nolan, "Examining Galvin Plan," *Globe*, Oct. 31, 1977, p. 1.

63. Gary McMillan, "Clear Voice from the Neighborhoods," *Globe*, Nov. 10, 1977, p. 25. Christine Rossell, "School Desegregation and Community Social Change," *Law and Contemporary Problems* 42 (Summer 1978): 178; Carol Surkin, "Busing Out as Issue, Quality In," *Globe*, Oct. 25, 1977, p. 24; Gary McMillan, "School Committee: Ad Blitz," *Globe*, Nov. 6, 1977, pp. 1, 10; Robert A. Jordan, "For Boston Voters, a Chance to Bring in Real Representation," *Globe*, Oct. 5, 1977; *Globe*, Nov. 19, 1977, p. 5.

64. William Lewis, "ROAR Regards Reagan as its Redeemer," *Herald*, Oct. 23, 1975; Weisman, "Wallace Aim: 'Send a Message,' " *Ledger*, Feb. 6, 1976, p. 7.

65. K. Marie Clarke, interview with author, June 27, 1984; in 1982 Clarke was a delegate to the Democratic state convention.

66. Alan Lupo, *Liberty's Chosen Home*, pp. 342–43 (the 1988 edition contains a new epilogue); David Nyhan, "Slow Healing Process Is Underway," *Globe*, June 24, 1984, pp. 1, 8; for Flynn's record in minority hiring, see Brian C. Mooney, "White-Minority Wage Gap in City Jobs Seen Closing," *Globe*, Mar. 1, 1989, p. 25.

67. For criticism of Flynn, see James Green, "The Making of Mel King's Rainbow Coalition: Political Changes in Boston, 1963–1983," in James Jennings and Mel King, eds., *From Access to Power: Black Politics in Boston* (Cambridge, Mass.: Schenkman Books, 1986), pp. 99–135. Thomas H. O'Connor, *South Boston My Home Town: The History of an Ethnic Neighborhood* (Boston: Quinlan Press, 1988), pp. 241–45; Jonathan Kaufman, "Public Housing Integration Moving Slowly," *Globe*, Dec. 28, 1988, p. 13; Brian C. Mooney, "Boston Sets a Slow Pace in Housing Desegregation," *Globe*, June 22, 1989, p. 27. For severe criticism of the Boston media, particularly the *Globe*, for having rewritten Ray Flynn's record on race relations and making him into a moderate, see William E. Alberts, "What's Black, White and Racist All Over?" in Jennings and King, *From Access to Power*, pp. 137–74.

68. Kevin Cullen, "South Boston Activists Leaving Home Turf After Attack," *Globe*, Dec. 30, 1987, pp. 17, 18; Lupo, *Liberty's Chosen Home*, p. 348.

69. Suzanne Perney, "Will the Real Jim Kelly Please Stand Up?" *Boston Sunday Herald Magazine*, Dec. 4, 1988, pp. 8, 18.

70. Ibid., pp. 6, 8, 9, 18; O'Connor, *South Boston*, pp. 238–39; Kevin Cullen, "Jim Kelly: From Southie Firebrand to Field General," *Boston Sunday Globe*, Mar. 13, 1988, pp. 29, 88; Brian C. Mooney, "Kelly Seen as Having Pivotal Role in Integration Process," *Boston Sunday Globe,* July 10, 1988, pp. 23, 26. These sources all cover the desegregation of public housing as well.

Chapter Nine

1. Janet Palmariello, phone interview with author, Jan. 11, 1988.

2. Christopher Jencks, review of *Schooling in Capitalist America: Educational Reform and the Contradictions of Economic Life*, by Samuel Bowles and Herbert Gintes, *New York Times Book Review*, Feb. 15, 1976, p. 17.

3. Howie Schrobe, "An Ex-Anti-Buser Speaks Her Mind," *Thursday: MIT*, Oct. 2, 1975, p. 3.

4. Mayor's Commission on Violence to Mayor Kevin White, June 23, 1976; *Boston Herald* (hereafter *Herald*), Oct. 29, 1976; Walter V. Robinson, "School Violence—the Worst May Be Over," *Boston Globe* (hereafter *Globe*), May 24, 1976. According to state representative Kevin Fitzgerald, in 1976 the Maurice Tobin School was "a shining example of busing that works." Kevin Fitzgerald, interview with John Mulkern, 1976.

5. Theresa M. Padula, president, et al., Home and School Association officers, to Judge Garrity, April 14, 1977, Clarke Papers. A file of letters, "School Closings—1977," in the Clarke Papers contains many similar letters, e.g.: Staff of Rochambeau School, to Thayer Fremont-Smith, April 15, 1977; and Cochairs of REPC and Home and School Association president, William McKinley Elementary School to Hon. W. Arthur Garrity, Jr., May 19, 1977. Examples from 1979: Robert Milling, President HSA, Edward Everett School to Whom It May Concern, Nov. 15, 1979; Robert Fuller, Vice President Kent School HSA [Charlestown] to Thayer Fremont-Smith, Nov. 13, 1979, both in Clarke Papers.

6. On the latter point, see David Gumpert, "Unwelcome Recess," *Wall Street Journal*, Apr. 7, 1975.

7. D. F. to Judge Garrity, Oct. 31, 1974, GL; the following are to Judge Garrity, in GL: A. D., Roslindale, Oct. 7, 1974; Mrs. R. F., Mrs. F. J., May 13, 1975; Mrs. E. E. W., West Roxbury, May 30, 1975; J. T., Hyde Park, Nov. 19, 1974; E. E., West Roxbury, June 30, 1976; F. T. C., Dorchester, Sept. 20, 1975; L. F. R., Oct. 5, 1976; see also "Despaired," July 15, 1977, and Mrs. M. M., Roslindale, June 19, 1975.

8. "A Worried Roslindale Mother" to Judge Garrity, Sept. 8, 1975, GL. "The rights of non-blacks to an equal education is [*sic*] being destroyed by lack of supervision in corridors, elevators, escalators, lunch rooms, and above all lavatories. Why must non-blacks be beaten, monies extorted for lavatory fees, girls insulted, threats of rape and assorted brutalities together with foul language. Must non-blacks suffer these indignities in the name of good education[?] . . .

How long will the grade school children have their lunches stolen, clothing stolen and live in fear of a beating if the authorities are told [?]" V. M., chairperson, Roslindale Improvement Association to Judge Garrity, Oct. 10, 1974, GL.

9. L. M., Hyde Park, to Judge Garrity, [Oct. ?], 1975; A. and E. G., Hyde Park, to Judge Garrity, Oct. 9, 1974, who wrote that their child would not go to school "to learn the black national anthem or foul language or even run the risk of being assaulted in these schools." In Canarsie many whites "viewed black street slang as a sign of blacks' reluctance to observe the most basic proprieties." Jonathan Rieder, *Canarsie: The Jews and Italians of Brooklyn against Liberalism* (Cambridge, Mass.: Harvard University Press, 1985), p. 60.

10. Thomas Fleming, *Rulers of the City* (New York: Doubleday and Co., 1977), p. 196.

11. One school official said that "85 percent of the city is against it, and 6,000 school department employees are trying to frustrate it." John Kifner, "Boston Politics and Patronage Playing Big Role in Complex Maneuvering in the School Desegregation Fight," *New York Times*, Dec. 23, 1975, p. 26.

12. Robert A. Dentler and Marvin B. Scott, *Schools on Trial: An Inside Account of the Boston Case* (Cambridge, Mass.: Abt Books, 1981), pp. 85–87, 104–20, 190–91, 196–201.

13. Ken O. Botwright, "Phase 2 Assignments Bring Flood of Protests," *Globe*, July 9, 1975; Muriel Cohen, "Garrity Phase 2B Plan: Evolution, Not Revolution," *Globe*, May 4, 1976, pp. 1, 21; James Worsham, "No Additional Busing in Garrity's Phase 2B Plan for Next Year," ibid., p. 20.

14. M. —. to Robert A. Dentler, July 28, 1977, GL; Fletcher Roberts, "Brighton Principal Quits: Reassignment One Reason," *Globe*, Nov. 4, 1977, p. 10; Diane Dumanoski, interview with author, June 17, 1983; Alan Lupo, *Liberty's Chosen Home: The Politics of Violence in Boston* (Boston: Beacon Press, 1988), p. 350. In Greensboro, North Carolina, after several years of desegregation, the percentage of white students in the public schools, due to birth rates, age structure, movement to suburbs, and flight to private schools, dropped from 68 to 55 percent. "Faced with the prospect of re-drawing attendance zones so that every school would have the same racial proportions, most parents—black and white —emphasized their commitment to the schools their children were then attending. In many instances, parents had invested hundreds of hours to make the new school pairings work for their children; now these parents were unwilling to go through the process all over again." William H. Chafe, *Civilities and Civil Rights: Greensboro, North Carolina, and the Black Struggle for Freedom* (New York: Oxford University Press, 1980), p. 345.

15. For Atkins's views: *West Roxbury Transcript* (hereafter *Transcript*), Dec. 4, 1974, pp. 1, 20; Walsh's: Robin Reisig, "Is Judge Garrity Failing?" *Real Paper*, Jan. 14, 1976, p. 20; Dentler's: Rowland Evans and Robert Novak, "Judge Garrity and Political Realities of School Administration," *Globe*, Dec. 7, 1977; Pettigrew's: Howard Husock, "Conversation: Thomas Pettigrew on Busing Resistance," *Boston Phoenix* (hereafter *Phoenix*), Sept. 28, 1976, p. 12; Christine H. Rossell, "School Desegregation and White Flight," *Political Science Quarterly* 90 (Winter 1975–76): 688.

The essentials of the controversy are laid out in an exchange between Rossell, Diane Ravitch, and David J. Armor, in "Busing and 'White Flight,'" *The Public Interest* 53 (Fall 1978): 109–15; also Ravitch, "The 'White Flight' Controversy," ibid., (Spring 1978): 135–49. See also, Michael W. Giles, "White Enrollment Stability and School Desegregation: A Two-Level Analysis," *American Sociological Review* 43 (December 1978): 848–64, and Christine H. Rossell, "White Flight: Pros and Cons," *Social Policy* 9 (November/December 1978): 46–51.

16. *Transcript*, Apr. 30, 1975, p. 6, and May 7, 1975, p. 10; Joseph Alsop, "The Second Battle of Bunker Hill," *Washington Post*, Oct. 20, 1975; John Kifner, "Boston Politics and Patronage Playing Big Role in Complex Maneuvering in the School Desegregation Fight," *New York Times*, Dec. 23, 1975, p. 26, reported the loss of at least a third of the white students the first year; Diane Ravitch, "Busing: The Solution that Has Failed to Solve," *Sunday New York Times*, Dec. 21, 1975, sec. 4, p. 3; Alan Eisner, "12,526 Pupils Leave Schools in Busing Crisis," *Herald*, Jan. 15, 1976, p. 1.

17. Muriel Cohen, "Collision Course on Busing," *Globe*, Sept. 4, 1985, p. 36; Rossell, "White Flight," 1978, p. 46, and pp. 48, 49; Dentler and Scott, *Schools on Trial*, pp. 224–27. David J. Armor found "substantial anticipatory effect the year *before* the start of desegregation," a finding that makes one of Rossell's methods "which predicts post-desegregation rates from pre-desegregation rates, very hazardous indeed, with a likely underestimation of 'white flight.'" Rossell, "Busing and 'White Flight,'" p. 115. White movement to the suburbs, of course, has always involved many causes besides school desegregation, see William H. Frey, "Central City White Flight: Racial and Nonracial Causes," *American Sociological Review* 44 (June 1979): 425–48.

18. Virginia Sheehy, interview with Lupo, Lupo Notes; Alan Dennis Burke, *Firewatch* (Boston: Little, Brown, and Co., 1980), p. 186. Archdiocesan representatives told the United States Commission on Civil Rights that the number of students in Catholic high schools in the city actually declined, though it rose in the suburbs. U.S. Commission on Civil Rights, *Hearing Held in Boston, Massachusetts, June 16–20, 1975* (Washington, D.C.: GPO, 1978), pp. 211–12. The conservative estimate here comes from James T. Hannon, "The Influence of Catholic Schools on the Desegregation of Public School Systems: A Case Study of White Flight in Boston," *Population Research and Policy Review* 3 (1984): 228–29; for more detail, see James T. Hannon, "The Catholic Church and School Desegregation in Boston," M.S. thesis, University of Wisconsin, Madison, 1980, pp. 64–76. Coincidentally, one of the schools identified by Hannon as a "likely violator" of the cardinal's policy, Mt. Alvernia, happened to be the elementary school where one of my interview sources, Emily DeCesare of Roslindale, sent her daughter after trying desegregation with unhappy results during 1974–75. DiCesare regarded Catholic education as "adequate" and "safe" but also as "narrow" and expensive, and she needed to contribute to a car pool. This was less inconvenient, however, than moving. Emily DeCesare, interview with author, June 11, 1984. According to Phyllis Igoe and Virginia Teehan, Catholic as well as public schools colluded with parents in falsification of addresses. Interview with author, June 11, 1984.

19. Irene Sage, "A Different System," *Globe*. Sept. 4, 1985, p. 35; Lupo, *Liberty's Chosen Home*, p. 352; Peter Anderson, "My Old School," *Boston Sunday Globe Magazine*, May 8, 1988, pp. 45, 46, 48, 52; Allan R. Gold, "Boston Ready to Overhaul School Busing Policy," *New York Times*, Dec. 28, 1988, p. 38; Diane E. Lewis, "Blacks in Boston: Looking Ahead: Roxbury's Rebirth Brings New Hope and Old Fears," *Boston Sunday Globe*, June 12, 1988, p. 30.

20. Lupo, *Liberty's Chosen Home*, p. 351; Dentler and Scott, *Schools on Trial*, pp. 218–21, 233. Dentler and Scott admitted that something resembling the bad old system of preferential treatment of schools crept back in through the magnet system, a problem which continues (pp. 140–42); Muriel Cohen, "4 Cities' Magnet Schools Are Said to Fail Minorities, Handicapped," *Globe*, Mar. 1, 1989. The major review of the impact of desegregation on student achievement in the mid-1970s found mixed and indeterminate results, see Nancy H. St. John, *School Desegregation: Outcomes for Children* (New York: John Wiley, 1975). An example of how businesses lost interest early on can be found in the case of Boston High School, a trade school integrated since 1966 that had served as a magnet school for "disadvantaged" and "needy" youths, providing basic skills and job opportunities. Under Phase 2, however, students were assigned who were too young for its work program and without motivation, so the school lost its credibility with businesses. K. Marie Clarke, Boston Home and School Association, to Hon. W. Arthur Garrity, Nov. 3, 1976, Clarke Papers.

21. "Parents United: Newsletter of Boston Public School Parents," vol. 4, no. 1, Jan.–Feb. 1979, pp. 1, 4; Peggy Hernandez, "Over 40% Drop Out of Hub High Schools," *Globe*, May 14, 1986, p. 23; *Globe*, June 13, 1986, p. 16; Lupo, *Liberty's Chosen Home*, p. 352; Jim Gomez, "Enrollment's Up in This Course, to School's Dismay," *Globe*, Jan. 9, 1988, p. 1.

22. Kenneth J. Cooper and Muriel Cohen, "Eight Years Later, Black Parents Reassess Boston's Desegregation Plan," *Globe*, Mar. 12, 1982; Larry Johnson and Robert Pressman, "Plaintiffs' Motion For a Freedom of Choice Desegregation Plan," Sept. 13, 1982, and "NAACP—S.C.F. [Special Contribution Fund] Comments on Behalf of Plaintiffs Concerning Draft Final Orders Issued by Court," with Thomas F. Atkins, Aug. 24, 1982, to Stephen Moynahan, Jr., Deputy Clerk, United States District Court, Boston, Clarke Papers; Lupo, *Liberty's Chosen Home*, p. 350; Kenneth J. Cooper, "After 8 Years, Garrity Prepares to Curtail His Role in Schools," *Globe*, Dec. 8, 1982.

23. Howard Husock, "Boston: The Problem That Won't Go Away," *New York Times Magazine*, Nov. 25, 1979, pp. 34, 90, 93. In March 1979, Larry J. Johnson referred to Hyde Park High School's "history of racial violence throughout court-ordered desegregation." Larry J. Johnson, Counsel for Plaintiffs, to Superintendent Robert Wood, Mar. 14, 1979, Clarke Papers.

24. *Boston Sunday Globe*, Feb. 1, 1987; Saragh Snyder, "Charlestown Calmer about Racial Change," *Boston Sunday Globe*, Mar. 1, 1987, pp. 1, 17; Peter J. Howe, "One Month Later, It's Life as Usual at Housing Project," *Globe*, Aug. 15, 1988, pp. 21, 23; Peter J. Howe, "Former BHA Chief Says Base Was Laid for Desegregation," *Globe*, Aug. 15, 1988, p. 23; Brian C. Mooney, "Black Family Moves into Old Colony," *Globe*, Aug. 20, 1988, p. 25; Alan Lupo, "Have You

Heard, Boston? Rumors of Change?" *Phoenix*, Sept. 13, 1983, p. 22; Lupo, *Liberty's Chosen Home*, pp. 342–43; David Nyhan, "Slow Healing Process Is Underway," *Globe*, June 29, 1984, pp. 1, 18. Flynn was endorsed by the minister of one of Roxbury's largest black congregations who said Flynn "has been our friend" and "can bring this city together." *Globe*, July 12, 1983, p. 16. Some former antibusers had bitter reactions to Flynn's "complete turnaround." Phyllis Igoe and Virginia Teehan, interview with author, June 11, 1984.

25. *Globe*, May 13, 1983, p. 6; Daniel Golden, "Hub's Racial Lines Remain in Place," *Globe*, Apr. 8, 1982; Lupo, *Liberty's Chosen Home*, p. 346; Charles Kenney, "The Politics of Turmoil," (Part 1), *Boston Sunday Globe Magazine*, Apr. 12, 1987, pp. 36, 39; ibid., (Part 2), Apr. 19, 1987, p. 26; *Globe*, May 1, 1986, pp. 29, 36; poll reported in Chris Black and Jane Meredith Adams, "Racial Climate Improved, Hub Residents Say," *Globe*, Mar. 9, 1987, pp. 1, 6; Steve Marantz, "Study Finds Racial Pattern in Lending," *Globe*, Sept. 1, 1989. In 1975, when the Vice President of the John Hancock Insurance Company was asked about the presence of minorities among the Hancock's 7,000 employees, he did not have figures "ready at hand," but conceded that "the highest proportion [were] at the clerical level." U.S. Commission on Civil Rights, *Hearing, 1975*, p. 187. At the 1985 forum on J. Anthony Lukas's book, "In Search of *Common Ground*: A Town Meeting on Race and Class in Boston," Sept. 28, 1985, John F. Kennedy Library, Ted Landsmark, the black lawyer and victim of the notorious attack on City Hall steps in April 1976, asked, "How many of you know a black realtor in this town?"

26. In chapter 1 I pointed to the similarities between Boston and New Orleans's attempts at school desegregation. Despite New Orleans's success the second time, its large black underclass remained segregated in residence in substandard housing and generally grim socioeconomic conditions. Race relations had improved, but despite the election of a black mayor in 1977 the black population was more segregated than in 1960. Blacks paid a greater proportion of their income for less worthy housing. Daphne Spain, "Race Relations and Residential Segregation in New Orleans: Two Centuries of Paradox," *The Annals of the American Academy of Political and Social Science* 44 (January 1979): 91, 93, 96.

27. *Herald*, Dec. 24, 1982, p. 1; "Garrity's Final Orders on School Desegregation [complete text]," *Globe*, Sept. 4, 1985.

28. *Herald*, Sept. 30, 1981, June 23, Dec. 23, 1982; Alan Lupo, "Insider: Facing the Facts About Busing," *Phoenix*, Mar. 30, 1982, p. 27; Daniel Terris and Michael Tierney, "There's Hope at South Boston High," *Boston Sunday Globe Magazine*, Nov. 4, 1984, pp. 74, 79, 80; *Boston Sunday Globe*, Apr. 27, 1986, p. 24. In June 1983 there was still graffiti on South Boston High, but not of a discernible racial import. See also, George V. Higgins, *Style versus Substance: Boston's Kevin White & the Politics of Illusion* (New York: Macmillan Co., 1985), p. 165; Mike Barnicle column, *Globe*, Jan. 18, 1985, p. 17.

29. Malloy, *Southie Won't Go*, p. 80; *Globe*, June 9, 1977, pp. 1, 16; *Time*, June 6, 1983, p. 50; D. M. Z. to Judge Garrity, Oct. 9, 1974, GL.

30. Charles L. Glenn, review of *Schools on Trial: An Inside Account of the*

Boston Case, by Robert Dentler and Marvin B. Scott, *Equal Education in Massachusetts: A Chronicle* 3 (December 1981): 10, 11; Winship remark made at "In Search of *Common Ground*: A Town Meeting on Race and Class in Boston," Sept. 28, 1985, John F. Kennedy Library.

31. Closing Southie High was one part of a plan favored by Mayor White's education adviser: Bob Schwartz to Mayor White, Bob Kiley, Dec. 19, 1974, City of Boston, Departmental Communication, Lupo File.

32. Robin Reisig, "Is Judge Garrity Failing?" *Real Paper*, Jan. 14, 1976, p. 13.

33. Andy Merton, "Boston's Least Liked man," *Boston Magazine*, Apr. 1975, pp. 89–90. James P. Sterba, "Denver School Busing Succeeds; Social Mixture Called a Factor," *New York Times*, Oct. 26, 1974.

34. John Kifner, "Boston Politics and Patronage Playing Big Role in Complex Maneuvering in the School Desegregation Fight," *New York Times*, Dec. 23, 1975, p. 26; Francis X. Quinn, "Marion Fahey . . . Without Apologies," *Boston Ledger*, Feb. 6, 1976, p. 5; James G. Colbert column, *Transcript*, Apr. 7, 1976, p. 11.

35. Joseph M. Cronin, et al., "Improving Boston Education," to Hon. Kevin White, Mayor, Sept. 17, 1976, Clarke Papers. As the number of students in the system fell more rapidly after 1974 than previously the excess numbers of teachers and other personnel became even more disproportionate, but the system's most egregious excess was at the top. Pamela Bullard, then a reporter for WGBH-TV, discovered that Denver and San Francisco, both under court-ordered desegregation, possessed comparable student populations. They had 412 and 312 administrators, respectively, compared to Boston's 1,045, and both were cutting back. San Francisco's superintendent's office had a staff of 3; Boston's central staff numbered 14, with 36 associate superintendents and 66 assistant superintendents. Radio Station WEEI editorial, Margaret Noonan, Feb. 5, 1976.

36. Gary McMillan and Fletcher Roberts, "What's Yellow, Costly, Late? A Boston School Bus," *Boston Sunday Globe*, Mar. 12, 1978, p. 1; Judge W. Arthur Garrity to Arthur J. Gartland, Chair, CCC, Dec. 24, 1975, personal correspondence, Clarke Papers. During 1976 the school committee became sensitive to charges that it was wasting money and issued a report defending itself. David Bernstein [director of school committee's Budget Management Program], "The City's Financial Crisis and the Boston School Department," Clarke Papers.

37. Frank Thompson and John Wilpers, "School Balance Cost: $77.1 M," *Herald*, July 2, 1978; *Transcript*, Dec. 17, 1975, p. 22. In September 1976 Boston's tax rate increased by $56.20, raising the per thousand rate to $252.90, the biggest single jump ever; school spending accounted for almost $40 of the $56 increase. J. Brian Sheehan, *The Boston School Integration Dispute: Social Change and Legal Maneuvers* (New York: Columbia University Press, 1984), p. 96.

38. *Herald*, July 2, 1978; *Christian Science Monitor*, Dec. 30, 1977; the cost of protecting the judge and his family over a period less than the first two years of desegregation was $147,752, *Herald*, Apr. 20, 1976.

39. Fred Salvucci, interview with author, Sept. 20, 1984; John Coakley, interview with author, June 5, 1984; for a different view, see Dentler and Scott,

Schools on Trial, p. 47; Judge Garrity believed in the martyr thesis, Judge Garrity, interview with author, Oct. 3, 1986.

40. Joe R. Feagin, "School Desegregation: A Political-Economic Perspective," in Walter G. Stephan and Joe R. Feagin, eds., *School Desegregation: Past, Present and Future* (New York: Plenum Press, 1980), p. 36; some of the relevant literature is discussed in Robert L. Turner, "Governing from the Bench," *Boston Sunday Globe Magazine*, Nov. 8, 1981, pp. 70–71.

41. D. Garth Taylor, *Public Opinion & Collective Action: The Boston School Desegregation Conflict* (Chicago: University of Chicago Press, 1986), p. 8.

42. Eleanor Roberts, "Cardinal Rejects City Leadership Role," *Boston Sunday Herald*, May 2, 1976, p. 1; ibid., May 6, 1976, p. 1; J. Anthony Lukas, *Common Ground: A Turbulent Decade in the Lives of Three American Families* (New York: Alfred A. Knopf, 1985), pp. 398–99.

43. Christine Rossell, "The Mayor's Role in School Desegregation Implementation," *Urban Education* 13 (October 1977): 255–56, 265–66; during the 1974 gubernatorial campaign, Dukakis favored "local control" while his principal opponent, Robert H. Quinn, campaigned as an opponent of "forced busing," which Dukakis did not do. John Kifner, "Massachusetts," *New York Times*, Sept. 8, 1974, and "Reform Democrat to Face Sargent in Massachusetts," *New York Times*, Sept. 11, 1974, p. 34. Judge Garrity saw White as always exaggerating the magnitude of the turmoil accompanying busing. Judge Garrity, interview with author, Oct. 3, 1986.

44. U.S. Commission on Civil Rights, *Hearing, 1975*, pp. 184, 185, 192.

45. Diane Ravitch, *The Great School Wars: New York City, 1805–1973* (New York: Basic Books, 1974), pp. xiii–xiv; J. Anthony Lukas, "All in the Family: The Dilemmas of Busing and the Conflict of Values," in Ronald P. Formisano and Constance K. Burns, eds., *Boston, 1700–1980: The Evolution of Urban Politics* (Westport, Conn.: Greenwood Press, 1984), pp. 241–57.

46. In the 1980s the defended neighborhoods were still battlegrounds in a war that, though less dramatic, was more threatening to their existence. Gentrification and development, which had entered into Charlestown earlier, had penetrated now even into South Boston. These changes, which occasionally resulted in a newspaper story, are potentially more far-reaching too than the limited desegregation of public housing that has begun in both neighborhoods. This was not the result, as some have suggested, of a plot by the same economic elite who promoted desegregation. In Southie, some former antibusers were now backing both gentrification and commercial development. Lupo, *Liberty's Chosen Home*, pp. 335–36, 347–48; *Globe*, Sept. 26, 1984, pp. 1, 10; David Rublin, "A Loaf of Bread, a Jug of Milk, and Megabucks," *Boston Sunday Globe Magazine*, Jan. 17, 1988, p. 56.

Chapter Ten

1. Gary Orfield, *Must We Bus? Segregated Schools and National Policy* (Washington, D.C.: Brookings Institute, 1978), discusses similar patterns in New York,

Los Angeles, Chicago, Philadelphia, and Detroit, pp. 151–62, 168–75.

2. Ira Katznelson and Margaret Weir, *Schooling for All: Race, Class and the Decline of the Democratic Ideal* (New York: Basic Books, 1985), pp. 183–89; see also, Alan B. Anderson and George W. Pickering, *Confronting the Color Line: The Broken Promise of the Civil Rights Movement in Chicago* (Athens: University of Georgia Press, 1986), pp. 72–102, 105–67, 326–36; Charles Wollenberg, *All Deliberate Speed: Segregation and Exclusion in California Schools, 1855–1975* (Berkeley: University of California Press, 1977), pp. 142–77; David Kirp, "School Desegregation in San Francisco, 1962–76," in Allan P. Sindler, ed., *America in the Seventies* (Boston: Little, Brown and Co., 1977), pp. 104–57, Larry Cuban, *Urban School Chiefs under Fire* (Chicago: University of Chicago Press, 1976); and Albert S. Foley, "Mobile, Alabama: The Demise of State Sanctioned Resistance," in Susan L. Greenblatt and Charles V. Willie, eds., *Community Politics and Educational Change: Ten School Systems under Court Order* (New York: Longmans, 1981), pp. 174–207.

3. Harold Cruse, *Plural but Equal: A Critical Study of Blacks and Minorities and America's Plural Society* (New York: William Morrow and Co., 1987), p. 20; "We are heading toward ghettoized education on a vast scale." Gary Orfield, "Why It Worked in Dixie: Southern School Desegregation and Its Implications for the North," in Adam Yarmolinsky, Lance Liebman and Corrine S. Schelling, eds., *Race and Schooling in the City* (Cambridge, Mass.: Harvard University Press, 1981), p. 40; David Tyack, Robert Lowe, and Elizabeth Hansot, *Public Schools in Hard Times: The Great Depression and Recent Years* (Cambridge, Mass.: Harvard University Press, 1984).

4. Arlen J. Large, "Congress Changes Its Busing Tune," *Wall Street Journal*, Oct. 7, 1975; "Busing: Why Tide Is Turning," *U.S. News & World Report*, Aug. 11, 1975, pp. 24–26; B. Drummond Ayres, Jr., "School Integration Drive Eases in South," *New York Times*, June 29, 1975; William K. Stevens, "Massive School Busing Program Near in Detroit," *Boston Herald* (hereafter *Herald*), June 29, 1975; David Plank and Marcia Turner, "Changing Patterns in Black School Politics: Atlanta, 1872–1973," *American Journal of Education* 95 (August 1987): 584, 600, 601.

5. Derrick Bell, "Civil Rights Commitment and the Challenge of Changing Conditions in Urban School Cases," in Yarmolinsky et al., *Race and Schooling*, p. 196. As a Justice Department official in the 1960s, Bell supervised as many as three hundred school desegregation cases across the South. He now puts a priority on attaining the best education possible for black children and is ready to reverse direction again if need be, as blacks have since the 1790s, as "they have sought education for their children alternately in separate and integrated schools." Bell, Foreword to Daniel J. Monti, *A Semblance of Justice: St. Louis School Desegregation and Order in Urban America* (Columbia: University of Missouri Press, 1985), pp. vii–viii.

6. Orfield, *Must We Bus?*, p. 4. For one example of Boston being mentioned as symbolizing failure, in this case by a liberal Democrat, see Susan Bickelhaupt, "Education Aid Sought for Lowell," *Globe*, Oct. 23, 1987, p. 20. In a 1986 novel set in a city other than Boston, the hero is a crusty old judge who refers to Boston

to illustrate his skepticism regarding busing. The sometimes radical, often conservative jurist opposes judicial activism consistently and speaks disparagingly of Judge Garrity "running the schools for more than a decade" with the result that the number of white students fell so drastically that "there were not enough white students left to provide racial balance. If that is success, what would it take to achieve failure?" Henry Denker, *Justice Spencer Dissents* (New York: William Morrow and Co., 1986).

7. Willis B. Hawley, "The New Mythology of School Desegregation," *Law and Contemporary Social Problems* 42 (Autumn 1978): 214; Lee A. Daniels, "In Defense of Busing," *New York Times Magazine*, Apr. 17, 1983, pp. 36, 97–98; Office of Information and Publications, United States Commission on Civil Rights, "Public Knowledge and Busing Opposition: A New National Survey," [1973], p. 17; Gary Orfield, "Research, Politics and the Antibusing Debate," *Law and Contemporary Social Problems* 42 (Autumn 1978): 153–54, 158–63. For an inspirational account of Charlotte-Mecklenburg that came to hand after this manuscript was completed, see Frye Gaillard, *The Dream Long Deferred* (Chapel Hill: University of North Carolina Press, 1988).

8. Richard A. Pride and J. David Woodward, *The Burden of Busing: The Politics of Desegregation in Nashville, Tennessee* (Nashville: University of Tennessee Press, 1985).

9. Pride and Woodward, *Burden of Busing*, p. 164; also pp. 145, 149, 151, 162. The retreat of social scientists from busing along the highway of cost/benefits calculation may be seen in two essay reviews of several books dealing with desegregation: Joseph F. Zimmerman, "Review Essay," *American Political Science Review* 80 (September 1986): 991–94, and Donald D. Cohen, "Essay Review: To Bus or Not to Bus? That Is the Question," *History of Education Quarterly* 27 (Fall 1987): 379–86. See also, David L. Kirp, *Just Schools: The Idea of Racial Equality in American Education* (Berkeley: University of California Press, 1982), and David L. Kirp, "Elusive Equality: Race, Ethnicity and Education in the American Experience," in Nathan Glazer and Ken Young, eds., *Ethnic Pluralism and Public Policy: Achieving Equality in the United States and Britain* (Lexington, Mass.: Lexington Books, 1983), pp. 85–107.

10. Christine H. Rossell, "White Flight: Pros and Cons," *Social Forces* 9 (November/December 1978): 50.

11. Leo Conway to Hon. W. Arthur Garrity, May 9, 1977, Clarke Papers. On this point generally the best source by far is Alvis V. Adair, *Desegregation: The Illusion of Black Progress* (Lanham, Md.: University Press of America, 1984). Cruse's outlook is similar to Adair's: "The 'equalization' of the two systems eliminated untold numbers of black schoolteachers, principals, and administrators from the formerly segregated schools, sending them into the ranks of the displaced and unemployed." Cruse, *Plural but Equal*, p. 21. Cruse believes the South made a great error by not investing in public education for blacks and whites after Reconstruction and that the NAACP erred in this century by pressing for integration rather than better black facilities: "By eliminating scores of black teachers and administrative personnel, the South was saved from allocating state funds for maintaining a *de facto* biracial school system that *should* have ab-

sorbed and financially supported all of those black teachers, principals, and administrators who were fired in order to implement the *Brown* decision (p. 22)." Pride and Woodward, *Burden of Busing*, p. 242; Hugh J. Scott, "Desegregation in Nashville: Conflicts and Contradictions in Preserving Schools in Black Communities," *Education and Urban Society* 15 (February 1983): 235–44; George R. Metcalf, *From Little Rock to Boston: The History of School Desegregation* (Westport, Conn.: Greenwood Press, 1983), pp. 91–93; William H. Chafe, *Civilities and Civil Rights: Greensboro, North Carolina, and the Black Struggle for Freedom* (New York: Oxford University Press, 1980), p. 345, regarding the loss of a black high school's and other black institutions' racial identity.

12. Fred Salvucci, interview with author, Sept. 20, 1984. Daniel Monti recommends tough treatment of school boards violating the law, arguing that their removal would have a reinvigorating effect. *A Semblance of Justice*, pp. 185–86.

13. Chafe, *Civilities and Civil Rights*, p. 353; see also Robert Coles, quoted in *Globe*, Apr. 11, 1976. Morton Inger, *Politics and Reality in an American City: The New Orleans School Crisis of 1960* (New York: Center for Urban Education, 1970), pp. 76–77, described the nonparticipation of New Orleans' traditional elite.

14. *Christian Science Monitor*, June 24, 1974; Orfield, *Must We Bus?*, p. 407. Lino A. Graglia, *Disaster by Decree: The Supreme Court Decisions on Race and the Schools* (Ithaca: Cornell University Press, 1976), pp. 203–57, discusses *Milliken v. Bradley* in detail, though from a point of view different from mine. For an excellent discussion of the original decision by Judge Stephen Roth and the reaction of Detroit's suburbs, see Metcalf, *From Little Rock to Boston*, pp. 162–67.

15. U.S. Commission on Civil Rights, *Hearing Held in Boston, Massachusetts, Oct. 4–5, 1966* (Washington, D.C.: GPO, 1967), pp. 140, 238–39, 241, 242, 247. In 1975 a West Roxbury lawyer and parent who had just witnessed the final hearing on the masters' plan observed of Garrity "that he will no way incur any burden or risk unto himself to try to effect a plan which may seek an optimum solution under the Constitution, because he fears the possibility of being overruled (better that a great multitude of people suffer than his reputation be vulnerable to a possible risk of being overruled)." Michael F. Donlon to Gov. Michael S. Dukakis, Apr. 23, 1975, Clarke Papers. In 1983 Logue visited Boston and declared that "Garrity acted like a Roman proconsul subduing the barbarians instead of a creative judicial statesman who could have . . . involved the whole of Greater Boston or at least the inner suburbs in a manner that would have caused no pain or strain." "Garrity's Impact and Other Thoughts on Boston," *Boston Globe* (hereafter *Globe*), May 2, 1983.

16. *Boston Sunday Globe*, Jan. 6, Dec. 12, 1965; *Herald*, Nov. 18, 1966; e.g., House Bill no. 731, March 21, 1972, "An Act Providing for the Establishment of a Metropolitan Plan for the Elimination of Racial Imbalance in Certain Cities"; *Globe*, June 11, 12, 1975; *Globe*, Jan. 22, 1975, afternoon edition.

17. James Green, "Searching for 'Common Ground': A Review Essay," *Radical America* 20 (1987), pp. 44–60, called METCO "an effort at community controlled busing," but also saw that it weakened the public schools (45, 54);

Mel King, *Chain of Change: Struggles for Black Community Development* (Boston: South End Press, 1981), pp. 86–87. Thomas F. Pettigrew echoed King's critique and used the phrase "black flight." "The Case for Metropolitan Approaches to Public-School Desegregation," in Yarmolinski et al., pp. 177, 178. Even one who administered the program in the 1970s had second thoughts about it in the 1980s, Charles Glenn, "Metropolitan Desegregation: A Fresh Appreciation," photocopy, 1982, pp. 3–4, 12 (Mr. Glenn kindly made available a copy to me). Mayor White asserted in 1975 that "one of the few common denominators that ties together the major actors on all sides of this issue—School Committee members, Commissioner of Education, NAACP leadership, Teacher Union, ROAR leaders, black social agency directors, the Mayor and City Councillors, the most vocal State Representatives and Senators—is that virtually *none* of us has children in the Boston Public Schools." "Statement of Mayor Kevin White for Possible Submission to the U.S. Commission on Civil Rights, June 19, 1975," Lupo File. Regarding blacks fleeing from public schools, see Mrs. R. E. G. to Judge Garrity, July 14, 1976, Dorchester, GL. Why would there not be "black flight"? Residential segregation usually has the result that middle-class blacks "must live in neighborhoods with fewer resources and amenities than whites of similar background. Specifically, they live in poorer, more dilapidated areas characterized by higher rates of poverty, dependency, crime, and mortality, and they must send their children to public schools populated by low income students who score badly on standardized tests." Douglas S. Massey, Gretchen A. Condran, and Nancy A. Denton, "The Effect of Residential Segregation on Black Social and Economic Well-Being," *Social Forces* 66 (Sept. 1987): 29.

18. Patricia Wen, "City Teachers Broaden Call for Return of Metco Students," *Globe*, Jan 12, 1989.

19. St. Louis's voluntary metro desegregation plan succeeded in infiltrating all the white suburban districts with blacks, but the in-city magnet schools designed to draw in whites attracted only a trickle. As with METCO, the suburban and magnet schools have drained the best black students and most active families. Those who remain behind seldom push for improvements. Robert A. Frahm, "St. Louis Desegregation Plan Holds Lessons in Success, Failure," *Hartford Courant*, Mar. 13, 1988, sec. A, pp. 1, 18.

20. William Julius Wilson, *The Truly Disadvantaged: The Inner City, the Underclass and Public Policy* (Chicago: University of Chicago Press, 1987), p. 56. Wilson's primary focus is on joblessness, which, he says, has an ever widening impact, a "vicious cycle perpetuated through the family, through the community, and through the schools" (p. 57).

21. Jennifer L. Hochschild, *The New American Dilemma: Liberal Democracy and School Desegregation* (New Haven: Yale University Press, 1984), pp. 155, 156.

22. Monti, *A Semblance of Justice*, p. 8, *passim*; Derrick Bell, *And We Are Not Saved: The Elusive Quest for Racial Justice* (New York: Basic Books, 1987), p. 63.

23. Joel Williamson, *The Crucible of Race: Black-White Relations in the*

American South since Emancipation (New York: Oxford University Press, 1984), p. 294; also pp. 292, 295.

24. Chafe, *Civilities and Civil Liberties*, pp. 51, 79. Across the South, the responses of political and economic elites to desegregation varied from reactionary to moderate: Numan V. Bartley, *The Rise of Massive Resistance: Race and Politics in the South during the 1950s* (Baton Rouge: Louisiana State University Press, 1969), pp. 313–15; in the black belt support for "massive resistance" cut across class lines and county elites often provided leadership, including many wealthy and prominent persons (pp. 82–107). See also, Elizabeth Jacoway and David R. Colburn, eds., *Southern Businessmen and Desegregation* (Baton Rouge: Louisiana State University Press, 1982). In St. Augustine, Florida, the business community's response began as reactionary and moved eventually to a withdrawal quite damaging to the fulfillment of the civil rights movement, see David R. Colburn, *Racial Change and Community Crisis: St. Augustine, Florida, 1877–1980* (New York: Columbia University Press, 1985), pp. 137–53.

25. Alan Lupo, Frank Colcord, and Edmund P. Fowler, *Rites of Way: The Politics of Transportation in Boston and the U.S. City* (Boston: Little, Brown and Co., 1971), p. 87.

26. Harry C. Boyte, *The Backyard Revolution: Understanding the New Citizen Movement* (Philadelphia: Temple University Press, 1980), pp. 18–19. To the Left, as Boyte refers to liberals and progressives, urban villages are places inhibited and marred by tradition. The Left devalues such places because of its worship of rationality and detachment from the traditional. But actual populist movements "inevitably draw on rich buried cultural themes from the past that coexist alongside repressive ones. They normally form in traditional institutions that retain some degree of political and organizational insulation from elite control—free social spaces" (p. 2).

27. Wilson Cary McWilliams, "The Meaning of the Election," in Gerald Pomper et al., *The Election of 1984: Reports and Interpretations* (Chatham, N.J.: Chatham House Publishers, 1985), p. 165. McWilliams said that Reagan understands the ordinary citizens' sense of grievance against the federal government, "the conviction that complex government works for the advantage of the powerful and clever, who understand the loopholes of law and the workings of power. . . . Reagan has reaped where the liberals and the New Left sowed. The critique of American policy in Vietnam and the exposures surrounding Watergate worked, for a time, to the advantage of the liberals and the left, discomfiting their immediate enemies. But the attack on public authority also had the effect of undermining confidence in the federal government as a whole, calling its benevolence into question as much as its competence." On the tensions, especially racial, disturbing "Middle Americans" in the 1960s and early 1970s, see Robert Coles and Jon Erikson, *The Middle Americans: Proud and Uncertain* (Boston: Little Brown and Co., 1971).

28. Bulger quoted in Ione Malloy, *Southie Won't Go: A Teacher's Diary of the Desegregation of South Boston High School* (Urbana: University of Illinois Press, 1986), p. 230. *South Boston Marshal*, 1982–83.

29. Boyte, *Backyard Revolution*, p. 36; Sara M. Evans and Harry C. Boyte, *Free Spaces: The Sources of Democratic Change in America* (New York: Harper and Row, 1986), p. 197.

30. Robert N. Bellah, Richard Madsen, William M. Sullivan, Ann Swidler, and Steven M. Tipton, *Habits of the Heart: Individualism and Commitment in American Life* (Berkeley: University of California Press, 1985), p. 23. In some ways antibusers resembled the "forgotten men" of the Depression who rallied to the likes of Father Coughlin, Huey Long, and other populist demagogues who articulated "vague anxieties that had afflicted their society for many decades—the animosity toward concentrated power, the concern about the erosion of community and personal autonomy." Alan Brinkley, *Voices of Protest: Huey Long, Father Coughlin, and the Great Depression* (New York: Random House, 1983), p. 262, also pp. 282–83.

31. The *Bakke* case of the early 1970s also showed how difficult it was to bring class issues rather than race to the forefront of public policy. After an older white applicant to the University of California-Davis medical school had been denied admission, he sued the school because some 12–15 places in the entering class of 100 had been set aside for minorities. Alan Bakke argued that some of those admitted did not have credentials as good as his, therefore he had been discriminated against. The Supreme Court in a mixed opinion ordered Davis to admit Bakke, while saying that affirmative action programs were allowable under certain conditions. The crucial point for this discussion is that the dean of the medical school also selected each year as many as five students who also may not have been qualified, but who were the children of wealthy alumni, rich donors, or powerful politicians. This information never surfaced at the trial, though the defense lawyers were well aware of it. Thus, class was ignored. "The real winners had been the country's economically and educationally privileged" (p. 228), and poor whites had grievances against the medical school admissions process that never were expressed. Naturally, race dominated the debate while class was ignored, and whites' hostilities resulting from this case were directed at blacks, not at the class structure. Joel Dreyfuss and Charles Lawrence III, *The Bakke Case: The Politics of Inequality* (New York: Harcourt, Brace, Jovanovich, 1979), pp. 10, 24–25, 43, 228–29, 261.

32. Edmund S. Morgan, *American Slavery American Freedom: The Ordeal of Colonial Virginia* (New York: W. W. Norton and Co., 1975). It is significant, in view of the argument here, that Morgan's emphasis on racial slavery as a solution to the problem of the poor, i.e., as a manifestation also of classism, often gets ignored.

33. Orfield, "Why It Worked in Dixie," p. 29; also, pp. 32–33, 38–39; Pettigrew, "The Case for Metropolitan Approaches to Public-School Desegregation," pp. 163–203. Wilson makes a recommendation similar to that made here: "The problems of the truly disadvantaged will have to be attacked primarily through universal programs that enjoy the support and commitment of a broad constituency. . . . The hidden agenda is to improve the life chances of groups such as the ghetto underclass by emphasizing programs in which the more advantaged

groups of all races can positively relate." Wilson, *The Truly Disadvantaged*, p. 120; also, pp. 120–24, 154–55.

34. Gary Orfield, *Public School Desegregation in the United States, 1968–1980* (Washington, D.C.: Joint Center for Political Studies, 1983), pp. 25, 59; Orfield, *Must We Bus?*, pp. 391–420.

35. The phrase "Berlin Walls" is from Thomas F. Pettigrew and Robert L. Green, "School Desegregation in Large Cities: A Critique of the Coleman 'White Flight' Thesis," *Harvard Educational Review* 46 (February 1976): 49.

36. Peter S. Canellos, "After 20 Years, Anti-snob Zoning Law Found Ineffective," *Boston Sunday Globe*, Jan. 1, 1989, pp. 1, 16, and "Changes in Rules, Attitudes Prescribed on Housing Logjam," *Globe*, Jan. 3, 1989, pp. 1, 5. "More and more Americans, including members of the working class, have been able to purchase particular kinds of public schools by purchasing specific kinds of residence areas protected by defensive zoning to ensure their homogeneity. Housing and schooling markets have displaced educational politics as key forums of decision making." Katznelson and Weir, *Schooling for All*, p. 27.

Index